Bourchier Wrey Savile

Revelation and science : in respect to Bunsen's biblical researches, the evidences of Christianity, and the Mosaic cosmogony

Bourchier Wrey Savile

Revelation and science : in respect to Bunsen's biblical researches, the evidences of Christianity, and the Mosaic cosmogony

ISBN/EAN: 9783337305215

Printed in Europe, USA, Canada, Australia, Japan

Cover: Foto ©Lupo / pixelio.de

More available books at **www.hansebooks.com**

REVELATION AND SCIENCE

IN RESPECT TO

BUNSEN'S BIBLICAL RESEARCHES,
THE EVIDENCES OF CHRISTIANITY, AND
THE MOSAIC COSMOGONY:

WITH AN EXAMINATION OF CERTAIN STATEMENTS PUT FORTH BY THE REMAINING AUTHORS OF

ESSAYS AND REVIEWS.

BY THE

REV. BOURCHIER WREY SAVILE, M.A.

CURATE OF TATTINGSTONE;
AUTHOR OF "LYRA SACRA," "THE FIRST AND SECOND ADVENT," ETC. ETC.

" Revelation and Science are both beams of Light from the same Sun of Eternal Truth."
   Dr. Pye Smith.
" Christianity has everything to hope, and nothing to fear, from the advancement of Philosophy."
   Dr. Chalmers.

LONDON:
LONGMAN, GREEN, LONGMAN, AND ROBERTS.
1862.

PREFACE.

THE object of the present work is to show the connexion which exists between the statements in the book containing the *Revelation* of the Divine will to man, and modern discoveries in the various departments of *Science*, in contradistinction to the views and opinions put forth in the well-known " Essays and Reviews."

The most prominent subjects which it has been thought advisable to consider separately are— *Bunsen's Biblical Researches*, in respect to the chronology of Scripture and the duration of man upon earth; the *Evidences of Christianity*, with special reference to the " Origin of Species," as determined by Holy Scripture; and the *Mosaic Cosmogony*, as being in perfect harmony with all that Science has brought to light by means of geological research. Hence we have selected the three Essays bearing those titles for separate and careful examination.

But, inasmuch as the four remaining Essays contain a variety of subjects which require much consideration, we have attempted to examine them under the separate heads of — 1. *Holy Scripture*, in its integrity, inspiration, and interpretation. 2. *Judaism*, as regards the present position of the Jews and their future prospects. 3. *Romanism*, viewed in its relation to real *Catholicism*. 4. On the distinction between the Ancient and Modern Creeds. 5. *Buddhism*, as having no claim to being termed "the Gospel of India." And, 6. *Rationalism*, in its negative aspect, as compared with the true theology which Scripture teaches.

These are the chief matters which have been handled in the following work. Our object has been to show, not only the all-perfect and instructive harmony which necessarily exists between *Revelation* and *Science*,— between God's Word and God's Works,— but how susceptible of confutation are the errors and mistakes of the several authors of "Essays and Reviews" in their denial of the same.

In thus exposing the failings of our clerical brethren, we have endeavoured, with what success our readers must judge, to avoid that rock on which theological controversialists are too often apt to split, as it has given rise to a well-known and unhappy proverb amongst us ; and the way by which some, especially platform orators, have sought the condemnation of the authors of "Essays and Reviews" is a melancholy illustration thereof. We sincerely deprecate such a mode of crushing all freedom of inquiry as unwise, impolitic, and as a serious infraction of that boundless and fathomless law of love, which is both the mainspring and the foundation of the Gospel of Christ. For, as one honoured name amongst us, whose writings bear the stamp of primitive catholicity more than perhaps any other writer of the present day, has most justly observed : — " Love is the sign of life, ' our safety in sacraments,' as St. Augustine writes ; the mark of Christ's disciples, the beginning and ending, the mother and foundation of all virtues, the earnest of the Spirit inviting and waiting for its fulness. Martyrdom, without love, were death to the soul; faith, the confession of devils; sacraments were received to our hurt; miracles, a testimony against us; the tongues of angels, a tinkling cymbal; the knowledge of mysteries, a swelling vanity; but love, as it cannot be without faith, so it gives or replaces knowledge, or wisdom, or speech, or (if they be not unlovingly laid aside) even sacraments themselves, for *God is love.*"

It is in this spirit, and with such an effective weapon of controversy, that we may best hope to succeed in confuting those with whom we, as consistent Churchmen, are necessarily at issue, according to the admirable advice so happily expressed by George Herbert:—

> " Be calm in arguing, for fierceness makes
> Error a fault, and truth discourtesy.
> Why should I feel another man's mistakes
> More than his sickness or his poverty?
> *In love* I should; but anger is not love,
> Nor wisdom neither; therefore, gently move."

If it be possible, without any infraction of that heaven-born principle, which, as St. Paul teaches, "covereth (στέγει) all things," to assign a reason for this tendency to "Negative Theology" on the part of those whose education and profession should alike forbid such ambiguous and defective teaching of the great Christian verities as the authors of "Essays and Reviews" have too clearly displayed, it is to be traced, we venture to think, to a deficiency of study of the *letter* of Scripture, on the one hand, and to a want of that true faith which inflames the heart, and invigorates the understanding, and inclines it to a right reception of the *spirit* of Scripture on the other. "The study of God's word," taught the great St. Bernard, "and the mere reading of it, differ as much as the friendship of such who every day converse lovingly together doth from the acquaintance with a stranger at an inn or a casual acquaintance whom he salutes in the street." What the saintly Augustine remarked concerning a spiritual understanding of the 119th Psalm is equally applicable to the whole of the Old and the New Testament. "The more open it seemeth, the deeper it seemeth to me; so that I cannot even show how deep it is."

So faith, which the *inspired* writer, as we must continue to call him, notwithstanding the denial of "Essays and Reviews," terms "the substance of things hoped for, the evidence of things not seen," and which alone is genuine, fruitful, and salvific, establishes the soul on Him who is the Rock of Ages, purifies the heart, empties it of the love of sin, and then fills it with the consolation of Christ and hope of eternal glory. It draws the heart as well as the head to a firm acquiescence in the truth of Scripture above all natural methods, and is, as St. Basil calls it, "the effect, not of geometrical conclusions, but the result of the energy of the Spirit." Well, therefore, would it be if every one with a leaning to the "Negative Theology" could sufficiently humble himself to receive and adopt the confession made by Anselm, Archbishop of Canterbury, during the period commonly known as "the dark ages:"—"I do not seek, O Lord, to penetrate thy depths; I by no means think my intellect equal to them; but I long to understand in some degree thy truth, which my heart believes and loves. For do not seek to understand that I may believe; but I believe that I may understand." For while humility on the one hand ranks right nobly and highly in the scale of Christian graces, on the other, faith, which is the grace of care and the antidote to scepticism, in its genuineness and power may be compared to the "bird, which rejoices in contending with wild, adverse winds, or balances itself on the bosom of the illimitable sky. Thus, even the difficulties that oppose it, faith meets unbaffled with a cheerful confidence; while on the incomprehensible nature of God it reposes as on a vast deep or a boundless heaven; awed with that vastness which is without limit, and at rest on that centre which hath no circumference." *

B. W. S.

---

* The beginning of the Book of Genesis, by Isaac Williams.

Tattingstone Rectory, Christmas, 1861.

CONTENTS.

CHAP.		PAGE
I.—Bunsen's Biblical Researches	. . . .	3
II.—Bunsen's Biblical Researches—*continued*	. .	53
III.—On the Study of the Evidences of Christianity	.	171
IV.—Mosaic Cosmogony	. . . . .	223
V.—Statements of the Remaining Essayists	. .	266

REVELATION AND SCIENCE

B

BUNSEN'S BIBLICAL RESEARCHES.

CHAPTER I.

THERE is a story on record of a certain author, who, after long hesitation, declined publishing his intended work, because he was unable to decide whether it should be commenced by a "Prefatory Introduction" or an "Introductory Preface." Had Dr. Temple so far followed this example, as to refuse to allow his Essay to be used as a suitable introduction or preface to that which subsequently follows, it would have been better for his fame as a minister of the Church of Christ. For if language, whether oral or written, is still to be accepted in its plain and unmystical meaning, and not used as a vehicle for *concealing* the thought, as the witty Italian[1] defined it, very wide is the difference between the theological bearings of the Essayist, whose work stands first, and those of the Reviewer of "Bunsen's Biblical Researches." For notwithstanding the disclaimer with which the "Essays and Reviews" are introduced "To the Reader" of there being any connexion between the respective authors, and which the continued republication of the work in its

---

[1] This *bon mot*, commonly attributed to Talleyrand, was originally from Aretino, an Italian of the 14th century.

original form makes it somewhat difficult to understand, it is, to say the least, unfortunate for Dr. Temple, that his Essay is the selected porch for the subsequent superstructure. Indeed, so objectionable do some of the statements appear in Dr. Williams's Essay, that we are afraid of breaking that precious and boundless law of Charity, which the Gospel so highly exalts, if we gave utterance to the feelings which spontaneously arise in the mind when reflecting on the lengths in scepticism which a professing Christian, much more an English clergyman, can permit himself to go antagonistic to that faith, and that revealed Word of God, which he is bound by every tie to defend. We, therefore, confine ourselves to calling attention to the notice bestowed upon this Essay by a *friendly* reviewer, who has with justice remarked that, "anything more 'unbecoming' than some of Dr. Williams's remarks we never have read in writings professing to be written seriously."[1]

It is necessary, however, to distinguish at the commencement between the statements of the Essayist himself, and those of the distinguished German, whose "Biblical Researches" have formed the ground-work of his own review.

Let us then consider what the Essayist says in *propriâ personâ*, and subsequently the Researches into Bible History of that great name under whose shadow he now presents himself to the world.

§ 1. Dr. Williams says, "Criticism reduces the strangeness of the past into harmony with the present. The truth itself may have been apprehended in various degrees by servants of God, of old, as now. Instead of, with Tertullian, *what is first is truest*, what comes of God is true" (p. 50). It is, we think, unfair criticism to make any distinction between Tertullian's golden canon and the

---

[1] Edinburgh Review, No. ccxxx. p. 479.

deduction of the Essayist. For the exact words of that father, in a work composed after his lapse, "Whatsoever was first, that is truth; whatsoever is later, that is adulterated,"[1] only affirm that He, who is revealed to us as "the Way, the Truth, and the Life," the God-man, Christ Jesus, promised the perpetual presence of the Holy Ghost to guide the Church into all truth, and to abide with her for ever, and that those who introduced novelties, which had not been taught "from the beginning," adulterated the truth, and were departing from Him who is the source of all truth. It would have been well had the Essayist remembered and applied the saying of St. Augustine to himself, when most unphilosophically writing about *the strangeness* of the past harmonising with the present. "What is truth?" exclaimed that great theologian, "Who can teach it me, save He that enlighteneth my heart, and discovereth its dark corners?"[2]

§ 2. "We cannot encourage a remorseless criticism of Gentile histories," argues Dr. Williams, "and escape its contagion when we approach Hebrew annals; nor acknowledge a Providence in Jewry without owning that it may have comprehended sanctities elsewhere. But the moment we examine fairly the religions of India and of Arabia, or even those of primeval Hellas and Latium, we find they appealed to the better side of our nature, and their essential strength lay in the elements of good which they contained, rather than in any satanic corruption" (p. 51). Those who, discarding Dr. Temple's theory of "occasional inaccuracy," or Mr. Wilson's of "the human element" of the Bible, believe that "the Hebrew annals," as forming a portion of God's word, have been as much inspired by Him, as the doctrinal or prophetic parts of Scripture, so that the sacred writers could not and did not record un-

---

[1] Adv. Praxeam, § 11.   [2] St. Aug. Confess., lib. xi. § 16.

truths, do not fear criticism, however "*remorseless*," so long as it is fair, when applied to any portion of the oracles of God. Nay, with unhesitating confidence we challenge it, being fully persuaded that every fresh discovery in the paths of Science can only tend to show its perfect harmony with Revelation, as we shall have little difficulty in proving when we come to examine the numerous charges which Bunsen brings against the genuineness of the historic statements of the Bible. Natural religion, independent of revelation, teaches us that an overruling Providence hath been recognised, external to "Jewry," during the first four millennaries of man's existence upon earth; but to say that criticism has discovered " sanctities elsewhere" during the period that God in His inscrutable wisdom confined the revelation of Himself to one favoured and chosen race, is alike contrary to Bible history and to fact. And we confidently appeal to any one who will "examine fairly" the religions either of India, Greece, or Rome, with the only true one, revealed whether in the Old or the New Testament, to say if such did really "appeal to the better side of our nature," or that they betrayed any signs of a divine origin. The anecdote of an Indian Brahmin, on returning a lent Bible to an English missionary, affords an admirable commentary of what Revelation declared respecting the religion of heathen Rome, as well as of testifying to its similarity with that of India. "You tell me, Padre," said the Brahmin, "that this book was written many hundreds of years ago, and you pretend that it is inspired by the unseen God, and that every part of it contains truth and nothing but the truth. Now, I will prove to you the falseness of this in one instance, at least. For I find in the Epistle of St. Paul to the Romans such a true and exact picture of the religion of my countrymen, that I am convinced it must have been written since you became acquainted with the people of India."

§ 3. "If," Dr. Williams declares, "we are to retain the old Anglican foundations of research and fair statement, we must revise some of the decisions provisionally given upon imperfect evidence; or if we shrink from doing so, we must abdicate our ancient claim to build upon the truth; and our retreat will be either to Rome, as some of our lost ones have consistently seen, or to some form, equally evil, of darkness voluntary. The attitude of too many English scholars before the last monster out of the deep is that of the degenerate senators before Tiberius. They stand, balancing terror against mutual shame. Even with those in our universities, who no longer repeat fully the required Shibboleths, the explicitness of truth is rare. He who assents most, committing himself least to baseness, is reckoned wisest" (pp. 52, 53). Passing over the accusations of cowardice which the Essayist thinks it becoming his position to bring against his rationalistic friends, and remembering the illustration afforded of the necessary results of shrinking from "research and fair statement" in the case of the brothers Newman, one of whom "retreated to Rome," and the other, after lingering for a time amongst the Plymouth Brethren, was eventually landed in the extreme regions of scepticism, a form doubtless of "equal evil," we would earnestly entreat him to consider whether he himself, and the leaders of this modern school of theology to which he is so firmly attached, desires to "retain the *old* Anglical foundations," or whether he is not seeking to introduce something modern and novel, and, therefore, untrue. "Some of the decisions provisionally given upon imperfect evidence" will, doubtless, require reconsideration and revision, but we may rest assured that every real discovery which the skill and wisdom of man has made, has tended, and ever will tend to show the perfect accord between Revelation and Science. We shall have frequent opportunities of proving this in our examination of other equally strange statements which have been put forth by the Essayists, being convinced that all research and all investigation carried out to its legitimate conclusion can only tend to show that—

> "Every science, power, and art
> Which tends to foster in the heart
> Knowledge of Nature's laws,
> Must, sanctified by grace divine,
> Precept on precept, line on line,
> Exalt the First Great Cause."

§ 4. In support of his view of the propriety of "research and fair statement," in order to keep members of the Church of England satisfied with resting upon "the old Anglican foundations," Dr. Williams writes, "that there was *a Bible before our Bible*, and that some of our present books, as *certainly* Genesis and Joshua, and, perhaps, Job, Jonah, Daniel, are expanded from simpler elements, is indicated in the book before us (*Bunsen's Gott in der Geschichte*) rather than *proved as it might be*" (p. 62). It would be well if the Essayist would apply this just remark on the work he is reviewing to the many strong statements which he and his Co-Essayists have put forth with the usual dogmatism of the school to which they belong, but which are often as devoid of *proof* as Bunsen's theory regarding the non-inspiration of Genesis and Joshua for *certain*, with the assumed possibility of other books of Scripture being so likewise. Dr. Williams cannot suppose that any one who has really made "Biblical Researches" into the genuineness and authenticity of the sacred writings, and with the spirit of a humble-minded believer in the existence of God, and the fact of His having made a Revelation of His will to man, will be satisfied with his criticism upon the hypothesis of his more daring and speculative brother.

§ 5. As a specimen of his qualifications for the office he so confidently assumes in defence of "the old Anglican foundations of research and fair statement," Dr. Williams continues his commendation of Bunsen by saying, " the famous Shiloh (Gen. xlix. 10) is taken in its local sense, as the sanctuary where the young Samuel was trained; which, if *doctrinal perversions* did not interfere, *hardly any one would doubt to be the true sense*" (p. 62). Believing that this is one of the many prophecies in the Old Testament, which may well be described as "directly Messianic," notwithstanding the effort of Dr. Williams, which we shall presently notice, to limit such to " two *doubtful* passages in Zechariah and Isaiah," we offer the following proof that, so far from it being a " doctrinal perversion " of the Christian Church to apply it, as she has invariably done from the days of the Apostles, by pointing its fulfilment to our Saviour, it was interpreted by the Jews of the expected Messiah before Christ appeared in the world; and it betrays a limited acquaintance with the subject on the part of the Essayist to assert, that no one ought to " doubt the true sense " of the prophecy to mean "the sanctuary where the young Samuel was trained." Let us hear the exact words of the dying Jacob, who was inspired to utter this prediction as an intimation to his descendants concerning future judgments and blessings. " The sceptre shall not depart from Judah, nor a lawgiver from between his feet, until Shiloh come." The word " Shiloh " signifies the Sent-one, or Apostle, and was evidently indicative of Christ's Apostleship, as the sacred writer expressly styles Him, Ὁ Ἀπόστολος (Heb. iii. 1). It was probably alluded to by Moses, when declining at first the mission which God ordered him to undertake at the Court of Pharaoh, " O my Lord, send I pray Thee by *the hand of Him whom Thou wilt send*," i.e. the promised Shiloh (Exod. iv. 13); in which we have the true meaning of the word as it is rendered in the Vulgate, *qui mittendus est*, " who is about to be sent." So a Rabbinical comment on Deut. xxii. 7, says, " If you keep this precept you hasten the coming of the Messiah, who is called *Sent*." All the three Targums, the Talmud, and many Jewish writers[1], both ancient and modern, agree in this, that, by the title " Shiloh," the Messiah is to be understood. R. Bechai expressly owns that " it is right to understand this verse of the Messiah, the last Redeemer, which is meant when it saith, *till Shiloh come*, i.e. his son proceeding from his seed. And the reason why the word *beno* is not used in this prophecy, but *Shiloh*, is because he (Jacob) would emphatically express a son, who should be brought forth of his mother's womb, after the manner of all those that are born of a woman." The true interpretation of this prophecy is so convincing, that, in order to evade the argument, the Jews have invented a great many tales of the power which they are said to possess in some remote parts of the world. They have written a book, entitled " The Voice of Glad Tidings," with that object in view. Their forefathers, however, who lived at the time when the prophecy was being fulfilled, and when the kingdom did in reality depart from them, by Herod the Idumean forcibly seizing the crown with the assistance of the Romans, are said to have shaved their heads, put on sackcloth, and cried, " Woe to us, because the sceptre is departed from Judah, and a lawgiver from between his feet." It remained for a German scholar, and an English presbyter of the nineteenth century, to discover that the ancient Jewish understanding of this famous prophecy was a " doctrinal perversion " of the Christian Church, and that so far from having any reference to the Saviour of the world, it should be understood of " the sanctuary where the young Samuel was trained," which no one ought to doubt is " the true sense " of Jacob's words !

---

[1] Zohar in Gen. fol. 32, 4. Bereshit Rabba, fol. 98, § 85. Jarchi and Baal Hatturim in loco. Abarbinel, Mashmiah Jeshuah, fol. 10, 1. R. Abraham Seba, Tzeror Hammor, fol. 36, 4.

§ 6. Dr. Williams, in his attempt to depreciate the genuineness and reality of Scripture prophecies, has thought it becoming to speak in the following manner of the author of the "Analogy of Religion," one of the profoundest theological works in the English language. "Even Butler foresaw the possibility that every prophecy in the Old Testament might have its elucidation in contemporaneous history; but literature was not his strong point, and he turned aside, endeavouring to limit it, from an unwelcome idea" (p. 65). It would have been well for the character of the Essayist if he had given some reasons, instead of his own inference respecting Bishop Butler's understanding of the prophecies, as after the specimens in the Essay of the author's qualifications, few will be disposed to pay much attention to his expressed opinion on such a subject. It would have been still better if he had avoided speaking of Bishop Butler in the contemptuous manner he has done, as it has only brought discredit upon himself, and exposed his own incapacity to handle the matter on which he writes. And it will be sufficient to our purpose if we adduce the testimony of one infinitely greater in intellectual power, as well as in theological worth than the Vice-Principal of Lampeter College, respecting the character of the traduced Bishop of Durham. "Butler," says Dr. Chalmers, "is in theology what Bacon is in science. The reigning principle of the latter is, that it is not for man to theorise *on the works of God;* and of the former, that it is not for man to theorize *on the ways of God.* Both deferred alike *to the certainty of experience,* as being paramount to all the plausibilities of hypothesis; and he who attentively studies the writings of these great men will find a marvellous concurrence of principle between a sound philosophy and a sound faith."

§ 7. Dr. Williams remarks on the subject of prophecy

generally, that "the declamatory assertions so easy in pulpits or on platforms, and aided sometimes by powers which produce silence rather than conviction, have not only kept alive, but magnified with uncritical exaggeration, whatever the fathers had dreamt or modern rhetoric could add, tending to *make prophecy miraculous*. Keith's edition of Newton need not here be discussed" (p. 66). We agree with the Essayist in thinking that the subject of prophecy is better suited for the calm of the study than the excitement of the platform. We can overlook the contemptuous way in which he speaks of one of the most distinguished of living authors on the subject of *fulfilled* prophecy, as the expression, "Keith's edition of Newton," betrays either a perverted mind or reprehensible ignorance on the part of a reviewer, who dogmatises on a subject which he is evidently incompetent to judge. And we invite attention to the patent infidelity of the writer in the lamentable expression which he, as a clergyman, thinks it becoming to use, "*tending to make prophecy miraculous.*" The very word "prophecy," as used alike in its conventional sense and according to its etymology, shows that it can be nothing but "miraculous;" for what human being ever possessed in himself power to foretell things to come? If the axiom of Lord Bolingbroke be true, that the history of the past "is philosophy teaching us by example," with no less truth may it be said that that prophecy, which Bacon termed "a kind of histriography," is the history of the future recorded by the authority of God. It is the essence of scepticism, to which the rationalistic school of the present generation is so zealously allied, to deny the genuineness and the authenticity of the prophetic portions of the Bible, especially those of Daniel, to which we shall presently call attention. The believer in a Revelation from God, however, is too well assured that in prophecy he has before him the thoughts of an Omniscient Being regarding the future, which it is his duty and his privilege to study and not to dispute. And deep must be the guilt, as well as incalculable the loss, of those who, in place of owning their ignorance and of seeking humbly by prayer and faith to know the mind of God, question, dispute, deny, and cavil at every clearly fulfilled prophecy which is displeasing to their vanity, but which has been accepted in all ages by the concurrent testimony of the Christian Church.

§ 8. Hence, Dr. Williams, after contending with deplorable pertinacity against the authenticity and genuineness of certain portions of those books which bear the names amongst the prophets of Isaiah and Zechariah (p. 68), gives us a specimen of his rationalistic conclusions concerning the former, in respect to the interpretation of the famous 53rd Chapter, that "the weight of arguments (in the master's hand) is so great, that *if any single person should be selected, they prove Jeremiah should be the one*" (p. 73). Adding immediately, "nor are they a slight illustration of the historical sense of that famous chapter, which *in the original is a history;*" and supporting his opinion in a foot note that "the tenses from verse 2 onward are rather historical than predictive; and in verse 8, "for *he was stricken,*" the Hebrew is נגע למו, *the stroke was upon them;* i.e. on the generation of the faithful, which was cut off, when the blood of the Prophets was shed on every side of Jerusalem." Although it is true that this strange interpretation of Isaiah 53rd, was anciently propounded by one Jewish Rabbi, Saadiah Gaon, who selects Jeremiah, just as other Rabbies had variously selected Abraham, Moses, King Josiah, Zorobabel, or the people of Israel in general for the fulfilment of the prophecy, Dr. Williams ought in common fairness to have stated that the Jewish Targum [1], to which he

---

[1] Dr. Williams declares that Bishop Pearson's "citations from Jonathan and from Jarchi are *most unfair.*" (Foot note, p. 72.) Did he

alludes in a foot note, distinctly refers it to the Messiah; "Behold, *my servant the Messiah* shall prosper;" and that the mere fact of its being compiled "in the fourth century of our era," or the Jewish compiler speaking of the Messiah "in the character of a Judaic deliverer," in place of "a Saviour," is only what we should have expected, and sufficiently contradicts his strange theory of the Spirit of God intending it for the Prophet Jeremiah. The Essayist, with lamentable taste, sneers at Bishop Pearson's understanding of the way in which the Rabbies dealt with this prophecy, yet the following extracts will prove that the Bishop was right. One of them says that "the section, which begins with these words, *He shall be exalted and extolled, and be very high*, is concerning the Messiah."[1] Another on the same passage, that "Messiah is exalted above Abraham, extolled above Moses, and made higher than the ministering angels."[2] A third remarks, "The kingdom of Israel shall be exalted in the days of the Messiah, as it is written, *He shall be* exalted and extolled."[3] The fact of the Jews omitting to read this prophecy in their public services, and the Rabbinical[4] denunciations against its being read in private, are sufficient to convince all persons, save those whose minds are warped by a morbid and unhealthy scepticism, that the interpretation of the Catholic Church since the day of

---

forget the "beam in his own eye"? or did he trust to Porson's *eulogy* upon that great theologian, that "he would have been a first-rate critic in Greek, *equal even to Bentley*, if he had not muddled his brains with divinity?"—*Baker's Lit. Anecd.* vol. ii. p. 24.

[1] Baal Hatturim in Lev. xvi. 14.
[2] Tanchuma apud Yalkut in loco.
[3] Pesikta apud Kettoreth Hassammim in Targum in Numb. fol. 27, 2.
[4] "It has lately been publicly declared by a Jew who professed and preached Christianity, that the Rabbies forbid the people to read this chapter with dreadful denunciations."—*Scott's Commentary in loc.*

Pentecost is indeed the true one. Further, the criticism of the Essayist on ver. 8 of the prophecy, when it comes to be analysed, is very far from supporting his opinion of applying it either to Jeremiah in particular, or to the nation in general. We admit the literal rendering of the present Massorete text to be as he says, "*the stroke was upon them;*" but we deny the correctness of the inference which he deduces therefrom. We have satisfactory evidence that such is not the true reading, which, by the *omission* of the letter מ[1], would read, as our translators in the margin, following the Syriac and Vulgate versions, have done "the stroke was upon *Him;*" or else by the *introduction* of the letter ה at the end of the sentence, we should accept the reading of the LXX, ἀπὸ τῶν ἀνομιῶν τοῦ λαοῦ μου ἤχθη εἰς θάνατον, "for the iniquity of my people was he smitten to death," which is supported by the Arabic and Coptic versions, and one Syriac MS., and which for the following reason we believe to be correct. Origen relates[2] that once, when in controversy with some learned Jews, having quoted at large the 53rd Chapter of Isaiah, concerning the Messiah, one of them replied then (as the rationalists contend now) that "the words did not mean one man, but *one people,* the Jews, who were smitten of God and dispersed among the Gentiles for the purpose of their conversion;" and that he (Origen) confounded them most by quoting the passage "smitten to death," according to the LXX, which could not apply to

---

[1] This is one of the most important of the 800,000 various readings which, according to Professor Moses Stuart, occur as to the Hebrew consonants in the different MSS. which have been examined. It is satisfactory, however, to know that the whole of them, *en masse,* do not materially affect any important precept, or even history, the generality of them being nothing more than a different way of spelling certain words, as, in the English language, *honour* or *honor.*

[2] Contra Celsum, lib. i. p. 370, ed. 1733.

the nation at large. Considering that Origen had laboriously compared the version of the LXX with the Hebrew text, and has recorded the necessity of arguing when in controversy with the Jews from such passages only where the texts of both agree, it is fair to conclude, both from Origen's argument and the silence of his Jewish adversaries, that the Hebrew text in those days read למות " to death," agreeable to the version of the LXX. Hence, we think that it would have been better for the Essayist if his " Biblical Researches " had extended somewhat further than the mere bringing forward of a questionable reading of the Massorete text, in order to contradict what the Christian Church has so long accepted as " the sure word of prophecy." It is not necessary to show at any length that this famous prophecy can refer to none other save our Lord and Saviour Jesus Christ, as every faithful Christian must be so fully persuaded of the same; and it ought to be sufficient to convince every professed minister, even though he be a most unreasonable rationalist, of his great error in the application of the prediction, that our Lord applied it to Himself the night before the crucifixion, as St. Luke records his words : " I say unto you, that THIS that is written must yet be accomplished *in me*, And *he was reckoned among the transgressors;* "[1] and that, when the Spirit of God directed the steps of the Evangelist Philip to the spot where the Ethiopian eunuch was reading from the prophecy of Isaiah, " He was led as a sheep to the slaughter ; and like a lamb dumb before his shearer, so opened he not his mouth : In his humiliation his judgment was taken away: and who shall declare his generation, for his life is taken from the earth," the same Spirit inspired him to reply to the natural question, " I pray thee, of whom speaketh the Prophet this ? " — none other

---

[1] St. Luke, xxii. 37.

than the name of JESUS. "Then Philip opened his mouth, and began at the same scripture, and preached unto him Jesus."[1] No one who allows the writings of the New Testament to be inspired by God, can hesitate in deciding to whom the term which the Essayist angrily uses, " such traditional *distortion* of prophecy" (p. 74), most appropriately belongs, when investigating either spiritually or critically the 53rd chapter of Isaiah.

§ 9. We invite attention to other "*distortions* of prophecy," which are so recklessly scattered throughout this review of "Bunsen's Biblical Researches." E. g. Dr. Williams says, " He may read in Psalm xxxiv. that 'Not a bone of the righteous shall be broken,' but he must feel a difficulty in detaching this from the context, so as to make it a prophecy of the crucifixion " (p. 68). The Essayist, or Baron Bunsen, for it is not quite clear from the construction of the sentence which is in fault, ought to quote with scrupulous nicety when endeavouring to set aside any portion of God's prophetic truth; for the words at ver. 20 read : " He keepeth all his bones : not one of them is broken;" and the same Spirit which "moved" David to foretell it, equally " moved " (though of course this Dr. Williams must consistently deny[2]) St. John to apply it in his account of the crucifixion, " These things were done, that the Scripture should be fulfilled, A bone of Him shall not be broken."[3] Dr. Williams's criticism is equally at fault in another of the Psalms. He continues, " If he accepts mere versions of Psalm xxii. 17, he may wonder ' piercing the hands and the feet ' can fit into the

---

[1] Acts, viii. 27—35.
[2] One of the Essayists writes, " Some critics think St. John's Gospel was not of a date anterior to the year 140, and that it presupposes opinions of a Valentinian character, or even Montanist, *which would make it later still.*"—*Essays and Reviews*, p. 161, *note*.
[3] St. John, xix. 36.

whole passage; but if he prefers *the most ancient Hebrew reading*, he finds, instead of 'piercing,' the comparison 'like a lion,' and this corresponds sufficiently with the 'dogs' of the first clause, though a morally certain emendation would make the parallel more perfect by reading the word ' lions' in both clauses" (p. 69). We think Dr. Williams is mistaken, and that our own "mere version," by its rendering of the disputed clause, "they pierced my hands and my feet," has retained the ancient and true reading. The whole difference lies, as is well known, between the Hebrew letters ׳ and ו, which, being so much alike, might easily be mistaken for each other; the former making the sentence "*like a lion*," the latter, "*they pierced*." In support of each reading there are various MSS. as well as eminent critics. The LXX., Syriac, Æthiopic, Arabic, and Vulgate, read it *they pierced*. The Chaldee and the Targum combine both by reading it, *biting as a lion my hands and my feet*. The Complutensian Polyglott has *they pierced;* but the Polyglotts of London, Paris, and Antwerp have *like a lion* in the text, and *they pierced* in the margin. In the small Masorah on this text, it is observed by the Jewish writer that the word is used twice, as it is here pointed, but in two different senses. This is one place; and Isaiah, xxxviii. 13, where the sense requires it should be read *as a lion*, is the other. Therefore, according to the author of that note, it should *not* be understood in this place of *a lion*. The larger Masorah, on Numbers xxiv. 9, observes the word is to be found in two places, in that and in Psalm xxii. 16, and adds to the latter, it is written, *they pierced*. Ben Chayim[1] confirms this reading, and says he found it so written in some correct copies, and in the margin, *as a lion*. All this, together with the knowledge

---

[1] In Maareath א, fol. 10, 2, ad Calc. Buxtorf. Bibl.

that the Jews themselves sometimes apply this passage from the Psalms to their Messiah, together with the fact that the undisputed reading of the LXX., which in reality is the safest guide when there is any doubt about the Hebrew, being ὤρυξαν, *they pierced*, is sufficient to decide the question against the perverted conclusion of the Essayist. Whether he believes in the fact of our Lord's hands and feet having been pierced at the time of the crucifixion simply because the Evangelists[1] have stated it, we cannot say; but we have independent evidence by both Jewish and Heathen writers, of the Crucifixion, where of necessity any one who suffered death in that form, must have had his hands and feet pierced.

Nor is Dr. Williams less at fault in his system of criticism upon the New Testament than we believe it to be upon the Old, as witness his treatment of the Book of Revelation. He observes that " the Apocalypse, if taken as a series of poetical visions, which represent the outpouring of the vials of wrath upon the city where the Lord was slain, ceases to be a riddle. Its horizon answers to that of *Jerusalem*, already threatened by the legions of Vespasian " (p. 84). As we gather from this that the Essayist advocates the *Neronic* date of the Apocalypse, we can only express our surprise at the confidence of any one claiming to be a critic, who can support in the present day so indefensible a theory. The attempts to set aside the force of Irenæus' testimony that " the Apocalypse was seen not very long ago, but almost in our age, *towards the end of the reign of Domitian*,"[2] have been so well exposed by the author of Horæ Apocalypticæ, that

---

[1] St. John applies the continuation of the disputed passage in Psalm xxii. 18, to the crucifixion, "That the Scripture might be fulfilled, which saith, They parted my raiment among them, and for my vesture did they cast lots" (xix. 24).

[2] Irenæus contra Hær. v. xxx. 3.

we need only refer any one wishing to investigate the subject to that valuable work, " in order to convince the intelligent and candid reader of their absurdity and extravagance."[1] The only *internal* evidence for such a theory rests upon the mention of the Temple of the Apocalypse, from which it is hastily concluded that as the Temple of Jerusalem was destroyed shortly after the termination of Nero's reign, therefore it must have been written before his death. But it might as well be argued that the nine concluding chapters of Ezekiel's prophecy, which contain a full description of some magnificent temple, could not have been written " in the 25th year of our Captivity," according to the prophet's statement[2], because the Temple of Jerusalem had been destroyed a few years before by Nebuchadnezzar's captain of the guard; whereas both Ezekiel and St. John undoubtedly refer to a temple of another sort and another age. Again, there can be no question that the locality around which the " poetical visions " of the Apocalypse may be said to centre, is not Jerusalem, but Rome. For to refer to St. John's definition of the woman as " that great city, which reigneth over the kings of the earth,"[3] to the former, instead of the latter, is as unwarrantable a speculation as that other conclusion in the opposite extreme, which refers it to a future Babylon on the river Euphrates.[4] It

---

[1] Hor. Apoc. Preliminary Essay on the Genuineness of the Date of the Apocalypse of St. John, chap. ii. By Rev. E. B. Elliott.

[2] Ezekiel, xl. 1.

[3] Revelation, xvii. 18.

[4] Mr. Newton, a writer amongst the "Plymouth Brethren," contends that the " seven-hilled " city, called " Babylon the Great " in the 17th and 18th chapters of Revelation, so far from referring to Rome, which the Spirit of God clearly points to as " that great city reigning over the kings of the earth " when St. John lived, must mean Babylon on the Euphrates, where Nebuchadnezzar dwelt. And the little difficulty of the " seven mountains " he gets over by supposing that, since

is true there is allusion in the Apocalypse to " the city where the Lord was slain." But a very little criticism enables us to decide that the reference in this instance, as in the previous one, is to Rome, and not to Jerusalem. The passage, on which we conclude the Essayist mainly rests, reads, " their dead bodies shall lie in the street (τῆς πλατείας) of the great city, which spiritually is called Sodom and Egypt, where also our Lord was crucified."[1] We know our Lord was crucified at Jerusalem, which is here called *the street* or *broadway* of that great city, whose empire at that time extended from Britain to the Euphrates; but the term, " the great city," can refer to nothing but Rome itself. And this is all that need be said on the subject.

§ 10. Dr. Williams makes a deeper plunge in the whirlpool of rationalistic doubts by observing, " When so vast an induction on the destructive side has been gone through, it avails little that some passages may be doubtful, one, perhaps, in Zechariah, and one in Isaiah, capable of being made *directly Messianic*, and a chapter possibly in Deuteronomy foreshadowing the final fall of Jerusalem. Even these few cases, the remnant of so much confident rhetoric, *tend to melt, if they are not already melted*, in the crucible of searching inquiry" (pp. 69, 70). If by this statement the Essayist means to assert that there are only two passages in the Old Testament which point to Christ as the foretold Messiah, and that even these must be given up after having passed through the critical alem-

---

" seven is used in Scripture as the number of completeness," it may refer to the perfection of wickedness and " governmental influence," which will be found in the *future* Babylon; or, if that interpretation does not please, it may possibly refer to the hanging gardens in the *old* Babylon!—*Babylon: its Future History.* By B. W. Newton, pp. 85—88.

[1] Rev. xi. 8.

bic of his fellow-rationalists, we can only recommend him to enter the nearest village school, and question the best instructed scholar therein, and if he has sufficient humility he will speedily discover what little progress his "Biblical Researches" have yet made. We have not time to answer this marvellous specimen of rationalistic unbelief. Nor is it needed, as any one moderately taught in that Book of books, wherein God has condescended to reveal His history of the past, and His will respecting the future, to fallen man, will have presented to his mind at once numberless passages which contradict and confute the patent infidelity of this daring announcement. It will be sufficient if we adduce the testimony of the Jewish Rabbies[1] subsequent to the time of our Lord's ministry on earth, who, although the veil is still on their hearts when reading the law of Moses, appear to have had a better understanding of the "Messianic" nature of Christ, as predicted in the Old Testament, than one English Presbyter has in the present day. "*In the Rabbinical version* of the History of Jesus," says Mr. Myers, himself a converted Jew, and now a clergyman of the Church of England, " it is *confessed* that He was born at Bethlehem, of the tribe of Judah, of royal descent — that he was very learned — that He asserted He was born of a pure virgin — that He said He was the Son of God, and applied to Himself the prophecy of Isaiah vii. 14, 'Behold a virgin shall conceive, and shall bear a son, and shall call his

---

[1] Buxtorf, in his Lex. Talm., gives above *sixty* passages where the Chaldee paraphrasts mention the Messiah; and though many of such interpretations would not be owned by Christian commentators, there are others of which there can be no doubt. They could understand Gen. i. 2, to be "directly Messianic" before "the crucible" of the rationalistic school was known. "The Spirit of God," as Zohar, Bereshith Rabba, and divers others declare, "is the Spirit of Messias."

name Immanuel,'— that He declared that He created the heaven and the earth — that many Jews worshipped Him as the Son of God — that He entered Jerusalem upon an ass — that the whole city came out to meet Him — that He applied to himself, Zech. ix. 9 — that He said He would sit at the right hand of God — that He was betrayed by Judas — that He was scourged, and crowned with thorns — that they gave Him vinegar to drink — that He applied to Himself Psalm lxix. 21, and Psalm xxii. 1 — that He said His blood should be an atonement for all mankind — that He said Isaiah, liii. 5, was fulfilled in Him — that He was put to death on the evening of the Passover — that He was buried before the Sabbath set in — that His followers increased after His death more and more — that they soon numbered tens of thousands — that He had twelve disciples who travelled into twelve kingdoms — that the Jews went after them; and that some of them were men of great learning and probity, and confirmed the doctrines of Jesus."[1]

§ 11. Speaking of the Prophet Daniel, Dr. Williams approves of Baron Bunsen's view, by his observation that " in distinguishing the man Daniel from our book of Daniel, and bringing the latter as low as the reign of Epiphanes, our author only follows the admitted necessities of the case. Not only Macedonian words, such as *symphonia* and *psanterion* . . . . . . and not only the minute description of Antiochus' reign, but the stoppage of such description at the precise date, 169 B.C., remove all philological and critical doubt as to the age of the book. But what seems *peculiar* to Bunsen, is the interpretation of the four empires' symbols with reference to the original Daniel's abode in Nineveh. The original place of the book amongst the later Hagiographa of the Jewish canon

---

[1] See "The Jew," by A. M. Myers, pp. 393, 4.

confirms this view of its origin (viz., at the time of the struggle against Antiochus); and if some obscurity rests upon details, the general conclusion, that the book contains *no predictions*, except by analogy and type, *can hardly be gainsaid*" (pp. 76, 77). Let us examine separately these marvellous statements. The question to be discussed is simply this. Was the Book of Daniel written by an inspired man living at Babylon during the 6th century before the Christian era, or by a forger of four centuries later, who usurped his name, and who recorded events after they had taken place? The Jews and the Christian Church have accepted the former, Baron Bunsen and Dr. Williams, with the rationalistic school generally, having disinterred the objections of an infidel (Porphyry, the Syrian of Bashan) of the third century of our era, who asserted that the book was a forgery of the time of the Maccabees, have adopted the latter. Such was also the view of the late Dr. Arnold, whose opinion is thus openly expressed: "I have long thought that the greater part of the Book of Daniel is most certainly a very late work, of the time of the Maccabees; and the pretended prophecy about the Kings of Grecia and Persia, and of the North and South, is mere history, like the poetical prophecies in Virgil and elsewhere."[1] It would be well if those who are apt to have their minds swayed by the character and estimable qualities of such men as Bunsen and Arnold[2], instead of rea-

---

[1] Life of Arnold, vol. ii. p. 195, 5th ed.

[2] The testimony of one of these eminent men regarding the other may be fitly introduced here as bearing upon the subject. "I could not," says Arnold, "express my sense of what Bunsen is without seeming to be exaggerating; but I think if you could hear and see him, even for one half hour, you would understand my feelings towards him. He is a man in whom God's graces and gifts are more united than in any person whom I ever saw. I have seen men as holy, as amiable, as able; but I never knew one who was all one in

soning as they unconsciously do, " If such learned persons did not own the authenticity of Daniel, they must have had good grounds for rejecting it," were to consider what those *grounds* are really worth. When an opinion is broadly stated *without any reason being assigned*, it carries far greater weight with the unthinking class than if *reasons* were given : in the latter case, the reasons for the opinion are judged; in the former, the opinion rests on some ground of unknown and undefined importance. Be it ours to endeavour to show as briefly as the extensive nature of the subject will allow, a few, out of many, *reasons* why we must contend for the genuineness and authenticity of the Book of Daniel.

(*a*.) Daniel *claims* to be its author no less than nine times, as the following texts declare, chap. vii. 1, 2, 28, and viii. 1, 15, 27, and ix. 2, and x. 2, and xii. 5. In any other writing this would be deemed sufficient proof conjointly with the mode of its having come down to us. It is a singular fact, that the abridged history of Rome by Velleius Paterculus has been transmitted to the time when printing was discovered by means of a single MS., and is alluded to by but one ancient author, viz., Priscian, a grammarian of the 6th century. It has been the same with the more important work of Tacitus, which was likewise preserved in a single MS., discovered in a monastery of Westphalia. It is needless to remark that the genuineness and authenticity of these two works are universally admitted, notwithstanding the scantiness of the evidence in their behalf. So in the last century, when Muratori discovered in the Ambrosian Library at Milan, a Latin fragment on the canon of the New Testament, it was at

---

so extraordinary a degree, and combined with a knowledge of things new and old, sacred and profane, so accurate, so profound, that I never knew it equalled or approached by any man."—Ibid. vol. ii. p. 140.

once received as a genuine work of the second century, as the nature of the case precluded imposture, and the internal evidence showed that the author of it lived about A. D. 140.

(*b.*) Ezekiel, a contemporary historian, independent of being an inspired Prophet, mentions Daniel three times, chap. xiv. 14 and 20, and chap. xxviii. 3, apparently as if he was a *well-known* person of that age, and as we find no other Daniel recorded in earlier ages, we must conclude that Ezekiel must refer to the prime minister of Darius the Mede, who succeeded Belshazzar on the throne of Babylon.

(*c.*) The First Book of Maccabees (originally written in Hebrew according to Origen and Jerome[1]) affords satisfactory evidence that the Prophecy of Daniel was, in the Maccabean age itself, received and used as being what it professed,— an authoritative revelation given to the Prophet at Babylon. For not only does the writer evidently quote from Daniel when he speaks of the servants of Antiochus Epiphanes having "set up *the abomination of desolation* upon the altar" (i. 54), but there are frequent allusions[2] to the fact that the canon of the Old Testament was closed, and that the Jews had *no prophet* amongst them, which they allowed Daniel to be. This we know from the testimony of Josephus, who speaks of him as "one of the greatest of the prophets — for the several books that he wrote and left behind him are still read by us till this time; and from them we believe that Daniel conversed with God; for he did not only prophesy of future events as the other prophets did, but he also determined the time of their accomplishment."[3] If the modern

---

[1] Origen apud Euseb. H. E. vi. xxv., and Jerome Prologus Galeatus.
[2] Macc. iv. 46; ix. 27; xiv. 41.
[3] Jos. Antiq. x. xi. 7.

Jews have endeavoured to lessen the value of Daniel's testimony by placing him in the כתובים or Hagiographa, though we do not know at what time this was done, or upon what principle the collection of sacred writings was arranged, it may be owing partly to its being an historical work as well as prophetic, partly to its having been written at Babylon, and partly to the clear but unwelcome testimony it bears to their treatment of the Messiah as fulfilled in the person of our Saviour. The Jews have a story concerning Jonathan ben Uzziel, when about to commence a paraphrase on the Hagiographa, in continuation of his previous one on the Prophets, having been forbidden by the *Bath-Kol*, or Voice from Heaven, because that in it was contained " the end of the Messiah and the exact time of his coming."[1] This was considered so clear by them, that one of their Rabbies, who lived in the century preceding the Christian era, asserted that " the time of the promised Messiah, as foretold by Daniel, could not be deferred *longer than fifty years*,"[2] which will account for what St. Luke records respecting Simeon at the expiration of that period, that " the same man was just and devout, waiting for the consolation of Israel: and the Holy Ghost was upon him. And it was revealed unto him by the Holy Ghost, that he should not see death before he had seen the Lord's Christ."[3] Aben Ezra and R. Jacchiades express the same opinion as Josephus does, respecting the value of Daniel as a prophet; and Maimonides[4], though, he says, the Book of Daniel by the general

---

[1] T. Bab. Megillah, fol. 3, 1.
[2] R. Nehumiah apud Grotium, de Ver. Relig. Christ., l. v. § 14.
[3] St. Luke, ii. 25, 26.
[4] More Nevochim, pt. ii. c. 45. The Hagiographa commence with the Psalms and terminate with the Chronicles. The Book of Daniel is placed between Esther and Ezra. That the Jews of our Lord's time admitted the authority of the book, we know from the fact that

consent of the Jews is placed amongst the Hagiographa, he owns that Daniel and the other writers of those sacred books, as David and Solomon, may be called prophets in general.

(*d.*) Had the Book of Daniel been composed by a forger of the Maccabean age, it must have been written between the period of Judas Maccabeus purging the Temple (when the Feast of Dedication, which our Lord subsequently observed, was appointed), B. C. 165, and the death of his successor, John Hyrcanus, B. C. 107, and must have come into general use within a few years of that last event. Now the Jews at the commencement of the Christian era must have *known* whether Daniel belonged to the Maccabean period or not; for that age was not so far removed from the time of our Lord, as to be sufficient to produce uncertainty, in a matter of such public importance and notoriety as the introduction and reception of a book of Holy Scripture. Melanchthon thus states the chronological connexion of the two periods:—"Simeon, who embraced Christ as an infant, saw, when a young man, the elders who had seen Judas Maccabeus."[1] Hence if the Book of Daniel had been a forgery of that age it must have been well-known as a fact at the time of our Lord's birth.

(*e.*) Every believer in the New Testament must necessarily deny the Book of Daniel to be a forgery of the Maccabean age, not only because the Scriptures[2] are

---

when Christ referred the expression in Daniel vii. 13, "the Son of Man," to Himself, the Sanhedrim charged Him, not with quoting an apocryphal work, but with blasphemy, as appropriating to Himself the title which they would only allow to the Messiah, and on that ground they condemned the Innocent, saying, "He is guilty of death." St. Matt. xxiv. 30, xxvi. 63—6.

[1] Quoted in Hävernick über Daniel, p. 390.

[2] E. g. St. Matt. xxii. 29; xxvi. 54. St. John, v. 39; x. 35. Rom. iii. 2; xv. 4.

appealed to so frequently as a collection of writings acknowledged by the Jews to have been inspired by God, and divided, according to Josephus[1], the contemporary of the Apostles, into twenty-two books, of which Daniel formed one; but our Lord expressly bore testimony to the genuineness, the authenticity, and the inspiration of Daniel by saying, "When ye, therefore, shall see the abomination of desolation, *spoken of by Daniel the prophet*, stand in the holy place (whoso readeth let him understand)."[2] What can be a stronger proof of the value of Daniel than this reference? Christ mingles his own predictions with a citation from this book, which shows that He did not understand Daniel as the historian of the *past*, but the Prophet of the *future* in the coming Roman desolation. This is authority to us of the genuineness and authenticity, even though denied by German scholars and English clergymen, without a shadow of proof for their untenable opinions, and on this ground alone, we may cast aside every objection in which captious critics may indulge, as of no weight when compared with the positive declaration of the Son of God.

(*f.*) The objection of Dr. Williams to the genuineness of Daniel, on the ground of "Macedonian words, such as *symphonia* and *psanterion*," translated " dulcimer " and " psaltery," is rather strange. The conclusion which we should draw on finding these words, would naturally be that such musical instruments were then known at Babylon as had been derived from the Greeks, and still retained their Greek names, just as we retain the well-known English word *flute*, derived from the German *flöte*. That the musical instruments mentioned by Daniel, iii. 5, as in

---

[1] Contra Apion, lib. 1, § 8.
[2] St. Matt. xxiv. 15. "The abomination of desolation" is referred to by Daniel three times; ix. 27; xi. 31; and xii. 11.

use at Babylon, had been known long before his time both in Egypt and Greece, we have inferential proof. E. g. Sir Gardner Wilkinson discovered a painting at Thebes, of an instrument very like the recently invented *concertina*, the attitudes of the players resembling those of the well-known Ethiopian serenaders. In a tomb at the same city a psaltery or harp was found, now removed to Paris, with twenty chords of catgut so well preserved that they still retained their sound after having been buried since the century previous to that when David's harp sounded aloud the praises of God on Mount Zion. Terpander is considered by the Greeks to have invented the flute, about 150 years before Daniel was a captive in Babylon; and Pythagoras, his distinguished contemporary, is said to have been an excellent performer, maintaining that music greatly conduced to health, and that to direct the morals and soften the lives of men by means of music was most beneficial.[1]

(*g.*) "The texture of the Chaldaic" is another of the Essayist's objections to the authenticity of Daniel, but not of much more force than a somewhat similar objection which has elsewhere been brought against that same book, in consequence of its having been *partly* written in Chaldee and part in Hebrew, but the objector forgets that the same thing is found in the Book of Ezra, and as such tells rather in favour of Daniel than the contrary. Had the Hebrew of Daniel been such as is found in the Prophecy of Isaiah, doubtless an objection would have been raised to it from the purity of the language, being such as a Jew in Babylon could not be expected to use, so easy is it for critics to endeavour to set aside the power of the Word of God by seeking to bring down truth inspired by the Infinite to the level of their own limited reason.

---

[1] Plutarch de Musicâ. Jamblichus de Vit. Pythag.

(h.) Dr. Wilhams apparently dissents from his friend's view of one portion of the Book of Daniel, remarking, "What seems *peculiar* to Baron Bunsen is the interpretation of the four empires' symbols with reference to the original Daniel's abode in Nineveh." Considering that the Assyrian empire was finally overthrown, and Nineveh destroyed (B. C. 625) nearly a century before Daniel wrote the prophecy "of the Four Empires," in the first year of Belshazzar's short reign, which terminated B.C. 538 — that there is not a shadow of proof to make us suppose that Daniel ever abode in Nineveh, even if it was still standing — that in the image-vision, which Nebuchadnezzar saw and Daniel interpreted, the same "four empires" are described under the symbols of different metals, "the God of Heaven" inspired Daniel to announce the Babylonian empire as the *first*, by his speech to the King, "Thou art this head of gold," when Gentile dominion had begun to be exercised over the people of Israel, and that the *fourth* is no less clearly marked out in Scripture as that of the Cæsars, which held sway in Judea when Christ commenced His ministry, and of which the Pharisees stood in such awe when they uttered unconsciously the prediction, "the Romans shall come and take away both our place and nation,"[1] and to which our Lord referred when He foretold that "Jerusalem shall be trodden down of the Gentiles until the times of the Gentiles be fulfilled"[2] — considering all these things and many other things in Scripture confirmatory of the same, we agree with the Essayist in thinking that Baron Bunsen's hermeneutical system of interpreting the Assyrian Empire as the *first*, and the Grecian, during "the sway of Alexander" the fourth, is very "*peculiar*" indeed, and completely disqualifies the

---

[1] St. John, xi. 48.   [2] St. Luke, xxi. 24.

learned German from being a safe guide to the understanding of prophecy.[1]

(*i*.) Dr. Williams sums up his own opinion respecting Daniel with these words : " The general conclusion that *the book contains no predictions*, except by analogy and type, can hardly be gainsaid" (p. 76) ; having previously written, "two results are clear beyond fair doubt, that the period of the *seventy weeks* ended in the reign of Antiochus Epiphanes, and that those portions of the book supposed to be specially predictive, *are a history of past occurrences* up to that reign" (p. 69). Probably in the whole range of the Biblical literature of this country, there never were so many misstatements comprised in so short a space as the above, and which recent discoveries in science (we refer to the reading of the cuneiform character by our distinguished countrymen, Sir H. Rawlinson and Dr. Hincks) enable us so easily to disprove. When Nebuchadnezzar, in the height of his glory, boasted of the magnificence of his world-renowned capital, " Is not this great Babylon that I have built for the house of my kingdom, by the might of my power, and for the honour of my majesty," Daniel records the *prediction* that in con-

---

[1] It is somewhat singular that another school of prophetic interpreters, of which the most prominent are the Jesuit Lacunza, under the *nom de guerre* of Ben Ezra, and Drs. Maitland and Todd, have attempted to set aside the ancient Catholic interpretation of " the four empires" of the prophecy of Daniel by an equally untenable theory, making the Babylonian and Persian united as the first, and the *fourth* an empire still future, on the ground the Persians did not subvert the empire of the Chaldeans at the time when Belshazzar was slain, but only changed the dynasty. Dr. Maitland attempts to support this theory by supposing a parallel in William of Orange having subverted the throne of his father-in law, James II. He might as well have argued that Queen Victoria is the Great Mogul, and that Hindostan still remains the same empire, as there has been nothing more than a change of dynasty.

sequence of this boast, a voice from heaven forewarned the king that he should be driven from men — that his dwelling should be with the beasts of the field — and *seven times* should pass over him, until he acknowledged " that the most High ruled in the kingdom of men, and gave it to whomsoever He willed." [1] Science has recently brought to light several things confirmatory of this remarkable *prediction*. Had Daniel, a resident in Babylon at the time, made the same statement which Berosus the Chaldean historian made nearly three hundred years later, that Nebuchadnezzar built his palace " for the honour of his majesty " in the incredibly short space " *of fifteen days*," it would have been doubtless alleged by German critics and English Essayists against the value of the prophet's testimony, though we do not recollect ever hearing of such an objection against Berosus, — but then he lived three centuries after the events he professes to record, and did not claim to be an inspired man.

A tablet at the India House in London, whose cuneiform inscription has been recently deciphered, affords a singular confirmation of this most unlikely statement. A portion of it reads thus:—" Nebuchadnezzar King of Babylon — I erected its walls, I finished it completely *in fifteen days* — its roofs I covered it." Similarly does another cuneiform inscription confirm the truth of the *prediction* respecting Nebuchadnezzar's madness. The Standard Inscription, according to Sir H. Rawlinson, reads as follows : " *Four years* — the seat of my kingdom in the city — which — did not rejoice my heart. In all my dominions I did not build a high place of power; the precious treasures of my kingdom I did not lay up. In Babylon, buildings for myself and for the honour of my kingdom I did not lay out." In the whole range of

---

[1] Daniel, iv. 30—32.

history there is probably no similar instance of a king recording so publicly his own inaction, which the believer in revelation is alone enabled to explain. Further, in the period of *four years* mentioned by Nebuchadnezzar, we receive the true explanation of *the seven times* recorded in Daniel, which has been a subject of prolific controversy amongst prophetic students. Theodoret informs us that the Persians used to distinguish their years into two seasons, winter and summer, and which was doubtless a similar custom with their neighbours at Babylon. Hence *the seven times* of Daniel must be understood as a period of three and a half solar years (a well-known period in Scripture), which will agree with the *four* (current) years mentioned in the inscription above.

We have another instance of the harmony between Revelation and Science in the *prediction* of Daniel respecting the overthrow of Belshazzar's kingdom, which was to be given to the Medes and Persians. It is written: "Then commanded Belshazzar, and they clothed Daniel with scarlet and put a chain of gold about his neck, and made a proclamation concerning him, that he should be the *third* ruler in the kingdom. In that night was Belshazzar the king of the Chaldeans slain."[1] Berosus, on the other hand, states that, when "Cyrus took Babylon in the seventeenth year of the reign of Nabonnedus," the king was not in the city, having previously fled to a place called Borsippus, where Cyrus subsequently besieged him, took him prisoner, treated him kindly, and "provided him with an establishment in Carmania, where he spent the remainder of his life."[2] Here the discrepancies between Daniel and Berosus are so great that it would have been impossible to reconcile them, had it not been for the

---

[1] Daniel, v. 29, 30.
[2] Berosus apud Euseb. Præp. Evang. lib. ix.

happy discovery of reading the cuneiform inscriptions. By means of these Sir H. Rawlinson has found that Nabonnedus, whom Berosus speaks of as king of Babylon at the time of Cyrus's attack, had previously admitted his son Bel-shar-ezar (the Belshazzar of Daniel) into partnership with him in the government, just as Nabopalasar had Nebuchadnezzar. This enables us to reconcile the statements of Daniel and Berosus completely. Nabonnedus retired to Borsippus before the final catastrophe; Belshazzar was feasting his lords as the prince regent, when Daniel interpreted the handwriting on the wall to foretell the downfall of his kingdom, and was slain in the night when the city was taken. And further, this remarkable discovery enables us to understand the expression, which has hitherto presented such a difficulty to commentators, that Daniel was made "the *third* ruler in the kingdom." Why not *second*, as Joseph had been made in Egypt? Now the answer is plain; Nabonnedus the father would naturally be reckoned *first*; Belshazzar, the son, *second*; and Daniel *third*. This is an undesigned coincidence as to the accuracy of Scripture statements in general, and to the genuineness and authenticity of Daniel in particular.

Dr. Williams, however, may contend that these are not *predictions* in the sense which he attaches to the word, and of which he says there is not one in the Book of Daniel, "except by analogy and type." We certainly have a lively recollection of a very interesting *prediction* recorded in the Book of Daniel; so interesting and so important that the greatest reasoner perhaps amongst the children of men, as well as an earnest student of prophecy, the illustrious Sir Isaac Newton, is reported to have said that "the foundation of the Christian religion rested upon it." We refer of course to the famous prophecy respecting the time of the death of the Messiah, or, as it is generally known by the name of "*the seventy weeks*," which the Essayist, with rare confidence in his own unsupported theory, with a determination to close his eyes to every historic statement that bears upon the subject, and with the incredible infatuation of his school that his marvellous ideas will pass unchallenged and unquestioned, has the amazing temerity to affirm "ended in *the reign of Antiochus Epiphanes.*" This he declares is "*clear beyond fair doubt.*" Let us examine this. The words of Daniel are as follows: "Seventy weeks are determined upon thy people, and upon thy holy city. . . . Know therefore and understand, from the going forth of the commandment to restore and to build Jerusalem, unto the Messiah the Prince, shall be seven weeks, and threescore and two weeks: the street shall be built again, and the wall, even in troublous times. And after *the* (Hebr.) threescore and two weeks shall Messiah be cut off,"[1] &c. Without noticing the endless interpretations of the whole of this famous prophecy, as being foreign to our object, we would direct attention to the one important point, viz. the cutting off of the Messiah, or, in other words, the crucifixion of Christ. Does it really *predict* this great event? and are these chronological signs sufficiently defined to enable us to compute with unerring accuracy when it was to take place, and thereby testify to the truth of the prophecy? Dr. Williams will, of course, deny that it has any reference to the crucifixion or to Christ at all, but that, as it was a mere record of events which occurred in the Maccabean age, it can only be understood to refer to something in the history of Judas Maccabæus. The first point to be settled in the consideration of this passage, is the meaning of the term translated "weeks," but which might be rendered more literally

---

[1] Daniel, ix. 24—26.

"sevens" or "hebdomads," as the word standing by itself might equally mean *a seven of days*, i.e. *a week*, or a *seven of years*, which would define the term "seventy weeks" to mean 490 years. That this latter is the true meaning, there can be no doubt, from the context; because if we were to accept the view of the Essayist, that it is a history by some forger of the Maccabean age, that the seventy weeks is to be understood as a period of about a year and four months, at the termination of which his Messiah, whether in the person of Judas Maccabæus, or some one else, was to be cut off, there is simply nothing whatever in that period of Jewish history which can in any way whatever be made applicable to the passage we are considering. There was no command to restore and rebuild Jerusalem, because it was not needed, the city and the temple having been rebuilt after the Babylonish captivity, about 300 years previous to the Maccabean age; the period during which the temple was profaned by Antiochus Epiphanes was not *seventy weeks*, but about three years, as the author of the first book of Maccabæus minutely records. Judas Maccabæus did not pretend to be the Messiah, nor any other Jew at that period; nor was he "cut off" or put to death as such. And if Dr. Williams, or any other critic of his school, can discover any appearance of application in the history of the Maccabean age, to what is stated in ver. 24, such as *finishing* or *restraining the transgression, making an end of sins*, or *bringing in everlasting righteousness*, he must possess spectacles of both telescopic and microscopic power, and be enabled to see farther into the *past* than any man, whether inspired or not, has ever pretended to look into the *future*. But in truth, so far from its being "beyond fair doubt that the period of the seventy weeks ended in the reign of Antiochus Epiphanes," the statement is in itself so monstrous, and the Essayist has so judiciously avoided attempting anything like *proof*, in support of his marvellous theory, that we feel it scarcely needs the brief refutation we have thought it right to give.

On the other hand, it is rather remarkable that another recent discovery in the department of Science, besides the interpretation of the cuneiform inscriptions — we refer to the reading of the Egyptian hieroglyphics — enables us to solve a difficulty which has hitherto baffled our commentators, in attempting to explain the time respecting the cutting off of the Messiah, according to the prophecy of the "seventy weeks." Without stopping to notice the endless attempts to reconcile history with prophecy in this instance, it will be sufficient to glance at the cause of the many failures, which we believe can be traced to the misunderstanding of Ptolemy's Canon respecting the commencement of the reign of King Artaxerxes, who granted the decree for restoring the broken-down wall of Jerusalem. We do not seek to depreciate the value of that canon, which is of immense value for a right understanding of the chronology of the interval between the Babylonish captivity and the Christian era, on which Scripture is silent; but we have certain proof that its chronology has been misapplied in this instance, by commentators seeking to unravel the truthful mysteries of this famous prophecy. According to Ptolemy's Canon, Artaxerxes Longimanus, the son of Xerxes, began to reign B.C. 465. Hence there has been a difficulty with respect to the commencement and termination of the prophecy, or rather that chief point in it which refers to the cutting off of the Messiah. Some referring the commencement to the decree given in the seventh year of Artaxerxes' reign, respecting the worship in the Temple [1]; others to the decree of the twentieth year of his reign, mentioned by Nehemiah [2]; some considering

---

[1] Ezra, vii. 11—28.   [2] Neh. ii. 1—20.

the cutting off of the Messiah to have taken place at the end of sixty-nine weeks, or 483 years; others at the end of "the seventy weeks," i.e. in all 490 years.[1] The results of such computations are as follows : If the commencement of the prophecy is to be dated from the 7th year (B. C. 458), it would terminateei ther A. D. 25 or A. D. 32, according to the mode of interpreting the termination at the end of 483 or 490 years; if from the 20th year (B. C. 445), then it would end either A. D. 38, or A. D. 45. Now there is no evidence that the crucifixion took place in any one of these four years. The eary A. D. 32 is nearest that of the commonly received chronology, which places that great event in the following year, but an error of one year would be more than sufficient to invalidate the force of any prophecy, which God in His wisdom has condescended to give for the edification of His inquiring and believing people. We have evidence, however, of the strongest and most satisfactory kind, in which Revelation and Science may be said to combine, to prove that the crucifixion or cutting off of the Messiah took place March 17th, A.D. 29.[2] Archbishop Usher, about two centuries ago, called attention to the fact, that Thucydides, who, as a contemporary historian must be a much greater authority than one who lived between five and six centuries later, placed the com-

---

[1] The eminent Dr. Lightfoot, however, differs from all these, as he dates the commencement of the *seventy weeks* in the first year of Cyrus, B. C. 538, and the termination with the death of Christ, A. D. 33, thus making the period 571 years. (See Hebr. and Talm. Exercitations upon St. Matt. iii. 6).

[2] The author has endeavoured to show this in his work on "The Introduction of Christianity into Britain," by adducing the scriptural, prophetical, historical, and scientific grounds at length, which prove, as he ventures to think, "beyond all fair doubt," the true year of the crucifixion.

mencement of Artaxerxes' reign nine years earlier than the Canon of Ptolemy, which gives twenty years as the length of Xerxes' reign, and forty for that of his son. The only way to reconcile these two authorities, is by accepting the suggestion of Whiston in the last century, that Xerxes must have taken his son Artaxerxes to share his throne, about the eleventh or twelfth year of his reign, just as we have already noticed Nabopalasar did Nebuchadnezzar, and Nabonnedus Belshazzar. Now we have evidence that such was the case. At Hammamet, on the Cosseyr road from Persia to Egypt by the Red Sea, some of the rare monumental records of the Persian rule in that country have been discovered, where a series of proscynemata have been engraved to the local divinity Khem, Lord of Coptus. The first of these is one of Adenes, a saris of Persia, who inscribes on shields, following each other, " the sixth year of Cambyses, the thirty-sixth year of Darius, and *the twelfth year of Xerxes*," and which evidently denote the length of time which each king reigned in Egypt, though, as Xerxes is last in order, it may only show the year of his reign when the record was made. There are also other inscriptions of the second, sixth, tenth, and *twelfth* years of Xerxes, but none beyond that *last*-mentioned year of his reign, save one, which is very remarkable, where the thirty-sixth year of Darius and the *thirteenth* of Xerxes, the son of Darius, are mentioned as synchronous years, the inscription under each cartouche or oval being " *Living like the sun for ever.*" [1]

By this we learn that the Persian sovereigns were accustomed to associate their sons in the regal power, and we conclude that Nehemiah and Thucydides alike

---

[1] Birch's Note in Loftus' Chaldæa, p. 411. Burton's Excerpta Hieroglyphica, pl. viii. and xiv. Lepsius, Denkmäler, iii. 283.

date the commencement of Artaxerxes' reign from the time when he was associated in the government with his father. Xerxes' *sole* reign, after the death of his father Darius, with whom he was associated, according to the hieroglyphic record, being just about twelve years (the thirteenth current), or the same length before he admitted his son Artaxerxes into partnership with him, and this agrees with the length of years allotted to him in the "Excerpta Latino-Barbara," as edited by Scaliger. That the decree of the twentieth year of Artaxerxes is the one from which to date the commencement of the prophecy, is evident from the fact of the previous decree referring to the way in which the worship in the temple was to be carried on, whereas the decree given to Nehemiah was solely in consequence of the ruined condition of the walls of Jerusalem, which had remained so since the time of Nebuchadnezzar, and which Artaxerxes gave him permission to rebuild. If, therefore, we have any respect to the words of Scripture, whether of Daniel or Nehemiah, we may compute with unerring accuracy the time which the prophecy foretold should elapse from rebuilding the walls of Jerusalem to the crucifixion of Christ, viz., a divided period of seven weeks and sixty-two weeks, or sixty-nine in all, equalling 483 years. Dating from the twentieth year of Artaxerxes, B.C. 455, as the commencement of the famous *prediction* in Daniel, respecting the time of the Messiah's appearing, and adding the 483 years, we are brought to the Passover of A.D. 29, in which year we have an overwhelming amount of evidence that the crucifixion occurred. It will be sufficient to adduce one sort of evidence on this point, but which is of the most satisfactory kind. The Acta Pilati, containing the report of Pilate's government in Judea to the Emperor Tiberius, and which existed when Justin Martyr and Tertullian wrote their respective Apologies in the 2nd century, specify the 17th of March as the day of the month in the Roman Kalendar when the crucifixion took place. This we learn from Epiphanius' account of the Quartadecimans of Cappadocia, who justified their observance of Easter at that date, as St. John and the other Apostles had done before, from the time having been so specified in the Acta Pilati. Hence, as we find by the astronomical tables, A. D. 29 is the only one of many years either before or after that time when the 14th day of the month Abib, or Nisan, as it was then called by the Jews, fell on the 17th of March, and as it is certain, from the unanimous testimony of the Evangelists, that "the Messiah was cut off" at the time of the Passover, which, by God's command to Moses, was kept on the 14th of Abib[1], we have one of the strongest proofs which Science affords to the truth of Revelation, that the prophecy or *prediction* recorded in Daniel was literally fulfilled at the time according to God's appointment.

Science affords us also another proof of what we believe may be fairly termed the marvellous exactness of the prophetic word respecting the time when the Messiah was to be cut off. We read in the Book of Nehemiah that it was "in the month Nisan, in the twentieth year of Artaxerxes," that Nehemiah informed the king of the ruined condition of the walls of Jerusalem; and supposing the decree for their restoration to have been dated on the 14th day of that month (Scripture does not specify the day), we may compute from that time unto the Passover of A.D. 29, when the prophecy would be accomplished in the cutting off of the Messiah; for the expression "after the threescore and two weeks shall Messiah be cut off," must mean at the termination of the

---

[1] Exodus, xii. 16, 17, xiii. 3, 4.

483 years, just as we understand the prophecy respecting Christ's resurrection, "after three days," to mean at the expiration of the time specified. Now we find from the astronomical tables that the time for observing the Passover in both B.C. 455 and A.D. 29, fell on the same day, viz., the 17th of March. If, therefore, we are justified in our inference respecting the decree of Artaxerxes having been dated on the 14th of the month Nisan, *on that very day* 483 *years afterwards*, the prophecy was fulfilled to the letter when the "Messiah was cut off" on Mount Calvary. With such a proof of the truth of God's word, is it not marvellous that any one claiming to be a critic of "Biblical Researches" should betray his scepticism and his incapacity alike, by avowing his "conclusion that the book (of Daniel) *contains no predictions*, except by analogy and type, can hardly be gainsaid"?

§ 12. Dr. Williams' treatment of the Prophet Jonah seems to manifest an equal amount of scepticism with that of Daniel. "It provokes *a smile on serious topics*," writes this English clergyman, "to observe the zeal with which our critic (Bunsen) *vindicates the personality of Jonah*, and the originality of his hymn (the latter being generally thought doubtful), while he proceeds to explain that the narrative of our book, in which the hymn is embedded, contains a late legend founded on misconception. One can imagine the cheers which the opening of such an essay might evoke in some of our own circles, changing into indignation as the distinguished foreigner developed his views. After this he might speak more gently of mythical theories" (p. 77). Whether a "smile" is the most becoming mode for a professed minister of the Church of Christ to testify the intensity of his disbelief in the miracles which are recorded in Scripture, we need not stop to inquire; but we think it would have been a happier avowal on the part of the Essayist, as well as more suitable to the obligations of his profession, if he had possessed both the knowledge and the faith of the old woman, of whom it is related that being taunted by a sceptical neighbour for believing that " a whale swallowed Jonah," very simply and justly replied, " If God had said Jonah had swallowed the whale, I would have believed it." We recollect once hearing an eminent English clergyman, who had been engaged in the whale fishery in his earlier days, express himself in a public lecture on this subject, in a manner which might provoke " a smile," though his object was the opposite to that fatal theory which seems to pervade the mind of the Essayist. Well knowing from personal experience that the throat of the *whale* is capable of admitting little more than the *arm* of an ordinary man, he thought to reconcile Revelation and Science by supposing that, as our Lord had compared the type and the antitype by declaring " as Jonas was in the whale's belly, so shall the Son of Man be in *the heart* of the earth ;" and as our Lord's body only lay on the *surface* of the earth, during the interval between his burial and resurrection, it was not to be understood that Jonah was *swallowed* by the whale, but that it was a sufficient miracle for the whale to have retained Jonah in his *mouth*, as that species of fish possessed one sufficiently large for the purpose, and moreover furnished with an " unruly member," equal in size to a sofa, and of a texture softer than velvet, on which the Prophet might comfortably recline during his three days and three nights' confinement. The good man, however, clearly forgot one or two things in his singular conclusion. In the first place, Scripture by no means describes the animal which received Jonah as a *whale*, but merely says, " The Lord had prepared *a great fish*," דג גדול [1], into whose " belly "

---

[1] Dr. Adam Clarke observes that "some have translated דג גדול by a *fishing cove*, or something of this nature ; but this is merely to get

the prophet undoubtedly went. And though it is true that the translators of the New Testament have introduced the word "*whale*," we all know that the Greek word κῆτος is merely significant of any *great fish*, and that as the *whale* was known in their day, as it is in ours, to be the greatest of marine monsters, they thought it allowable to use such a word, without meaning it to be understood in its present common signification. We may question if that species of "great fish," from which our domestic article *whalebone* is obtained, was known to the civilised world before the time of King Alfred, in the ninth century, when some Norwegian fishermen are said to have discovered it; and it is certain that the whale is not a native of the Mediterranean Sea, where the miracle in all probability took place. We say "in all probability," unless we accept the dictum of an Archbishop of Lisbon, who once gravely contended in the pulpit against the right of priority in the discovery of the Cape of Good Hope, which was generally attributed to his distinguished countryman Vasco de Gama (though by the way the Phœnicians had circumnavigated the Cape ages before, according to Herodotus), since Jonah had previously performed the same voyage in the belly of the whale, which, by safely landing him at the mouth of the Tigris, enabled him to perform the remainder of his journey by water to Nineveh! Further, the comparison of Jonah being in the *mouth* of the whale, as our Lord was buried on the surface of the earth, is rather beside the mark; for the expression, "the heart of the earth," referred doubtless to our Lord being laid in a tomb dug out of a rock, as St. Matthew records, which would be suitably defined as

---

rid of the miracle, for, according to some, the whole of Divine Revelation is a forgery, or it is a system of metaphor or allegory, that has no miraculous interferences in it."—*Comment. in loco.*

belonging to the *heart* of the earth as distinct from the upper surface, or what geologists term the post-tertiary system. But the question which really concerns us is the possibility of there being any species of sea-monster inhabiting the Mediterranean Sea with a throat sufficiently large to swallow, and a belly to contain, a human being; for though, in the exercise of His miraculous power, God could as easily enlarge the throat of a whale, and place him in any sea to which naturally he does not belong, we have no reason to suppose that He goes unnecessarily out of His way to perform a *second* miracle, in addition to what His own word declares. Now we have evidence that there is a " great fish " common to these latitudes, in which men have been discovered whole. Without accepting the wonderful tales of Pliny[1], who speaks of whales 600 *feet long and* 360 *feet broad*, or of Pomponius Mela[2], who relates that at Joppa they used to show the skeleton of a huge sea-monster, which was afterwards exhibited at Rome during the ædileship of M. Scaurus (though, as these are not writers of Scripture, possibly their stories will have more weight with some than Christians would feel right to allow), we have the explicit testimony of credible writers that in more than one instance a fish of the species called *carcharias*, or dog-fish, has been taken in the Mediterranean, in whose belly was found the body of a soldier armed *cap-a-pie*. In Linnæus' System of Nature by Müller, a fact is mentioned which may be considered as illustrating the miracle of Jonah. At the close of the last century, during a storm in the Mediterranean, a sailor fell overboard, and was instantly received into the throat of a *carcharias*. An officer on deck having a gun at hand, fired instantly at the monster's head, and the shot taking effect, the creature disgorged

---

[1] Nat. Hist. lib. ix. c. 5.   [2] Lib. i. c. 7.

the sailor comparatively speaking uninjured. This "great fish" was subsequently captured, and found to weigh 4000 pounds. We have, therefore, good reason to believe in the miracle recorded in the Book of Jonah; but we have no reason to credit "the mythical theories" of the rationalistic school in general and of Essayists in particular, who seek to bring the miracles of Scripture down to the level of their own finite understandings.

§ 13. On the grand doctrine of Justification by Faith, Dr. Williams asks, "Why may it not have meant the peace of mind, or sense of Divine approval, which comes of trust in a righteous God, rather than *a fiction of merit by transfer?* St. Paul would then be teaching moral responsibility, as opposed to sacerdotalism; or that to obey is better than sacrifice. Faith would be opposed, not to the good deeds, which conscience requires, but to works of appeasement by ritual. It is not a fatal objection to say that St. Paul would thus teach natural religion unless we were sure that he was bound to contradict it; but it is a confirmation of the view if it brings *his hard sayings* into harmony with the Gospels and with the Psalms, as well as with the instincts of our best conscience" (pp. 80, 81). Again he remarks, " Our author (Bunsen) believes St. Paul, because he understands him *reasonably.* Nor does his acceptance of Christ's redemption from evil bind him to repeat traditional fictions about our canon, or to read its pages with that dulness which turns symbol and poetry into materialism" (p. 83). How any man who has sworn to teach that "we are accounted righteous before God, only for the merit of our Lord and Saviour Jesus Christ by faith, and not for our own works or deservings,"[1] and that " the offering of Christ once made is that perfect redemption, propitiation,

---

[1] Art. xi.

and satisfaction, for all the sins of the whole world, both original and actual; and there is none other satisfaction for him *but that alone*,"[1] can reconcile the avowal of the above opinions with his retention of the status of an English clergyman, we are at a loss to imagine. But it will be sufficient to notice the fatal mistake of which Dr. Williams is guilty, in supposing that there is any difference in the teaching of St. Paul from that of the Evangelists in the New Testament, or of David in the Old. That the doctrine of the *atonement*, or the way by which we fallen creatures are "at one mind" (as the word etymologically signifies) with the Great Creator, by the mutual transfer of our sins to Christ and Christ's righteousness to us, as well as the doctrine of *Justification by Faith*, or God's righteous way of righteously accounting unrighteous man righteous, is taught alike in the Old and New Testament, the one leading on to the other, needs not much " Biblical Research" to discover. For as Bishop Horsley truly remarked, " That man is justified by faith without the works of the law was the uniform doctrine of the first Reformers. It is a far more ancient doctrine. It was the doctrine of the whole college of Apostles. It is more ancient still. It was the doctrine of the Prophets. It is older than the Prophets. It was the religion of the Patriarchs." So the ancient fathers interpreted these great doctrinal verities; e. g. Cyril of Alexandria, in the 5th century, writes, "He who formed the earth, and men upon it, He who adorned the heavens with stars, raised up for us as righteousness Jesus, who gratuitously redeems (for we have been justified by faith), releasing from chains and captivity, spiritually building the intellectual Jerusalem, and founding the Church, so that it shall be unmoved by the gates of hell, and unsubdued by enemies."[2] Chry-

---

[1] Art. xxxi.
[2] Cyr. Arch. Alex. Glaphy. ii. p. 55; Tom. i. Lutet. 1638.

sostom in the preceding century had written : " God doth not say He made Christ a sinner, but *sin*, that we might be made, not righteous, but righteousness, even the righteousness of God. For it is of God, since it is not of works (which would require spotless perfection) but by grace we are justified, where all sin is blotted out."[1] We think we can trace the confusion which is so evident in the reasoning of the Essayist, to the mistake he makes of the different objects which St. Paul and St. James have in view. Both alike bring forward the case of Abraham, in whom Scripture was fulfilled, when he " believed God, and it was counted or imputed ($ἐλογίσθη$ is used by both) unto him for righteousness." St. James concludes : " Ye see then how that by works a man is justified, and not by faith only."[2] St. Paul writes : " We conclude that a man is justified by faith without the deeds of the law."[3] Yet this apparent difference is in reality perfect harmony, when we remember that it is by faith only and not by works that man is accounted righteous in heaven, while it is by works only and not by faith, that a man is esteemed righteous upon earth. " Non sunt sibi," taught the saintly Augustine, " contrariæ duorum Apostolorum sententiæ Pauli et Jacobi, cum dicit unus justificari hominem per fidem sine operibus. Quia ille dicit de operibus quæ fidem præcedent, iste de his quæ fidem sequuntur." When, therefore, we find a professed Minister of Christ, like the Essayist, terming " merit by transfer *a fiction*," and commending another for " understanding St. Paul (the most prominent teacher of the important doctrine of ' Justification by Faith ' in Scripture) *reasonably*," we cannot but see a striking fulfilment of the Apostolic declaration : " The natural man receiveth not the things of the Spirit of God:

---

[1] Chry., Hom. ii. on 2 Cor. v.
[2] St. James, ii. 23, 24.   [3] Rom. iii. 28.

for they are foolishness unto him; neither can he know them, because they are spiritually discerned."[1] Had the Essayist more spiritual discernment respecting the doctrine of the atonement, he would surely have avoided the use of such objectionable language respecting it, when he says "The angels who hover with phials, catching the drops from the cross, are pardonable in art, but make a step in theology towards transubstantiation. Salvation from evil through sharing the Saviour's Spirit, was shifted into a *notion of purchase from God* through the price of His bodily sufferings." (p. 87.)

§ 14. The mode in which Dr. Williams speaks of another fundamental doctrine of our religion, viz. that of the Trinity, which the Jews, though they refuse to recognise the Messiahship of Christ, have rightly termed "the mystery of faith,"[2] is scarcely less objectionable. "With the mere speculative fathers," says he, "the doctrine of the Trinity was a profound metaphysical problem, wedded to what seemed consequences of the incarnation. But in ruder hands it became a materialism almost idolatrous, or an arithmetical enigma. Even now, different acceptors of the same doctrinal terms hold many shades of conception between a philosophical view which recommends itself as easiest to believe, *and one felt to be so irrational, that it calls in the aid of terror.* 'Quasi non unitas, *irrationaliter* collecta, hæresin faciat; et Trinitas *rationaliter* expensa, veritatem constituat,' said Tertullian" (p. 87). We cannot accept Tertullian's definition of the doctrine of the Trinity, simply because the work (Adversus Praxeam) from which the quotation is taken, though valuable so far as its object of exposing the Patripassian heresy is carried out, was composed after its author had deserted Catholicism for Montanism, and he cannot here be a safe guide

---

[1] 1 Cor. ii. 14. [2] Zohar in Gen. fol. 12, 4.

to us in our search after Divine truth. And we must express our surprise at the mode in which Dr. Williams speaks of the Athanasian Creed, as we naturally conclude his rod *in terrorem* refers to that wondrous definition of the faith, when he talks of one of many shades of conception of the doctrine being "felt to be so irrational, that it calls in the aid of terror." The "Catholic Faith," or the "Right Faith," as it is likewise termed in the Athanasian Creed, in its sound and proper definition of the truth, "calls in the aid of terror" no further than the Word of God itself. "The Catholic faith is this, that we worship one God in Trinity, and Trinity in Unity. The right faith is, that we believe and confess that our Lord Jesus Christ, the Son of God, is God and man — who suffered — descended — rose — ascended — from whence He shall come to judge the quick and the dead. At whose coming all men shall rise again with their bodies, and shall give account for their own works. And they that have done good shall go into life everlasting: and they that have done evil, into everlasting fire. This is the Catholic Faith, which except a man believe faithfully he cannot be saved." It is difficult, however, to understand exactly what Dr. Williams means in his attempted definition of this great doctrinal verity, which, though it may be above our reason, is not contrary to it. When he quotes from Hippolytus that "the Unity of God, as the Eternal Father, is the fundamental doctrine of Christianity," we accept it as a true expression of the Catholic faith, because it includes the Triune personality in the one undivided Jehovah, just as man is one, consisting of these three several parts, body, soul, and spirit. So the Godhead in its incomprehensibility is revealed to us in the person of the Father; in its comprehensibility in that of the Son; and in its communicableness in that of the Holy Ghost. But when he asserts that "the primitive Trinity represented neither three original principles nor three transient phases, *but three eternal subsistences* in one Divine Mind" (p. 88), we cannot tell whether he means to deny or to recognise the separate personality of the Father, the Word, and the Holy Ghost, who, whatever value we may attach to the genuineness of 1 John v. 7, unquestionably compose the heavenly witnesses, and "these three are one." We think enough has been adduced from Dr. Williams' Essay to show the propriety of applying the epithet "*painfully sceptical*," which he rightly supposes some would consider applicable to Bunsen's "Biblical Researches" (see p. 434), more peculiarly to his own criticisms on the doctrines, the prophecies, and the histories in Scripture; and we gladly turn from this unwelcome task, of exposing a brother's failings, to consider how far Bunsen himself is a safe guide to a right understanding of the Word of God.

CHAP. II.

WHILE we would fain bear in mind, whether of Baron Bunsen or of any other who has been taken hence, the value of the old Latin adage, " De mortuis nil nisi *bonum*," we cannot but admit the necessity of the proposed emendation, " De mortuis nil nisi *verum*." And this is truly needful here, when we recollect the just admiration which this distinguished German scholar excited during his life, of which we have already seen an instance in the manner in which Dr. Arnold used to speak of his friend, together with his sincere Christianity, as exemplified (if we may judge from M. de Presense's affecting record of his last hours on earth) in his death. Of all the works which Bunsen published, and which Dr. Williams has generalised under the term " Biblical Researches," the one on which his fame will rest is undoubtedly his " Egypt's Place in Universal History," a work that is still incomplete, as far as the translation is concerned; though the concluding volume, there is every reason to believe, may be expected during the present year in its English dress. Putting aside the great talent and varied learning displayed in the work itself, as well as the many and attractive qualities of its author, so long known and deservedly esteemed in this country as the popular Prussian Ambassador, how melancholy to find this eminent scholar, this able investigator, this student in " Biblical Researches," denying that there is any *chronological element in Revelation*," which Dr. Williams has commended as combining the incongruous qualities of *quaintness* and *strength*. "He (Bunsen) says with quaint strength, 'there is no chronological element in Revelation'" (p. 57). On this point, as believers in Revelation, we are necessarily at issue with this distinguished German, and our object will be to show not only how groundless are his views respecting the Chronology of Scripture, but how satisfactorily Science aids Revelation in proving, with regard to "times and seasons," the truth and accuracy of God's Word. And in order that we may not be unjust, let us hear, first of all, his own words respecting the "chronological element in Revelation."

"As regards the Jewish computation of time, the study of Scripture had long convinced me, that there is in the Old Testament no connected chronology prior to Solomon. All that now passes for a system of ancient chronology beyond that fixed point, is the melancholy legacy of the 17th and 18th centuries; a compound of intentional deceit and utter misconception of the principles of historical research. .... It is in Egyptian history, if anywhere, that materials are to be gathered for the foundation of a chronology of the oldest history of nations."[1] .... "Whoever adopts as a principle that chronology is a matter of revelation, is precluded from giving effect to any doubt that may cross his path, as involving a virtual abandonment of his faith in revelation. He must be prepared not only to deny the existence of contradictory statements, but to fill up chasms; however irreconcilable the former may appear by any aid of philology and history, however unfathomable the latter."[2] .... "For the period of the sojourn in Egypt there existed neither historical chronology nor even his-

---

[1] Egypt's Place in Universal History, vol. i. pref. viii.
[2] Ibid. vol. i. p. 161.

tory." .... "It ought long ago to have been a settled point, that our present popular and school chronology is *a fable strung together by ignorance and fraud, and persisted in out of superstition and a want of intellectual energy.*"[1] .... "We think we may say that *the chronology of Egypt which we have set up is verified when confronted with the Bible* and with the Greek accounts of Egypt and Babylon, and we may also now add the cuneiform inscriptions of Nineveh."[2] .... "The chronology of the Exodus can only be ascertained from the Egyptian monuments. .... We are certain to find in this quarter systematic contradiction to everything historical. For the date as here fixed is at issue with the Jewish-Christian calculation, and at the same time attacks long-established prejudices and hierarchical pretensions. We may, therefore, take for granted that any synchronism which can be proved historically will be disputed and mistrusted a few years longer 'for the glory of God.' Any one who knows nothing about, and does not wish to know anything about, philological research, may, without any difficulty, believe everything which he will, or is told to believe. Any one who has no rational grounds for his belief can never be at a loss for a doubt about anything historical. Doubt becomes his nature, because he lives in the unhistorical and in untruth."[3] .... "The ordinary chronology we declare to be devoid of any scientific foundation; *the interpretation*, indeed, by which it is accompanied, when carefully investigated, *makes the Bible a tissue of old women's stories and children's tales, which contradict each other.* When confronted with authentic chronology, it generally leads to impossible results. It

---

[1] Ibid. vol. ii. p. 440.
[2] Ibid. vol. iii. p. 20.   [3] Ibid. vol. iii. pp. 23, 24.

does not harmonise with anything which historical criticism finds elsewhere, and which it is under the necessity of recognising as established fact. It is, as regards the religious views of educated persons, the same thing as the stories in the Vedas about the world-tortoise are to those who are supposed to believe them — a stone of stumbling, and it will become more and more so every ten years. For it contradicts all reality, and necessitates the denial of facts which are as clear as the sun; or if it does not succeed in that, compels them to be passed over altogether as matters of no moment. In countries where research cannot be prohibited by the police, or is not punishable by excommunication, this indeed in the long run becomes exceedingly laughable, but it does not on that account cease to be immoral."[1] . . . . " In the Egyptian we have obtained a fixed chronological point, and in fact the highest in general history. In it we find a perfectly formed language, which *we can prove* to have been in existence about the middle of the fourth millennium B.C. We, therefore, arrive at the very threshold of the formation of language."[2] . . . . " The chronology of Egypt shows still more clearly than the traditions preserved in the Biblical book of the Origines, that the flood of Noah could not have taken place later than about 10,000 years B.C., and could not well have taken place much earlier."[3] . . . . " It is obvious that if the attempted interpretation of the Biblical narratives about the early world be correct, it must be verified by an examination and restoration of the Hebrew traditions about the commencements of the post-diluvian world. It may be considered as a settled point that the Biblical narratives have taken their

---

[1] Egypt's Place in Universal History, vol. iii. pp. 348, 349.
[2] Ibid. vol. iv. p. 45.
[3] Ibid. vol. iv. p. 51.

legitimate place among the other traditions and records of general history. The real and eternal signification of the strictly ideal portion of Biblical tradition may now be thoroughly understood. No man can honestly deal with the present chronology, when, by the dates of the pyramids and other contemporaneous monuments, he must go back to nearly 4000 B.C., or the Judaic date of creation, in order to arrive at Menes."[1] . . . . " It ought strictly speaking, to be unnecessary, not to say unseemly, to adduce any proof that if there be historic truth in this tradition, it never can have meant that individual men lived six, eight, or nine centuries. Had this been the case, the statement ought to have been declared intrinsically impossible. But our analysis has shown us that the original account meant no such thing. And still some who serve at the altar and in the halls of science, *either from cowardice or superstition (not to impute to them worse motives)*, are not only not ashamed of avowing their own unbelief, but even call upon other Christians, at the peril of being declared outcasts and infidels, to hold as true Christian faith *the absurdities of their assumptions.* It is one thing to say 'I believe the Biblical account, although I cannot explain it;' another, *to set up as an article of faith an absurd explanation, the child of ignorance or of unbelief in the spirit.* . . . . We have good reason to believe that what we have is only the misunderstanding of the earliest records of Biblical tradition. Even in the time of Solomon, the original tradition about Seth and Enoch had ceased to be understood. . . . . . . Christian writers, from Eusebius the Bishop of Cæsarea downwards, began to act on the offensive, and to enter into the domain of falsehood. For any one who states that he knows a thing to be historical which he has not

---

[1] Egypt's Place in Universal History, vol. iv. p. 402.

inquired into, and consequently does not know, is guilty of lying. .... Shortly after, all intellectual culture and learning perished in the West, and even the compilation of Eusebius was too much for the Western World of Rome. With that miserable epitome they were contented in the Middle Ages, that is during a thousand years. When in the 15th and 16th centuries men's minds were awakened, there rose the masters of research, but the necessity of political self-defence against persecution prevented them from carrying out fully their researches and fighting out the great intellectual battle. The 17th century, that triumph of bigotry and of tyranny in most countries, although beginning with so much light and hope, endeavoured to stifle its own conscience and that of the future by a display of learning, partly sophistical and partly spiritless, without ideas and without real erudition. The 18th century avenged itself, for the opprobrium to which it was obliged to submit, by suicidal mockery; and the 19th has in the last thirty years witnessed, together with immortal discoveries, *the most senseless and shameless attempts to re-establish in the world ancient and modern fraud, falsehood, and nonsense, and pass it off as orthodoxy.* Posterity will find in the noble love of truth and the fearless faith of *German research*, an atonement and consolation for political follies and despotic violence. We must take care not to relax our steps, nor to turn round, but to go on in the course of restoration with all boldness and all the aids of research, not for the purpose of destroying an existing fabric, but of building *up one that has been crushed by its own falsehood.*"[1]

Thus much respecting Bunsen's Biblical Researches, with reference to "the Chronological Element in Revela-

---

[1] Egypt's Place in Universal History, vol. iv. pp. 395–7.

tion." Some will naturally conclude that the severity of his invective betrays a conscious weakness of the cause which he adopts, and which he with deplorable violence of language seeks to defend. Believing for our own part notwithstanding, that the Chronology of Scripture is as much inspired, and, therefore, necessarily as true, as the doctrines or the history or the prophecies found in the Bible, we propose to adduce every species of scientific proof in order to corroborate Scripture Chronology, and to disprove by the very means on which he boastingly relies, viz. "Astronomy" and "Historical Synchronisms,"[1] the "quaint" and extraordinary theory by which he endeavours to overthrow the plainest and most positive statements in God's Word.

The great authority on which Bunsen mainly relies for upsetting the Chronology of Scripture is Manetho, the Egyptian priest, who flourished in the days of Ptolemy Philadelphus, B.C. 285, and about thirteen centuries later, be it remembered, than Moses. Yet so infatuated is the learned German with this Sebennyte scribe, whose History of the Thirty-one Dynasties of the Kings of Egypt is known to us from the *fragments* preserved by Josephus in his treatise against Apion, as well as in the Chronicles of Syncellus, which are compiled from the earlier works of Eusebius and Africanus, in whose time the history itself was probably extant, that he thinks the authority of Manetho is amply sufficient to overthrow the contemporary witnesses in Scripture, leaving out the question of inspiration; and all this, notwithstanding his admission that "the Egyptians possessed no work on history among their sacred books, nor had they any *connected chronology* like that of the years of Nabonassar, the Olympiads, or the building

---

[1] Egypt's Place in Universal History, vol. i. pref. xli.

of Rome."[1] Indeed so boundless is his admiration for the Egyptian historian, that he can scarcely find language sufficiently eulogistic to express himself:—

> "Grateful I offer to thee whatever through thee I have learned;
> Truth have I sought at thy hand; Truth have I found by thy aid."[2]

The difference in his estimate of the writers of Scripture and Manetho[3] are so great that we can only express it by describing him as a giant in scepticism as regards the one and an infant in credulity as regards the other. As Bunsen follows Manetho, so the Essayist follows his leader. "Our own testimony is," says Dr. Williams, "where we have been best able to follow him, we have generally been most able to agree with him. But our little survey has not traversed his vast field, nor our plummet sounded his depth :

> "And when those fables strange, our hirelings teach,
> I saw by genuine learning cast aside,
> Even like Linnæus kneeling on the sod,
> For faith from falsehood severed, thank I God."

Dr. Williams' following of Bunsen, as he does Manetho, reminds us of the way in which quotations are frequently diverted from their true origin. The well-known and

---

[1] Egypt's Place in Universal History, vol. i. p. 24.
[2] Ibid. vol. ii. p. 392.
[3] Bunsen's grand error is seen in his determination to make Manetho's dynasties successive, instead of contemporary, as many of them unquestionably were. This may be proved, not only from the authority of Manetho himself, who speaks of the "kings of Thebaïs and of the other provinces of Egypt," but the monuments themselves decide this point by the mention of the years of one king's reign corresponding with those of another, according to the conclusion of our most eminent Egyptologer, Sir G. Wilkinson. See *Rawlinson's Herod.* vol. ii. c. viii. app. book ii.
[4] Essays and Reviews, p. 93.

very beautiful saying, "God tempers the wind to the shorn lamb," has been supposed by many to be found in Scripture. Those who knew better, generally credited it to Sterne; but he stole it from George Herbert, who translated it from the French of Henri Estienne. So the errors of the Egyptian, having been adopted by the German, have been faithfully acknowledged by an English clergyman. We must not, however, omit to notice that Eratosthenes, the Grecian chronicler of Egyptian history, is relied upon by Bunsen, as well as Manetho, for the purpose of contravening Biblical chronology. And it is the enormous discrepancies which exist between these two contemporary authorities, as we gather from the fragments which have come down to us, which prevent our placing much reliance upon them, especially when they are used by clever advocates to set aside the consistent testimony of the inspired writers of Scripture. For example, *the difference*[1] between Manetho and Eratosthenes in the duration of those dynasties which reigned in Egypt from Menes (the same as Mizraim the son of Ham, Gen. x. 6) the first king unto Amuthantæus, who preceded the XVIIIth dynasty, when " the king which knew not Joseph arose," *is upwards of* 3000 *years*. The former reckons it at 4055 years, the latter at 1050. So likewise in the statements of Manetho himself, as they have been transmitted by the two Christian chronologers, Africanus and Eusebius, there is *a difference of* 400 *years* in the duration of the first eleven dynasties, the former giving 2285 years, the latter 1876. Further, the different conclusions to

---

[1] Diodorus Siculus notices the great difficulty of ascertaining the truth in regard to Egyptian history, as he observes of one of their kings, "not only do the Greek writers differ among themselves about him, but likewise the Egyptian priests and poets relate various and different stories concerning him."—*Hist.* lib. i. c. iv.

which distinguished Egyptologers in the present day have come respecting most important periods in history, shows the utter vanity of the attempt to reject the testimony of Scripture on the question of chronology. The Hyksos period, as it is commonly called, representing the interval between Amuthantæus and the XVIIIth dynasty, lasted, according to Lepsius, 500 years, Bunsen, 1000, and Viscount de Rougé 1900. Hence Bunsen very *naïvely* remarks that he finds a "*difficulty* in coinciding either with the views of Lepsius or De Rougé in respect to the period which intervened between the 12th and 18th dynasties."[1] On the other hand Osburn, in his very valuable work "The Monumental History of Egypt," has shown the mythical nature of the so-called Hyksos period altogether ; that in reality it was a struggle between the kings of Memphis and Thebes, who equally claimed descent from Menes, the proto-monarch of the whole of Egypt[2], and that the probable duration of the period between the 12th and 18th dynasties could not have been more than about 150 years.

The chronological and historical differences are so great between ancient and modern writers on Egypt, that we shall have a good idea of the same by drawing an ideal comparison of the way in which events in English history might in future ages be recorded. Let us suppose Lord Macaulay's New Zealander (not by the way his original idea) sitting on the broken arch of London Bridge, A.D. 2862, and meditating the history of the mighty nation,

---

[1] Egypt's Place in Universal History, vol. ii. p. 427.

[2] Three eminent authorities, Sir Gardner Wilkinson, Dr. Hincks, and Mr. Stuart Poole, agree in considering that after the reign of Menes the kingdom became divided, and while the remaining kings of the 1st and 2nd dynasties reigned in Upper Egypt, the 3rd and 4th reigned at Memphis, in Lower Egypt. See *Rawlinson's Herodotus*, vol. ii. p. 163.

which once flourished, like Babylon and Tyre, and then had entirely passed away. He might learn from the few fragments of her history which remained in his day, that it was very difficult to decide who "the great king" meant, occasionally referred to by early historians; whether it meant Alfred the Great, Edward III., or Oliver Cromwell; for thus do historians dispute respecting the whereabouts of Sesostris the Great: that it was impossible to decide whether the Saxon Heptarchy meant contemporary or successive kings, and the same of the sovereigns of the Northern and Southern parts of the Isle of Great Britain, known as Scotland and England; for thus some dispute about the dynasties reigning in Upper, Middle, and Lower Egypt: that it is not certain how long the Danes continued in England, whether 90 or 1440 years, for that is the difference between the two great authorities Bunsen and Lepsius, who reject Scripture testimony respecting the duration of the children of Israel in Egypt: that it is disputed whether the interval between the death of Alfred the Great and the Norman Conquest represented a period of 500 or 1900 years; these being, as we have already noticed, the two extremes which Lepsius and De Rougé give for the duration of the so-called Hyksos period, which in reality was only about 150 years: that it is difficult to decide whether the celebrated William of Orange lived in the 7th or 17th century after Christ; for that is the difference between Bunsen and Osburn, respecting the time of a very distinguished Pharaoh called Phiops-Apappus, to whom Joseph was prime minister, one placing him in the 6th dynasty the other in the 16th, there being an interval of about a thousand years between the two: that it is disputed whether the reigns of the first three Georges of the Hanoverian dynasty lasted 87 or 192 years; for thus do Manetho and Eratosthenes differ respecting the length of the reigns of the three kings who were distinguished as the builders of the Pyramids of Gizeh, and who succeeded each other. These things will afford some faint idea of the inextricable confusion which exists on important portions of Egyptian history, and amply sufficient to convince us of the impossibility of accepting it when it contradicts the plain and consistent statements of Scripture. We readily admit its value, as we shall now endeavour to show, when confirmatory of Scripture; but we affirm, without the slightest doubt, that it is most unphilosophical and most unscientific to imagine, as the German rationalists have done, that their numberless contradictions respecting the chronology and history of Egypt are likely to supplant the well-established chronology of the Word of God. In order that we may see at a glance the difference which exists between Scripture chronology and that which has been adopted and so zealously defended by Bunsen, we present a tabular view of some of the important epochs in the history of the world.[1]

	The Bible. B.C.		Bunsen. B.C.	
1. The Creation of Man	4,100		20,000	
Interval		1,657 years.		9,000 years.
2. Noachian Flood	2,443		11,000	
Interval		102 years.		4,000 years.
3. Babel Dispersion	2,341		7,000	
Interval		326 years.		4,123 years.
4. Call of Abraham	2,015		2,877	
Interval		215 years.		122 years.
5. Joseph's Rule in Egypt	1,800		2,755	
Interval		215 years.		1,435 years.
6. Time of the Exode	1,585		1,320	
Interval		566 years.		306 years.
7. Building of the Temple	1,019		1,014	

[1] When Dr. Hales, in his great work on Chronology, observed that "no less than 120 authors give a different period for the epoch of the creation of the world, the extreme range of difference between

We propose to examine these several statements, and we think we can show reasons for confirming the chronology of Scripture and rejecting that which Baron Bunsen has proposed to substitute in its place. But before attempting this, it may be well to define what is meant by Biblical Chronology. Which are we to accept as inspired and genuine, the longer computation of the LXX., or the shorter chronology of the Hebrew Text? The difference between the two, as well as that of the Samaritan, may be briefly stated as follows:

	Hebrew.	LXX.	Samaritan.
From the Creation to the Deluge . . years	1,656	2,262	1,307
From the Deluge to the Birth of Abraham . . . . ,,	352	1,002	1,002
	2,008	3,264	2,309

The following reasons will suffice to show that the Hebrew Text contains the true Chronology, and that the other two are not to be depended upon: 1st. The LXX. and the Samaritan version abound *in various readings* with respect to their different chronologies, and frequently contradict themselves; whereas the Hebrew is uniform and consistent in all its copies. 2nd. The Hebrew claims to be the inspired original, transmitted by those who were chosen by God to be " witnesses and keepers " of His Word, to whom, as St. Paul says, " were committed the oracles of God;"[1] whereas the Samaritan Pentateuch was a translation, or rather another version in a different dialect, made about 900 years after the great original; and the LXX. was a translation into another language, made in another country, about four centuries later still.

---

them amounting to no less than 3,268 years," he little anticipated how soon an extension of 13,000 further years would be required to satisfy the speculative researches of the German school.

[1] Rom. iii. 2.

3rd. The variations between the original and the translation in the duration of the lives of antediluvian patriarchs, which is our only mode of computing the chronology of the world's history in those early times, appear to be not the effect of accident, but of design, on the part of the latter; because the years before the father begat a son, and the residues in all the cases, agree with the totals of lives; e.g. it is said in the Hebrew, "Adam lived 130 years, and begat a son," after which he lived "800 years;" and "all the days that Adam lived were 930 years," for $130 + 800 = 930$; whereas in the LXX., it is elongated before the birth of a son, and curtailed subsequently, thus "Adam lived 230 years and begat a son," after which he lived "700 years;" and "all the days that Adam lived were 930 years," for $230 + 700 = 930$. By this means the LXX. translators in Egypt were enabled to lengthen the antediluvian period, and thus to bring it nearer to that fabulous system of chronology which the Egyptians adopted, without any material difference from the original, as regards the duration of the Patriarchal lives, which they equally with their brethren in Judæa, acknowledged to be inspired of God. One manifest error in this mode of computation is seen in the fact of the LXX. making Methuselah *live fourteen years after the deluge;* whereas it is abundantly clear that none but Noah and his family lived through that awful judgment. The Hebrew Chronology very properly places the death of Methuselah in the year of the deluge, as indeed his name Meth-u-shelah—" He dieth and it is sent "—which his father the Prophet Enoch, was doubtless inspired to give him, seems to signify. 4thly. The account in Scripture of the dispersion of mankind 102 years after the Deluge, is in favour of the shorter computation of the Hebrew Text. That dispersion was effected by the immediate interposition of God, in opposition to the wishes of mankind, who desired to dwell together at a time when they " all spoke one language," as it is written, " They said, Let us build a city and a tower—*lest we be scattered abroad upon the face of the whole earth ;*"[1] from which it is manifest that the dispersion was commanded while they were yet few in number. It was evidently directed with a view to prevent the evils which would arise from over-crowded numbers in a limited space. But at the time assigned to this event by the LXX., more than 500 years after the Deluge (the Paschal Chronicle dates it 659 years after), it is clear from the average rate of the increase of mankind, that such was no longer the condition, and their dispersion would have been no longer a matter of choice, but of necessity. And as the dispersion took place in the days of Peleg, who flourished in the second century after the Deluge, according to the Hebrew Chronology, and when the human race, springing from three pairs, the children of Noah, would, according to the usual rate of increase, have amounted to about 50,000 persons, a suitable number for the population of one large city,—we have in this a reasonable proof of the correctness of the Hebrew text in opposition to that of LXX.

St. Augustine, however, though advocating the Hebrew Chronology in preference to that of the LXX., which had been generally received by the earlier Fathers, accounts for the difference between the two on this wise,—" It is incredible that such honourable men, as those who translated the Septuagint were, would record an untruth. If I should ask them whether it be likely that a nation so large, and so far dispersed as the Jews, should all lay their heads together to forge this lie, and subvert their own truths ; or that the LXX., being Jews also, and all

---

[1] Gen. xi. 4.

shut up in one place (for Ptolemy had gotten them together for that purpose), should be envious that the Gentiles should enjoy their Scriptures, and put in those errors by a common consent — who sees not which is easier to effect? But God forbid that any wise men should think that the Jews (however forward), could have such power, or so many and so far-dispersed books, or that the LXX. had any such common intent to conceal the truth of their histories from the Gentiles. One might easier believe that the error was committed in the transcription of the copy from Ptolemy's Library, and so that it had a successive continuation dispersed through all future copies."[1]

Accepting then the chronology of the Hebrew Bible, as much a matter of *Revelation* as any other portion of God's Word, and therefore of necessity to be preferred to that of the LXX., we proceed to challenge the startling conclusions to which Baron Bunsen has come, and which he has advocated with so much learning, but which we think may be set aside, as it will be our endeavour to show, in a variety of ways, by recent discoveries in the departments of *Science*. It will be necessary, however, at the outset, to explain our meaning of "the Chronology of the Hebrew Bible." We do not mean the chronology which is to be found at the headings of the authorised version, and which bears the name of the very learned and devout Archbishop Usher, but rather that of Clinton, the most eminent amongst English chronologers of the present century, as set forth in his admirable work the "Fasti Hellenici." The difference between the two may be thus stated. Usher dates the creation of man B.C. 4004, Clinton B.C. 4134. The cause of this difference is to be accounted for by the uncertainty respecting the exact

---

[1] De Civitate Dei, xv. 11.

interval between the time of the Exode and the building of the Temple, in which, as Clinton observes[1], "two breaks occur in the series of Scripture dates," which compel us in a measure to be conjectural, though only to the amount of a few years, and which we are obliged to endeavour to rectify by profane testimony. We shall, therefore, show cause in its proper place, why we have dated the Creation B.C. 4100 in preference to the thirty-four years' earlier date according to the computation of Clinton.

§ 1. We propose to show some reasons for concluding that the Creation of man is to be dated about 4100 B.C., and then to examine the grounds on which Bunsen dates that great event 16,000 years earlier. Those who believe with regard to chronology that there is more than a "human element in the Sacred Books," and accept the superiority of the Hebrew text over that of the LXX., will naturally acknowledge that the mere addition of the numbers mentioned in the Bible for the several epochs between the time of the Creation and the fall of Babylon, where sacred and profane testimony may be said to meet, will give as the result something more than 4000 years as the B.C. date for the Creation of man. The analogy we draw from the record of Creation compels us to reject so early a date as 20,000 B.C., which Bunsen adopts for that event. The very general impression in past ages, both amongst Jews and Christians[2], supports the interpre-

---

[1] Clinton makes the remark with reference to the extended period from the time of Abraham's birth to the destruction of the Temple, B.C. 587; but, in reality, the two breaks are included within the shorter interval, viz., the time of Joshua's rule over Israel, and the uncertainty how to reckon the number of years allotted to Saul and Samuel respectively. See *Fasti Hellenici*, vol. i. app. c. 5.

[2] So with regard to the opinions of the heathen, Suidas mentions the history of an ancient Tuscan author, who represented the six days' creation as so many thousand years.

tation of St. Peter's words that "one day is with the Lord as a thousand years, and a thousand years' as one day,"[1] as referring to the 6000 years' period from the Creation to the end of this age, previous to the expected Millennium. Thus amongst the Jews an ancient tradition of the house of Elias computes the duration of the age: "2000 years empty, 2000 years the law, and 2000 years the days of the Messiah."[2] Rabbi Katina, in the Gamara, observes, "the world is to endure 6000 years." Rabbi Eliezer, in his commentary, refers to the common opinion amongst his nation that "the world would continue 6000 years, and then a perpetual Sabbath would begin, typified by God's resting on the seventh day and blessing it." The Cabalists rather fancifully concluded that the world would last 6000 years, because "the Hebrew letter א, which stands for 1000 is found six times in Genesis i. 1;" and also because "God having taken six days in the work of Creation, and 'a thousand years in Thy sight are but as yesterday when it is past,' therefore, after 6000 years' duration of the world, there would be a millenary Sabbath of rest." Thus amongst the early Christians the author of "the Epistle of Barnabas," written probably in the second century, says, "God made the works of his hands in six days; the meaning of which is, that in 6000 years the Lord will bring all things to an end" (ch. xv.). Irenæus, Contra. Hær. v. xxviii. 3; Lactantius, Divine Instit. vii. 14; St. Augustine, De Civitat. Dei. xx. 30; interpret the teaching of what is said in Scripture, respecting the time of Creation, in the same manner. The ancient Persians appear to have entertained similar ideas respecting the longevity of this age, as we learn from the Eastern romance, entitled, *Caherman Rame*, in which the hero is represented as conversing with a griffin, named

---

[1] 2 Pet. iii. 8.   [2] Talm. Tract. Sanhedr. cap. Halec.

Simurgh, who tells him that, " she had already lived to see the earth *seven times* filled with creatures, and *seven times* reduced to a perfect void. That the age of Adam would last *seven thousand years,* when the present race of men would be extinguished, and their place be supplied by creatures of another form and more perfect nature, with whom the world would end."[1] We may fairly draw an inference from *Science* in support of the duration of this age lasting 6000 years. Speaking astronomically, the accurate adjustment of what is called the Gregorian year, by which the true solar or tropical year is found to consist of 365 days, 5 hours, 48 minutes, and 57 seconds, whence it fell short of the Julian computation of 365 days, 6 hours, by an interval of 11 minutes and 3 seconds, proves that at the termination of 6000 years from the time of the creation of man, *a further correction of the calendar will then be necessary,* as the deficiency of 11 minutes 3 seconds, or 663 seconds, will amount to 1 hour and 40 minutes every 400 years. For in fifteen such periods, as $15 + 400 = 6000$ years, this deficiency will amount just to *one day and one hour.*

Now, if we come to examine Bunsen's theory for extending the period of the creation of man to 20,000 B.C., we find it resting upon these three grounds. (*a*.) He considers that it would require that length of time for the formation and perfection of the various languages in use amongst the civilised nations of the earth. The question which virtually arises is this. Shall we prefer the *inference* of a learned scholar in the present day, to the *positive statement* of an inspired man made between 3000 and 4000 years ago? Concerning the time of about 100 years after the deluge, it is written, " The Lord said, Behold the people is one, and they have all one language.[2]

---
[1] Hyde's Religio Veterum Persarum.
[2] Professor Max Müller, in his 8th Lecture (1861) " On the Science

Let us confound their language, that they may not understand one another's speech. Therefore is the name of it called Babel ; because the Lord did there confound the language of all the earth ; and from thence did the Lord scatter them abroad upon the face of all the earth."[1] Very possibly, the "one language" known to man until that time, according to the Scriptural account, was composed of monosyllables, each one having a distinct ideal meaning, and one meaning only. When this simple monosyllabic language prevailed, men would necessarily have simple ideas, and a corresponding simplicity of manners.[2] The language of the Chinese, a nation as old as, and with authentic history still older than that of Egypt, is exactly such as this ; and the Hebrew, when stripped of its vowel points (a comparatively modern invention), of its prefixes, and its suffixes, nearly answers to this character in its present state. The Arabic, Chaldee, Syriac, and Ethiopic languages, bear a most striking resemblance to their parent, the Hebrew. The account which Scripture gives, of the miraculous formation of other languages, besides the primeval one, and of the intention of God in

---

of Language," justly concludes that, "however dissimilar the various classes might appear, they are all nevertheless derived from one primeval language." Thus will it ever be found that Revelation and Science go hand in hand.

[1] Genesis, xi. 6—9.

[2] Bunsen gives his opinion on the gradual formation of language with mathematical precision in the following complicated style :— "Formation and deposit of Sinism, B.C. 20,000. Primitive language, spoken with rising or falling cadence ; elucidated by gesture, B.C. 15,000. Pure agglutinative formation of polysyllabic words by means of the unity of accent, B.C. 14,000. Formation of stems into roots, producing derivative words, B.C. 11,000. Invention of hieroglyphic signs ; the phonetic element introduced, by means of the establishment of ideographs, to express a syllable, without reference to the original meaning." —*Egypt's Place in Universal History*, vol. iv. 485—487.

the execution of His purpose, has been quaintly expressed by an ancient French poet, which we introduce here, in order to show its natural effect upon designing and self-opiniated man.

> " Some speak between the teeth, some in the nose,
> Some in the throat their words do ill dispose;
> 'Bring me,' quoth one, 'a *trowel*, quickly, quick!'
> One brings him up a *hammer*. ' *Hew this brick*,'
> Another bids; and then they *cleave a tree*.
> '*Make fast this rope*,' and then they *let it flee*.
> One calls for *planks*, another *mortar* lacks;
> They bear, the first a *stone*, the last an *axe*.
> One would have *spikes*, and him a *spade* they give;
> Another asks a *saw*, and gets a *sieve*.
> Thus crossly crost, they *prate* and *pout* in vain;
> What one hath *made*, another *mars* again.
> These reasons then, seeing the storm arrived
> Of God's just wrath, all weak and heart-deprived,
> Forsake their purpose, and, like frantic fools,
> Scatter their stuff and tumble down their tools." [1]

No one, who really believes the Bible to be a revelation of God to man, can accept the vain theory of Bunsen respecting the length of time required for the formation of languages, as sufficient to overthrow the plain and positive statement of Holy Scripture.

(*b*.) Another ground which Bunsen takes for maintaining so early a date for the creation of man, is the marvellous stories of Manetho and other Egyptian chroniclers, respecting the reigns of the gods and the demi-gods in Egypt, previous to what are termed the historic periods. Eusebius writes, " Among the Egyptians there is a certain tablet called the Old Chronicle, containing thirty dynasties in 113 descents, during the long period of 36,525 years." [2] This same number is also mentioned by Jamblichus, in connection with Egyptian history, as the

---

[1] Du Bartas.—*Babylon*.   [2] Euseb. Chron. vi.

number of the Hermaic books, perhaps allowing a book to each year; as he says, "Hermes wrote it all in 20,000 books, according to the account of Seleucus; but Manetho, in his history, relates that they were completed in 36,525.[1] Eusebius in another place observes, that "the years (he considered they meant *lunar* years) which the Egyptians allow to the reigns of the gods, the demi-gods, and the manes, are 24,900."[2] We do not think that the Egyptians meant *lunar* years, as Eusebius supposed, and we trust to be enabled to show the grounds why they fixed upon some of those numbers mentioned above, when we come to examine Mr. Goodwin's Essay on "the Mosaic Cosmogony," but it will be sufficient at present to mention it in order to show its striking improbability, as one of the reasons for Bunsen's date of B.C. 20,000, for the creation of man. The fabulous statements of Manetho and the Egyptian chroniclers, carry with them their own refutation; as it is very evident that had *man* existed on earth at that early period, the tradition of the deluge, as we shall presently see, when we come to notice what has been handed down through other nations besides the Jews respecting it, would not have been omitted in the account of the reign of ideal gods and demi-gods.

(*c.*) Bunsen likewise finds support for his theory upon the ground "that Egypt was inhabited by men who made use of pottery about 11,000 years before the Christian era;" adding very properly that as this opinion "may appear *startling* to the general reader, who has taken for granted that the existence of man does not date beyond six or seven thousand years, the author feels it his duty to state, as clearly and succinctly as possible, the particular grounds on which the above conclusions are based,

---

[1] De Mystag. § 8. c. i.   [2] Euseb. Chron. A.M. 200.

and to show that it is not a *speculative geological*[1], but a positive *historical research* with which we have to deal."[2] Let us now examine how far it is really "historical research," on which this conclusion can be said to rest. Some attempts having been made near Cairo, at the suggestion of Mr. Leonard Horner, who does not appear to have assisted in person, or even to have been in the country, with a view to throw light upon the geological history of the alluvial soil of Egypt, by excavating the deposits of the Nile mud at the foot of the colossal statue of Rameses II. in the area of Memphis, he concluded, from the known rate at which such deposits are annually formed, that some specimens of *pottery*, which were brought up from a depth of thirty-nine feet, proved the existence of men upon earth long anterior to the time which Scripture assigns for the commencement of that event, though Mr. Horner says with becoming diffidence at his marvellous conclusions, which appear to have convinced the credulous Bunsen, "*if there be no fallacy in my reckoning*, this fragment of pottery found at a depth of thirty-nine feet, must be held to be *a record of the existence of man* 13,371 years before A.D. 1854;"[3] adding at the

---

[1] One of the most eminent of living geologists, Sir Charles Lyell, mentions, in contradistinction to Bunsen's opinion, that " Bishop Berkeley, a century ago, inferred on grounds which may be termed *strictly geological*, the recent (i.e. the Scriptural) date of the Creation of Man."—*Principles of Geology*, c. xlviii. p. 764. 9th edition.

[2] Egypt's Place in Universal History, vol. iii. pref. xii.

[3] Sir G. Wilkinson justly observes that although " the accumulation of alluvial soil at the base of the obelisk of Osirtasen at Heliopolis, as around the sitting colossi in the plain at Thebes (Rameses II.), has been often appealed to for determining the rise of the alluvial soil within a certain period, as there is no possibility of ascertaining how far it stood above the reach of the inundation, when first put up, we have no base for any calculation."—See *Rawlinson's Herod.* ii. p. 8.

same time, "in the boring at Bessousse *fragments of burnt brick* and pottery were brought up from the lowest part, viz., fifty-nine feet from the surface."[1] As at the same rate of deposit manufactured articles found at a depth of fifty-nine feet would give an additional[2] 7000 or 8000 years for man's existence on earth, we see Bunsen's reason for concluding not merely so early a date for the creation, but that there were Egyptian potters and burners of brick in active employment some 20,000 years before the Christian era. Unfortunately, however, for the advocates of this ingenious hypothesis, there are several ways of accounting for the presence of manufactured pottery, and fragments of burnt brick in the deposits of the Nile, any one of which is sufficient to overthrow the theory of Messrs. Horner and Bunsen, which certainly at first sight looks an imposing structure, but which when tested is found to be resting on a very weak foundation. Herodotus (ii. 99) mentions that Mên or Menes (the Mizraim of Scripture) the first king of Egypt, and founder of Memphis, *circa* B.C. 2350, was believed to have diverted the course of the river Nile eastward by a dam about twelve English miles south of the city, and thus to have dried up the old bed. As we know not the ancient course of the river, these recently discovered fragments found near the statue of Rameses II. *circa* B.C. 1450, which probably may stand on the old bed itself, doubtless dropt through some of the large fissures caused by the summer sun, in the deposits made by the inundation of the Nile, *centuries*

---

[1] Egypt's Place in Universal History, vol. iii. pref. xxv.
[2] Mr. Darwin enlarges upon this fanciful theory by asking, after alluding to the manufactured pottery of the valley of the Nile, "13,000 or 14,000 years ago," as a probable record of civilised man,—"Who will pretend to say *how long before these ancient periods*, savages, like those of Tierra del Fuego or Australia, who possess a semi-domestic dog, may not have existed in Egypt?"—*Origin of Species*, p. 18.

after the time of Menes. Moreover, we know from the testimony of Makrizi that *less than* 1000 *years ago* the Nile flowed close to the western suburbs of Cairo, from which it is now separated by a plain extending more than a mile in width, in which there would be no difficulty, by *digging twenty or thirty feet, in finding fragments of pottery less than* 1000 *years old.*

But there is a still more conclusive reply to Bunsen's theory concerning the fragments of *burnt brick* found at the same depth with pieces of pottery. Just as a coin, dug up in England some thirty feet below the present surface, of the reign of Cunobelinus, an ancient British king, with an inscription in Roman characters, would be a conclusive proof that it must have been struck some years *after* the Roman dominion had existed in this country; so the presence of *burnt brick* in the deposits of the Nile, however deep, betray the same comparatively recent origin. For it is an undoubted fact that *there is not a single structure of burnt brick from one end of Egypt to the other earlier than the period of the Roman dominion.* These fragments, therefore, of *burnt brick*[1] and pottery must have been deposited in the alluvial soil of Egypt *after the Christian era,* and instead of establishing the existence of man on earth some thousands of years before the Scripture record allows, supply a convincing proof of the untenableness and frailty of Bunsen's theory, as well

---

[1] A casual remark by a recent historian of Egypt concerning an event during the eighteenth dynasty, i.e. *circa* B.C. 1600, confirms our opinion respecting the comparatively modern origin of burnt bricks in that country. "This fact appears on the stamps of *unburnt* bricks at Gournow."—*Osburn's Monumental Hist. of Egypt,* ii. 193. In the Cosmogony of Sanchoniatho, Technites and Geïnus Autochthôn are represented as having "discovered the method of mingling stubble with the loam of bricks, and of *baking them in the sun,*" showing that in those early days *burnt bricks* were unknown to the Phœnicians.

as tend to confirm inferentially the Chronology of Scripture. We think we have already adduced sufficient proof, though we propose to add more as occasion requires, in confutation of his "four theses," which he endeavours to establish, as he says, "*by records peculiar to the history of Egypt.* First: that the immigration of the Asiatic stock from Western Asia (Chaldean) is antediluvian. Secondly: That the historical deluge, which took place in a considerable part of central Asia, cannot have occurred at a more recent period than the tenth millennium B.C. Thirdly: That there are strong grounds for supposing that that catastrophe did not take place at a much earlier period. Fourthly: That man existed on this earth about 20,000 B.C., and that there is no valid reason for assuming a more remote beginning of our race."[1]

§ 2. If we are right in fixing the date of the creation of man at B.C. 4100, as the Scripture account gives exactly 1657 years as the interval from that epoch to the Noachian or historical deluge, the latter must be dated B.C. 2443. Bunsen on the other hand fixes upon B.C. 11,000, as the correct date for that stupendous event.[2] Moreover, in order to be consistent with his theory of a greater length of time being required than even B.C. 1100 for the formation of language, as well as of man having existed in Egypt before that period, he denies the universality of the deluge, not in the sense in which that expression is generally used with reference to its extent[3],

---

[1] Egypt's Place in Universal History, pref. xxviii.
[2] Ibid. vol. iv. 480.
[3] We must be careful to distinguish between what Scripture teaches respecting the destruction of the human race, and the extent which the waters overflowed the earth. For though Scripture affirms that "all the high hills that were under the whole heaven were covered," we may limit the word "all" just as we are compelled to do in other parts of the Bible; e.g. it is said of Nebuchadnezzar, that

but with regard to the destruction of the human race. Now what saith Scripture on the subject? "All flesh died that moved upon the earth — *and every man:* All in whose nostrils was the breath of life, of all that was in the dry land, died. And every living substance was destroyed which was upon the face of the ground, both *man* and cattle, and the creeping things, and the fowl of the heaven; and they were destroyed from the earth; and *Noah only remained alive, and they that were with him in the ark.*"[1] It is as impossible to conceive plainer language in support of the generally received opinion that the whole human race was destroyed at the time of the deluge with the exception of the eight persons in the ark, which St. Peter teaches[2], as it is to receive the "painfully sceptical" opinion of Bunsen, whose theory compels him to deny it. In order to confirm the testimony of Scripture on this subject, we may notice the traditions that have been handed down through various nations respecting it.

(*a.*) The Phœnician Sanchoniatho, the oldest historian next to Moses and the Scripture annalists, who lived, it is

---

" wheresoever the children of men dwelt, God had made him ruler over them *all,*" Dan. ii. 38. And St. Paul wrote, in the first century, of the Christian era, that " the Gospel was preached to every creature under heaven," Col. i. 23. It is sufficient for our purpose to know that *Science* is silent on what *Revelation* does not require; and if so much of the earth was overflowed as was occupied by the human race, both the physical and moral ends of that tremendous judgment were fully answered. Bishop Stillingfleet justly observes, " The flood was universal as to mankind; but from thence follows no necessity at all of asserting the universality of it as to the globe of the earth, unless it be sufficiently proved that the whole earth was peopled before the flood, which I despair of ever seeing proved." — *Origines Sacræ*, b. iii. c. iv. § 3.

[1] Genesis, ii. 21—23.
[2] Compare 1 Pet. iii. 20 and 2 Pet. iii. 6.

supposed, about the 12th century B.C., though not expressly recording the deluge, represents what is worthy of note, that *mankind sprung from one pair*, reckons ten generations from them inclusive through the line of Cain, and places Mizraim, the grandson of Noah by name, in the 12th descent, agreeably to the history of Scripture.[1]

(*b.*) Berosus, the Chaldæan, records two traditions respecting the deluge, the separate details of which are in marvellous agreement with the statement in Scripture. He relates that "there was one amongst the giants who reverenced the gods, and was more wise and prudent than all the rest, whose name was *Noa*, dwelling in Syria with his three sons, Sem, Japet, Chem, and their wives, the great Tidea, Pandora, Noela, and Noegla. This man, fearing the destruction which, he foresaw from the stars, would come to pass, began in the seventy-eighth year before the deluge to build a ship, covered like an ark. After the seventy-eight years were expired, the ocean suddenly broke out, and all the inland seas and rivers and fountains bursting from beneath (attended by the most violent rains from heaven for many days) overflowed all the mountains; so that *the whole human race was buried in the waters, except Noa and his family*, who were saved by means of the ship, which being lifted up by the waters, rested at last upon the top of the Gendyae, or mountain, on which, it is reported, there now remaineth some part, and that men take away the bitumen from it and make

---

[1] Euseb. Præp. Evang. lib. i. c. 6, 9. Eusebius gives the following account of Sanchoniatho from Porphyry, that " he related in his history Jewish affairs with great veracity, and *agreed entirely with their history* in the names of places and men; having his accounts from Jerobaal (Gideon, Judges vii. 1), servant of the God Jehovah, and dedicated his work to Abibalus, king of Berytus; and his history was allowed to be true both by the king and by those who were appointed to examine it."

use of it by way of charm or expiation to avoid evil." Another tradition which Berosus records is to this effect: "In the time of Xisuthrus (the 10th in descent from the first of the Chaldæan kings[1]) a great deluge happened, which is thus described. The deity, Cronus, appeared to him in a vision, and warned him that *upon the 15th day of the month Dæsius there would be a flood by which mankind would be destroyed*. He, therefore, enjoined him to build a vessel, and take with him into it his friends and relations, and to convey on board everything necessary to sustain life, together with all the different animals, both birds and quadrupeds, and trust himself fearlessly to the deep. He obeyed the divine admonition, and built a vessel five stadia in length and two in breadth. Into this he put everything which he had prepared; and last of all conveyed into it his wife, his children and his friends. After the flood had been upon the earth, and was in time abated, Xisuthrus sent out birds from the vessel, which not finding any food, nor any place whereupon they might rest their feet, returned to him again. After an interval of some days, he sent them forth a *second* time, and they now returned with their feet tinged with mud. He made a *third* trial with these birds, but they returned to him no more; from which he concluded that the surface of the earth had appeared above the waters. He, therefore, made an opening in the vessel, and upon looking out, found that it was stranded upon the side of some mountain; upon which he immediately quitted it with his wife, his daughter, and the pilot. Xisuthrus then paid his adoration to the earth, and having constructed an altar, offered

---

[1] Cosmos Indicopleustes, an Egyptian monk, relates from Timæus Locrus, that ten kings had reigned in the island Atlantis before it was sunk in the sea by a deluge. This seems to be some imperfect account of the Chaldæan ten kings before the flood. — *De Mund.* lib. xii. p. 340.

sacrifices to the gods, and, with those who had come out of the vessel with him, disappeared. The place wherein they then were was the land of Armenia."[1]

(c.) In China they have a tradition of two great floods, one of which happened in the reign of the Emperor Jao, *circa* B.C. 2300, but which, they say, did not reach to China, nor even so far as India. Another, concerning which it was believed, as the very learned Sir William Jones describes it, that "just before the appearance of Fohi in the mountains, a mighty flood, which first flowed abundantly, and then subsided, covered for a time the whole earth, and separated the higher from the lower age of mankind."

(d.) The same great authority relates the Hindu tradition respecting the deluge as follows: "An evil demon having stolen the sacred books from Brahma, the whole race of men became corrupt *except the seven Rishis*, and especially *the holy Satyavrata*, who was once visited by the god Vishnu, and thus addressed: "In seven days *all creatures who have offended me shall be destroyed by a deluge*, but thou shalt be saved in a large vessel miraculously formed. Take, therefore, all kinds of herbs and grain for food, and, together with the seven holy men, your respective wives, and pairs of all animals, enter the ark without fear." Vishnu then disappeared, and after seven days, during which Satyavrata had conformed to the instructions given him, the deluge commenced, during which Vishnu preserved the ark by taking the form of a fish and tying it to himself; and when the waters had subsided, he communicated the contents of the sacred books to Satyavrata, after having slain the demon who stole them. It is added, however, that on one occasion after the deluge, having drank too much he fell asleep un-

---

[1] Euseb. Chron. v. 8.

clothed, when Charma, one of his three sons, finding him in that condition, called on his two brothers to witness the shame of their sire. By them, however, he was covered with clothes, and recalled to his senses, when, knowing what had passed, he cursed Charma, saying, ' Thou shalt be a servant of servants.' "

(*e.*) There is a tradition amongst the Dyaks of Borneo to the following effect. They call themselves " poor simple fools," which they say was owing to an occurrence at the time of the great deluge, very long ago, *when all mankind was destroyed* save a pair of whites, a pair of Chinese, a pair of Malays, and a pair of Dyaks, who all endeavoured to preserve the book which was to teach everything. The white man placed the book on his head, which was thus preserved perfectly free from wet. The Chinaman placed it on his shoulder, and the other under his arm, by which each had his book partially injured. The Dyak tied his round his waist, and all having to swim for their lives, his book was thoroughly wetted and completely spoiled.

(*f.*) Thus much for the traditions in *Asia* respecting the deluge. If we turn to *Africa* we find in the hieroglyphic records of ancient Egypt, the name of *Noah*, variously written as *Nh*, *Nuh*, and *Nou*, and worshipped as " the god of water," which Mr. Birch has truly identified with him who was entitled " the father of the gods" and "the giver of mythic life to all beneath him."[1] According to Plutarch's treatise of Isis and Osiris, it would appear as if tradition had represented Noah under the name of the latter; when Typhon, a personification of the ocean, enticed him into an ark, which being closed was forced to sea through the Tanaïtic mouth of the Nile. " These things," Plutarch reports, " were done upon *the* 17*th day*

---

[1] Osburn's Monum. Hist. of Egypt, i. 239.

of the month Atayr, when the sun was in Scorpio, in the 28th year of Osiris' reign."[1]

(*g.*) The tradition of Europe is still more precise. Lucian, in his work *De Deâ Syriâ*, represents the idea of a great deluge entertained by the Greeks, as follows: " The present world is peopled from the sons of Deucalion. The previous race were men of violence, to whom mercy was unknown, and on this account were doomed to destruction. For this purpose there was a mighty eruption of water from the earth, attended with heavy rains from above, so that the rivers and sea overflowed, till the whole earth was covered with a flood *and all flesh drowned*. Deucalion, on account of his piety, was alone preserved to people the world. His preservation was effected by placing all his family, both his sons and their wives, into a vast ark which he had provided, and he then entered it himself. At the same time animals of every species — whatever lived upon the face of the earth — followed him by pairs; all of which he received into the ark, and experienced no evil therefrom." Plutarch confirms this tradition by adding that "as the voyage was drawing to a close Deucalion sent out a dove, which, returning in a short time, showed that the waters still covered the earth, but which on a second occasion failed to come back, or, as some say, returned with mud-stained feet, and thus proved the abatement of the flood." We have a confirmation of this Greek tradition in what is known to antiquarians as the Apamæan medal, struck in the fourth century B.C., which represents a man and woman seated in a floating ark, on which is inscribed the familiar name of *Noe*, while a dove on the wing is seen returning to the ark bearing an olive branch.

---

[1] Plutarch De Iside et Osiride, § 13.

(*h.*) Nor is *America*[1] less devoid of traditionary records of the deluge than exist as we have seen in *Europe, Asia*, and *Africa*. Herrera, a Spanish historian, relates that the aborigines of the *Brazils* had some knowledge of a general deluge; and in *Peru*, the ancient Indians believed that many years before there were any Incas, *all the people were drowned by a great flood, save six persons*, who were saved on a float; that amongst the ancient inhabitants of *Cuba*, the current tradition was to this effect, that "an old man, knowing the deluge was to come, built a great ship, into which he entered with his family, and many animals; and that, being wearied at the long continuance of the flood, he sent out a crow, which at first did not return, staying to feed on the dead bodies, but afterwards came back bearing with it a green branch." The Indians of North America hold that the common father of their tribes, being warned in a dream that a flood was coming, built a raft, on which he preserved his family, and pairs of all animals, which drifted about for many months, until at length a new earth was made for their reception by the "mighty man above." Humboldt in his wanderings in South America, found amongst the wild Indians of the wilderness surrounding the Orinoco, traditions of the deluge still fresh and distinct. Amongst others he relates, that "when the Tamanees are asked how the human race survived this great deluge, they say,

---

[1] That the Ancients had a knowledge of America some two thousand years before its discovery by Columbus, is evident from what Diodorus relates of the Phœnicians, of whom he says that, when "sailing beyond the Pillars of Hercules, they were driven by great tempests far into the (western) ocean, and being tossed about it many days by the violence of the storm, at length they arrived at a great island in the Atlantic Ocean, which lies many days' sail distant from Africa to the west. The soil was fruitful, the rivers navigable, and *the buildings sumptuous*." By which we conclude it must have been peopled long before.—*Diodorus Siculus*, lib. v.

a man and woman saved themselves on a high mountain called Tamanacu, situated on the banks of the Asivern, and casting behind them over their heads the fruits of the mauritia palm tree, they saw the seeds contained in those fruits produce men and women who repeopled the earth."

Thus the traditions of the deluge, which have been handed down amongst different nations in the four quarters of the globe, are in complete accordance with the Mosaic record respecting the destruction of the whole human race, the family of Noah excepted, and contradict thereby the unfounded theory of Bunsen, who limits its effects, not merely in locality, but in regard to God's judgment upon mankind. Moreover, we have some evidence which may throw light upon the disputed time of this great deluge, whether it should be dated in the 25th century B. C., or whether, with Bunsen, as having occurred B. C. 11,000.

We have seen that Berosus, the Chaldean historian, mentions that Xisuthrus was warned that the flood would commence "*on the 15th day of the month Dæsius;*" and as we know from Callisthenes[1], that there were at Babylon astronomical observations which extended over 1900 years prior to the time of Alexander the Great, in whose reign Berosus flourished, which would carry the authentic chronology of the Babylonians as high as B. C. 2233, i. e. within about a century of the building of the tower of Babel, we may reasonably infer that their tradition respecting the time[2] for the commencement of the great

---

[1] Callisthenes sent his account of this from Babylon to his uncle and master Aristotle, who had desired him to procure it; and Porphyry gave the account from Aristotle, which Simplicius has preserved.— *Simplic. Conv.* 46, in lib. ii. *Aristot. de cælo.*

[2] It is a singular confirmation of the correctness of this chronology, that the *origin* of those ceremonials of solstitial sacrifice, which were celebrated on the accession of the Ethiopian monarchs, in

deluge was correct. Now the Scripture account gives "*the* 17*th day of the second month*,"[1] as the exact time when the Noachian flood commenced; and as the Jews and Babylonians had a different mode of computing their months and years, just as Christians and Mahomedans have in this present day, if we can find on any one single year that "*the* 17*th day of the second month*," amongst the Jews, agrees with "*the* 15*th day of the month Dæsius*," amongst the Babylonians, we may infer that we have very strong grounds for concluding that such must be the true year when the deluge took place. According to our mode of computing Scripture chronology, we believe B. C. 2443, to have been the date of this important event. It is not difficult to calculate any occurrence mentioned in Scripture when the day and month are given, as in this instance, because the Jews were commanded to regulate their years and months in a certain prescribed form; and Moses, writing for their instruction, would necessarily record such an event as the Deluge, though happening eight centuries before his time, in a way which they would understand. The beginning of the Jewish year commenced with the new moon of the vernal equinox; consequently, by referring to the astronomical tables, we can compute what we should call the March new moon of the year B. C. 2443, as having happened on the 23rd of that month. Hence, the first day of the second month would answer to our April 22nd, and the 17th day to

---

honour of Cush, the grandson of Noah, and the probable founder of that kingdom, has been traced back to B.C. 2282, which well accords with our date of the dispersion of the human race and the foundation of the Egyptian kingdom, B.C. 2341. The mode of computing this, which is dependent upon astronomical calculations and a right understanding of certain Phœnician cylinders and scarabæi, has been admirably worked out by Landseer in his *Sabæan Researches*.

[1] Genesis, vii. 11.

the 8th of May, on which day "all the fountains of the great deep were broken up, and the windows of heaven were opened." The Babylonians appear to have had a different mode of computing the commencement of their year. With them it was a fixed festival, as it is with us; only, instead of the first of the Roman month Januarius being their New Year's day, it was the vernal equinox itself which regulated the beginning of the year; and this, in the time of Berosus, happened on the 25th of March. As they reckoned thirty days to a month, Dœsius, which was the name of their *second* month, would fall on the 24th of April, or two days later than, as we have just seen, was the case with the second month of the Jews on that year; consequently, "the 15th day of the month Dœsius" would fall on the 8th of May, as "the 17th day of the second month" did, according to the Jewish mode of reckoning; and thus we have one of many instances where *Revelation* and *Science* are shown to be in harmony one with the other.

It is also worthy of note, if we are right in supposing that the Egyptian legend respecting Osiris and Typhon, which has been already noticed, is a tradition of the Noachian deluge, that the embarkation of Osiris is said by Plutarch to have taken place "*on the 17th day of the month Athyr.*" As Athyr was the third month in the Egyptian calendar, and the first month Thôüt was not fixed, like our January, but varied according to the heliacal rising of Sothis, we are unable to conclude anything from Plutarch's mention of the name of the month, as we know not whether he referred to the time when he lived, or the period of which he was speaking, but it is a singular historical synchronism that the day of the month, viz., the 17th, should be the very day mentioned in Scripture, when Noah and his family entered the ark.

The tradition of so many different nations in the four

quarters of the globe, varying in minor details, and yet agreeing with much that is mentioned in Scripture, is sufficient to assure us that one and all refer to the Noachian deluge. None, however, specify the exact time when this event was supposed to have occurred. But the Phœnician tradition respecting Mizraim, the founder of the kingdom of Egypt, being the twelfth in descent from the first pair of the human race; and the Chaldæan tradition, which made the hero of the flood, that destroyed all mankind, whether under the name of Noa the Syrian, or Xisuthrus, the tenth in descent from the first king, as Noah was from Adam; and the Chinese traditions respecting two floods, one of which was deemed universal, and the other not so extensive, to have happened in the reign of the Emperor Jao, *circa* B.C. 2300, are sufficiently in accordance with the chronology of Scripture, to warrant our rejection of Bunsen's theory, who places it, as we have seen, B.C. 11,000. It has been considered by some that we have a clue to the correct date of the Noachian deluge, from the recent decipherment of a cuneiform inscription by M. Oppert, who considers he has detected on a Babylonian cylinder records of the deluge and the confusion of tongues, and who gives the following from a Khorsabad inscription: "The destruction of the city of L-ka took place when the planet Venus eclipsed the star Al-debarn, which is in the constellation Al-debar. Al-debar is opposite the six stars, and near the flying horse. This was fifty-four years from the sun's entry into Shor — the Bull." The late Mr. Ormsby, in a letter to the Journal of Sacred Literature, July, 1857, remarks that "the city referred to is L-ka on the Tigris, the first Eastern Semite colony, now known as Nimroud, and the *date is thus precisely given* (supposing there was an occultation B. C. 2420), as it refers to the periplus of Noah, the flood of the sacred Scriptures." Having, however, been favoured by a communication from the Astronomer-Royal (in reply to a request that he would examine the question respecting the inference which has been drawn from this cuneiform inscription), in which he assures me "the result of calculations" shows "that an occultation of Aldebaran by Venus was *impossible*," it can be no longer contended that B. C. 2420 is the "precise" date of the periplus of Noah, though of course it in no way affects our computation for that event, and which, according to Biblical chronology, we have dated more than twenty years before, or in other words at B. C. 2443. The testimony of the grammarian Censorinus, a very exact chronologer of the third century, confirms this opinion. When computing the pre-Olympic times, he says: "From the first or Ogygian flood to the first Olympiad is not clearly known, but is thought to be *about* 1600 years."[1] The date of the first Olympiad being fixed B. C. 776, we get B. C. 2376 for the supposed date of the flood, as traditionally reported amongst the ancient Romans, which is sufficiently near the Scriptural date for that event.

§ 3. The interval between the Noachian deluge and the dispersion of the human race on the attempt to build the tower of Babel, is, according to Scripture, 102 years. As it is written: "Shem begat Arphaxad two years after the flood, who lived thirty-five years and begat Salah, who lived thirty years and begat Eber, who lived thirty-four years and begat Peleg;" .... "Unto Eber were born two sons; the name of one was Peleg (i. e. *division*), for in his days was the earth divided."[2] Now 2+35+30+34=102. Consequently, if our time of the Noachian deluge B. C. 2443 be correct, the dispersion from Babel

---

[1] Censorinus, De Die Natali, cap. xxi.
[2] Genesis, x. 25; xi.

must be dated B. C. 2341. Bunsen, on the other hand, dates the flood B. C. 11,000, and the dispersion B. C. 7,000, leaving an interval of 4,000 years between the two events. Respecting the commencement of the kingdom of Egypt, which almost all authorities agree was founded by Menes, the Mizraim of the Bible, eldest son of Ham, and grandson of Noah, at the time of the dispersion from Babel, Bunsen writes: "History of Egyptian Deposit. Beginning of elective kings B. C. 7230. Duration of these, according to Manetho, 1817 years, end B. C. 5414. Beginning of hereditary kings in Lower Egypt, B. C. 5413 . . . Menes, king of all Egypt, B. C. 3623."[1] This will afford a distinct idea of the difference which exists between the chronology of Scripture after the deluge, and that system which Bunsen has adopted solely upon the authority of Manetho, and which, without any attempt at proof, he considers sufficient to overthrow the same. These 4000 years Bunsen finds in the fabulous reigns of the gods and demigods recorded by Manetho, and invites our acceptance of them, though contradicted by the unbroken and consistent testimony of Scripture. But further than this, we learn, from what history has transmitted concerning the three empires of Egypt, Babylon, and China, and of which we have more ancient and more complete records than any other kingdoms of the world, that they not only do not afford any grounds for Bunsen's ideal theory, but that they are in perfect accord with the chronology of the Bible. The histories of Herodotus, Diodorus Siculus, Josephus, and others, the lists of Manetho himself, and the canon of Eratosthenes, give the name of Menes, or Mizraim, as the first *man* who reigned in Egypt, the date of which we infer from Scripture to have been about 100 years after the flood, when the dispersion took place B. C.

---

[1] Egypt's Place in Universal History, vol. iv. p. 490.

2341. The testimony of the existing monuments is strictly in accordance with this inference. The name of Menes, written in hieroglyphics, occurs at the head of the tablet recording the ancestors of Rameses-Sesostris, in a relief on the roof of the Ramesseum, or Memnonium, as it is more commonly called, a royal palace near Gournou, in Western Thebes. It is also found in hieratic characters[1] in the Turin papyrus, brought from Thebes by Drovetti, and supposed to have been written in the fifteenth century B. C. If there were any foundation for Bunsen's theory of a long line of kings reigning in Egypt for 4000 years previous to Menes, there surely would have been some memorial of the same in the imperishable monuments of that wonderful country, or some traditionary legend, of which early historians would have heard, and mentioned in their writings; but there has never yet been discovered a sign of such mythical heroes, and therefore we are bound by all the laws of critical research to reject his unfounded and untenable idea. Champollion, the father of Egyptology, has distinctly affirmed his own conviction of the absence of any chronological discrepancy between the records of Scripture and the facts recorded on the monuments. Alluding to the adversaries of revelation in his own day, he writes: "They will find in this work an absolute reply to their calumnies, since I have demonstrated that no Egyptian monument is really older than the year 2200 before our era. This certainly is a very high antiquity, but it presents nothing contradictory to the sacred histories, and I venture to affirm that it establishes them on all points;

---

[1] The hieratic mode of writing was a sort of tachygraphy or hieroglyphic short-hand adopted by the Egyptian priests, and distinct from the third sort, called the demotic or enchorial, which bore the same relationship to it as our hand-writing does to print.

for it is, in fact, *by adopting the chronology and the succession of kings given by the Egyptian monuments, that the Egyptian history wonderfully accords with the sacred writings.*" Some writers[1] have considered that the long period of *years*, which Manetho and the Egyptian chroniclers have given to their ideal heroes, as reigning in Egypt previous to Menes, are to be understood of *months*, and by this mode of reduction understand them as descriptive of the antediluvian periods; but even this would make it too long for Scripture chronology, as the 36,000 lunar years of the Egyptian chronicle would give about 3000 solar years as the duration of time previous to the first mortal king in Egypt, and make the date of creation B. C. 5343, in place of its true date B. C. 4100. We believe there is a way of explaining this lengthened period, which we reserve for our examination of the Mosaic cosmogony, as we hope to be able to show from it a fresh instance of the agreement between *Revelation* and *Science*.

If we turn to the history of Babylon, as extracted from Berosus, we find that the duration of the various dynasties from the time of Nimrod, its founder, to its capture by Cyrus B. C. 538, supports the chronology of Scripture respecting the date of the dispersion.

						B.C.
1. The Median Dynasty of 8 kings reigned	224 yrs.	2341—2117.
2. First Chaldean	,,	11	,,	141[2]	,,	2117—1976.
3. Second Chaldean	,,	42	,,	458	,,	1976—1518.
4. Arabian	,,	9	,,	245	,,	1518—1273.
5. Assyrian	,,	45	,,	526	,,	1273— 747.
6. Lower Assyrian	,,	8	,,	122	,,	747— 625.
7. Babylonian	,,	6	,,	87	,,	625— 538.

[1] Jackson's Chronological Antiquities, ii. 119.

[2] This date is conjectural. Professor Brandis of Bonn gives 258; but as the average length of each reign in the succeeding Chaldean dynasty is only 9 years, we think it too high to estimate, as he does, the average length of each at 23 years, and have therefore been content with about 13, which is more likely to be correct.

Chinese chronology accords with this deduction, if we admit the testimony of the best Chinese writers, such as Xu-king, Confucius, and Mencius, who make the empire begin with Yau, the commencement of whose reign, according to Martinus and Couplet, is placed B. C. 2319 [1], about twenty-four years after the time of the dispersion, according to Scripture, and a very natural period for mankind to spread from western to eastern Asia, and to establish an empire which has proved the most lasting of all the kingdoms of the world. Thus the profane testimony respecting the three great empires of antiquity, Egypt, Babylon, and China, confirm and support the chronology which we find in the Hebrew Scriptures.

§ 4. The next point we have to consider is the time when Abraham's call, and his journey to Egypt took place, as forming a very important epoch in the history of the world, with whom Bunsen, as Dr. Williams expresses it, "reasonably conceives that the historical portion (of Scripture) begins [2] where the lives become natural and information was nearer" (p. 57). From the time of the deluge until Abraham's call, according to the Hebrew chronology, exactly 428 years elapsed, expressed by the number of descents from father to son, as well as the age of

---

[1] The learned chronologer Jackson, though an advocate of the chronology of the LXX., and who dates the reign of Yau nineteen years higher than Martinus and Couplet, bringing it thereby to B.C. 2338, within four years of our date for the dispersion, observes that "Chinese chronology from the reign of this emperor is fixed with great and undeniable certainty by a cycle of sixty years, and is continued from his reign without interruption to this day; and this computation can no more be doubted of than the reckoning of the Greeks by their Olympiads."—*Chron. Antiq.* ii. 28.

[2] Another of the Essayists differs from this inference. Mr. Wilson observes that "previous to the time of the divided kingdom, the Jewish history presents little which is thoroughly reliable. The taking of Jerusalem by 'Shishak' is for the Hebrew history that which the sacking of Rome by the Gauls is for the Roman" (p. 170, *note*).

each parent at the birth of his child. Deducting the 102 years from the interval between the flood and the dispersion at Babel, which has already been considered, we have 326 years left, which brings us down to the year B. C. 2015, as the Scripture date for the time when Abraham took his journey to Egypt after his father's death. Bunsen makes an interval of more than 8,000 years between these two events, and dates "the immigration of Abraham B. C. 2877."[1] In computing this part of Scripture chronology, a dispute has arisen respecting the age of Terah at the time of Abraham's birth, which we must not omit to notice. Josephus places it when Terah was in his 70th year; while Usher and Clinton more correctly adjudged it to have taken place sixty years later, when he was 130 years old, for this reason: It is clear from Acts vii. 4, that Abraham removed from Charran to Canaan *after* his father's death; and from Gen. xii. 3—5, that at the time of this immigration he was 75 years old. Terah died in Charran aged 205, according to Gen. xi. 32. Now 205—75=130 the age of Terah when Abraham was born. Usher observes, "When Terah had lived 70 years, there was born to him the eldest of his three sons (Gen. xi. 26), and he, not Abram (who came not into the world till sixty years after), but Haran, father-in-law of the third brother Nachor, died and left a daughter married to her uncle Nachor . . . . Sarai, who was also called Iscah, the daughter of Haran, Abram's brother (Gen. xi. 29), was ten years younger than her husband Abraham."[2] Clinton adds to this conclusion, that "the erroneous date for the birth of Abraham, placing the call of Abraham into Canaan sixty years before the death of his father, is contrary to Gen. xi. 32;

---

[1] Egypt's Place in Universal History, vol. iv. p. 492.
[2] Usher's Annals in loc.

xii. 1, 4 ; and on this account in the Samaritan copy, *the life of Terah is reduced to* 145 *years*, that his death might be adapted to the supposed time of the call."[1] We cannot hesitate to accept this as the correct mode of computing the age of Abraham at the time of his father's death, when he left Charran and took his journey to Egypt. The difference between Scripture chronology and Bunsen's, with regard to Abraham, is nearly 900 years, between the dates B. C. 2015 and B. C. 2877. One result of his system, which we shall presently have to notice, is that it requires us to prolong the sojourning of the children of Israel in Egypt from 215 years, according to Scripture, to over 1400 years, and necessarily carries its own confutation. What other testimony have we, confirmatory or contradictory, of the time of Abraham, according to the statements in Genesis? The first thing mentioned in Scripture, after his leaving Charran or Haran and dwelling in Canaan for a time, is that " he went down to Egypt to sojourn," on account of a grievous famine in Canaan, and that when there he was hospitably entertained, for Sarah's sake, by the reigning Pharaoh, who gave him " *sheep* and oxen, and he-asses, and men-servants and maid-servants, and she-asses and camels."[2]

---

[1] Fasti Hellenici, vol. i. p. 290.

[2] Gen. xii. 10, 16. V. Bohlen, a German rationalist, having endeavoured to deny the genuineness of the Pentateuch on the ground that no *sheep* existed in Egypt (though in another place, forgetful of his previous objection, he speaks of that animal being esteemed sacred by the Egyptians), it is remarkable that just before the period of Abraham's visit we have monumental evidence of their belonging to the country. In a tomb hewn in a rock near the pyramids of Gizeh, bearing the name of Suphis or Cheops, *circa* B.C. 2050, there is a representation of a shepherd giving an account of the flocks committed to his charge. First come oxen, over which is the number 834, cows 220, goats 3,234, asses 760, *sheep* 974. See *Sir G. Wilkinson's Ancient Egyptians*, i. 130, 2nd series.

Have we any evidence in Egyptian history by which we can ascertain the name of the reigning Pharaoh at the time of Abraham's visit? Josephus relates, in addition to what is stated in Scripture, that God arrested Pharaoh's designs against Sarah by "sending a sedition against his government;" and mentions that "whereas the Egyptians were formerly addicted to different customs, and despised one another's sacred and accustomed rites, and were very angry with one another on that account," Abraham acted the part of a wise mediator, and made peace between the contending parties. Moreover, Josephus says that Abraham taught them "arithmetic, and the science of astronomy; for before he came into Egypt they were unacquainted with that sort of learning."[1] In order to estimate aright the value of Josephus' testimony respecting any events in Egyptian history, we should remember that his chief literary opponent, Apion, was a custodian of the Temple records in Egypt; and that had he stated anything untrue, or without due authority, his enemies wanted neither the will nor the power to expose his errors. We may reasonably conclude, therefore, that their forbearance sufficiently proves its truth. What then is the lesson we may learn from Josephus respecting the time of Abraham's visit? The description of Abraham as a pacificator, after some religious contest had been carried on amongst the Egyptians, seems to point very distinctly to the cessation of the war respecting the limbs of Osiris, which Plutarch mentions[2], and which was parallel six or seven centuries later amongst the Jews in a civil war between the house of Benjamin and the children of Israel. We are unable to offer the lengthened proof required in order to show the grounds from Egyptian history upon which this conclusion rests, but we will content ourselves

---

[1] Antiq. I. viii. § 2, 3.   [2] De Iside et Osiride, § 18, 19.

with quoting from Osburn's valuable History of Egypt, who considers it " a well-established synchronism of much value, that Abram went into Egypt in the reign of Pharaoh *Acthoes*, and that the treaty which terminated the war for the limbs of Osiris was ratified during his sojourn there."[1] Moreover, as Josephus relates that Abraham taught the Egyptians arithmetic and astronomy, which was very natural when we remember that he was a native of Chaldea, where the science of astronomy originated, it is worthy of note that *there does not exist a single record of king or subject with a date previous to the time of Pharaoh Acthoes;* whereas tablets and papyri, with dates inscribed upon them of Amenemes, the son and immediate successor of Acthoes, and on whose monuments the names of the Egyptian months *first* occur, are not uncommon. Now, in the celebrated sepulchral grottoes of Benee-Hasan, in Middle Egypt, there are two hieroglyphic inscriptions, executed by or for persons living in the reigns of Amenemes I., Sesertesen I., Amenemes II., and Sesertesen II., Pharaohs belonging to Manetho's 12th dynasty, wherein special mention is made of the " Panegyry of the First Year," referring, as Poole in his learned work on Egypt very justly concludes, to the commencement of the Tropical Cycle, i. e. a perfectly exact cycle of the sun, moon, and vague year, which the science of astronomy fixes to B. C. 2005.[2] Now, considering that Amenemes I. was the son of Pharaoh Acthoes[3], in whose reign Abra-

---

[1] Monumental History, i. 375.
[2] Poole's Horæ Ægypticæ, pt. I. sec. ii.
[3] Though Pharaoh Acthoes was reigning at the time of Abraham's visit, it is not certain that he was the king with whom Abraham had intercourse, as there were for a very long period in Egyptian history two or more contemporary Pharaohs. The one with whom Abraham had dealings was a Sebennyte Pharaoh of the 10th dynasty, probably Imephthis, the contemporary of Acthoes. To understand the compli-

ham visited Egypt, according to Scripture chronology B. C. 2015, we have a very remarkable confirmation of its accordance with what *Science* reveals, that the son of this Pharaoh was on the throne ten years later, and on whose monuments we have proof of Abraham's instructions having been attended to by the introduction of months and dates, as well as the commencement of an important chronological cycle.

We have further proof of Abraham having lived about B. C. 2000, and not 850 years earlier, as Bunsen thinks fit to place him. In the Scripture record [1] of the war which Abraham had to undertake in order to recover Lot, " his brother's son, who was taken captive," mention is made of two kings, Amraphel, king of Shinar (Babylon), and Chedorlaomer, king of Elam (Persia), the time of whose reigns accords with Biblical chronology, as we may judge from other testimony besides that of Moses. According to Abydenus, there was a king reigning at Babylon of the name of Arbel or Arabel, the same, we have little doubt, as the Amraphel of Moses. Abydenus speaks of him as the father of Ninus, whom Diodorus Siculus from Ctesias describes as the great conqueror of Babylon and the adjoining nations of Egypt and Phœnicia.[2] Now, Manetho relates that when an army of Shepherds from Phœnicia conquered Egypt and made *Salatis* their leader, he fixed his seat at Memphis, and fortified most strongly the parts towards Chaldea, " foreseeing that the *Assyrians, who were then grown powerful,* would sometimes be inclined to

---

cations of Egyptian history, we should remember that, besides the two contemporary Pharaohs just mentioned, there was then a third, in all probability named Salatis, who built Avaris, and whose capital was Memphis, and who is commonly but erroneously termed the founder of the Hyksos dynasty, or Shepherd Kings.

[1] Genesis xiv. 1—16.
[2] Euseb. Arm. Chron. Diod. Sic. lib. ii. c. 1.

invade the kingdom of Egypt."[1] This Salatis, though in reality a descendant of Menes, and chief of the opposing dynasty to his rival at Thebes, had doubtless availed himself of the assistance of the Phœnicians in the civil war in Egypt, which may account for Manetho's strange story of what is called the Hyksos period, and which Osburn, in his Monumental History of Egypt has so skilfully unravelled. Salatis was the ancestor of Aphophis, the Pharaoh of Joseph, as we shall have occasion to show, and the duration of those kings whom Manetho mentions as reigning between Salatis and Aphophis accords with the 215 years spoken of in Scripture between the time of Abraham and Joseph. We have thus established an historical synchronism between Arabel or Amraphel, the father of Ninus, and king of Shinar (Babylon), and Abraham, from profane testimony, which is valuable so far as it confirms the accuracy of the Book of Genesis.

The same may be said in respect to *Chedorlaomer* king of Elam (Persia), whose name has been deciphered by Sir H. Rawlinson from a cuneiform inscription as "*Kudurmabuk*" (the latter word in Hematic being the exact equivalent of Laomer in Semitic), a king of Elamitic origin in Babylonia, who bears the remarkable title of *Anda-Martu*, or "Ravager of the West," which is very applicable to the account which Moses gives of his smiting the Rephaims, the Zuzims, the Emims, and the Horites in the fourteenth year of his reign, previous to his capture of Lot.[2] The celebrated Persian historian Mohammed Khavendschah, commonly called Mirkhond, has given in his Universal History two dynasties of Persian kings, reaching from the earliest times to the subversion of the empire by Alexander the Great. The second king of the first dynasty is named *Hushang*, or *Houscheuk Pischdad*,

---

[1] Josephus contr. Apion, i. 14. [2] Genesis, xiv. 5, 6.

or *Chedorlaomer*, who appears to have been on the throne, according to Hale's mode of adjusting the chronology of the Persian historians *Mirkhond, Firdusi*, and others cited in *Herbelot's Bibliothèque Orientale*, during the twenty-first century B. C., which accords with the Biblical account of the time of Abraham. Thus, the evidence from profane testimony is most conclusive against the date which Bunsen assigns to Abraham, viz. B. C. 2877.

§ 5. The next chronological epoch we have to notice is the time of Joseph's rule in Egypt, the consideration of which will necessarily bring to light the deplorable pertinacity with which Bunsen seeks to set aside the plain statements of Scripture. Nothing can be clearer than the Biblical record respecting the interval between Abraham's visit to Egypt and his great-grandson Joseph's rule in the same country, which we gather from Scripture to amount to 215 years, and which Bunsen, without the slightest reason for so doing, curtails to 122. In order that we may make this very apparent, we give a tabular statement of the genealogy of the four generations of that period as recorded by Moses.

Events.	Years old.	Year of the call.	
Abraham's call from Haran and visit to Egypt when	75	1	Gen. xii. 4, 10.
Isaac born when Abraham was	100	25	,, xvii. 1, 21.
Isaac married Rebecca when he was	40	65	,, xxv. 20.
Jacob born when Isaac was	60	85	,, xxv. 26.
Abraham's death at 175 when Jacob was	15	100	,, xxv. 7.
Joseph's birth when Jacob was	91	176[1]	
Joseph sold into Egypt when he was	17	193	,, xxxvii. 2.
Isaac's death at 180 when Joseph was	29	205	,, xxxv. 28.

---

[1] As this is not stated, we can only infer Jacob's age when Joseph was born, from the fact of the son being 39 at the time the father was 130, as will be seen in the accompanying table.

Events.	Years old.	Year of the call.	
Joseph made viceroy of Egypt when he was	30	206	„ xliv. 46.
End of the seven years of plenty when Joseph was	37	213	„ xliv. 53.
Jacob and his sons go down to Egypt in the second year of the famine, when Joseph was	39	215	„ xlv. 6.
Jacob stood before Pharaoh when he was	130	215	„ xlvii. 9.

Joseph's rule in Egypt began in the 206th year after Abraham's call, and was at its height in the 215th, when he presented his aged father at the court of Pharaoh, and gave him and his brethren as a possession "the best of the land of Egypt, in the land of Rameses, as Pharaoh had commanded." This sufficiently disposes of the erroneous chronology of Bunsen, who, by dating "the Immigration of Abraham B. C. 2877," and "Joseph Viceroy of Egypt B. C. 2755,"[1] curtails it, without the slightest attempt at proof, to 122 years. And this he does notwithstanding his admission that "the personality of Abraham is unquestionable, and all the important circumstances related of him and his race are strictly historical. .... Isaac is as certainly the bodily son and Jacob the bodily grandson of Abraham, as Joseph is the bodily son of Jacob and great-grandson of Abraham."[2] Bunsen considers Adam, Noah, and those patriarchs who are represented in Scripture as having lived for centuries, to be representative of races, and not descriptive of individuals, which justifies him, as he thinks, in prolonging the period from 4000 to 20,000 B. C. for the creation of man; though his attempted proofs for this are not, as we have already seen, of a nature calculated to inspire confidence in the writer;

---

[1] Egypt's Place in Universal History, vol. iv. p. 492.
[2] Ibid. vol. iv. p. 421.

indeed, we may say, they are most illogical and unphilosophical. But since he allows that "modern history begins with Menes and Abraham," and "it is with Abraham that the strictly historical tradition commences,"[1] we cannot understand upon his own showing, if Manetho, the historian of Menes, is to be believed, why the testimony of Moses, the historian of Abraham, is to be rejected. It is true that he makes a distinction between the *ages* which Moses says the patriarchs *attained* and the *events* which are recorded in the Book of Genesis, as he observes that "no instance can be adduced demonstrably historical of any one reaching the age of 180,"[2] and affirms it to be an "infatuation" and "purely childish delusions" to credit the ages of the antediluvian patriarchs as recorded in Scripture, "persistence in which can only be," he adds,

---

[1] Egypt's Place in Universal History, vol. iv. p. 377, 410.

[2] We may adduce two instances in modern times and in our own country of persons, one of whom lived nearly as long as Abraham or Isaac, and the other longer than Jacob or Joseph. "Old Parr" reached the age of 156, and Henry Jenkins, who was taken as a boy from the plough to carry arrows for Lord Surrey's army to the battle of Flodden Field, A.D. 1513, and appeared as a witness in the Court of Exchequer, A.D. 1665, died at Bolton in Yorkshire, where a tomb during the last century was erected to his memory, A.D. 1670, aged 169. See a pamphlet *On the great age of Henry Jenkins*, by Mrs. Ann Saville. There is another well-authenticated instance of longevity in the Countess of Desmond, who was born in the reign of Henry VI., A.D. 1464, danced at her wedding with Richard III., and testified that he was not "humped-backed," according to the popular idea. She renewed her teeth twice in the course of her long pilgrimage, and having lost her property by attainder, she came from Ireland in the 140th year of her age, to claim justice at the hands of James I. She marched on foot from Bristol to London, through inability to afford a conveyance, and on her return to Ireland met with a violent death when she was 140 years old; for "shee must needs climb a nutt-tree to gather nutts, soe, falling down she hurt her thigh, which brought a fever, and that brought death," A.D. 1604.—*Sidney Earl of Leicester's Table Book.*

"productive of doubt and unbelief.'" Bunsen describes *the events* recorded in Scripture as the "historical element," and therefore to be believed; but *the ages* are scornfully set aside, as interfering with his own theory, and termed "the Rabbinical view, which is as untenable critically as it is absurd philosophically." He adds that "the Biblical tradition must be understood according to the spirit, on the basis of the letter rightly understood; a method which has been *triumphantly discussed and settled by research and science during a century.*" Having previously declared it to be a "false or childish, not to say Godless notion of there having been a mechanical communication of the sacred books to a single man of God (that is, in the present instance, to Moses), for the purpose of transmission," he boasts that "we come to this conclusion by *sound science and research* as much as by methodical thought."[2] We frankly avow that however great may be the learned German's "*research*," we have not yet met with a single specimen of "*sound science*" in support of his wild notions, so contradictory of the plainest statements of Holy Writ. We hope to be able to show this more distinctly than we have yet done in the consideration of our next historical epoch.

§ 6. It will be more convenient, in considering the true interval between the time of Joseph's rule in Egypt and that of the Exode, which Scripture defines at 215 years, to include the longer period from the call of Abraham, bringing to bear all that *Science* has yet enabled us to learn respecting the much-mooted question respecting the presence as well as the duration of the children of Israel in the land of Egypt. We propose first of all to notice what is said in Scripture respecting the length of their

---

[1] Egypt's Place in Universal History, vol. iii. 340.
[2] Ibid. vol. iv. 384, 392.

sojourn, and then to adduce the testimony of Bunsen and others, for the purpose of seeing which system of chronology is most in accordance with what *Science* has recently revealed respecting the existence of the Israelites in Egypt.

In the Book of Exodus, xii. 40, it is said that " the sojourning of the children of Israel, who dwelt in Egypt, was 430 years." This is explained by St. Paul in his Epistle to the Galatians, iii. 16, 17, who shows that the law which God gave to Moses at Mount Sinai was " 430 years after " the promise was originally made to Abraham. It is evident, then, from Scripture respecting the duration of the Israelites in Egypt, that we are to reckon the " 430 years " from the call of Abraham unto the Exode, and not, as some have erroneously done, from the time when Jacob and his sons went down to Egypt, which, we have already seen, took place in the 215th year after the call, leaving the same number of years for their actual dwelling in the land of bondage. On the other hand Bunsen endeavours to make out that the children of Israel were more than 1430 years in Egypt, as he dates the time of Joseph as viceroy B. C. 2755, and the Exode B. C. 1320.[1] Lepsius writes just as decidedly that " only about 90 years intervened from the entrance of Jacob to the Exodus of Moses, and about as much from the entrance of Abraham into Canaan to Jacob's Exodus ;"[2] while Osburn contends very strongly that the sojourn of the children of Israel from the time of the descent of Jacob and the patriarchs until the Exode lasted the whole " 430 years " mentioned in Exodus.[3] Let us briefly notice the Scripture grounds

---

[1] Egypt's Place in Universal History, vol. iv. 492, 493.
[2] Lepsius' Letters, translated by the Misses Horner, p. 475.
[3] Monumental History of Egypt, ii. 625, *et sequitur*. As Mr. Osburn's work on Egypt is one of an entirely opposite character to that of Bunsen's as regards the due recognition of the supremacy of Scripture

for affirming that "the 430 years" can refer to nothing else than the whole period from Abraham to the Exode.

(*a*) The Hebrew text does not say that the sojourning in *Egypt* lasted 430 years, but that "the sojourning of the children of Israel, who dwelt in Egypt," was for that period; wherein is a distinction which it behoves us carefully to observe. Just as that much disputed passage in St. Luke, ii. 12, "This taxing was first made when Cyrenius was governor of Syria," can only be properly understood by accepting Lardner's interpretation of St. Luke's words, "This was the first assessment of Cyrenius, who was governor of Syria," meaning that it was the first assessment made by Cyrenius in Syria, who subsequently became its governor: so we understand, when Moses is speaking of the sojourning of the children of Israel, that he includes the sojourning of Abraham and Isaac and Jacob in the land of Canaan, before their descendants came into possession of the promised inheritance

---

on matters of chronology and history, though we believe in this instance he has mistaken the meaning of Exodus xii. 40, it may be an act of justice to mention, since Bunsen has endeavoured to depreciate the work in question, by affirming " from a critical point of view it has no value whatever " (Egypt's Place, iii. 31), that he has not disdained to make use of at least fifteen discoveries connected with the history of Egypt which have appeared nowhere else than in Osburn's work, and has transferred them *unacknowledged* to his own. Bunsen's treatment of another distinguished Egyptologer, whose great offence is that he adheres to the chronology of the Bible, is marked with similar injustice, and deserves exposure. Speaking of Mr. Poole's Horæ Egypticæ, which we have quoted above, Bunsen, with the usual superciliousness of the rationalistic school, says "his historical research is a failure from beginning to end. He has allowed himself the most incredible latitude of arbitrary assumption, in order not to disturb the Rabbinical system of ecclesiastical chronology in respect to the age of man upon the earth, which he has taken under his protection " (Egypt's Place, p. 31). Few who believe in *Revelation*, and have studied *Science*, will pay any heed to this unbecoming invective.

at the time appointed, as it is said in Hebrews xi. 9, "By faith Abraham sojourned in the land of promise as in a strange country, dwelling in tabernacles with Isaac and Jacob, the heirs with him of the same promise."

(b) The Samaritan Pentateuch, which is allowed by many learned men to exhibit the most correct copy of the Pentateuch, reads the passage, "Now the sojourning of the children of Israel, *and of their fathers, which they sojourned in the land of Canaan*, and in the land of Egypt, was 430 years."

(c) The best copies of the LXX., e. g. the Codex Alexandrinus in the British Museum, which we should regard as of some weight in the question, as being the authoritative version of the Scriptures and used by our Lord and His Apostles, read the passage in the same way.

(d) St. Paul, being an inspired man, and writing under the influence of Him who was promised to guide the Church into all truth, so understood the passage, as we have already noticed, in his Epistle to the Galatians.

(e) The Jews of old understood the meaning of the text in the same way, as may be proved from both the Talmuds; one of which[1] reads "in Egypt, and in all lands," and the other[2], "in Egypt and in the rest of the lands." So Aben Ezra interprets the words; and Joseph Ben Gorion, a Rabbinical writer of the 10th century, says, "The dwelling of the children of Israel in Egypt *and other lands* was 430 years. Notwithstanding they abode not in Egypt but 210 years, according to what their father Jacob told them, רדו '*descend*,' which in Hebrew signifies 210. Furthermore, the computation of 430

---

[1] T. Hieros. Megillah, fol. 71, 4.   [2] T. Bab. Megillah, fol. 9, 1.

years is from the year that Isaac was born, which was the holy seed unto Abraham."[1]

(*f*) The chronology of Scripture requires only 215 years from the time of Jacob and his sons going down to Egypt until the Exode, and forbids our understanding that interval as being 430 years. For if the space from the descent of the patriarchs to the Exode, when Moses was 80 years old, had been 430 years, there would have been 350 years to his birth. But the mother of Moses was the daughter of Levi[2], who, as he was 49 years of age at the time of the descent, and 137 at the time of his death, according to Exodus, vi. 16, must have lived in Egypt 88 years; and if 350 years had intervened between the descent into Egypt and the birth of Moses, *his mother would have borne him* 262 *years after her father's death*, which is impossible; whereas by accepting 215 years as the true interval, Moses' birth would have occurred within the more reasonable period of 47 years after his grandfather's death.

(*g*) The connexion of the affliction of Israel for "400 years," together with its termination "in the fourth generation," mentioned in Genesis, xv. 13, 16, shows that the sojourn in Egypt can only be understood of about half that period. The four generations being respectively represented by 1, Levi, who went down to Egypt with his brethren; 2, Kohath, Levi's son; 3, Levi's grandson Amram, who married his aunt Jochebed; and, 4, Levi's great-grandson Moses, who led the children of Israel out of Egypt "in the fourth generation," according to the promise of God. Stephen, in his address to the elders of Jerusalem, refers to the bondage of the children of Israel

---

[1] Historie of the latter tymes of the Jewes Commonweal, by Joseph Ben Gorion. Translated by Peter Morwing. Oxford, 1567, pp. 2, 3.
[2] Compare Exodus, ii. 1, vi. 20. and Numbers, xxvi. 59.

and their suffering "evil 400 years;"[1] but he does not affirm they were in Egypt for that period, any more than the passage in Genesis does. And that passage does not affirm it, because it limits their stay to the fourth generation, and the ages of these four generations are delivered by Moses himself, the last of the four; from which it is plain that the 400 years in round numbers includes the sojourning in Canaan. Clinton justly observes on the subject that "these facts show that some modern writers have very unreasonably doubted this portion of the Hebrew chronology, as if it were uncertain how this period of 430 years was to be understood. Those who cast a doubt upon this point refuse to Moses, an inspired writer (in the account of his mother and father and grandfather), that authority which would be given to the testimony of a profane author on the same occasion."[2] All these things are quite sufficient to assure us that the sojourning of the children of Israel in Egypt from the time of the descent unto the Exode was not more than 215 years, according to the teaching of Scripture. And we shall find in confirmation of this, satisfactory evidence from the monuments of the existence of the Israelites in Egypt during that period, *and neither before nor after it*. This is of the very highest importance to a right understanding of the testimony which *Science*, by the recent discovery of the key to the hieroglyphic inscriptions, bears to the truths of *Revelation*. We must, however, notice an objection which has been made against the great increase in the descendants of the Patriarchs during so short a period as their 215 years sojourn in Egypt. At the commencement "all the souls of the house of Jacob which came into Egypt were threescore and ten;"[3] at the

---
[1] Acts, vii. 6.
[2] Fasti Hellenici, App. Scripture Chronology, c. 5.
[3] Genesis, xlvi. 27.

termination they had increased to "about six hundred thousand on foot that were men, beside children."[1] Dr. Baumgarten of Kiel has fairly reasoned out this statement as follows: "If 30 years are to be taken for a generation, the sixth generation begotten in Egypt is born in the 180th year, and, consequently, at the Exode was above 20 years old. This generation, therefore, comprises the majority of the 600,000 men. If, then, we deduct from the 70 souls who came into Egypt, 14, namely Jacob, his 12 sons, and Dinah, there remain 56 pair who produced children."[2] Bunsen has endeavoured to set aside this reasonable conclusion according to his usual custom, and with the same failure of success, by a mixture of scepticism and ridicule. "This remainder of 56 pair out of 70 souls puts us very much in mind of Falstaff's mode of reckoning. Dr. Baumgarten shows that from these 56 pairs, giving each a family of six children, which is a moderate progeny for Goshen in the sixth generation, 4,000,000 could so easily have been born in 200 years, that we may really wonder that the number of the children of Israel at the Exodus was not greater. I do not think this is good theology; but I will confine myself to history, and say that the old Rabbis have hardly been more absurd."[3] Had the learned sceptic really confined himself to history, he would have avoided exposing himself in the way he has done. A very high authority has shown from experience that the Israelites could have increased as rapidly during their sojourn in Egypt as Scripture affirms they did. "According to a table of Euler," says Malthus, "the period of doubling will be only $12\frac{1}{3}$ years. And this proportion is not only a possible supposition, *but has*

---

[1] Exodus, xii. 37.
[2] Theological Commentary on the Old Testament, pt. i. p. 476.
[3] Egypt's Place in Universal History, vol. i. p. 178.

actually occurred for short periods. Sir W. Petty supposes a doubling possible in so short a time as 10 years."[1] And the same author, quoting Short's Observations on Bills of Mortality, p. 259, observes, " It is calculated that the Israelites in Egypt doubled their numbers *every fifteen years* during the period of their stay."[2] We may, therefore, consider it settled beyond the power of contradiction, as taught in God's Word and confirmed by experience in other instances, that the children of Israel increased during their 215 years' sojourn in Egypt from 70 souls to upwards of 2,000,000, their probable number, including their women and children, when they came up out of the land of bondage.

Our object now must be to show that there is satisfactory evidence from the monuments of Egypt of the existence of the Israelites at the period when Scripture chronology supposes them there, and we search in vain for similar indications at any other period in the history of that country. If we can establish our point, we need scarcely say how completely it is subversive of Bunsen's theory upon his own chosen ground of the value of historical synchronisms, respecting the interval between Abraham and Moses being upwards of 1400 years. "All persons," (i. e. all Christian chronologists), says George Syncellus, an eminent chronographer of the eighth century, "are agreed that *Joseph was in power in the reign of Apophis.*" Who was this Pharaoh of whom tradition thus speaks? According to Josephus, he was the fourth king out of six who formed what was commonly termed the dynasty of the Shepherd Kings. Africanus places him the last of the six. Eusebius places him the third out of four kings, to which he limits the dynasty. And Syncellus reverses this order by making him the fourth and

---

[1] Malthus' Essay, vol. i. p. 8. [2] Ibid. vol. ii. p. 190.

last king. The two former authorities give him sixty-one years as the length of his reign; the two latter shorten it to fourteen. This affords a fair specimen of the exceeding difficulty of understanding Egyptian history from the variations of different authors; at least with regard to times anterior to the eighteenth dynasty, when history is more certain, and during which the Exode of the Israelites took place. Before, however, entering upon the history of the patron of Joseph, it may be convenient if we insert a list of the two races of Pharaohs who were reigning contemporaneously in Egypt from the time of Abraham's visit until the death of Joseph, when a new king arose, according to Scripture, who "knew not" the Israelites as heretofore, and which event can only be explained of the conquest of Memphis by Amosis, the termination of the civil war, erroneously called the Hyksos period or invasion of the Shepherd Kings, and the rise of the renowned eighteenth dynasty. We should remember that those two Pharaohnic races had each more than one capital at different periods, just as the Emperor of Russia may be said to possess three in this present day; the capital of Upper Egypt being either Thebes, or Coptos, or Abydos; and of Lower Egypt, either Memphis, or On (Heliopolis), or Avaris; and that these Pharaohs *de facto* often assumed titles *de jure*, to which they conceived themselves entitled, just as the kings of England bore the title of kings of France until the beginning of the present century, or as the kings of Sardinia have added the titles of Cyprus and Jerusalem to their European dominions, which will account for the king of Upper Egypt frequently bearing the title of Lower Egypt as well, and *vice versâ*, without any *de facto* power in that part of the country, which refused allegiance to their rule. Bearing this in mind, we may, by comparing Manetho's list of dynasties, as transmitted by Josephus, Africanus, Eusebius, and Syncellus, with the

A DOUBLE LINE OF PHARAOHS. 113

discoveries from the *hieroglyphic* inscriptions on the monuments, especially in the chamber of Karnak[1] and on the tablet of Abydos, or from the *hieratic* reading of the Turin papyrus, ascertain the succession of these two lines of Pharaohs, as follows :—

Kings of Upper Egypt.	Kings of Lower Egypt.
Achthoes.	Imephthis.
Amenemes I.	Othoes.
Sesertesen I.	Salatis.
Amenemes II.	Mæris.
Sesertesen II.	Apophis.
Sesertesen III.	Melaneres.
Amenemes III.	Jannes.
Amenemes IV.	Asses.
Sebacon.	
Amosis.	

It is impossible to give with any degree of certainty the length of each individual reign of these kings, on account of the endless disagreements between the fragmentary notices of such on the monuments, and the statements of Manetho and Eratosthenes. Even in Manetho's history alone the variations are very great as transmitted by the different Greek annalists. The contrast which this exhibits with the plain and consistent statements of Biblical history, omitting for a time the question of inspiration, for there is no difference between the readings of the Hebrew and the LXX. after the time of Abraham, ought to be sufficient to satisfy every candid inquirer of

[1] The chamber of Karnak, containing the ancestral tablet of Thothmes III. of the 28th dynasty, with portraits and names of sixty-one kings, to whom he is sacrificing, was discovered by Mr. Burton, and given to the public by the discoverer in his *Excerpta Hieroglyphica*, A. D. 1824. The tablet of Abydos, which represents Rameses-Sesothis, the great king of the 19th dynasty, receiving homage from fifty of his royal predecessors, was discovered by Mr. William Banks in 1818, and now forms a part of the splendid collection of Egyptian antiquities in the British Museum.

I

the untenableness of Bunsen's theory, which seeks to elongate the well-ascertained period of 430 years into 1440. The reign of Amosis, or of his son Chebron-Amenophis, synchronised with the birth of Moses, which took place eighty years before the Exode, and the termination of the 430 years from the call of Abraham. And the improbability, may we not say the *impossibility*, of Moses, the seventh in descent from Abraham, omitting so lengthy a period as Bunsen's hypothesis requires, may be seen by supposing an English author of the present day, in writing the history of his country since the discovery of printing in the fifteenth century, were to be accused of having omitted *all notice of the previous* 1000 *years*. Such reveries stand self-convicted by their own improbability. But happily we can do more; we can show by undeniable proofs from the Egyptian records, by the tests of astronomical science, and by the historical synchronisms of other nations, that the chronology of Scripture is true, and that of Bunsen is utterly unfounded and wrong. The time between the visit of Abraham to Egypt and the termination of the civil war in the capture of Memphis by Amosis, who may be likened unto our Henry VII. in English history, and who, being the founder of the famous 18th dynasty, was "the king that knew not Joseph," must be reckoned as 350 years. For Moses was born, according to the statement in Exodus, soon after the rise of that dynasty, and his birth preceded the Exode by eighty years. Now, if we search into Egyptian history, such as we have, of the two Pharaohnic races who were reigning contemporaneously during this period in Upper and Lower Egypt, we find an agreement with Scripture chronology sufficiently strong to satisfy us of its truth. As regards the kings of Upper Egypt, Osburn, who has analysed the hieroglyphic inscriptions with equal skill and far greater success than Bunsen, in his Monumental

History of Egypt, gives as the probable duration of the period from the death of Amenemes I., the son of Achthoes, and founder of what is termed the 12th dynasty, unto the death of Sebacon, the father of Amosis, the founder of the 23rd dynasty, 285 years, which, by allowing the remaining 65 years, the difference between 285 and 350, for the reigns of Achthoes and Amenemes I. at the beginning of the period, and of Amosis (concerning whom all the Greek lists agree in giving 25 years as the length of his reign, and there is a hieroglyph of his twenty-second year) at its termination, we have a very satisfactory approximation to the chronology of Scripture.[1] It is the same with the kings of Lower Egypt. Josephus gives 260 years, Africanus 284, as the duration of the six Shepherd Kings (as they were subsequently called by the successful faction), from the time of Salatis, who was reigning at Memphis, when Sesertesen I. was reigning at Thebes, unto Asses, who probably fell, like Richard III. at Bosworth, when Amosis captured Memphis, and united in his own person and family the two kingdoms of Upper and Lower Egypt. Bunsen denies this striking confirmation of the truth of Biblical chronology in the history of the kings of Egypt, by endeavouring to make an interval of many centuries (though he appears undecided, as we have before noticed, whether it should be 500 or 900 years, a curious admission for any one pretending to be a correct chronologer) between Amuntimæus (Amenemes III.), the last king

---

[1] Eusebius in his canon makes the beginning of Amosis' reign synchronise with the 294th after the call of Abraham, and as Manetho's history was then in existence, his authority ought to have some weight, even with Bunsen; but as he was only a Christian bishop, and not a profane author, German rationalism seeks to write him down as an intentional falsifier of history. Josephus, notwithstanding Bunsen's deserved eulogy of him elsewhere, is treated in the same way.

mentioned in the canon of Eratosthenes, and the time of Amosis. We believe the real period to be about one century; and we may take this opportunity of observing that it is impossible either to understand an important epoch in Egypt's history, or to see its complete agreement with Scripture chronology, as long as we acknowledge that *fable* of the Hyksos dynasty, which was probably originated by Manetho, the historian of the successful faction in ancient times; and which has been amplified as well as misunderstood by Bunsen[1], the advocate of the rationalistic school in modern days. Osburn has satisfactorily decided the question, and with great skill proved that the invasion of the Shepherds, and the establishment of the Hyksos dynasty, is nothing more than another race of native Pharaohs reigning in Lower Egypt, and claiming equally descent from Menes, though doubtless assisted by Shepherd soldiers from Phœnicia, during their constant wars with their contemporary kings in Upper Egypt. It has been assumed by some that, because mention is made in Scripture at the time of Joseph's brethren going down to Egypt of "every shepherd being an abomination to the Egyptians,"[2] it implies an allusion to the Hyksos or Shepherd dynasty, and a time subsequent to their expulsion. But even were there any truth in the fabulous story of the Hyksos dynasty, it would not necessarily have such a meaning, for we know from Diodorus that the lower orders of the Egyptians

---

[1] As a specimen of Bunsen's fondness for amplification, in order to lengthen his chronology thousands of years beyond Scripture testimony, or fact, or any attempt at proof, he gravely argues, "No place is anywhere found for an old monarch in the Book of the Dead, King *Goose*, in Egyptian *Sent*, whose scutcheon we give phonetically and figuratively. *He may as well have been one of the unchronological kings before Menes*"!!!—*Egypt's Place, &c.*, vol. ii. p. 112.

[2] Gen. xlvi. 31.

were divided into "*shepherds,* husbandmen, and artificers,"[1] and it appears from the context to the passage we have quoted that after Joseph's brethren were announced to Pharaoh as tending cattle by occupation, he commanded that *the best of the land* in Goshen should be allotted to them. The phrase, "every shepherd," must be understood to mean "foreign shepherds," who were accustomed, as the Israelites, to sacrifice those very animals, such as sheep and oxen, which the Egyptians held sacred. Hence Tacitus, in his description of the Jews, observes, "They sacrifice the ram in order to insult Jupiter Ammon; and they sacrifice the ox, which the Egyptians worship under the name of Apis."[2]

We may see in the amazing differences between those who have made Egyptian history and these hieroglyphic inscriptions their life study, how little dependence can be placed upon any who leave the sure ground of Scripture chronology for their own crude and contradictory theories. Osburn gives for the period between the 11th and 18th dynasties, as we have already noticed, and which he modestly describes as "the *probable* duration," the sum of 285 years, and which, as being in accordance with what Scripture relates respecting the visit of Abraham to Egypt, and the rise of that dynasty "which knew not Joseph," we have no doubt is the true chronology. For the same period Leipsus allows "500 years;" Bunsen, "perhaps nine centuries;" and De Rongé, "about nineteen centuries." When writers of the same school are so much at variance amongst themselves as to differ about fourteen centuries for an historical epoch, we may reasonably ask to be excused rejecting the consistent chronology of the Bible, and accepting their wild theories in its place, at all events until they are agreed as to what

---

[1] Hist. lib. i. c. vi. [2] Hist. lib. v. § 4.

they really mean. And the very language in which Bunsen indulges on this subject, sufficiently betrays a conscious weakness of the cause he seeks to uphold. "Professed scholars even," says he, "especially in Germany, do not blush to parade before all Europe a scandalous ignorance of Egyptian research, and to talk with caste-arrogance of 'so-called contemporary monuments,' and 'pretended explanations of the hieroglyphics.' When, however, that will not answer their purpose any longer, they come forward, especially in England, with theological suspicions and charges of infidelity. All such persons rush eagerly to attack our assumption as to the length of the Middle Empire (i. e. the period of dispute) with the arms, so often victorious, of positive denial, and by referring to great names of those who lived before the discovery of the hieroglyphics."[1] Now we propose to test the accuracy of his chronology, not by "the great names" of past times, nor by those "German scholars" of the present day, whom he appears to hold in such little esteem on account of their adherence to the testimony of Scripture, but *by himself.* We think we can show from his own words some reasons for disregarding his *chronological* theory on this portion of Egyptian history. Referring to Viscount De Rougé's translation of the Sallier papyri, an hieratic document of great importance with reference to this period, Bunsen observes, "This, as I learn from himself, contains a description of the negotiations between the Theban 'Prince,' a king of the 17th dynasty, and his contemporary and foe, a king *Apophis,* at Abara (Uara, Avaris)."[2] Now, who was this king *Apophis,* residing at

---

[1] Egypt's Place, &c. vol. ii. p. 417, 418.
[2] Egypt's Place, &c. vol. iii. p. 32. For a fuller account of this historical synchronism, see the *Exodus Papyri,* by the Rev. D. Heath, chapter ii. Sallier i. By "Avaris," we conclude "Heliopolis," one of the three

Abara or Avaris, the contemporary and foe of a Theban king of the 17th dynasty, according to Bunsen, and who must have lived not very long before the time of the 18th dynasty, the commencement of which is recognised by all, speaking generally, as about 1700 B. C.? According to Manetho, we read: "There was once a king of ours, named Timæus (or Amun-Timæus, the same as Amenemes III.), in whose reign men of ignoble birth out of the east invaded our country, and made of themselves a king, whose name was Salatis, who rebuilt the city of *Avaris;* he reigned thirteen years; then Beon, forty-four years; then Apachnos, thirty-six years and seven months; after him *Apophis reigned sixty-one years;* then Janias, fifty years and one month; after all these reigned Apis, forty-nine years and two months. This whole nation was styled *Hycsos,* i. e. *Shepherd Kings;* for the first syllable *Hyc,* according to the sacred dialect, denotes a *king,* as *sos* signifies a shepherd. The kings of Thebes and of the other parts of Egypt rose in insurrection, and a long and terrible war ensued between them. They were finally conquered by Alisphragmuthosis (i. e. Tethmosis or Amosis,

---

capitals of Egypt, is meant, where the Pharaoh of Joseph certainly held his court. Sir Gardner Wilkinson observes that "the name of Heliopolis was ĉi-ù-re, 'the abode of the sun,' from which the Hebrew On or Aôn, corrupted into *Aven* (Ezek. xxx. 17), was taken;" or it may be understood as describing the city where the Jews dwelt in Egypt, the same great authority remarking, "it is not impossible that the name of the city of *Abaris* may point to that of the Hebrews or *Abarim* (Gen. xi. 15)."—*Rawlinson's Herodotus,* ii. § 8 and § 136. Osburn shows that the rival faction were fond of ridiculing all names relating to their enemies, and it is possible it was done in this instance by corrupting the On of Scripture, the same as Heliopolis, into Abara, or Avaris, or Aven. Ewald in his "Geschichte des Volkes Israel," p. 450, contends that the word philologically means "city of the Hebrews." If so, it may only mean another name for the city which was called by the Egyptians *On,* and by the Greeks *Heliopolis.*

as he is variously termed, the head of the 18th dynasty 'which knew not Joseph'), and shut up in the place named *Avaris*, containing 10,000 acres.[1]" Manetho says, in addition, that this Shepherd kingdom, as he terms it, and which we have before explained to mean the rival Pharaohnic kingdom in Lower Egypt to the kings of Thebes [2], lasted 511 years, which may help to account for Bunsen's theory of nine centuries, or De Rongé's of nineteen, for this period[3] of Egyptian history; but this is evidently an incorrect reading, as the united sums of the various reigns of this Shepherd dynasty, as given by Manetho, amounts to only 254 years, which may be shown to be true, inasmuch as it harmonises with what we gather from Scripture. Comparing then the statement of Manetho respecting Pharaoh *Apophis*, in the city of *Avaris*, who died about 100 years before the rise of the dynasty " which knew not Joseph," with the fragmentary notice in the Sallier papyri of a Theban king of the 17th dynasty negotiating with a *king of the same name and residing at the same place*, we have as decisive proof as we can need, that this king *Apophis* was reigning in Lower Egypt at the time when Joseph was first brought there as slave, and subsequently raised to the post of second ruler in that kingdom. It likewise refutes the theory of Bunsen, who dates the Exode of the Israelites

---

[1] Manetho apud Josephus contra Apion, i. 14.

[2] Osburn says, " the *proof* that the Shepherd invasion was a slanderous perversion of the conquest of Memphis by the Lower Egyptian Pharaohs is very complete."—*Mon. Hist.* vol. ii. p. 56.

[3] Bunsen admits that " the tablet of Abydos jumps over the whole Hyksos period" (Egypt's Place, &c. vol. ii. p. 254), a concession which is as fatal to his own system of chronology as it would be to an author of the present day who should assert that Louis XVIII. succeeded *de facto* to the throne of France on the death of Louis XVII., and that the twenty-five years of the Revolution and the reign of Napoleon I. were mere myths, which never had existence.

1000 years earlier, according to his system of anti-Biblical chronology.

Apophis, Phiops or Apappas (for by these different names in the lists the same individual is meant), the patron of Joseph, appears from the monuments to have been one of the most magnificent of the Pharaohs. He ascended the throne early in life, or rather reigned conjointly for a period of more than sixty years with his father and grandfather, and lived to an advanced age. The monuments of this king that have yet been discovered are but few, in consequence, as Osburn naturally concludes, of Memphis and Thebes being still covered with sand. The only exploit of this king of which there is any monumental record, is the defeat of the Egyptians of the rival kingdom, which is said in the hieroglyphic inscription to have taken place in the mountains of Western Thebes. This feat of arms is commemorated in a superb tablet sculptured on the face of one of the granite cliffs in the Sinaitic peninsula. It is in two compartments. In one Apophis is represented as wearing the crown of Lower Egypt, and in the other that of Upper Egypt; showing that at one period of his reign he must either have possessed or claimed the whole kingdom.[1] In the hieroglyphic genealogy, as given in the tablets belonging to the chamber of Karnak, Apophis is declared to be king of Lower Egypt, at the time that Sebacon, the successor of Amuntimæus, was king in Upper Egypt. The few

---

[1] Though Pharaoh Apophis was probably king of both Egypts at one period of his reign, it does not follow that the mere claimant of that title implies possession of the whole country; e. g. in a tablet on the Cosseyr road from Persia to Egypt, by the Red Sea, which is given in Burton's Excerpta Hieroglyphica, an inscription relating to Amenemha I. reads, " The Lord of all Egypt, Neb-tete-ra, living for ever, like the Sun, says, I will establish his Majesty — King Amenemha with soldiers in *Upper Egypt.*"—*Poole's Horæ Egypticæ,* pt. ii. sec. iii.

remains of his reign, which have been found at Abydos, are of exquisite beauty. Egyptian art had attained, perhaps, at that period its highest perfection. The tombs of his princes and courtiers, especially of one amongst them, to which we shall presently allude, appear to have surpassed, both in dimensions and in beauty of execution, those of the famous 12th dynasty, to which the great Sesostris (Sesertesen I.) belonged, and whose rival capital was the famous city of Thebes. The following reasons show conclusively, as it appears to us, that this Apophis was the veritable Pharaoh who advanced Joseph to the place of second ruler in the kingdom of Egypt.

(1.) There seems to have been a very general agreement amongst the Greek writers that Apophis was the king who befriended Joseph. Syncellus says, it is admitted by all; and specifies that " in the fourth year of his reign Joseph is said to have come into Egypt, and in his seventeenth to have been advanced to the highest honours."[1] And the chronological agreement between the reign of Apophis, as set forth in Manetho, together with what is said in Scripture respecting the time of Joseph, confirms this view.

(2.) When Joseph was raised to power, it is said in Scripture that " Pharaoh called his name *Zaphnath-paaneah;* and he gave him to wife *Asenath,* the daughter of *Poti-pherah,* priest of *On.*"[2] Several interpretations have been offered for the Egyptian name of Joseph. In the margin of our English Bible it is rendered, " A revealer of secrets." Rosellini interprets it to mean, " Saviour of the age;" Gesenius and others, "Sustainer of the age;" and Cory considers it to refer to the fabulous Phœnix, or Hermes. Osburn more correctly reads it from the hieroglyphic language as " Tsaphnath-Phehnuk," and which signifies, "One with Neith, the god-

---

[1] Syncel. p. 104. B. [2] Genesis, xli. 45.

dess of wisdom—he who flees from adultery,"—the interpretation of the first word being very apposite to Pharaoh's address to Joseph, "There is none so discreet and wise as thou," just before giving him his Egyptian name; and that of the second accords with the well-known story of Joseph's purity.[1] The name of Joseph's first master was Potiphar, and his subsequent father-in-law was called Potipherah. Both are derived from the Egyptian word *pteophre*, signifying "the sun worshipper." Potiphera was the chief priest or prince of On, which the LXX. translates as Ἡλιόπολις, the city of the Sun, one of the three chief cities of Egypt[2], where justice was administered, and which at that time, in all probability, formed the chief residence of Pharaoh Apophis and his court. The name of Asenath, who was given him to wife, was long ago identified by Champollion, and signifies, "she who sees Neith," the goddess of wisdom; an appropriate title for the spouse of him who was acknowledged by the king to be wiser than all his subjects.

(3.) There is a well-known monumental painting which, notwithstanding all that has been said against it, may possibly refer to the arrival of the family of Jacob in Egypt. At Benee-Hasan, on the Nile, about 100 miles north of Thebes, there has been discovered the tomb of

---

[1] An hieratic MS. belonging to Mrs. Daubeny of London, and translated by De Rongé, has proved to be a romance of the time of Sethos II., the last king of the 19th dynasty, founded upon the lives of two brothers, who are represented as *feeders of cattle*. The younger brother has an adventure with his elder brother's wife, which Osburn declares is "*identical in every particular* with Joseph's adventure with the wife of Potiphar." If so, as it must have been written five or six centuries after the occurrence to which it is supposed to refer, it would bear the same relative proportion in chronology to Sir Walter Scott's romance of Ivanhoe, in which another descendant of Abraham forms a prominent feature in the work.

[2] "Heliopolis, Thebes, and Memphis."—*Diod. Sic.* lib. i. ch. vi.

Nevôtp, an officer of high rank under Sesertesen II. On this tomb there is a representation of an occurrence in the sixth year of that monarch, in which two Egyptians are presenting to their master a party of strangers of a race called "Mes-stem," or "Mes-strem," consisting of ten males, four females, with two children on a donkey, and a lad bearing a spear. The inscription calls them "The great foreign prisoners;" and the hieroglyphic figures, thirty-seven, seem to indicate the whole number, of which the seventeen painted only formed a part. No one who has seen the magnificent work of Lepsius[1], which has been published at the expense and by the liberality of the Prussian government, in which the paintings on the Egyptian monuments are copied with extreme fidelity, can for a moment doubt that these strangers bear on their features the strongly-marked characteristics of the Jewish race, so well known throughout the world. The force of this argument seems to be irresistible. When, moreover, we find, according to our chronological arrangement of the rival sovereignties of Upper and Lower Egypt, that Sesertesen II. was ruling at Thebes when Pharaoh Apophis was at the commencement of his long reign, we think this remarkable painting may refer to the arrival of the family of Jacob in Egypt. Though called "prisoners," they are not represented in the guise of prisoners, but armed and at liberty, which would seem to intimate that they were an honorary deputation from Lower Egypt, to an officer of the rival dynasty in the Upper country, during an interval in the civil war. This may account for their being called Mes-stem or Mestrem, and not Jews or Israelites, as they might be regarded by the inhabitants of Upper Egypt as belonging to the Lower country; and

---

[1] Denkmaeler aus Egypten und Æthiopien, Band v. Abth. ii. Bl. 131.

Josephus says, "We call Egypt Mestre, and the Egyptians Mestreans."[1]

(4.) Scripture records a noticeable fact which affords a clue to the time of Joseph's viceroyalty in Egypt. In consequence of the great famine which then desolated Egypt, and which caused the people to offer their land to Joseph in return for that bread which he had provided in anticipation of the distress he was gifted to foresee, it is said, "Joseph bought all the land of Egypt for Pharaoh; for the Egyptians sold every man his field, because the famine prevailed over them; so the land became Pharaoh's: only the land of the priests bought he not; for the priests had a portion assigned them of Pharaoh, and did eat their portion which Pharaoh gave them; wherefore they sold not their lands."[2] We quote from the work of a distinguished Egyptologer, to which we have had frequent occasion to refer in confirmation of the accordance between *Revelation* and *Science* (in the reading and understanding of the hieroglyphics), on the political change which ensued in consequence of the seven years' famine in Egypt. "The monumental proofs," says Mr. Osburn, "of the occurrence of this modification in the social condition of Egypt are just as striking as any of those which have engaged us. The tombs of the eras that follow that of Apophis bear unequivocal testimony to a great political change having taken place in the condition of the inhabitants of Egypt at this period, when we compare them with those of the preceding epochs. In old Egypt scarcely an act of any Pharaoh is recorded in the tombs of his subjects. Nor does his name appear at all, save in the names of their estates, and sometimes in their own names. But in the tombs of the new kingdom, or that of the times that followed Joseph, *all this is re-*

---

[1] Antiq. Jud. i. v. 2.   [2] Genesis, xlvii. 20—22.

versed. There is scarcely a tomb of any importance, the principal subject of which is not some act of service or devotion performed by the excavator to the reigning Pharaoh. We shall have abundant opportunities, in the course of the inquiry before us, of showing the reality of this remarkable change, the cause of which we so plainly discover in the legislation of Joseph. Nor is this difference confined to the secular princes of Egypt only. . . . We found the priest's office in old Egypt to be a mere appendage to the secular functions of the princes and nobles, performed invariably, in the cases where the performance is depicted, by proxy and by the hands of menials and dependents. *The contrast to this presented by the monuments of the later epoch is marvellously perfect.* The priest has risen greatly in authority and importance in the state. His office becomes more and more exclusive and hereditary, until at length he ascends the throne of the Pharaohs, and rules Egypt by a dynasty (the 21st) of Priest-kings. For all this the inspired narrative gives us the amply-sufficient cause in the forbearance of Apophis to exact payment for corn supplied to the temples during the famine. . . . We find from Diodorus that the tripartite division of the soil, so clearly implied in the Scripture account of the reforms of Joseph, was in full force at the time of his visit to Egypt. . . . The existence of the same proprietorship of the soil is just as plainly assumed in the Rosetta[1] inscription, where the land of the priests is exempted from the taxes imposed on the rest of Egypt. Thus clearly does the Greek tradition testify to the reality of the arrangement specified in the sacred

---

[1] On the Rosetta stone now in the British Museum we read that " Ptolemy Epiphanes ordered that the revenues of the temples, and the annual contributions to them in corn and money, should remain everywhere as usual . . . . and with respect to the priests, that they should pay nothing more for the completion of their order than they had paid to the first year of his father."—*Greek Inscrip.* lines 14 and 16.

text, to the effect of which, on society, the preceding and following monuments bear evidence just as unequivocal."[1] If this argument be worth anything, and we believe it to be of great importance in confirmation of the harmony which exists between Egyptian history as deducible from the hieroglyphic monuments and the Scripture record, it amply refutes the erroneous chronology of Bunsen, who places the viceroyalty of Joseph about 1,000 years before it really took place.

(5.) We have now to consider a matter of still greater importance in deciding on the chronological dispute between the language of Scripture and the theories of Bunsen. The latter lays very great stress upon what he considers confirmatory of his own system, and it behoves us to examine with care the remarkable statement to which he calls public attention. Speaking of the fact and the time of Joseph being viceroy of Egypt, Bunsen observes, " Joseph might just as well have been made vicegerent by the second or third, as by the first Sesortosis (Sesertesen). *The question is settled, however, in favour of the first by a very unexpected and singular discovery.* There is authentic proof that in his reign a terrible famine raged in Egypt. We are indebted to Birch for this unforeseen confirmation and more accurate determination of the synchronism of Joseph and the first Sesortosis, by deciphering a remarkable tomb inscription of the lieutenant of Amenemha (co-regent with Sesertesen I.), which was published in the great work of the Prussian expedition. The person entombed states that he was governor of a district in Upper Egypt under the above king, and is made to say,—

" ' *When in the time of Sesortosis I. the great famine prevailed in all the other districts of Egypt, there was corn in mine.*'

---

[1] Monumental History of Egypt, vol. ii. p. 104—107.

"Nobody would venture to build up a synchronism upon such a notice as this; but admitting that Joseph was vicegerent of one of the three Sesortosidæ, and that he owed his power and consideration to his foresight in providing against the seven years of scarcity, no one will contend that such a notice is not deserving of very great attention, and it must turn the scale in favour of Sesortosis I. But the more I think over the development and chronology of Egypt, the more convinced I am that the juxtaposition of these two personages is certain and incontrovertible. The proof is completed by the present restoration of the Jewish chronology in the periods between Abraham and the immigration of Jacob, and from thence to the Exodus, as the sequel will show."[1]

Now, we are prepared to show upon other testimony beside that of Scripture that the learned Baron is as wrong in his inference respecting this Egyptian famine as he is in his chronology concerning the duration of the Israelites in Egypt. We have seen that he contends for 1435 years as the interval between Abraham and Moses, in place of 430 years, which the Sacred Record so distinctly affirms. Even Dr. Williams can hardly receive Bunsen's speculations on this subject, as he says, "The idea of bringing Abraham into Egypt as early as 2876 B.C. is *one of our author's most doubtful points, and may seem hardly tenable.* But he wanted time for the growth of Jacob's family into a people of two millions, and he felt bound to place Joseph under a native Pharaoh, therefore before the Shepherd Kings. He also contends that Abraham's horizon in Asia is antecedent to the first Median conquest of Babylon in 2234. A famine, *conveniently mentioned* under the 12th dynasty of Egypt, completes his proof."[2]

---

[1] Egypt's Place in Universal History, vol. iii. p. 334.
[2] Essays and Reviews, pp. 57, 58.

While lamenting the spirit in which Dr. Williams appears to notice this brilliant discovery of Birch, though erroneously applied by Bunsen, let us inquire how far this "conveniently mentioned" famine is a *proof* of the existence of Joseph in Egypt, and of its referring to the seven years' famine which he was enabled to foretell. We observe, first of all, that the hieroglyphic record specifies that the famine in the time of Sesertesen I. did not extend to a certain district in Upper Egypt, though prevailing in all other parts of the country. Now, what saith Scripture respecting the famine which occurred when Joseph was the viceroy of Pharaoh, and when he had laid up corn for the people at On (Heliopolis), one of the chief cities of Lower Egypt? " And the seven years of dearth began to come according as Joseph had said : and *the dearth was in all lands; but in all the land of Egypt there was bread. And the famine was over all the face of the earth. And all countries came into Egypt to Joseph for to buy corn ; because that the famine was so sore in all lands.*"[1] No two records can be more unlike, and it is surprising that so acute a reasoner as Bunsen could have discovered, or supposed, in the one any reference to the other. It affords a fresh instance of how easily men—even German rationalists — will jump at a hasty conclusion in support of a wrong and indefensible theory. For without laying any stress on the proof which has been already adduced, that the Pharaoh under whom Joseph ruled Egypt was named Apophis, and not Sesertesen I., and that the latter preceded the former by a full century (Bunsen's system requires 1000 years), or that *Lower* Egypt was the locality where the corn had been carefully preserved, by Joseph's orders, for the use of the people, instead of there being corn in

---

[1] Genesis, xli. 54, 56.

a district of *Upper* Egypt, as was the case in the time of the great famine to which the hieroglyphic inscription refers, it is certain, from the Scripture record, that the seven years of famine was *universal*, not merely in Upper Egypt, but throughout Asia as well as in Africa, wherever man was to be found. The great famine alluded to in the hieroglyphic inscription may refer to another one recorded in Scripture, and we think very probably it does, as it is said to have occurred in the time of Sesertesen I., whose reign synchronises with what took place in the time of Isaac. We read in Scripture, "There was a famine in the land (of Canaan) beside the first famine that was in the days of Abraham," which we may conclude was a very severe one in Egypt as well as in Canaan, for it is added, " The Lord appeared unto Isaac and said, *Go not down into Egypt*, but dwell in the land which I shall tell thee of." [1] This famine appears to have occurred about the 105th year of the call of Abraham, when Jacob was fourscore years old, and Jacob and Esau had come to man's estate, which would answer according to the Bible chronology, B. C. 1910. And as the reign of Sesertesen I. preceded that of Apophis by about 100 years, and Joseph's rule in Egypt is dated B. C. 1800, we find the great famine which is recorded as having happened in his reign synchronises with the time mentioned in Scripture when Isaac was forbidden to go to Egypt, doubtless on account of the severity of the famine which then prevailed. In addition to this we have independent testimony of the fact of a severe famine having occurred in the eastern extremity of Asia at that period, and which we believe fully confirms the accuracy of the sacred record. In the Chinese annals it is related that, " In the beginning of the reign of the Emperor Ching-tang, the founder of the

---

[1] Genesis, xxvi. 1, 2.

second dynasty in China, "*there happened a drought and famine all over the empire, which lasted SEVEN YEARS, in which time no rain had fallen.*"[1] The reign of Ching-tang commenced, according to Martinius and Couplet, B.C. 1766, and the seven years' famine in Egypt, according to our conjectural estimate of Scripture chronology, ended B.C. 1795. If we were certain that these two dates were correct, it would prove that the famines thus recorded in Scripture and the Chinese annals referred to different events. But inasmuch as we are not absolutely certain of the Scripture chronology within a few years, on account of being in a measure compelled to make a conjecture on one or two periods in the interval between the Exode and the building of Solomon's Temple, which we shall have presently to consider, and much less so of the exactness of the chronology of Martinius and Couplet, as deduced from the Chinese annals, we think, considering that the duration of the famine in both countries having been exactly *seven years*, and that the Scripture record particularly specifies it was not confined to Egypt or Africa, but was "in all lands," and "over all the face of the earth," we may fairly conclude that they both refer to the same event. If so, it is not only a remarkable testimony to the truth and accuracy of Biblical history, but also completely subversive of the extraordinary system of chronology which Bunsen has thought fit to adopt.

(6.) The discovery of Joseph's tomb affords another clue to the time of the existence of the Israelites in Egypt. We read that Joseph before his death "took an oath of the children of Israel; saying, God will surely

---

[1] Jackson's Chron. Antiq. vol. ii. p. 455. Analysis of the History and Chronology of the Emperors of China, from Martinius, Couplet, and Du Halde.

visit you, and ye shall carry up my bones from hence. So Joseph died, being 110 years old: and they embalmed him, and he was put in a coffin in Egypt."[1] In this state the body of Joseph must have remained 144 years, as he became viceroy at the age of thirty, in the 206th year of the call, and 206+80 to the time of his death +144 to that of the Exode, complete the number of 430 years. It is natural to conclude that during that prolonged period of nearly a century and a half the immense blessings which Joseph had bestowed upon Egypt would have been gratefully commemorated by the reigning dynasty and the people with a magnificent tomb; especially as it was the custom of the Egyptians to erect their sepulchres during life, as we do our houses, preparatory to their subsequently becoming receptacles for the dead. There are still in existence at Sakkara, opposite Memphis, in Lower Egypt, the ruins of the tomb of a distinguished personage, whose name in hieroglyphics accords with that of *Joseph*. It is close in the vicinity of the largest pyramid[2] of the group, which Osburn considers to have been the tomb of Apophis, and his father Meris. Another pyramid of this group bears the significant title of Mustabet el Farûn, "the throne of Pharaoh." On the relief of the tomb referred to, the names and titles of Joseph appear in great beauty, as may be seen in the accurate copies of Lepsius' magnificent work.[3] The name is written in hieroglyphics *ei-tsuph*, signifying " he came to save." The title under which Joseph's power was inaugurated, as we

---

[1] Genesis, l. 25, 26.

[2] It is curious to find an allusion in the Book of Job to these royal sepulchres. "Then had I been at rest," says Job, " with kings and counsellors of the earth, which build *desolate places* (הרבות *Pyramids*, probably a Semitic version of an Egyptian word) for themselves." Job, iii. 14.

[3] Denkmaeler, No. 15, Sakkarah Abt. ii. Bl. 101.

read in the book of Genesis, by the people crying, *Ab-rech*, "Bow the knee," appears likewise on the tomb, under the hieroglyphic *tib-resh*, signifying "royal priest and prince." Amongst other titles mentioned, there is one peculiarly suitable to both the person and office of Joseph. He is called "Director of the granaries of the chiefs of both Egypts." We have thus monumental evidence of the existence of Joseph in Egypt, honoured by the king and people to whom he had proved himself so great a benefactor, and in accordance with both the history and chronology set forth in Scripture.

(7.) One more synchronism must be noticed in confirmation of the agreement between the Bible and the hieroglyphic inscriptions. We read in the book of Exodus, that after the death of Joseph and his brethren, and all that generation, "there arose up a new king over Egypt, which knew not Joseph."[1] The time of Joseph's death has already been computed. It occurred 144 years before the Exode, which we place B.C. 1585. The date of his death would therefore be $1585+144=1729$ B.C. Moses was born eighty years before the Exode. The interval between the death of Joseph and the birth of Moses would consequently be sixty-four years, during which time the new king appeared, "which knew not Joseph." We are not able to compute to a year when this took place, as it is not stated in Scripture to have occurred until "all the generation of Joseph" were dead, as well as himself, which time is not specially mentioned. We may conclude that it took place within a very few years after Joseph's death, as he was the youngest but one of Jacob's large family, and himself lived to the age of 110 years. Levi, who was ten years older than

---

[1] Exodus, i. 6, 8.

Joseph, as may be easily computed, attained the age of 137 years [1]; consequently he did not die until seventeen years after Joseph, and as his age is the only one of Joseph's generation which is specially mentioned in Scripture, we may fairly infer that Levi was the last of that generation, which died before the rise of the new dynasty. This would give about 127 years before the Exode, and must be dated, according to our interpretation of Bible chronology, B. C. 1712.

Let us now consider the amount of evidence we have from the monuments in confirmation of Scripture history respecting the sojourn of the Israelites in Egypt. The "new king that knew not Joseph" is clearly a record of a very important event in the history of Egypt. Josephus, who had better authority for what he wrote than we have now, from Manetho's History and the Temple records being then in existence, says "the Egyptians having in length of time forgotten the benefits they had received from Joseph, particularly the crown being now come into another family, ill-treated the Israelites." [2] That the rise of this new king or family refers to none other than Amosis, the chief of the famous 18th dynasty, who captured Memphis, and put an end to the civil war which had so long raged between the kings of Upper and Lower Egypt, just as Henry VII. of England terminated the Wars of the Roses at the battle of Bosworth, we are fully persuaded, as the historical and chronological proofs of this may be seen in a twofold way by reckoning both backwards and forwards. We find three kings reigning in Lower Egypt after Apophis, the patron of Joseph, and before Memphis was lost to that dynasty. *Melaneris*, the son of Apophis, a great and magnificent monarch, whom

---

[1] Exodus, vi. 16.   [2] Antiq. II. ix. § 1.

doubtless Joseph continued to serve with the same success as he had served his father. *Jannes*, or *Unas*, apparently of another family, at all events not the son of Melaneris, succeeded. A cartouch at Hamamat is the only hieroglyphic record of his name; and the tomb of one of his princes is still found at Sakkara. He was succeeded by his son Asses, whose monumental fame is equally slight, and in whose reign Memphis was lost, and the dynasty came to an end. Manetho relates that, "In his reign a king of Upper Egpyt, named Alisphragmuthosis (Amosis) confederated with other princes of Egypt, drove them out of Memphis, and shut them up in a place called Avaris; and eventually expelled them from Egypt."[1] This accords with the statement in Scripture, that a new king or dynasty had obtained power in Lower Egypt, where the Israelites had been so long located, "who knew not Joseph." The three intervening reigns between Apophis and the capture of Memphis by Amosis, would naturally agree with the ninety-seven years according to Scripture between the viceroyalty of Joseph and the death of his brethren and all that generation. According to our computation of the time of the death of Levi, the last survivor of that generation, we have 127 years left for the remainder of the Israelites' sojourn in Egypt. The chronology would stand thus:

Events.	Year of the call of Abraham.	B.C.
Joseph made viceroy of Egypt at 30 years of age	206	1809
Joseph died at 110	286	1729
Levi died 17 years later, at 137	303	1712
The new king which knew not Joseph	303	1712
The birth of Moses	350	1665
The Exode	430	1585

---

[1] Josephus contr. Ap. i. § 15.

The other prominent events of the whole period may be thus chronicled:

Events.	Year of call.	B C.
Call of Abraham	1	2015
Descent of the patriarchs to Egypt in the second year of the famine	215	1800
The death of all that generation	303	1712
Interval of 127 years.		
The Exode	430	1585

Consider now the evidence we have from Manetho and the hieroglyphic inscriptions of the sojourn of the Israelites in Egypt during those 127 years, and the name of the Pharaoh by whom they were released at the appointed time. Even in this period of Egyptian history, which commences with the famous 18th dynasty, the differences, variations, and contradictions of such distinguished authors as Josephus, Eusebius, and Africanus, in ancient times, and their still more eminent followers of modern times, such as Champollion, Rosellini, Wilkinson, Birch, Osburn, Sharpe, Poole, Felix, Bunsen, Lepsius, and De Rougé, whether in regard to the exact number of sovereigns during these 127 years, or the order of their reigns, or the century in which they lived, are so patent as to make it a matter of very serious difficulty to show the harmony which really exists between the historical records of Egypt and the statements in Scripture. By comparing the Greek lists with the monuments we may infer as most probable that the order of the first seven kings of the 18th dynasty would stand as follows:

  1. Amosis.   5. Tuthmōsis III.
  2. Amenōphis I. 6. Amenōphis II.
  3. Tuthmōsis I.   7. Tuthmōsis IV.
  4. Tuthmōsis II.

No dependence can be placed upon the exact number of years to be allotted to each separate reign, on account of the variation in the Greek lists. And, though twenty-five years are generally allotted to the reign of the

Amosis, the chief of the dynasty, it is of no use in our computation of the 127 years, because we know not in what year of his reign the capture of Memphis and the overthrow of the rival dynasty was effected. The fact of Africanus omitting to notice the years of his reign would seem to imply that it was one of the last acts of his life. And the interval between the death of Amosis and the death of Tuthmōsis IV. (the Pharaoh who, we believe, was drowned in the Red Sea,) is sufficiently near according to the Greek lists to satisfy us of its synchronism with the required 127 years. All the assistance which the monuments afford us respecting the length of any individual reigns of these seven sovereigns is the discovery of twenty-two years belonging to Amosis, twenty-seven to Tuthmōsis III., and seven to Tuthmōsis IV. Bunsen computes 122 years as the interval between the death of Amosis and Tuthmosis IV.; and supposing Amosis had captured Memphis five years previous to his death, this would harmonise with the numbers required according to Scripture chronology[1]; but he considers that Amosis reigned twenty-five years *after* the capture of Memphis. An inscription, explained by Rosellini (*Monum. Storici* i. 195), rather favours the opinion, though we admit it is not certain, that it must have occurred towards the close of his reign, as a stile, hewn out of the rock at Mokattam, near Cairo, states that "in the 22nd year of the reign of Amosis, the quarries were opened for the restoration of the temples at Memphis and the temple of Ammon at Thebes;" and if his conquest of Lower Egypt had taken place at the commencement of his reign, it is not likely he would have delayed twenty-two years before attempting the restoration of those sacred edifices which it must have been his interest at once to have repaired.

---

[1] Egypt's Place in Universal History, vol. iii. p. 109.

There has also been a remarkable discovery made by Mr. Birch, of the British Museum, respecting the interval between Tuthmōsis III. and Tuthmōsis IV., which would necessarily refer to the reign of Amenōphis II. Among the historical notices on the Karnak obelisk, which now stands in the Piazza Laterana at Rome, the following chronological fact is recorded; that "*after the death of Tuthmōsis III., the obelisk was thirty-five years in the hands of the workmen till the reign of Tuthmōsis IV.*" It is not stated in what year of Tuthmōsis IV., but we may conclude it remained until the fourth or fifth of his short reign, as all the chroniclers of Manetho agree in allotting thirty-one years to the reign of Amenophis II., though, strange to say, they make him the *successor*, instead of the *predecessor* of Tuthmōsis IV., as he must have been, since he was his father. What little evidence, therefore, we have from the monuments respecting the chronology of this period of Egyptian history, harmonises with what is deducible from Scripture, as the interval between the "new king which knew not Joseph," and the Exode of the children of Israel.

We must notice in addition the harmony which exists at this period of history, by comparing the incidents mentioned in Scripture, with the fragments that have been transmitted to us, either by the Greek writers, or with what has been discovered on the monuments.

(1.) In the Alexandrian Chronicle, the Pharaoh, under whom Moses was brought up, after having been preserved by his daughter, is called *Kenebron*, which obviously refers to the name of the second king of the 18th dynasty, the son of Amosis. The prenomen, or name in Lower Egypt of Amenophis I., the successor of Amosis, reads Chrp-k-ra, *i. e.* "he who consecrates his person to the sun." Chebron, or Kenebron, is the Hellenized version of this prenomen, which with the nomen in full, *Chebron*

Amenophis is found on a pair of sandals now in the Berlin Museum. A fine picture in stucco of this Pharaoh and his mother, was taken from a tomb at Gourmon, the burial-place of Thebes, which is now in the same museum. Lepsius' great work contains a beautiful representation of this painting, which has the names of *Chebron* and his mother *Amosis-nfr-atri*, in the usual cartouches. The Greek lists make two sovereigns out of this name, which the hieroglyphics confine to one; but the chief historical import of the name, is to notice the connection which some of these writers, such as the author of the Alexandrian Chronicle, make between the time of Chebron and the youth of Moses, which would thus bring the reign of the former within eighty years of the Exode.

(2.) Between the reigns of Chebron, Amenophis I., and his successor and kinsman Tuthmōsis I., a regency took place, as discovered from the monuments; when *Amessis*, as she is called by Manetho, or *Set-amen*, as read in hieroglyphics by Lepsius, the daughter of Amosis, governed either in her own right, or in behalf of her younger relation.[1] On an obelisk erected by her at Thebes, and which is one of the most splendid monuments of the country, she bears amongst other titles such as "royal wife," "lady of both countries," "great royal sister," the significant one of "*Pharaoh's daughter*,"[2] the same which she is so repeatedly called by Moses. The mention in the Epistle to the Hebrews of "Moses, when he was come to years, refusing to be called the son of Pharaoh's

---

[1] English history affords something parallel to this difficulty about the non-recognition in the Greek lists of Set-Amen, "the daughter of Pharaoh," as Queen Regent. The empress Matilda, the daughter of Henry I., rightly conveyed the throne to her son Henry Plantagenet, and exercised regal power at one time during the interval, though the reign of Stephen is the only one recognised in English history.

[2] Rosellini, Monum. Stor. t. iii. pt. i. p. 158.

daughter,"[1] seems to show that the daughter of Amosis, and successor of Chebron, Amenophis I., not having children of her own, adopted Moses, after she had preserved him from the effects of her father's cruel edict,— which required the destruction of all the male children of Israel, and that in consequence of his refusal the throne passed to Tuthmōsis I., who, though generally considered as a younger brother of Amenophis I., never appears on the monuments as the son of Amosis, and was probably only a near kinsman. Josephus mentions that when "Pharaoh's daughter," whom he calls *Thermuthis*, presented Moses to her father, "she thought to make him her father's successor, if it should please God she should have no legitimate child of her own;"[2] and that one of the priests, on seeing the infant, forewarned the king that by his instrumentality the kingdom would be brought low, and earnestly recommended his destruction, which was prevented by the interposition of Pharaoh's daughter. The notice in Scripture of Moses being "learned in all the wisdom of the Egyptians," can only be accounted for on the supposition that his adopted mother was really a queen regent of Egypt, who had power to compel a jealous priesthood to initiate her supposed heir in the science of the times. Moreover, it is said that Moses, during that period of his life, was "mighty in words and *deeds*,"[3] which Josephus explains by recording his success as a general of the Egyptian army in the war against the neighbouring country of Ethiopia.[4] Irenæus, who

[1] Hebrews, xi. 24.
[2] Antiq. II. ix. § 7.
[3] Acts, vii. 22.
[4] Antiq. II. x. § 2. Josephus gives a curious story of Moses' "mighty deeds" in Ethiopia, and the way by which he obtained an Ethiopian princess as his wife after his conquest of the country; but it accords with the statement in Scripture, that "Moses married an Ethiopian woman."—*Numbers*, xii. 1.

flourished in the century following Josephus, speaks likewise of the war which Moses waged against the Ethiopians, when commanding the army of the reigning Pharaoh.[1] This seems to be confirmed by an inscription on one of the obelisks at Karnak, erected by Tuthmōsis I., who succeeded Chebron Amenōphis I., according to Manetho, and who must have been the reigning Pharaoh during the early part of Moses' life before he retired to Midian, where Tuthmōsis I.[2] is styled, amongst other titles, " *Conqueror of the Ninebows*," referring to Libya, the Coptic name of which is *Na-pa-ut*, " The Ninebows." Lybia and Ethiopia may be understood in the same sense as England and Scotland form together a country known as Great Britain. But further than this, Birch, in his most valuable account of the statistical tablet of Karnak, has discovered a reference to a captain of this period, the inscription on whose tomb shows that he served under Amenōphis I. against the *Ethiopians*, and in the following reign accompanied Tuthmōsis I. in his campaigns to *Ethiopia* and Naharaina (Mesopotamia), which confirms the account which Josephus gives of Moses' " mighty acts" being exhibited in his wars with the people of that country.

(3.) At Gournou, near Thebes, there is still standing the tomb of one of the nobles of the court of Thothmōsis III., the son of Tuthmōsis I., and brother of the second king of the same name. The owner of this tomb bears the name of *Ros-she-ra*, which signifies, " A Prince like the Sun." The paintings of this tomb, which are given with great fidelity in Lepsius'[3] magnificent work, to

---

[1] Fragmenta de Perdit. Iren. Tractat. ed. Grabe, p. 347.

[2] Sir G. Wilkinson observes, " The Egyptians evidently overran all Ethiopia in the time of the 18th and 19th dynasties."—*Rawlinson's Herod.* ii. § 110.

[3] Denkmaeler, Abt. iii. Bl. 40.

which we have so often referred, afford indisputable proof, not only of the Israelites being in Egypt at this period of history, but of being forcibly engaged in the very occupation to which Scripture informs us they were compelled by the jealousy of the Pharaohs of that dynasty "which knew not Joseph."

One of the hieroglyphic inscriptions on this tomb reads, "The reception of the tribute of the land brought to the king by the captives in person." Another, "The bringing of the collections of the unclean of *the* land of Phenne (which is supposed to refer to the Sinaitic peninsula), which they bring in unto the footstool of his majesty King Thothmosis everliving." A third, "The bringing in of the offerings of the unclean races *of the two lands of Arrad and all the north.*" The races of prisoners are represented as engaged in the occupation of *making bricks*, and carefully watched by *Egyptian taskmasters*. One appears to belong to the country of Lower Egypt, which people are always distinguished by their red complexion. The other, of a different colour, and cast of features, clearly belong to the *Jews*. The same degraded race is represented everywhere throughout the tomb of *Ros-she-ra*, performing acts of drudgery under the coercion of taskmasters; their degradation being further symbolised by their torn and patched garments. It is needless to remark, how strikingly this accords with the treatment which the Israelites received from the dynasty "which knew not Joseph," according to the statement of Scripture.

(4.) The chronology of this period of Egyptian history agrees sufficiently well with that of Scripture to convince us of our application being correct. Lepsius, who has fully discussed the general question of the absolute dates on the Egyptian monuments in his "Book of the Kings," (pp. 151—169), and who appears, as we have seen, to ignore Scripture chronology entirely, so that his testimony is in this respect of greater value, has calculated from the fragment of a calendar worked into the wall of the present quay of Elephantina, grounding his computation upon the well-known commencement of the last Sothiac cycle B.C. 1322, that the first year of the reign of Tuthmosis III. should be placed B.C. 1613. Without admitting the exact correctness of this date, as it would bring us within thirty years of the true date of the Exode, and the obelisk at Rome speaks of thirty-five years intervening between Thothmosis III. and Thothmosis IV., still it is sufficiently near to adduce it as independent testimony in confirmation of the truth and accuracy of Scripture chronology.

(5.) The reign of Amenōphis II. the son of Tuthmosis III., presents nothing remarkable in connection with the Israelites in Egypt, save that on the dilapidated remains of a palace at Karnak, there is a representation of the Deity Ameen-Ra, addressing this king, in which *mention is made of a shepherd race*, possibly referring to the Jewish people, and promising "*that he shall restrain them within their own territories*," which appears to accord with the apprehension of the dynasty "which knew not Joseph" respecting that people. Pharaoh is represented in Scripture as saying, "Behold the children of Israel are more and mightier than we: come on, let us deal wisely with them, and so get them out of the land."[1]

(6.) The reign of Tuthmosis IV., his son and successor, affords many indications of his being the Pharaoh whose dealings with Moses and Aaron are so fully recorded in Scripture, and who was eventually destroyed with his army in the Red Sea. E.g. The statement respecting this Pharaoh's harsh treatment of the Israelites

---

[1] Exodus, i. 9, 10.

in compelling them to "gather straw for themselves," in order to complete their required "tale of bricks," is singularly confirmed by a remark of Rosellini, that "the bricks which are now found in Egypt belonging to the period of Tuthmosis IV. have *always* straw mingled with them, although in some of those most carefully made it is found in very small quantities."[1]

Tuthmōsis IV., whose name in Lower Egypt reads *mn-chru-ra*, "Sun fertile in creations;" and in Upper Egypt *tot-ms-sha-u*, "born of Thoth of the festivals," is the last Pharaoh *in whose reign there are any indications of the existence of the children of Israel in Egypt*, and this negative sort of proof, combined with other more positive, convinces us that he is none other than the proud king, who withstood the power of Jehovah, until finally his career was terminated at the Red Sea. Osburn identifies him with Armais, another sovereign of the same dynasty, according to Manetho's list, remarking that such confusions in the lists are "sure signs of troublous times in Egypt;" and adding, "we are prepared for the circumstance that Armais (who is generally named Tuthmōsis IV.) appears from the monuments to have had a turbulent reign."[2] Such must have been the case with the Pharaoh of the Exode. We have not any monumental inscriptions to prove the exact length of his reign (one has the number vii.), though sufficient to show that it was a short one, which also agrees with the inference from Scripture, as we read, that when "the king of Egypt, (Amenophis II. the father of Tuthmōsis IV.) died, under whom the children of Israel sighed by reason of the bondage, and they cried, and their cry came up unto God by reason of their bondage, and God

---

[1] Rosellini, ii. p. 259.
[2] Monumental History, vol. ii. p. 317.

remembered his covenant with Abraham, with Isaac, and with Jacob."[1] Moses prepared to return from Midian to Egypt, which return resulted in the Exode. A conspicuous tablet between the paws of that wonderful work of art, the great Sphinx of Ghizeh, has an inscription in which there is mention of the first year of Armais, and there is another of the seventh year of his reign, recorded on a granite rock opposite the island of Philæ on the Nile, when he was engaged in a war with the Phutim. There is a singular circumstance connected with this inscription. After the mention of the usual boasting titles, it stops short suddenly with the disjunctive particle "*then*," evidently pointing to defeat and disaster, which was the prominent characteristic of this Pharaoh's reign. The inference of his being the Pharaoh who was drowned in the Red Sea is further confirmed by the fact, that after the many careful researches of modern explorers, *no trace has been found of this king's tomb* in the royal burial-place near Thebes, in which the sovereigns of the eighteenth dynasty lie. And this is the more remarkable as the tomb of his son and successor Amenophis III., who carried out the measures in which his father was engaged, has been discovered.[2]

Another circumstance connected with Tuthmōsis IV. seems to afford confirmation of his being the Pharaoh of the Exode. On the walls of the palace of Luxor there is a sculpture, which is given in Lepsius's work, representing the birth of a son of this king, whom we naturally assume to be his "first-born." His wife, Queen Mautmes, who subsequently governed the kingdom during the minority of her son[3], is receiving a message

---

[1] Exodus, ii. 24.
[2] Sir G. Wilkinson's Thebes, p. 88.
[3] Sharpe's History of Egypt, vol. i. p. 65.

through the god Thoth, that she is to give birth to a child. The mother is placed upon a stool, while two nurses chafe her hands, and the babe is held up by a third. If this be a representation of the birth of the eldest son of the Pharaoh of the Exode, as we believe it to be, it is certain that this child could not have succeeded his father to the kingdom. For, "it came to pass that at midnight the Lord smote all the first-born in the land of Egypt, from *the first-born of Pharaoh that sat on his throne* unto the first-born of the captive that was in the dungeon."[1] Now, in one of the many very valuable works published by Sir G. Wilkinson[2] on the subject of Egypt, there is a reference to an *elder brother* of Amenophis III., the son and successor of Tuthmōsis IV., whose name does not appear in any list of kings, and whose exclusion from his rightful inheritance can only be accounted for by supposing him to be "*the first-born*" of Pharaoh's children, on whom the dreadful judgment fell; and if so, the infant-hero of the sculpture described above. It is, however, right to state what I have learnt from a private communication, with which Sir G. Wilkinson has favoured me, that he is not now prepared to abide by his early opinion respecting the supposed relationship of this "stranger king" to Amenophis III. The confusion in the Greek lists, and the different traditions respecting Armais (Tuthmōsis IV.), although they increase the difficulty of verifying the true history of his reign, nevertheless tend to support the opinion of identifying him with the Pharaoh of the Exode. It is clear from the monuments that during the reign of Armais Egypt underwent severe disasters, and that his successor, Amenophis, changed his religion, or rather introduced a new deity, viz. that of the Sun, as the substitution

---

[1] Exodus, xii. 29.   [2] Materia Hieroglyphica, Plate i.

of his new name, which reads *Bek-en-aten*, " the servant of the disc of the sun," in place of his old one which is everywhere erased, sufficiently discloses. After the failure of the Egyptian priests to withstand Moses and Aaron, and the heavy judgment upon the nation generally, we can readily conceive that nothing would be more natural than for the succeeding Pharaoh to try the power of some new deity.

Moreover, the Armenian Chronicle[1] of Eusebius speaks of Armais being the same person as Danaus, who was expelled from Egypt in the fifth year of his reign by his brother; and that he fled to Greece, where he established another kingdom. According to some authors, the ship in which Danaus came to Greece was called *Armaïs*[2], the first which had ever appeared there. Other authorities state that Cecrops was the first who led a colony from Egypt to Greece, and established a kingdom. This, according to the Parian chronicle, or the Arundelian Marbles, as more commonly called, a work of the very highest authority, occurred B.C. 1582, and, singular enough, answers to within two or three years of the date which we have computed from Scripture to be that of the Exode. Connecting all these traditionary legends respecting Armais' end, we have very strong grounds for assuming that he was indeed the Pharaoh overthrown with his mighty host at the Red Sea. Bunsen, with his usual disregard of the authority of Moses, denies this, as he observes, with surprising confidence, " *If there is any*

---

[1] Chron. Canon. Liber Prior, cap. xx.

[2] Sir G. Wilkinson says, " The flight of Armais was perhaps confounded with that of the ' stranger kings,' who ruled about the close of the eighteenth dynasty. Their expulsion appears to agree with the story of Danaus leading a colony to Argos, which Armaïs, flying from his brother, could not have done; and one of the last of their kings was *Toónh*."—Note in *Rawlinson's Herod.* ii. § 107.

historical fact well established, it is this,—that, however great the loss sustained by the Egyptians in horses and riders in their hasty pursuit through the foaming waves, *the Pharaoh himself did not perish.*"[1] And he gives his reason for this extraordinary conclusion. He declares "the Exodus must have taken place in the first five or six years of Menephthah (B.C. 1320, i. e. nearly three hundred years later than it really did). For he was thirteen years out of the country, and a conflict ensued upon his return;" and forming his opinion upon this fatal mistake, says, "the readers of a philosophical work or a history will not fail to ask for an explanation how it was that a king of Egypt, possessing a large army, which a few centuries before had made all Asia to tremble, did not pursue the Jews still farther, and annihilate them in the wilderness?" He then complacently adds, "I hardly think they will be satisfied with the simple answer that Pharaoh and his host were all overwhelmed in the Red Sea."[2] Of those who approve of Bunsen's fantasies, and the liberties which he takes with contemporary history, we say, " Probably they will not." But others who believe that the language of Scripture has definite meaning, and who gladly welcome the discoveries of real science in behalf of Revelation, will assuredly give credence to such a statement as this—" And it was told the king of Egypt that the people fled: and Pharaoh made ready his chariot, and took his people with him—600 chosen chariots, and all the chariots of Egypt, and captains over every one of them. And the Lord said unto Moses, I will get me *honour upon Pharaoh*, upon his chariots, and upon his horsemen. And the Egyptians pursued, and went in after them to the midst of the sea, even all Pharaoh's horses,

---

[1] Egypt's Place in Universal History, vol. iii. p. 265.
[2] Ibid. vol. iii. pp. 203, 264.

his chariots, and his horsemen. . . . The Lord overthrew the Egyptians in the midst of the sea—*there remained not so much as one of them.* Then sang Moses—The horse and his rider hath he thrown into the sea. *For the horse of Pharaoh went in with his chariots* and with his horsemen into the sea."[1] Such are the effects of speculating upon history at the expense of truth. Bunsen's system of chronology, which places Abraham about nine centuries earlier than Scripture does, and detains the Israelites in Egypt for 1,300 years after the descent of Jacob and his sons, required him to date the Exode as late as B.C. 1320, nearly three centuries after its actual occurrence; and in order to support this impossible theory, he seeks to find in Menephthah a king of the nineteenth dynasty, the Pharaoh of the Exode; and supposing that he lived several years after his assumed date of the departure of the Israelites under Moses, Bunsen endeavours to support his opinion by ridiculing the idea of the destruction of Pharaoh in the Red Sea. But more than this, spurning alike the history recorded in Scripture and the statements of Manetho, on whom he generally relies, he asserts that Moses and "his fellow conspirators," as he terms them, "quietly made preparations in the peninsula to insure the success of their vast undertaking," at the same time referring to Manetho as having given an account of the previous expulsion of the Hyksos races from the territory of Egypt.[2] Those who know what Manetho really wrote respecting the expulsion of the Hyksos from Egypt, as transmitted in the works of Josephus, with his annotations thereon, and compare his confused historical jumble with the recently discovered fact of the Hyksos period being more or less fabulous from beginning to end, cannot

---

[1] Exodus, xiv. and xv.
[2] Egypt's Place in Universal History, vol. iii. p. 266.

fail to perceive the singular testimony which the Temple Records of Egypt afford to the sojourn of the Israelites in, as well as their departure from, the country. When we find Manetho recording that "the Jews had come into Egypt — subdued its inhabitants — remained for a long period — revolted under the leadership of one of the priests of Heliopolis, called *Osarsiph* (from Osyris, the god of that city, and having subsequently changed his name to *Moses*), who required them upon oath to give up all Egyptian customs, and to destroy the sacred animal, and not to worship the Egyptian gods — went out of Egypt in the reign of *Tuthmōsis*, and settled in that country which is now called Judea, and there built Jerusalem and its temple;"[1] — we believe him because it accords with the history of that period written by Moses himself, a contemporary witness and chief actor in the events described. But when Manetho jumbles together these events with others which he mentions as having happened three centuries later, in the reign of the son of Ramesses (Menephthah), which Bunsen, with such marked want of discrimination accepts as true history, we are content to leave the matter in the hands of Josephus, who very properly denounces the same as "incredible narrations" and "arrant lies;" adding, with regard to the "leprous race," which Menephthah expelled from Egypt, and which Bunsen refers to the Exode of the Israelites, "that Moses who brought the Jews out was not one of that company, but lived *many generations earlier*, I shall endeavour to demonstrate from Manetho's own accounts themselves."[2]

We have never heard of but two reasons in favour of so late a date for the Exode, which it may be right to notice. It has been contended that, as the children of Israel were employed by the "new king which knew not

---

[1] Josephus contr. Ap. i. 26—28.
[2] Ibid. § 11.

Joseph" to build certain "treasure-cities, Pithom and *Ramesses*,"[1] therefore the Exode could not have occurred until some time in the reign of the nineteenth dynasty, which bore that name from its distinguished founder Ramesses I., whose accession Bunsen places B.C. 1413. As, however, there are 127 years more to be accounted for between that period and the Exode, it ought to be dated B.C. 1286. But Bunsen having adopted the novel idea of placing that event in the *middle* of the reign of Menephthah, the son of Ramesses II., only reckons that interval at eighty-three years[2], as his date for the Exode is B.C. 1320, which alone is sufficient to refute the argument grounded upon the idea that the treasure city *Rameses*, was called after the first king of that name; for according to Bunsen's chronology the rise of the king or dynasty "which knew not Joseph" must be placed about forty years later than the time in which the Jews were supposed to be so employed. But in truth the refutation of such an argument may be placed in a much stronger light than even this. For the same word *Ramesses* (the spelling varies in the English version, though exactly the same in the Hebrew) is met with at the period when Jacob and his sons first went down to Egypt; as we read that "Jacob placed his father and his brethren *in the land of Ramesses*, as Pharaoh commanded."[3] If, therefore, the argument be of any force, it would prove that *Pharaoh Ramesses must have lived*

---

[1] Exodus, i. 8—11.

[2] Bunsen in reality reduces these numbers still farther by asserting that "the opening remark (Exod. i. 2), 'they set over them taskmasters,' is clearly referred to Ramesses II.," and not to his grandfather, Ramesses I., which opinion he endeavours to support, by throwing a doubt, as usual, upon a Scriptural statement respecting this period, observing, "*We can hardly take literally the statement as to the age of Moses at the Exodus.*"—*Egypt's Place, &c.* vol. iii. p. 184.

[3] Genesis, xlvii. 11.

before the time of Joseph, which Bunsen places in the twenty-eighth century B.C., and which, according to the Biblical computation, cannot be placed later than the eighteenth century before Christ; whereas all parties are agreed that the dynasty of the *Ramesses* cannot be earlier than the fourteenth century. Therefore, the inference drawn from the name of *Ramesses* that the Exode must be dated, as Bunsen and others have done, in the fourteenth century is destitute of the slightest foundation.[1] The mistake has originated, probably, in supposing that " the treasure city," *Ramesses*, derived its name from the king or dynasty instead of the reverse. The LXX. in translating the passage in Exodus i. 11, have introduced " *On*, which is *Heliopolis*," as a third treasure city or fortress built by the Israelites. But Jablouski[2] has, with good reason, supposed that *Ramesses* and *Heliopolis* are in reality the same city, for *Ramesses* in the Egyptian tongue signifies, " The field of the Sun," as *Heliopolis* meant " The city of the Sun," and the name would therefore include both the territory and its capital, just as in modern times the names *Naples* and *Rome* include both. This agrees with what Benjamin of Tudela says of his visit to Egypt, that when he came to the fountain of *Al-shemesh*, or *the Sun*, which is *Ramesses*, he there found the remains of the buildings of our fathers, even towers built of brick."[3] Moreover, the testimony of Sir G. Wilkinson, that " the *first* individual called *Ramesses* mentioned on the monuments, was a person of the family

---

[1] Lepsius, though differing from Bunsen upwards of twelve centuries with regard to the duration of the Israelites in Egypt, agrees with him in respect to the time of the Exode, and makes the utmost of this argument concerning the name of *Ramesses*. See "Letters from Egypt," by Dr. Richard Lepsius, translated by the Misses Horner, pp. 426, 450.

[2] De Terrâ Goshen, Dissert. 4, § 8.

[3] Itinerar. p. 120.

of *Amosis* the first king of the eighteenth dynasty"[1] is satisfactory proof that the name *Ramesses* was known in Egypt at the very time that *Amosis*, " the king who knew not Joseph," was compelling the children of Israel to build " a treasure city," which was called by that name.

Another argument has been brought forward against the Biblical history and chronology of this period, that as there is monumental evidence of the nineteenth dynasty, viz. that of the *Ramesses*, having extended their conquests to Palestine and Syria, we must accept it as a proof that " no great empire (of the Israelites) then existed"[2] in that country, and that consequently the Exodus, and the settlement of the Israelites in the Land of Promise, could not have taken place until after that period. There happens to be far clearer proof of the kings of Egypt having extended their conquest as far as Assyria in the time of the eighteenth dynasty, than in that of the succeeding dynasty, some two or three centuries later, as Bunsen's theory requires. E. g. we have before noticed the campaign of Tuthmōsis I. in Mesopotamia (see p. 141); and at Arban on the Khabour River, a few miles north of Nineveh, Mr. Layard found some Scarabæi engraved with hieroglyphics, having the names of Tuthmōsis III. and his great grandson Amenophis III., who records amongst his conquests As-su-ni (Assyria), Naharaina (Mesopotamia), Saenkar (Shinar or Babylon), and Pattana (Padan-aram, where Laban dwelt), with other titles, such as " Lord of the Earth," " Sun rising in all lands," referring to his claim to universal dominion.[3] Tuthmōsis III. was, as we have shown from the Egyptian monuments, the Pharaoh who com-

---

[1] Note in Rawlinson's Herod. ii. § 121.
[2] Egypt's Place in Universal History, vol. iii. p. 165.
[3] Birch's Note in Layard's Nineveh, p. 281.

pelled the Israelites to make bricks without the needful supply of straw; and Amenophis III.'s conquests in Assyria, and the land of Canaan, must have occurred during the forty years' wandering of the Israelites in the Desert, God having thus employed the armies of Egypt to lessen the power of the tribes of Canaan previous to the children of Israel taking possession of their promised inheritance. But admitting the truth of the conquests of the *Ramesses* in Palestine, the inference, that the Israelites must have entered the land subsequently, because no great empire could have then existed, is not borne out by the historical statements in Scripture. For the repeated conquests of the Israelites by surrounding tribes during the first 400 years of their national existence, and the fact of Jerusalem being occupied by the Jebusites until the time of David[1], shows that the Bible does not suppose any " great empire " in Syria for several centuries after the Exode. Moreover, the evidence we have respecting the Egyptians in Syria at this period affords a clue to an historical synchronism between the histories of Egypt and Israel, which is of some importance. Herodotus mentions that an Egyptian king named Sesostris was in the habit of recording on pillars his conquests of certain nations, adding, when they were easily subdued, " emblems to mark they were a nation of women, i. e. unwarlike and effeminate." Herodotus likewise says, that " these pillars have for the most part disappeared, but in the part of Syria called Palestine, I myself saw them still standing, with the writing above-mentioned, and the emblems distinctly visible."[2] Manetho, who lived about two centuries after the time of Herodotus, mentions the same thing respecting

---

[1] 2 Sam. v. 6, 7.   [2] Herodotus, ii. 102, 106.

Sesostris.[1] Bunsen endeavours to show, and we think successfully, that so far from this referring to Sesostris (king of the twelfth dynasty according to Manetho, and the same as Sesertesen I., who reigned shortly after Abraham's visit to Egypt, which would invalidate the argument respecting the conquest of Syria being several centuries later), it must be understood of *Ramesses II.* the father of Menephthah, whom Bunsen considers to be the Pharaoh in whose reign the Israelites quitted Egypt. For the stelæ seen by Herodotus, who could not interpret the hieroglyphic characters, were doubtless those which are *still extant* on a rock near Beyroot at the mouth of the river Lycus, engraved by Ramesses II. The only inscription now legible is a mere fragment containing these words, "Pharaoh the powerful — king of kings, *Ramesses*, to whom life has been given like the Sun."[2] On referring to Scripture we find satisfactory proof of the effeminacy of some of the tribes or nations of Syria at that exact period of history. For in the well-known story of Deborah, that famous "mother in Israel," when "Jabin was king of Canaan," and Sisera the captain of his host, who came "with his chariots and his multitude against Israel," it is emphatically recorded in the Book of Judges, that they were conquered "*by the hand of a woman.*" It is likewise added, "So God subdued on that day Jabin the king of Canaan before the children of Israel."[3]

According to our computation of Biblical chronology,

---

[1] Eusebius Chron. Can. Liber Prior, cap. xx.
[2] Sir Gardner Wilkinson's Note to Rawlinson's Herodotus *in loco*. The reign of Ramesses II., according to a legible hieroglyph in the British Museum, extended over the long period of 66 years, B. C. 1392 —1326.
[3] Judges, iv. 7, 9, 23.

"the forty years' rest," which Israel had after the overthrow of Sisera and his host by the hand of Deborah, would be dated B.C. 1377—1337, and very well synchronises with the supposition that, in the fourteenth century B.C., the Canaanites were an effeminate race, whom *Ramesses II.* had easily overthrown, and who recorded his conquest of them as such, in a way which Herodotus and Manetho impute to an earlier king, of whose campaigns in Syria we know nothing, but which modern skill by reading the hieroglyphic inscriptions still extant shows can be applied to none other than a sovereign who was reigning during that century. We do not find any other reasons advanced for contradicting the date of the Exode as set forth in Holy Writ; and we must therefore reject, as unfounded and unsupported, either by Scripture or the monuments of Egypt, the conclusion of Bunsen and Lepsius in placing it so late as B.C. 1320.

§ 7. The duration of the interval between the Exodus and the building of the Temple is the concluding chronological difference between the sacred annalists and Bunsen, which it will be necessary to notice, as the latter event is placed by him so nearly[1] with our computation of Scripture chronology, that we are glad to find ourselves at length in accord with this distinguished scholar.

Bunsen observes, "Our readers may naturally ask: What becomes of the chronology between Moses and

---

[1] Bunsen's date for the building of the Temple is the same as that of Archbishop Usher, viz. B. C. 1014. We compute it four or five years higher on account of the years allotted to the several kings of Judah from Solomon to Jehoiakim (in whose reign the seventy years' captivity in Babylon commenced), being reckoned as *complete* years, instead of *current*, as by Usher's system we are compelled to do with four reigns, in order to obtain a supposed synchronism with some of the kings of Israel.

Solomon? What are we to do with the Bible dates of 440, 480, 593 years? The difficulties encountered in the first book as to each of the three Biblical dates, has proved to us that, if the Jewish chronology between Solomon and Moses can be restored at all, it can only be done by confronting it with Egyptian history."[1] Of course, if Bunsen's date of the Exode, B.C. 1320, be right, and his Pharaoh who let the Israelites go (in the *beginning* of a tolerably long reign) be correct, leaving only 300 years, in place of nearly six centuries, between that event and the building of the Temple, the so-called "Biblical dates" of 440, 480, or 593 years, must be one and all wrong. But can such be really termed "Biblical dates?" We are unable to discover upon what grounds he fixes upon the *first* of 440 years, unless it be the incorrect reading of the LXX.; as certainly there is no authority for such a date from the Hebrew. We have *proof* that the *second* of 480 years is not really any part of the sacred text.[2] And the *third* is one of several dates found in our present copies of Josephus, which so far vary as to give 592, 609, 612, and 632 years[3], for the interval between the Exode and the Temple. Seeing, therefore, the manifold mistakes which beset Bunsen's system on every side, when he attempts to make it harmonise with Scripture chronology, we are prepared for the way in which he treats the opinion of the early Christian writers, as well as of Josephus, who are unanimous in dating the Exode about the middle of the eighteenth dynasty, which was natural, considering that such, as we have shown, alike agrees with the history on the monuments, with the fragments of Manetho, and with the chronology of Scripture. "If,"

---

[1] Egypt's Place in Universal History, vol. iii. 205.
[2] See remarks on this in Chapter V.
[3] Clinton's Fasti Hell. vol. i. Appendix, p. 311.

says Bunsen, "we examine carefully the notion of the Fathers, that it took place in the eighteenth dynasty, we shall find that it was based simply on two wholly unfounded assumptions. One is, that it coincided with the evacuation of Avaris by the Shepherds. The other assumption is, that the middle or beginning of the eighteenth dynasty really coincided, or, at least, may *by some manœuvring* be made to synchronise with the 480th (or 440th) year before the building of the Temple, at which date the Biblical narrative places the Exodus."[1] Though we do not, as we have before remarked, admit that the Bible chronology places the Exode either 480 or 440 years before the Exode, we cannot think that Bunsen is justified in accusing the advocates of the Usserian chronology of "*manœuvring.*" It is not a suitable word for so distinguished a scholar to make use of towards those with whom he is at issue. The difference between 480 years and 566, which latter we believe to be the true interval between the Exode and the Temple, is not so great as the 300 years disagreement which exists between Scripture and Bunsen on the time of the Exode. And, as we have shown there are unmistakable evidences, both from the monuments and Manetho, of the existence of the Israelites in Egypt up to the middle of the eighteenth dynasty, we look in vain for, and we unhesitatingly challenge Bunsen's followers to show, a single scrap of proof *in favour of their continuance in Egypt after that period*, or during the 300 years in dispute between us.

Adopting, as we have done, 566 as the number of years between the Exode and the building of the Temple, we proceed to consider the authority we have for accepting the same. Since it is clear that the passage (1 Kings vi. 1), in which it is said that Solomon began to build the

---

[1] Egypt's Place in Universal History, vol. iii. p. 145.

Temple "in the 480th year after the children of Israel were come out of the land of Egypt," is not genuine, and it is admitted on all hands that there are two chasms [1] during that period in the Scriptural account of the Old Testament, by which we are prevented from accurately determining its duration; we turn first to the New Testament, to see what help is there afforded us in our search. St. Paul, in his speech before the rulers of the synagogue at Antioch, makes mention of this period, which he thus divides;—

	Years.	
The Israelites in the Wilderness	40	Acts, xviii. 18.
To the division of the land, not mentioned	0	,, 19.
Duration of the Judges "*about*"	450	,, 20.
Length of Saul's reign	40	,, 21.
Length of David's reign	40½	2 Sam. v. 5.
Temple begun in the fourth year of Solomon	3½	1 Kings, vi. 1.
Total	574 years.	

We cannot, however, gather anything decisive from this computation; because, in the first place, no time is allotted for the division of the lands, which, we gather from Joshua xiv. 7, 10, must have amounted to certainly five years, and which would raise the period to 579 years; and in the second, as St. Paul says, "*about* 450 years" for the time of the Judges, we are at liberty to lower the period to a certain extent. There is likewise another reading of this passage, which has the high authority of the Codex Alexandrinus, and which reads as follows:—"He divided

---

[1] Clinton, who leans rather to the longest period given by Josephus, says, "The interval between the death of Moses and the first servitude may be pretty accurately filled, although the years will be assigned upon *conjecture*, and not upon testimony. ... We then arrive at a *second chasm*, between the death of Samson and the election of Saul."—*Fasti Hell.* vol. i. App. pp. 303-4.

to them their land about 450 years, and after that he gave them judges," which renders it more difficult than ever to make a chronological computation from such a sentence. The traditional number current amongst the Jews for this period is one of those adopted by Josephus[1], viz. 592 years. Bunsen remarks that "the Jews of China and Cochin-China are said to adhere to it."[2] But it is rather singular, and we venture to say almost suspicious, in regard to the reckoning of Josephus for this period, that while he quotes from the Tyrian records as an independent testimony to the truth of Scripture, there is in our present copies a very remarkable omission. He observes, "that there are public writings among the Tyrians *kept with great exactness,* in which it was recorded, that the Temple was built by king Solomon at Jerusalem 143 years and eight months before the Tyrians built Carthage; and in their annals the building of our Temple is related; for Hiram, the king of Tyre, was the friend of Solomon our king, and had such friendship transmitted down to him from his forefathers."[3] Now why did Josephus omit to give the number of years which the Tyrian records mention, as having elapsed during the interval between the Exodus and the Temple, unless it be that he found they militated against his own computation, and he thought it better to be silent upon the subject? Theophilus, bishop of Antioch, who lived in the second century, observes, "About the building of the Temple in Judea,

---

[1] " Solomon began to build the Temple 592 years after the Exodus out of Egypt; . . . . and from Adam, the first man, until Solomon, there were in all 3002 years."—*Joseph. Antiq.* VIII. iii. § 1. This disproves the oft-quoted opinion of Josephus having adopted the longer reckoning of the LXX. in preference to the shorter but truer chronology of the Hebrew.

[2] Egypt's Place in Universal History, vol. i. p. 189.

[3] Jos. cont. Apion, i. § 17.

which *king Solomon built* 566 *years after the Jews went out of Egypt there is an account among the Tyrians;*[1] from which we gather that the Tyrian records were still in existence in the time of Theophilus, and that *they stated the exact number of years* which had elapsed from so marked a period in the history of the Israelites as the Exode, until that time of the close connection between the kingdoms of Israel and Tyre, as existed in the days of Solomon and Hiram, but which Josephus, for the reasons we have supposed, omitted to mention.

We accept, then, the authority of the Tyrian annals, for deciding the duration of the period from the Exode to the Temple, for it accords with the chronology of Scripture as far as we are able to test it, and enables us to fill up in a general way the two chasms alluded to above, which prevent our speaking decidedly within one year of the Biblical date, and enables us to understand the meaning of St. Paul's " about 450 years " for the rule of the Judges.

The harmony between the record of Scripture and the Tyrian annals in the chronology of this period, would stand as follows:—

	Years.
Israelites in the wilderness	40
To the division of the land	5
Rule of the Judges ("about 450")	437
Reign of Saul	40
Reign of David	40½
To the fourth year of Solomon	3½
	566

Moreover, there is an historical synchronism of much value for this period in our comparison of Egyptian history with Scripture testimony, which it may be well to notice. It is written that, "in the 5th year of king

---

[1] Theophil. ad Autolyc. § 22.

Rehoboam, Shishak king of Egypt came up against Jerusalem." Solomon reigned thirty-six years after building the Temple, therefore the fifth year of his son and successor must be computed as forty-one years after that event. Now, if we compare what we gather in Scripture respecting the whole period from the death of Levi, the last of Joseph's generation, in the 303rd year of the call of Abraham, and, consequently, 127 years before the Exode, which synchronised, as we have shown, with the rise of the new king, or eighteenth dynasty, "which knew not Joseph," unto the fifth year of Rehoboam, when he was attacked by Pharaoh Shishak, with the chronology of the different dynasties which reigned in Egypt according to Manetho during that time; we shall find it sufficiently near to satisfy us, in the main, of the correctness of our conclusion regarding one, by its undesigned coincidence with the statements of the other.

	Years.
From the rise of the 18th dynasty unto the Exode	127
From the Exode to the building of the Temple	566
From the Temple to the fifth year of Rehoboam	41
	734

According to Manetho, as transmitted by Africanus, whose authority is probably the best of the Greek annalists, the dynasty stands thus —

		Years.
The 18th dynasty lasted		262
The 19th "		209
The 20th "		135
The 21st "		130
		736

Pharaoh Shishak was the first king of the twenty-second dynasty, so that there are only two years' difference be-

---

[1] 1 Kings, xiv. 25.

tween our computation from Scripture and the chronology of Manetho of a synchronism of no slight importance in verifying the history of this period, and sufficiently near, without design, or " manœuvring" as Bunsen would describe it, to convince us of the truth.

Thus we find ourselves approaching the confines of the historic period according to the admission even of one of the Essayists. "Previous," says Mr. Wilson, "to the time of the divided kingdom, the Jewish history presents little which is thoroughly reliable. The taking of Jerusalem by 'Shishak' is for the Hebrew history, that which the taking of Rome by the Gauls is for the Romans."[1] We leave it to the consideration of others to decide how far this statement is correct, and whether we have not adduced some independent testimony, and proved some synchronisms between Egypt and Israel previous to the time of Shishak, sufficient to assure us that "Jewish history," in other words Holy Scripture, is more "reliable," both in its early as well as its later periods, than Mr. Wilson is disposed to admit.

We conclude with a summary of the differences, we have thus noticed between the chronology of Bunsen and that of Scripture. We have seen that Scripture allows about 6000 years for the existence of man upon earth, and that Bunsen's theory for prolonging that period to B.C. 20,000, grounded upon the fact of pottery being discovered in the Nile-mud, is unfounded and of no weight whatever; and that his inference concerning the many years being required for the formation of language is contrary to both *Revelation* and *Science*. We have learnt from Berosus the harmony which exists between the Chaldæan traditions and the Biblical statements respecting the Noachian Deluge; and from Calis-

---

[1] Essays and Reviews, p. 170, note.

thence with regard to the commencement of astronomical observations at Babylon; from Champollion's interpretation of the hieroglyphic monuments of Egypt; and from the history of China by Confucius, that there is nothing of the nature of scientific *proof* to contradict the statement of Scripture respecting the dispersion of mankind, and its time, about 100 years subsequent to the Flood. We have found independent evidence of two of Abraham's contemporaries, Amraphel king of Babylon and Chedorlaomer king of Persia, as existing at the time mentioned in Scripture, and not eight or nine centuries earlier according to the requirements of Bunsen's system. We have shown that the duration of the period from Abraham to the Exode is distinctly declared in Scripture to be 430 years, and not 1440, nor 200, nor 600 years, as those learned authorities Bunsen, Lepsius, and Osburn respectively reckon. Further, we have brought forward such evidence as has been discovered by the interpretation of the monuments in proof of the existence of the Israelites in Egypt from the time of Joseph to Moses; and we confidently challenge proof of their being in that country at any other period than that which accords with the statements of Scripture. The details are peculiarly interesting, and it is with no slight satisfaction that the earnest student of Bible and Egyptian history is enabled to discover the harmony which exists between them, and thus to see, in such undesigned coincidence, the truth and accuracy of both. If Scripture does not give any clue to the precise time of Abraham's visit to Egypt, Josephus, who possessed the records of Egyptian history which are now wanting, specifies that he instructed the people there in the science of astronomy, and was instrumental in healing some religious feuds which existed when he went down. The monuments show that a civil war was raging at the time, when, according to Scripture chronology, Abraham's journey was undertaken, and in the succeeding reign, we have the *first* indications of the advance in science, on the part of the Egyptians, by the hieroglyphic proof of their division of the year into months. We can meet the objection of a German rationalist that no sheep existed in Egypt, contradicting thereby the statement of Pharaoh having supplied Abraham with "sheep and oxen and asses, for Sarah's sake," by pointing to a tomb-painting at Gizeh of a period only a few years anterior to the time of Abraham, in which these several animals are represented as having belonged to the occupant of that tomb. If the monumental record of a "great famine in Egypt" does not support the hypothesis of Bunsen as to being the one which desolated Egypt in the time of Joseph, through failure both in chronology and of other details given in Scripture, we can adduce the Chinese annals in proof of a "seven years'" famine having extended as far as the extremities of Asia, at a time which synchronises with Joseph's vice-royalty in Egypt according to Biblical chronology. A tomb in Upper Egypt of that period reveals the existence of certain strangers from Lower Egypt, whose Jewish cast of countenance apparently indicates the coming of the children of Abraham into that country. We have independent testimony of a change in the Egyptian priesthood at that period, which harmonises with what Scripture relates as having happened under the rule of Joseph. And a tomb has been discovered belonging to the age of that Pharaoh, whom the Greek authorities are unanimous in naming as the reigning sovereign, with the name and titles ascribed to Joseph in Scripture, and whose body, after having been royally embalmed, must have remained 144 years in Egypt previous to its removal at the time of the Exode to the land of Canaan. We have found from the monuments proofs of the rise of a new dynasty, at the termination of a long civil war between the two Egypts, which Bunsen and others have so perseveringly misrepresented as the Hyksos period of *one* or *two thousand years* (for its advocates are not agreed which is the right chronology), in perfect harmony with the Scripture record of that period, that there arose " a new king which knew not Joseph." And that the chronology of the first seven kings of that dynasty, from the time of Amosis the chief of the dynasty, to the last year of Tuthmōsis IV., the Pharaoh who was drowned in the Red Sea, is in exact accordance with the remainder of the 430 years from the death of all Joseph's generation unto the Exode. We have pointed out the Greek tradition, that Moses was educated in the court of a Pharaoh called Kenebron or Chebron, and the monuments show that the successor of Amosis bore that name, and that his sister Amesses, or "Set-Amen," can be no other than "the Pharaoh's daughter," who saved Moses from the water, as an obelisk which still exists at Thebes testifies to her being called by that very name. And the fact of her having been queen-regent for some years during the minority of her successor, sufficiently explains the Scripture statement of Moses having been "learned in all the wisdom of the Egyptians;" as also the addition of his having been " mighty in words and deeds" is explained by the statement of Josephus respecting Moses having conquered Ethiopia for the king of Egypt, which event is confirmed by one of the titles which Tuthmōsis I., the reigning Pharaoh, bore according to a monumental inscription. We have seen, further, on the tomb of a court officer of Tuthmōsis III., a representation of the Jews engaged in making bricks, with taskmasters overlooking them, and have adduced the statement of Rosellini that all the bricks stamped with the name of that king have invariably a portion of straw in them, as a significant proof of the mode of their manufacture. We have noticed several things respecting the grandson of Tuthmōsis III., called Armais or Tuthmosis IV., whom we believe to be the Pharaoh drowned in the Red Sea; that Egypt underwent severe disasters during his reign; that no trace of his tomb has been discovered in the royal burialplace of the sovereigns of his dynasty; that he does not appear to have been succeeded by his eldest son; and that, for some cause or other, his younger son and successor, Amenophis III., made a change in the national religion, as if to signify that the priesthood of his father's reign had failed to preserve Egypt in the hour of danger. We have shown that Manetho's confused and contradictory account of the expulsion of those, whom he calls "Hyksos," or Shepherds, from Egypt, by a king named "Tuthmosis," can refer to none other than a perverted account of the Exodus of the children of Israel, as Josephus, who lived before the Temple records of Egypt were destroyed, and who has transmitted to us the fragments of this portion of Manetho's history, strongly contends is the case. We have proved that the rapid rate of increase in the children of Israel during their 215 years sojourn in Egypt, from seventy souls (the number at the time when Jacob and the patriarchs went down) to the 600,000 men "besides children," making in all it is calculated upwards of 2,000,000, whom Moses led out of Egypt, so far from being impossible, as Bunsen and others have contended in opposition to the plain statements of Scripture, accords with a similar rate of increase at other times, and in other countries, under less favourable circumstances than those with which the Israelites were favoured. We have pointed out that an argument which has been brought forward respecting the necessity of dating the Exode about 300 years later than Scripture allows on account of the monumental evidence of the conquests of Ramesses II. having extended to Canaan, has not the weight which its advocates desire, but that the significant import of that evidence rather supports our inference, that his war in Canaan took place at the time when Deborah was judging Israel, by which the chronology of Scripture and the monumental history of Egypt are found to agree. We have sought in vain, and have challenged the opponents of Biblical chronology to the proof, for any monumental evidence or sign of the existence of the children of Israel in Egypt *after* the time when Scripture teaches they had quitted the country. And finally, we have brought forward the independent testimony of the Tyrian annals, respecting the exact interval from the Exode to the building of the Temple in confirmation of Scripture chronology, and in contradiction of the unfounded theory which Bunsen has advanced, that it was only about half the duration which the Bible assigns to that period.

Under these circumstances, we are constrained to place a limited reliance upon the "Biblical Researches" of so eminent a scholar and so attractive a man as Baron Bunsen. When we recollect the theories these "Biblical Researches" have led him to adopt—viz. that man's existence on earth may be computed at 20,000 years B.C. in place of 4,000; that the ages of the antediluvian patriarchs, as given in Scripture, do not mean individual men, but represent certain epochs; that the Noachian deluge was not universal as regards the human race; that the interval between Abraham and Joseph's rule in Egypt was only a little more than 100 years, in place of over 200; that the time from Abraham to the Exode, is not to be reckoned as 430 years, according to the positive and repeated statements of Scripture [1], "chro-

---

[1] Egypt's Place in Universal History, vol. iii. p. 247.

nology being foreign to the purpose and vocation of the
Sacred Books," but must have embraced the prolonged
period of 1,440 years; that "if there is any historical
fact well established, it is that Pharaoh himself did not
perish"[1] in the Red Sea; and that Moses only led the
children of Israel for twenty years through the wilderness, instead of forty, as Scripture so repeatedly
affirms[2] :— when we remember such and similar instances of his mode of treating Scripture, we are compelled to reject his skilful but untenable hypotheses.
And it is with unfeigned sorrow that we find his language at times to be such as to receive, what it really
merits, the disapprobation of even his reviewer, Dr.
Williams. "When Bunsen asks: How long shall we
bear this fiction of an external revelation? All this is
delusion for those who believe it; but what is it in the
mouths of those who teach it? Is it not time, in truth,
to withdraw the veil from our misery? to tear off the
mask from hypocrisy, and destroy that sham which is
undermining all real ground under our feet? to point out
the dangers which surround, nay, threaten already, to
engulf us? —*there will be some who think his language too
vehement for good taste.*" But if we can so far agree with
the Essayist, we must no less dissent from his opinion respecting the meed of merit to be attributed to Bunsen, and
the justice of his comparison between the twelfth and the
nineteenth centuries, as well as his interpretation of what
truth really means, "Others," continues Dr. Williams,
" will think burning words needed by the disease of our
time. These will not quarrel on points of taste with a
man who in our darkest perplexity has reared again the

---

[1] Egypt's Place in Universal History, vol. iii. p. 265.
[2] Ibid. p. 258.

banner of truth, and uttered thoughts which give courage to the weak and sight to the blind. If Protestant Europe is to escape those shadows of the twelfth century, which with ominous recurrence are closing round us, to Baron Bunsen will belong a foremost place among the champions of light and right."[1]

---

[1] Essays and Reviews, pp. 92, 93.

ON THE STUDY

OF

THE EVIDENCES OF CHRISTIANITY.

CHAP. III.

THE same remark which we were constrained to make respecting the author of the "Biblical Researches," at the opening of the first chapter, applies equally here. Professor Baden Powell, the author of the Essay, "On the Study of the Evidences of Christianity," has been called away since this work was first published; while, therefore, in this as in every other instance, we would not be unmindful of the *nisi bonum* principle, truth compels us to expose, with all the rigour which the cause demands, the fallacies of the Essayist, which are doubly objectionable considering the quarter whence they come.

It is certainly a singular phenomenon of the present day, considering the striking contrast which all countries, that have received the Christian religion, present to the outer world, to think that it should be necessary in the nineteenth century to bring forward proofs in favour of the *Evidences* of Christianity. But so it is. And no faithful follower of our Divine Master conscious of the overwhelming amount of proof in behalf of that religion which He came on earth to establish, can hesitate for a moment to meet an adversary on his chosen ground, even though that adversary, sad to think, was a professed minister of the Church of Christ, which, therefore, he was bound by every moral obligation to uphold and defend.

Professor Baden Powell, at the outset of his Essay would fain discard all controversy on the subject, observing "The present discussion is not intended to be of a controversial kind, it is purely contemplative and theoretical; it is rather directed to a calm and unprejudiced survey of the various opinions and arguments adduced, *whatever may be their ulterior tendency*, on these important questions."[1] Notwithstanding this disclaimer, and bearing in mind our full persuasion that controversy may be conducted without any violation of the law of love — as one of our own poets has finely advised —

> "Be calm in arguing, for fierceness makes
> Error a fault, and truth discourtesy.
> Why should I feel another man's mistakes
> More than his sickness or his poverty?
> *In love I should:* but anger is not love,
> Nor wisdom neither; therefore, gently move,"—[2]

we must point out that "the ulterior tendency" of the learned Essayist's "calm and unprejudiced survey" is, in our humble opinion, of so dangerous a nature, that we feel constrained to notice it, and to the best of our power to endeavour to refute it.

"The Evidences of Christianity," which in other words mean the truth of our religion and its claim to unhesitating acceptance, may be said to rest upon these three separate proofs: — I. PROPHECY; II. MIRACLES; III. SCIENCE.

Let us investigate each one in its turn.

I. By *Prophecy*, we mean that portion of a Revelation from on high, as contained in the Bible, the interpretation of which in its literal accomplishment as regards

---

[1] Essays and Reviews, p. 100.   [2] George Herbert.

past events, is an assurance of the same with reference to the *future*. The Essayist speaks of the threefold manner in which Revelation in general is understood — " by the Romanist, who regards it as of the nature of a standing oracle, accessible to the living voice of the Church; by the Anglican theologians, who ground their faith on the same principles of Church authority divested of its divine and infallible character; by the Protestant, who regards it as once for all announced, long since finally closed, permanently recorded, and accessible only in the written divine word contained in the Scriptures;"[1] but these remarks are not applicable to the *prophetic* portions of Revelation, as there is no difference between the three with regard to the *fact*, however much there be in the interpretation and application of those facts. E. g.: In the first promise made to man after the fall, as recorded in God's revealed word (Gen. iii. 5), we have in the declaration of the " enmity between the Serpent and the Woman," a distinct prediction or prophecy respecting the mode of man's recovery from the effect of Adam's transgression; the fulfilment of which was accomplished 4000 years after the occurrence, and about 1600 years after Moses recorded it for the instruction of his own people. It is true that the Romanist in defence of his system of Mariolatry has perverted the prophecy, and has wrongfully applied, in defiance of all criticism and grammar, to a fallen creature like ourselves, though properly termed " blessed " by all nations, what was exclusively fulfilled by the Incarnate Son of God; but the error of the Church of Rome does not invalidate the truth and reality of the prophecy as understood both by the Jews in ancient, and by the Christians in modern times. We can point to this as one of many evidences

---

[1] Essays and Reviews, p. 101.

of the Bible being what it professes to be, — the will of God revealed through the instrumentality of men of old, who were moved by the Holy Ghost to speak the truth both of the past and the future.

Similarly must we understand the prophecy which the aged patriarch Jacob, when dying in Egypt, delivered respecting the expectation of Him, who was to bruise the Serpent's head. "The sceptre shall not depart from Judah, nor a lawgiver from between his feet, until Shiloh come; and unto Him shall the gathering of the people be."[1] Supposing for a moment that Jacob was no other than some mythical personage, such as some of the ideologists delight to imagine; still, the fact of Moses, who lived, according to Bunsen even, more than thirteen centuries before the Christian era, having recorded a prediction that his people, who were in his time in the position of bondsmen to their Egyptian masters, should become a nation, possess a sceptre or kingdom, and retain it up to a certain time, when, on the appearance of Him who in the prophecy is called "Shiloh,"[2] it should depart from them; when, according to all natural reasoning, we might suppose their power would be rooted firmer than ever. Surely this is what no man, unless inspired, would or could have imagined by himself for a moment, as the result of those promises which God had given before to Abraham.

Or consider what prophecy records concerning one of the oldest and mightiest kingdoms of the earth, whose history we have already noticed at length. We find a writer living at the commencement of the 6th century B.C., at a time when Egypt retained much of its original

---

[1] Genesis, xlix. 10.
[2] For an explanation of the word "Shiloh," and its application here, see pp. 9, 10.

power, and nearly seventy years before the Persian conquest, declaring that "it should be the basest of the kingdoms; that it should no more rule over the nations; that it should become desolate: and that *her cities shall be in the midst of the cities that are wasted;* . . . . for thus saith the Lord God, I will also *destroy the idols*, and I will cause their images to cease out of Noph[1] (Memphis); and there shall be *no more a prince of the land of Egypt*."[2] Here are three predictions, which it was absolutely impossible for man to foretell, and which have been literally and fully accomplished. The present position of Egypt, unlike all other countries, shows that her modern cities are verily in the midst of her ancient wasted cities, and that her extensive system of idolatry, which was probably the cradle of the later religions of Greece and Rome, is a thing of the past. Her history shows that more than twenty centuries have rolled by since a native prince has swayed the sceptre of that once magnificent empire. Persians, Greeks, Romans, Saracens, Mamelukes, and Turks, have in turn ruled over, trampled down, and despoiled that unhappy country. And it only required the testimony of two such sceptical and therefore unexceptionable witnesses as Volney and Gibbon, to show the accuracy with which the prophecy has been fulfilled. The former, after describing Egypt's loss of her "natural proprietors" for so many centuries, goes on to say, "The Mamelukes purchased as slaves, and introduced as soldiers, soon usurped power, and elected a leader. If their first

---

[1] In the chamber of Karnak there is an hieroglyphic inscription recording an expedition of Thothmosis III. against Canaan, the spoils of which are described as being brought to *Memphis*, which is written, not with its ordinary Egyptian name, but as it was known in Canaan, *Noph*.
[2] Ezekiel, xxix. 15; xxx. 7, 13.

establishment was a singular event, *their continuance is not less extraordinary.* They are replaced by slaves brought from their original country. The system of oppression is methodical. Every thing the traveller sees or hears, reminds him he is in the country of slavery and tyranny."[1] "A more unjust and absurd constitution," observes the latter, "cannot be devised than that which condemns the natives of a country to perpetual servitude, under the arbitrary dominion of *strangers and slaves.* Yet such has been the state of Egypt above 500 years. The twenty-four beys, or military chiefs, have ever been succeeded, not by their sons, but by their servants."[2] Although the reign of the Mamelukes has now ceased, Egypt is not governed by a native prince in this present day, and we may feel assured, she never will be again.

These few predictions we have noticed, a selection from a large number equally convincing, are sufficient evidence of the truth of the Old Testament being what it professes to be, a portion of the revealed word of God. And if the fulfilment of such prophecies affords evidence of their truth in regard to the *past,* we may fairly conclude that the New Testament predictions will equally be accomplished in the *future.* Hence the lesson we draw respecting such which we believe are now in the course of fulfilment.

The most important prophecies of the New Testament relate to the destruction of Jerusalem, and the restoration of the Jews; to the rise and fall of the Roman ecclesiastical power; and to the return of Him who once appeared as a "man of sorrows," and who will one day appear as

---

[1] Volney's Travels, vol. i. p. 198.
[2] Decline and Fall, ch. lix.

King of Saints.[1] The historic evidence respecting the first and most completely fulfilled of these several events may be briefly stated as follows. Irenæus, writing soon after the middle of the second century, states that the Apostle St. Matthew wrote a gospel amongst the Jews in their own language, while Peter and Paul were founding the Church at Rome. The testimony of Irenæus is probably the most valuable of any of the writers of that age, from the exact way in which it may be traced for nearly 150 years. Writing to Florinus, he says, "When I was yet a boy, I saw thee in company with Polycarp, in Asia Minor; for I remember what took place then better than what happens now. What we hear in childhood grows with the soul, and becomes one with it, so that I can describe the place where the blessed Polycarp sat and spoke . . . how he told of his intercourse with John, and with the rest who had seen the Lord; how he reported their sayings, and what he had heard from them respecting the Lord, His miracles, and His doctrines.[2] In the gospel of St. Matthew, which was written, according to the best evidence, not long after the Crucifixion, and several years before the fall of Jerusalem, our Lord is represented as having forewarned His disciples of its destruction. And so specific were His warnings, which were to usher in the judgment, that it is well known those who regarded them escaped the heavy judgment which then fell upon that doomed race. Josephus[3] records that after the unaccountable retreat of the Roman army under Cestus, which

---

[1] "To the Christian Church the second coming of Christ stands where His first coming stood to the Jewish — in the very centre of the field of prophetic light; and a participation in the glories 'then to be revealed' is even limited to those who in every age are devoutly 'looking for Him.'"—*Natural History of Enthusiasm*, p. 108.

[2] Fragm. Deperdit. Op. S. Irenæi, p. 340. Paris, 1710.

[3] Jud. Bel. II. xx. 1.

delayed, but did not prevent the destruction of Jerusalem, "many of the most eminent of the Jews swam away from the city, as from a ship when it was going to sink." Epiphanius[1] and Eusebius[2] both relate that the Christians fled to Pella in Peræa, a mountainous country, where they found safety, in accordance with their Master's exhortation, "Then let them which be in Judea flee into the mountains."[1] It is unnecessary to detail how literally our Lord's prediction was fulfilled, but we may adduce the unexceptionable evidence of the Talmud, which mentions, that "Rufus, the captain of Titus' army did with a ploughshare tear up the foundations of the Temple; and thereby signally fulfilled those words in Micah iii. 12. "Therefore shall Zion for your sakes be ploughed as a field, and Jerusalem shall become heaps, and the mountain of the house as the high places of the forest." The same spirit which foretold the fall of the Jews, has likewise prophesied their national restoration to that land which God gave to Abraham and his seed as an "everlasting possession." This, the prophets of the Old Testament are full of, as we find it taught *literally* in Jeremiah xxxi. 38—40; *symbolically* in Ezekiel xxxvii. 15—22; *figuratively* in Isaiah lxvi. 10—13; and this is what St. Paul, in his Epistle to the Romans, seems to point to; and certainly the signs of the times teach a very convincing lesson of the changed condition of the Jews, and the altered feeling of the nations of the Gentiles towards them from what it was at the commencement of the present century.

There is an ancient tradition amongst the Jews, that their national restoration would synchronise with the destruction of the Roman power. "Currente sexto," writes Abraham Sebah in his commentary on Gen. i., "annorum mundi millenaris Romana evertendam et Judæos

---

[1] Adv. Hæres. xxix. 7.   [2] Ecc. Hist. iii. 5.   [3] St. Matt. xxiv. 16.

reducendos." And this appears to accord with what we gather from the writings of the New Testament, which necessarily are of no authority amongst the Jews. In St. Paul's Epistle to the Thessalonians and to Timothy, and in the Apocalypse of St. John, we have a detailed and exact account of the rise and fall of that ecclesiastical system which has alike excited the admiration and indignation of so many ages. What human power could have foreseen that a Church whose "faith" was so bright in the first century as to be "spoken of throughout the whole world," should be guilty in after ages of apostasy[1], idolatry, and cruelty of so deep a die that humanity shudders at its recital. If we understand "the apostasy," defined by St. Paul, 2 Thess. ii. 3, &c., which in our authorised version is rendered "a falling away," or the parallel passage in 1 Tim. iv. 1, that "some should depart (lit. *apostatise*) from the faith," in the sense in which the word is elsewhere used in the New Testament, viz. Heb. iii. 12, and in many places of the Old, according to the LXX., we have an exact definition of the term, which means *a defection on the part of those to whom true religion has been revealed from the worship*

---

[1] "I am convinced," said Bishop Van Mildert in the House of Lords, A.D. 1829, "and that upon no light or superficial grounds, but after many years of studious consideration and inquiry, that the religion of Popery is distinctly pointed out in Scripture as *the one great apostasy* from the truth, the declared object of Divine displeasure." It is a matter of great importance to bear in mind the twofold judgment upon Rome, as declared so plainly in the 17th and 18th chapters of Revelation; the one from man, which we see in the present day, as she is being deprived of her temporalities by the powers of the earth; the other and more terrible judgment, which is coming, when God will pour out the vials of His wrath upon her, as He once did upon Sodom and Gomorrha, which will be fully accomplished when "her sins have reached unto heaven, and God hath remembered her iniquities — and with violence she be thrown down, and shall be found no more at all." Rev. xviii. 5, 21.

of Him whom we are commanded to serve "only," not by rejecting God, but by adding the worship of dead and deified mortals. Such was the sin of the Jews after their settlement in the Land of Promise, when ensnared by the false but attractive religion of the surrounding heathen nations; such has been the sin of the Church of Rome, which, after the first six centuries of her existence, gradually paganised Christianity, or as some would say, developed Roman Catholicism, by exchanging the pantheon of the Greeks for the worship of the Virgin Mary and all the Saints. It is unnecessary now to enter upon the details of those two famous prophecies in St. Paul's Epistles, as they have been so often and so fully considered; but it will be sufficient to remark, that if language has any definite meaning, if the characteristic marks which the Spirit of God has thought fit to reveal, are to be received in their plain and literal meaning as a guide to our understanding thereof, then assuredly, notwithstanding the unceasing attempts of two schools in the present day, those who are commonly called *Futurists*[1], and those who follow the teaching of the Essayists, such as Pro-

---

[1] The Futurists commonly deny the application of St. Paul's prediction in 2 Thess. ii. to the Papacy, on the grounds that the power there depicted claims obedience as the performer of "lying wonders," which they interpret to mean "true miracles in support of a falsehood," while some of them admit that *the miracles* of the Church of Rome are not true, but false or pretended ones. In thus reasoning they have betrayed their incompetency as critics, as well as their inefficiency as prophetic interpreters; for the expression which St. Paul uses, τέρασι ψεύδους, is one of the many Hebraisms found both in the Old and New Testament, and can have no other meaning than "false or fictitious miracles," which exactly suits the unfounded pretensions of the Church of Rome. It is right to remember that the *Futurist* interpreters of prophecy are also divided into two schools; the one leaning to Romanism, the other to extreme Puritanism, such as the tenets held by the "Plymouth Brethren." Both, however, are alike hostile to the Catholic teaching embodied in the formularies of the Church of England.

fessor Jowett, to evade the force of the predictions, we have no hesitation in affirming that they can have no other application than to the apostate and idolatrous Church of Rome.

If the rise and fall of what may be termed the *spiritualities* of the Roman Church have been predicted by St. Paul, no less fully have the *temporalities* been by St. John, to whom it was revealed that a great Ecclesiastical power, with the aid of the secular arm should persecute the followers of Him whose place she usurped and whose vicar she pretended to be, with such cruelty that the Apostle could not forbear to express his wonder and amazement. "I saw the woman (upon whose forehead was a name written, *Mystery, Babylon the great, the Mother of Harlots and abominations of the Earth*) drunken with the blood of the saints, and with the blood of the martyrs of Jesus: and when I saw her I wondered with great admiration."[1] When we remember that the Bull of Pope Pius III., A.D. 1536, entitled "Bulla in cœnâ Dei," which is still read every Maundy Thursday in the presence of the reigning Pontiff, "excommunicates and curses *all heretics, under whatever name they may be classed*, as well as those who secede from obedience to the Roman Pontiff for the time being;"[2] and that the Council of Constance in the previous century had decreed that "*heretics were to be burnt alive*," which decree had been enforced practically by the council in the martyrdom of John Huss and Jerome of Prague; when we recollect what history records as to the way in which the massacre of so many thousands in France on St. Bartholomew's day was welcomed at Rome, as the walls of the Vatican testify to this hour, we can in some measure understand "the wonder" which the vision

---

[1] Rev. xvii. 5, 6.　　[2] Mag. Bull. Rom. A. D. 1536.

must have excited in the Apostle's mind, when he saw by revelation the professed Vicar of Christ persecuting unto death those who gloried in His name. Heathen Rome doing the work of heathenism in persecuting the Church was no mystery. It required no prophetic eye to foresee that, after the burning of Rome and the Neronic persecution, which has been so graphically described by the pen of Tacitus, that Christians would suffer cruelly from the heathen powers; but that a Christian Church, calling herself "Mother and Mistress of all others,"[1] should in time become "the Mother of Harlots," and "drunk with the blood of saints," this was indeed a mystery. This was a prediction, which nothing but Omniscience could have foreseen or foretold, and as such it is evidence of the New Testament being, what it claims to be, the written testimony of men moved by the Holy Ghost to declare the revealed will of God.

If we contrast the prophecies recorded in Scripture, which are so self-convincing that scepticism has sought to obviate their force by vainly affirming them to be history of the *past* instead of predictions of the *future*, with the boasted oracles of the heathen, we see at once the falsity of their pretensions in the ambiguity of their answers. When Crœsus sought the assistance of the Delphic oracle to know his fate in the event of invading the Persian empire, he received this ambiguous reply: "By crossing the Halys, Crœsus will destroy a great empire."[2] When

---

[1] Concil. Trident. sess. x. Hard. x. 53.

[2] According to Herodotus, i. § 47, Crœsus had previously tested and, as he thought, proved the value of the Delphic oracle, when it related his actions in the well known story of the lamb and the tortoise in the brazen kettle; but there was this important distinction between the two cases: the *first* related to *things present*, in which the Pythian priestess might have been assisted by an evil spirit; the *second* related to *things future*, and therefore all that the spirit of divination could do was to veil his ignorance by intentional ambiguity. Rawlinson accounts for

Pyrrhus, King of Epirus, contemplated the invasion of Italy, he was induced by the oracular response,

" Aio te, Æacide, Romanos vincere posse,"

(which the peculiarity of the Latin construction reads, either "that *you* may conquer the Romans," or "the Romans may conquer *you*,") to interpret it in his own favour, and thus hurried on to his ruin. And if we believe the testimony of Plutarch, who admits the failure of oracles in his own time, we have an interesting account of their cessation about the time of the introduction of Christianity, and which he explains by supposing that the demons who conducted those oracles, though longer lived than men, were now dead. " In the time of Tiberius," he relates, " some persons embarking from Asia for Italy, towards the evening, sailed by the Echinades, where, being becalmed, they heard from thence a loud voice, calling one *Thamus*, an Egyptian mariner amongst them, and after the third time, commanding him, when he came to the Palodes, to declare that *the great Pan*[1] *was dead*. With the advice of his company, he resolved that if they had a quick gale when they came to the Palodes, he would pass by silently; but if they should find themselves becalmed there, he would then perform what the voice had commanded. But when the ships arrived thither, there was neither any breeze of wind nor any agitation of the water. Whereupon *Thamus*, looking out of the stern

---

the success of the answer by supposing that either the Pythoness really possessed an evil spirit, as in the instance mentioned in Acts, xvi. 16—18, or by Mesmerism. See Rawlinson's Herod. *in loco*.

[1] In the name of *Pan*, and the allusion to *an Egyptian* mariner alone of all the crew there might be a reference to the celebrated inscription on the Temple at Sais in Egypt, to Neith, the Goddess of Wisdom :—
" I am all (παν) that hath been, and is, and shall be,
And no mortal hath yet lifted my veil."
Plut. de Isid. et Osir. § 9.

towards the Palodes, pronounced these words, with a loud voice, '*The great Pan is dead,*' which he had no sooner done, than he was answered by a chorus of many voices, making a great howling and lamentation, not without a mixture of admiration."[1] Plutarch also says that Tiberius took pains to ascertain the truth of this extraordinary story, and, like Herod the Great, he inquired diligently of the wise men who this " great Pan " could be. But whether it be a real occurrence or not, it is a notable tradition current amongst the heathen with regard to a cessation of their oracles at a time when, according to the Gospels, the demons who afflicted men recognised the omnipotent power of Jesus, the Son of God.

Modern times, however, have witnessed no less than ancient, a fondness for dealing in prophetic utterances, but which upon investigation, present a very different appearance from the predictions recorded in Scripture, and can claim the title of only being happy guesses of the future. We all recollect the excitement caused by the republication of Fleming's work on Prophecy, A.D. 1848, in which the writer had stated that that year would see the end of the Papacy. Now, though it was true that Europe was convulsed from one end to the other at that period, and the Pope for a time was obliged to quit Rome, several years have since glided away, and the Papacy still exists. So at the commencement of the Russian war a few years subsequently, the following " cock and bull" story, said to have been written in the middle of the fifteenth century, was put forth respecting the contemplated fall of the Turkish Empire :—

> " In twice two hundred years the *Bear*
> The *Crescent* will assail ;
> But if the *Cock* and *Bull* unite,
> The *Bear* will not prevail.

---

[1] Plutarch, De Defect. Orac.

In twice ten years again
Let Islam know and fear,
The *Cross* shall stand, the *Crescent* wane,
Dissolve and disappear."

Certes, the middle of the nineteenth century witnessed a great war, in which England and France were united on behalf of Turkey against Russia. We know Christianity will last, and we believe Mahometanism will disappear; but we very much doubt whether the sobriquet of "John Bull" was known in the fifteenth century, or that the epithets of *Cock* and *Bear* were applied in that period to France and Russia respectively. It is true that there has been for many ages a popular notion that Russia is to obtain possession of Constantinople. Gibbon[1] relates that as early as the eleventh century an equestrian statue, which had been originally brought from Antioch, and was supposed to represent either *Joshua* or *Bellerophon* (an odd dilemma), stood in the square of the Taurus, on which was inscribed a prophecy how the Russians in the last days should become masters of Constantinople. The events, however, of late years, seem to show that this "prophecy," though its fulfilment has been so long and so anxiously sought by the Russians, is further removed than ever.

In the Augustinian Library at Rome, there is a work, which we believe is still to be seen, containing another of these curious predictions, though not claiming an antiquity of above two centuries. The author must have certainly possessed the mind of a far-seeing statesman, when he wrote as follows:—" Before the middle of the nineteenth century, seditions will be excited everywhere in Europe. Republics will arise; kings will be put to death, together with the nobility and ecclesiastics; and the religious will desert their convents. Famine, pestilence, and earthquakes will spread desolation over many

---

[1] Decline and Fall, ch. lv.

cities. Rome will lose her sceptre by the invasion of false philosophers. The Pope will be made captive by his own people, and the Church of God will be placed under tribute, divested of its temporal possessions. In a short time there will be no Pope. A prince from the North will overrun Europe with a great army, destroy the republics, and exterminate all rebels. His sword, wielded by God, will vigorously defend the Church of Christ, uphold the orthodox faith, and subdue the Mahomedan power. A new pastor, the final one, will come by a heavenly sign from the shore, in simplicity of heart, and in the doctrine of Christ, and peace will be restored to the world." Though some things in this very curious prediction have certainly come to pass, no one would be venturesome enough to pin his faith on the fulfilment of the rest, except so far as they are inferences from the revealed word of God; and therefore, like the others already noticed, they necessarily stand in a different category from those prophecies of Scripture, the literal accomplishment of which is both an evidence to their truth with reference to the *past*, and a warrant to assure us of their fulfilment in the *future*.

II. *Miracles*, as well as prophecy, are unquestionably one of the evidences of the truth of the Christian religion. If we have not misapprehended Professor Baden Powell's meaning, he seems, in the Essay before us, to reproduce the scepticism of Hume respecting miracles with the usual complacency of his school, not only as if the arguments he adduces were of the force which he supposes them to be, but as if they had not been answered, and that most satisfactorily, over and over again. We are reminded of what Bishop Horne used to say respecting the cavillers in his day. "Pertness and ignorance may ask a question in three lines, which it will cost learning and ingenuity thirty pages to answer; and when this is done *the same question shall be triumphantly asked again the next year, as if nothing had ever been written on the subject.*" When Hume stated the case of miracles to be a contest of opposite improbabilities, i. e. a question whether it be more improbable that the miracle be true or the testimony false, Paley properly exposed the " want of argumentative justice " in the reasoning of that noted infidel, by showing that he "suppressed all those circumstances of extenuation, which result from our knowledge of the existence, power, and disposition of the Deity."[1] Considering that the same author in his masterly work brought forward " an accumulation of historical testimony " in confirmation of the truth of the Christian religion in general, and of the writings of the New Testament in particular, it is a poor way of attempting to evade their importance, by quoting with approbation, as the Essayist does, the opinion of " a very able critic," that " the last age *erroneously* denominated such testimonies *the* Evidences of Christianity." Had this critic been better acquainted with the subject which he was treating, he would have known that " the last age," as well as the present age, was fully justified in accepting " historical testimonies," or what Bunsen calls " historical synchronisms," like prophecy, or miracles, or science, as valuable and undesigned proofs of the truth of the Christian religion. Professor Powell's inability to comprehend the Evidences of Christianity is apparent in the following monstrous asseveration, in which he is venturesome enough to declare that, " the extreme ' Evangelical ' school, strongly asserting the literal truth of the Bible, seeks its evidence wholly in spiritual impressions, *regarding all exercise of the reason as partaking in the*

---

[1] Paley's Preparatory Considerations to the Evidences of Christianity, p. 5.

nature of sin."[1] It is unnecessary to reply to this gratuitous mistake, which is only to be paralleled by another statement of the same writer (the confusion of whose mind is so evident) in the wonderful announcement, that "if a number of respectable witnesses were to concur in asseverating that on a certain occasion they had seen *two and two make five, we should be bound to believe them.*"[2] In comparing this with the case of Scripture miracles, it is difficult to decide which is most apparent, the profanity or the absurdity of the remark. Had the Essayist been less self-satisfied with his overpowering scepticism, he would have avoided the many blunders which pervade his Essay. Who but a sceptic of the deepest dye could have committed himself to such a statement as this — " testimony is but a blind guide, *testimony can avail nothing against reason?* "[3] We admit such testimony as that of his ideal arithmetician, whose first principles enable him to add up two and two and to produce five as the correct result, is of that unreasonable or rather impossible kind, that the slightest modicum of common sense compels us to reject it; but since the miracles of the New Testament, as evidences of Christianity, stand on a very different footing, the attempt at argument on the part of the Essayist refutes itself.

Dr. Johnson was right when, after alluding to Hume's proposition he declared that " the Christian revelation is not proved by *miracles alone*, but as connected with *prophecies* and with the doctrines in confirmation of which miracles were wrought."[4] The Essayist indeed quotes this truthful saying, but only for the purpose of dismissing it with the somewhat contemptuous remark, " What is it but to acknowledge the right of an appeal, superior

---

[1] Essays and Reviews, p. 120.   [2] Ibid. p. 141.
[3] Ibid. p. 141.   [4] Boswell's Life, vol. iii. p. 169.

to that of all miracles, to our own moral tribunal, to the principle that 'the human mind is competent to sit in moral and spiritual judgment on a professed revelation,' in virtue of which Professor F. W. Newman, as well as many other inquirers, have come to so very opposite a conclusion."[1] And he adopts this theory, that " if miracles are made the sole criterion, then amid the various difficulties attending the scrutiny of evidence, and the detection of imposture, an advantage is clearly given to the shrewd sceptic over the simple-minded and well-disposed disciple, utterly fatal to the purity of faith."[2] Without dwelling upon the theory of miracles being made *the sole criterion* of faith, which no Christian worthy of the name attempts to maintain, this reasoning is palpably erroneous, simply because he who adopts it has failed to notice the difference between true miracles, such as God alone can perform, and those pretended ones, with which men have sought to support their false religions, and which might be more properly denominated " mysteries " or phenomena which cannot be explained; and which are sometimes real, and sometimes the reverse. " All inexplicable phenomena," observes the Essayist, " are in fact *miracles, or at any rate mysteries*. We are surrounded by miracles in nature, and on all sides encounter phenomena which baffle our attempts at explanation, and limit the powers of scientific investigation; phenomena whose causes or nature we are not, and probably never shall be, able to explain."[3] We see in this the confusion in the writer's mind. " Miracles " are one thing, " mysteries " are another. There is as much difference between the two, as between God and man. The proper definition of a miracle is the exercise of Almighty Power, manifested either in person, or entrusted to His servants,

---

[1] Essays and Reviews, p. 122.   [2] Ibid. p. 123.   [3] Ibid. p. 109.

or permitted to His enemies, as was the case with the Egyptian Magi, in the past, and as will be the case, we conclude from Rev. xvi. 14, with "the spirits of devils working miracles" in the future. "Mysteries," or inexplicable phenomena, may be such as the Essayist has described in his curious jumble of "the martyrs, who spoke articulately after their tongues were cut out[1]; the angel seen in the air by two thousand persons at Milan; the miraculous balls of fire on the spires at Plausac; Herodotus' story of the bird in the mouth of the crocodile; narratives of the sea serpent, marvels of mesmerism, electro-biology, and *vaccination*."[2] We think it is a sad jumble to place the *sea serpent* and *vaccination* in the same category, when arguing against miracles as an evidence of Christianity, though it may betray the unhappy bias of the writer's mind, since it proves that he disdains not to use the weapons of banter and ridicule in his antagonism to the truth. What can be more offensive for a professed minister of the Church of Christ than the bold declaration of the Essayist on this subject? "In nature and from nature, by science and by reason, we neither have nor can possibly have any evidence of a *Deity working miracles;* for that, we must go out of nature and beyond science. If we could have any such evidence *from nature,* it could only prove extraordinary *natural* effects which would not be *miracles* in the old theological sense, as isolated, unrelated, and uncaused; whereas no *physical* fact can be conceived as unique, or without analogy and relation to others, and to the whole system of natural causes."[3] If we were content to meet this broad piece of scepticism by a general denial of the

---

[1] If we recollect aright, Gibbon gives some credence to this as a "miracle," notwithstanding the tone of ridicule which Professor B. Powell adopts.

[2] Essays and Reviews, p. 137. [3] Ibid. pp. 141, 142.

same, we could not do better than quote the language of the late much lamented Professor Archer Butler, who has justly observed, " You may deny the story of miracles, but can you destroy the miracle of the story? You may discredit this volume of miracles,—for the Spirit of God does not now descend to silence its gainsayers, — but can you *unmiracle* the obstinate fact of the volume itself?"

We would, however, prefer to specify two distinct events recorded in the New Testament, as evidences of the truth of Christianity, about which there can be no mistake and no deception, if we accept the testimony of the sacred writers as readily as we do that of another accredited historian when an eyewitness of what he records, and whose statements are subsequently confirmed by unwilling adversaries. They are these, 1st, the power of raising the dead; 2ndly, that unlettered persons should instantly be able to speak in languages before unknown to them, so as to be understood by those whom they addressed. This is what the New Testament claims for our Lord and His disciples, and the existence of Christianity to this day in place of overthrown Paganism sufficiently confirms its truth. If, therefore, a small company of unlearned men should declare that at a certain period an individual appeared in the world, claiming to be " the Son of God," telling them, as his followers, that he should suffer a cruel death, and that after lying three days and three nights in the grave he should rise from it, and that at the appointed time all this came to pass; that they were eyewitnesses of such events, and that this holy Being appeared to them three days after they had seen him crucified, and had watched beside the place where he was buried; that after his ascension to heaven, of which they were also eyewitnesses, they had gone forth in obedience to their Master's commands, to deliver the message with which he had entrusted them, to all who would listen to them; and that for the execution of this work they found themselves in the possession of certain powers, — such as raising the dead and speaking the various languages of the nations amongst whom they laboured with as much ease as their own and without any previous study, — which he had foretold should accompany their work; and finally that many of them laid down their lives in testimony of the truth of their story, which they otherwise might have preserved had they felt so disposed: when we remember these things it is impossible to explain them otherwise than by accepting it as the true history of " Deity working miracles " in behalf of that religion which He designed to establish among men. The effective testimony of such an unexceptionable witness as Tacitus to the spread of Christianity at Rome in the latter half of the first century[1]; the confident appeal of the converted philosopher Justin Martyr[2] to the Roman Senate in proof of the origin of Christianity at the commencement of the second century, as their own archives bore witness; the striking declaration of Tertullian[3] respecting the marvellous increase of Christianity throughout the empire at the close, and which was done always at the risk and often at the expense of life: all these are evidences to the fact, as well as to the proof that nothing less than " Deity working miracles " in behalf of His love towards mankind could have effected so wonderful a change in the condition of the Roman empire.

It is curious to observe how differently the testimony of two of the authors referred to above is accepted by a

---

[1] Tac. Annal. xv. 44.
[2] Apol. Prima, pp. 65, 72. Ed. Ben.
[3] " We are but of yesterday, and by to-day are grown up and overspread your empire; your cities, your islands, your forts, towns, assemblies, and your very camps, wards, companies, palace, senate, and forum, all swarm with Christians." — *Tertul. Apol.* c. xxxvii.

distinguished historian of modern times, but whose mind is of a "painfully sceptical" tendency. Commenting upon the description which a pagan has given of the sufferings of the early Christians, under Nero, Gibbon observes: "The most sceptical criticism is *obliged to respect the truth* of this extraordinary fact, and the integrity of this celebrated passage of Tacitus. The former is confirmed by the diligent and accurate Suetonius, who mentions the punishment which Nero inflicted on the Christians, a sect of men who had embraced a new and criminal superstition. The latter may be proved by the consent of the most ancient manuscripts; by the inimitable character of the style of Tacitus; by his reputation, which guarded his text from the interpolations of pious fraud; and by the purport of his narration, which accused the first Christians of the most atrocious crimes, without insinuating that they possessed any miraculous, or even magical powers, above the rest of mankind."[1] When, however, he has a Christian author to deal with, his reception and treatment of the same is somewhat different.[2] "The Apology of *Tertullian*," he relates, "contains two very ancient, very singular, but, at the same time, *very suspicious* instances of imperial clemency: the edicts published by Tiberius and by Marcus Antoninus, and designed not only to protect the innocence of the Christians, but even to proclaim those stupendous miracles which might perplex a sceptical mind. We are required to believe that Pontius Pilate informed the emperor of the unjust sentence of death which he had pronounced against an innocent, and, as it appeared, a divine person;"[3]

---

[1] Decline and Fall, ch. xvi. § 1.
[2] Porson, in his famous eulogy of Gibbon, remarks, that "his humanity never slumbers except when women are ravished and Christians persecuted."
[3] Decline and Fall, ch. xvi. § 4.

and so Gibbon adds, in a foot note, "The testimony given by Pontius Pilate is first mentioned by *Justin*."

Now, considering that the Apologies of both *Justin* and *Tertullian* were addressed to "the Roman senate," and that they continually appealed to the state documents, which must have been in existence when they wrote, in proof of what they asserted—as the former twice repeats his appeal to the senators—"that these things were so done, or done by him, *you* may know from the acts made in the time of Pontius Pilate;"[1] the latter declares, "this wonder of the world (viz. the supernatural darkness at the time of the crucifixion) you have related, and *the relation preserved in your archives*[2] *to this day*. . . . . . Pilate, who in his conscience was a Christian, sent Tiberius Cæsar an account of all the proceedings relating to Christ;"[3] and after speaking of Tiberius' proposition to enrol Christ amongst the Roman deities, which was rejected by the obsequious senate, on the ground that the emperor had declined the honour for himself, Tertullian continues, in agreement with the statement of Tacitus, "*Consult your annals*, and there you will find that Nero was the first emperor who dyed his sword in Christian blood, when our religion was just rising at Rome."[4] Considering all these things, we need only call attention to the manifest want of fairness on the part of a professed

---

[1] Just. Apol. Prima, pp. 65, 72. Ed. Ben.

[2] Gibbon contends that as Tertullian's "mention of this prodigy is found in *Arcanis* (not *Archivis*) vestris, he *probably* appeals to the Sibylline verses, which relate it exactly in the words of the Gospel."—*Decline and Fall*, ch. xv. *ad finem* foot note. The force of Gibbon's "probably" is lessened by the fact that some authorities (e. g. Nic. Rigalt. T. C.) read "Archivis" and not "Arcanis;" and it is far more rational to infer that Tertullian (whichever word he used) referred to the genuine Acta Pilati than to the "Sibylline verses," which were forged a little before his own age, and of which he must have been well aware.

[3] Tertul. Apol. c. xxi.   [4] Ibid. c. v.

rationalist, such as Gibbon, when he has two different measures for Christian and pagan authors. To any candid mind, uninfluenced by scepticism, and therefore impartial, when investigating a matter, such as this, on which concurrent evidence exists, the very fact of the writers appealing confidently to the State documents of their adversaries, in proof of their assertions, would be sufficient to satisfy it of the truth; and in this instance, we may, and ought to be satisfied with the evidence of such eminent philosophers as Justin Martyr and Tertullian, even though Christians, in favour of the truths which they assert.

Thus then, we reply to the unbecoming remark of the Essayist, that "the champions of the 'evidences' of Christianity have professedly rested the discussion of the miracles of the New Testament, on the ground of precise evidences of witnesses, insisting on the *historical* character of the Gospel records, and urging the investigation of the truth of the facts, on the strict principles of criticism, as they would be applied to any other historical narrative,"[1] by pointing out the confirmation which the historical records of the time for *external*, and the undesigned coincidences of the New Testament for *internal* proof, afford to the truths of the Gospel. And it betrays a conscious weakness of the rationalistic cause, as well as ignorance of the true foundation of Christianity, to assume, as Professor Powell has done, that "if we attempt any uncompromising, rigid scrutiny of the Christian miracles, on the same grounds on which we should investigate any ordinary narrative of the supernatural or marvellous, we are stopped by the admonition not to make an irreverent and profane intrusion into what ought to be held sacred and exempt from such unhallowed criticism of human reason." As a specimen of the Essay-

---

[1] Essays and Reviews, pp. 110, 111.

ist's incompetency to understand the nature of miracles, as an evidence of Christianity, we need only refer to the case which he quotes of Henry Martyn among the Persian Mahometans. "They believed readily," he says, "all that he told them of the Scripture miracles, but *directly paralleled them by wonders of their own;* they were proof against any argument from the resurrection, because they held that their own sheikhs had the power of raising the dead" (p. 118). Did they "parallel" them by wonders *as true* and *as real* as those recorded in Scripture? Had the Mahometan sheikhs "the power of raising the dead?" —not merely asserting their ability to do so, but actually doing it? In this lies the great distinction between the Christian religion and all other human systems which have captivated and deluded mankind. To compare one with the other is as unreasonable as it is to imply a parallel between the sober and consistent statements of the Evangelists respecting the resurrection and ascension of Christ, and the fabulous "night journey" of the impostor Mahomet, "from the sacred temple of Mecca to the farther Temple of Jerusalem," as recorded in the Koran.[1]

The Christian religion, being divine, is, of necessity, miraculous. It is likewise a rational religion, in the proper sense of the term, not contrary to, though it may be above our finite reasoning powers. Therefore the faithful Christian not only need fear no "investigation" of its realities and its truths, but challenges such, well assured that every fresh attempt, whether conducted by friend or foe, will bring the religion he loves, and knows to be true, triumphant through the ordeal. It is only such irrational sceptics as "Theodore Parker, who denies miracles, *because* 'everywhere (as he says) I find law the constant mode of *operation of an infinite God,*' or Wegscheider, who asserts the belief in miracles is irre-

---

[1] Koran, ch. xvii. v. 1.

concilable with the idea of an eternal God consistent with himself" (p. 114), that need fear "investigation" of the evidences of Christianity, as the result must necessarily be to convince every candid mind, that the hypothesis of miracles being irreconcilable with a consistent God is too preposterous to need refutation.

"Miracles," then,—the miracles of the New Testament, as distinguished alike from those pretended ones whereby Rome captivates her deluded votaries, and from the "mysteries or inexplicable phenomena," such as animal-magnetism, or any other of the many *isms* with which this sceptical age abounds,—are an evidence of the truths of Christianity. And when we find men representing the *rejection* of the miracles of Scripture as an indication of mental superiority, we need not feel surprised; for we are assured that "there shall come in the last days *scoffers*, walking after their own lusts, and saying, Where is the promise of his coming? for since the fathers fell asleep, all things continue as they were from the beginning of the creation. For this they *willingly* are ignorant of, that by the word of God the heavens were of old, and the earth standing out of the water and in the water," &c. It is this *willing* ignorance that has led the rationalistic school astray; and this it behoves every Christian to remember, in accordance with the warning,—" Seeing ye know these things before, beware lest ye also, being led away with the error of the wicked, fall from your own stedfastness."[1]

III. If *Prophecy*, and *Miracles* afford, as we contend they most clearly do, very strong evidence in favour of the truths of Christianity, with no less truth do the undesigned and incidental allusions to *Science*, which are occasionally met with in Scripture, afford proof of the same. Such, however, was not the opinion of Professor

[1] 2 Peter, iii. 3, 4, 5, 17.

Powell, as we gather from his brief references to the subject. "An evidential appeal, which in a long past age was convincing as made to the state of knowledge in that age, might have not only no effect, but even an injurious tendency, if urged in the present, and referring to what is at variance *with existing scientific conceptions*, just as the arguments of the present age would have been unintelligible in a former" (p. 117). Again, the same author observes,—" The first dissociation of the spiritual from the physical was rendered necessary by the palpable contradictions disclosed by *astronomical discovery with the letter of Scripture*. Another *still wider* and more material step has been effected by the discoveries of geology. More recently, the antiquity of the human race, and the development of species, and the rejection of the idea of creation, have caused *new advances in the same direction*" (p. 129).

Reserving the proof of the Scripture references to "Geology" being in accordance with real *Science*, for our examination of the Essay on the "Mosaic Cosmogony," we propose to consider the scientific accuracy of the Bible in general, and its agreement with modern " astronomical discoveries " in particular. We must, however, as a preliminary, distinguish between " scientific conceptions," which the Essayist admits are varying from age to age, and true science, in other words, the understanding and application of the irreversible laws of the Creator, which are unchangeable. We have a notable instance of this in relation to geology, according to the statement of a French author, who mentions that, " in 1806, the French Institute numbered eighty geological systems, all hostile to the Mosaic record, not one of which has stood the test of time and research."[1] All real *Science*, being true, is like

---

[1] La Bible et la Science Moderne par le Pasteur Ed. Panchaud, p. 13.

God's word, unchangeable, and, therefore, we are not surprised to find men, with limited understanding and finite reasoning power, compared with the Creator of all things, constrained to confess their ignorance, by fresh discoveries in *Science* eventually confirming those truths of *Revelation*, which at first they were supposed to contradict. Let us consider some illustrations of this as set forth in Holy Scripture.

§ 1. Gen. i. 3.— In that sublime speech, which Moses records respecting the creation of light, and which so highly excited the admiration of the great heathen critic [1], when God spake " Let there be light, and there was light," we note that this is said to have been done three " days " *before* the sun, which men considered for so many ages the sole source of light, was appointed to rule the day. Had Moses been a mere man, well up to the " scientific conceptions " of his own day, and without inspiration from above, he would have recorded the creation of the sun as anterior to that of light. But we see in this seeming inconsistency, a testimony to the divine authority of the Pentateuch; for modern science has at length discovered that the sun, though supreme, is not the only source of light, but that there is, throughout the endless regions of space, a fine, subtle essence, called ether, which, restrained by no limits, washes the remotest shores of the universe with an invisible ocean, and which is of so refined a nature, that the stars move through its depths without encountering any resistance. Hence arise those waves, or undulatory motions, which, spreading with excessive velocity in every possible direction, produce, according to the theory of Huygens, the effect of light.

§ 2. Leviticus xvii. 11.—" The life of the flesh is in the blood." What Moses taught in plain language, and

---

[1] Dionysius Longinus, Treatise concerning the Sublime, § 9.

what Solomon, more than 500 years later taught in figurative, " or ever the silver cord be loosed, or the golden bowl be broken, or the pitcher be broken at the fountain, or the wheel broken at the cistern,"[1] *Science* has at length, after the labour of 3000 years, taken credit for having been the first to discover. That the blood actually possesses a *living* principle, and that the life of the whole body is derived from it, as was demonstrated by Dr. Harvey in the seventeenth century, and established by the celebrated Dr. John Hunter in the eighteenth, is a truth of Divine Revelation, set forth and declared thousands of years before the skill and ingenuity of man enabled him to discover the same.

§ 3. Deuteronomy xxxii. 2.— " My doctrine shall drop as the rain, my speech shall distil as the dew." The scientific accuracy of this beautiful allusion, is very striking, as we learn by *Revelation* the true theory of the formation of dew, as distinguished from that of rain. The dew does not fall, as was supposed for many ages, but, as the experiments of a French chemist have recently shown, is merely the condensation of the watery vapour floating in the colder region of the air, and especially near the surface of the ground. In the same chapter, v. 24, there is an allusion to the dreadful scientific fact, which has only been lately pointed out by the celebrated Liebig, that when a person is starved to death, he is undergoing the process of being slowly *burned up*, as Moses foretold the judgment upon the guilty children of Israel, " they shall be *burnt with hunger*," and which was literally accomplished in the two-fold siege of Jerusalem.

§ 4. Job xiv. 7, 8, 9. — Nothing but the modern discovery of the microscope has enabled man to learn the action of vapour upon the respiratory organs and secretionary vessels in the leaves of plants, which they inhale

---

[1] Eccles. xii. 6.

from the air for their nourishment. This is another instance of scientific accuracy with which Scripture is written, as we find Job refers to this interesting discovery in the following language : " There is hope of a tree, if it be cut down, that it will sprout again, and that the tender branch thereof will not cease. Though the root thereof wax old in the earth, and the stock thereof die in the ground, yet through the scent of water it will bud, and bring forth boughs like a plant."

§ 5. Job xxvi. 7.—What uninspired man ever had certain knowledge of the real shape of this world which we inhabit until a few centuries ago? The Hindoo legend of the tortoise and the elephant was the limit of man's skill during several thousand years before being able to decide what now appears to us so simple and so plain. It is true that the Pythagoreans, according to the report of Philolaus of Croton, taught the progressive movement of a non-rotating earth, and that Aristarchus of Samos, and Seleucus of Babylon, are said to have taught that the earth not only rotated on its axis, but also moved round the sun, but these ideas were so much in advance of the age, that they were rejected by the greater names of Plato and Aristotle, who imagined that the earth neither rotated on its axis, nor advanced in space, but that, fixed to one central point, it oscillated, like a half-filled balloon, from side to side. Eratosthenes, the most celebrated philosopher of the Alexandrian school, believed that there was an " external sea surrounding all continents ;" but the world required 2000 years more education before it could receive the truth as set forth by Copernicus. Yet Job, as we read in probably the most ancient book of Scripture, was enabled by the inspiration of God to declare, " He stretcheth out the north over the empty place, and *hangeth the earth upon nothing ;*" thereby stating a scientific truth 3000 years before the ingenuity of man had enabled him to discover it.

§ 6. Job xxviii. 23—25. — Who ever, previous to the time of Galileo, imagined that the air around us possessed the property of *weight*? Yet the same inspired writer is represented as asserting, " God understandeth the way thereof to make *the weight for the winds ;* and He weigheth the waters by measure." God has given an atmosphere to the earth, which, possessing a certain gravity exactly suited to the fauna and flora of the present age, is the cause in His hand of preserving animal and vegetable life throughout all creation ; for by this means blood circulates in the veins of the one, and juices in the tubes of the other. Without this pressure of the atmosphere, there could be no respiration, and the elasticity of the particles of the air, without this superincumbent pressure, would rupture the vessels in which they are contained, and destroy both kinds of life. So admirably contrived is this " *weight of the winds* " by Him who doeth all things well, that we find in the mean that it is neither too light to prevent the undue expansion of animal and vegetable tubes, nor too heavy to compress them to the injury of their health and life.

§ 7. Job xxxviii. 31. — " Canst thou bind the sweet influences of Pleiades ? " was one of the questions wherewith the Lord answered Job when demanding a recognition of His almighty power. What is the meaning of this " influence of the Pleiades ? " Some commentators have considered that there is a reference to the influence which the stars were formerly supposed to have upon the seasons, forgetful of the declaration of Moses that God had appointed the sun and the moon, as the " two great lights for signs and for *seasons,* and for days and years."[1] And until the science of astronomy had made the very great advance which it has in our day, partly

---

[1] Gen. i. 14—16.

through the improvement in the telescope, it was impossible for man to imagine what this "influence" could mean. Recently this has been explained by one of the most wonderful discoveries in that department of *Science*. After infinite labour the revolution of the whole solar system around some central sun is recognised as a scientific truth just as much as the revolution of the earth in its orbit. The "influence" of this central sun upon our solar system must be proportionally as great as that of the sun upon the earth and the planets, according to the law of gravitation. Professor Maedlar of Dorpat, a distinguished Russian astronomer, who has for years devoted his attention to the subject, has determined the "influence" which the Pleiades have upon the earth, as they form the central group of our whole astral system, including the Milky Way, though exclusive, it is believed, of the most distant nebulæ; and that Alcyone, or γ Tauri, as it is named by astronomers, is the star of this group which appears most probably to be the true central sun. Light, which flits through space at the amazing rate of 192,000 miles each second of time, takes 537 years in reaching our earth from that distant centre.[1] And it has been estimated that it would require a period of

---

[1] The known speed at which light travels is the only way by which our finite minds are enabled to conceive the enormous magnitude of creation. Thus, e.g. the moon, our nearest neighbour in the skies, reflects on us the ray of light which it has received from the sun, *in less than one second of time*. The rays of the sun require about nine minutes in their transit to the earth, and rather more than four hours to Neptune, the farthest planet (*first* discovered by Professor Adams, be it remembered, and not by Le Verrier, as foreigners vainly boast) yet known in our solar system. It takes three years for light to pass to us from α Centauri, the nearest of the fixed stars; 537 years, as we have noticed above, from the chief star in the Pleiades; and, according to the estimation of Sir William Herschel, the long period of 330,000 years from the outer extremity of the Milky Way.

18,200,000 years for our solar system to complete one single revolution, although progressing annually at the rate of 154,185,000 miles around the central sun. May we not exclaim at the contemplation of the power of Him, who has called all these into being, and has regulated them by His wisdom, in the language of one of our own poets?—

> "These be Thy glorious works, Thou Source of good,
> How dimly seen, how faintly understood."

§ 8. Psalm cxlvii. 16. — "The Lord giveth snow like wool." Modern discovery has shown there is a deeper meaning in this expression of the Psalmist, than was formerly supposed. Hence the Jews very naturally, as in the Targum and Rabbi Kimchi, considered the similarity to refer to *colour*, snow and wool being in this respect alike. The ancients used to call snow "woolly water,"[1] and Martial, the Roman poet, gives it the name of "*densum vellus aquarum*,"[2] a thick fleece of waters. But the comparison refers, we cannot doubt, to the admirable manner in which the Creator of all things has ordered that snow falling upon the earth should cover it, and warm it, and cause it to fructify for the use of man. Snow maintains its internal heat exactly in the same way as wool on the sheep's back; the minute fibres entangle the air, and, forbidding its escape, prevent the introduction of cold.

§ 9. Proverbs viii. 27.—"When He prepared the heavens, I was there: when He set a compass upon the face of the deep." The expressions in this verse and the context, seem to indicate a measured progress in the act of creation, as well as an arrangement of pre-existing materials, which accords with the discoveries of modern

---

[1] Eustathius in Dionys.   [2] Epigram, lib. iv. ep. 3.

Science, that this earth was fitted up for the habitation of man many ages after it was originally called into being. The declaration that the Creator set a compass upon the face of the deep, or as it is expressed elsewhere, "compassed the water with bounds,"[1] points alike to the fact of this world being in form a terraqueous globe (so long unknown to civilised man), as well as to the law of gravitation by which all the particles of matter, tending to a common centre, would produce in all bodies the orbicular form, which we see them have, so that even oceans and seas are not only retained within proper bounds, but are subjected to the circular form like other parts of matter. Thus Solomon, the wisest of men in ancient times, by the inspiration of God, stated a scientific fact thousands of years before Newton the most gifted of men in modern times was enabled by his own unaided skill to discover it.

§ 10. Ecclesiastes, i. 5, 6. — "The sun ariseth, and the sun goeth down, and hasteth to his place where he ariseth; he goeth toward the south, and turneth about unto the north. The wind whirleth about continually, and returneth again according to its circuits." It will be seen that we have not, in this passage, adhered exactly to our noble authorised version, which has attributed to the wind, what *all other versions* agree in referring to the sun, by applying the first clause of verse 6 to the former, instead of to the latter, contrary to the original text. If then we read it according to the Hebrew, we find the course of the sun truly and scientifically stated, and somewhat different from the popular belief of the Iberians of old, a race on the western extremities of Europe, who affirmed that they used to hear the sun hiss as it nightly sank into its watery bed; though not

---

[1] Job, xxvi. 10.

to be wondered at when the learned of those times considered that the shape of the earth was merely that of a plate. The inspired son of David, however, could describe the apparent diurnal and annual course of the sun, without contradicting anything that *Science* has subsequently found true. In the passage we have quoted he notices two things : 1. Day and night, marked by the appearance of the sun above the horizon, travelling from east to west, where he is lost to sight during the silent hours of the night. 2. The annual course of the sun through the twelve signs of the zodiac, when, from the equinoctial, he proceeds southward to the tropic of Capricorn, from which he " turneth about to the north," until he reaches the tropic of Cancer. Moreover, what is said in the above passage respecting the " wind whirling about continually, and returning again according to its circuits," clearly indicates the rotatory theory of storms, viz. that hurricanes and storms do not blow, as formerly imagined, in a straight line from a single point, at a great distance, but that they are vast eddies in the air, which whirl about like the eddies of a stream of water, according to the inductions of modern science.

§ 11. Ecclesiastes, i. 7.—Solomon continues: " All the rivers run into the sea, yet the sea is not full ; unto the place from whence the rivers come, thither they return again." Thus scripture shows, long before the ingenuity of man had discovered it, the great system of aqueous circulation which is constantly going on. How comes it that the sea is not full, since so many gigantic rivers are unceasingly pouring into its depths such mighty streams of water? The reason is, as *Science* teaches, that nothing goes into it, either by the rivers or rain, which does not come from it. Water exhaled from the sea by evaporation, is collected in the clouds, then it is condensed into rain, then it descends to the earth, and percolates through its surface, then it rises in springs, the commencement of mighty streams, and finally is carried by these into the seas from whence it was first derived.

§ 12. John xix. 34.— " One of the soldiers with a spear pierced his side, and forthwith came thereout blood and water." It was at one time the custom for sceptics to affirm that the Evangelist's account (notwithstanding it was that of an eyewitness of the fact, as " he that saw it bare record, and his record is true," v. 35) of the issue from the Saviour's wound could not have been correct, as, if His frame had been " made in all things like " to our own, it would necessarily have been blood only. But, as Fullom, in his valuable work on " The Marvels of Science," remarks, " Here science has risen up, like a holy apostle, to testify to the truth of Christianity." For it has now been discovered that the heart is invested by a hollow membrane, somewhat like a purse, called the pericardium, containing a small quantity of clear water, and consequently the issue from the Saviour's wound must necessarily, according to the inspired record, have comprised both " *blood and water.*" It is by such seeming accidents, or rather undesigned coincidences that the genuineness, the authority, and the truthfulness of the Scriptures are established and vindicated.

Having thus noticed some of the many incidental allusions in *Revelation* to subjects which modern *Science*, after thousands of years of toil and labour, has at length discovered and admitted to be true, we must examine one more question which the Essayist has mooted, wherein he endeavours to show " the palpable contradictions disclosed by (modern) discovery with the letter of Scripture," as he asserts that " more recently the antiquity of the human race, and the development of species and the rejection of the idea of ' creation,' have caused new advances in the same direction " (p. 129). Further on he again speaks of "that *enormous length of time* which modern discovery has now indisputably assigned to the existence of the human race" (p. 139). It is unnecessary to repeat what we have already considered at length in our examination of "Bunsen's Biblical Researches," but it may be satisfactory to state that the more we investigate the discoveries of real science, the more confirmed we are in our belief that there is not the shadow of a *proof* in contradiction of the Scripture statement respecting the age of man on earth. Bunsen's theory from the pottery deposits in the Nile mud is the strongest argument which the rationalistic school has adduced in contradiction of Scripture on this point, but we have already seen that when the objection is fairly investigated it has no force whatever, for it tends rather than otherwise to confirm the historic statement of the Bible. The Essayist, however, not content with the error he has committed respecting the *age* of the human race on earth, has made a gigantic stride in the direction of scepticism by his theory, or rather his quoting approvingly another man's theory, respecting the mode of *creation*. "It is now acknowledged," says Professor Powell, "under the high sanction of the name of Owen, that 'creation' is only another name for our ignorance of the mode of production; and it has been the unanswered and unanswerable argument of another reasoner that new species *must* have originated *either* out of their inorganic elements, or out of previously organised forms; *either* development *or* spontaneous generation *must be* true: while a work has now appeared by a naturalist of the most acknowledged authority, Mr. Darwin's masterly volume on 'The Origin of Species' by the law of 'natural selection,' — which now substantiates on undeniable grounds the very principle so long denounced by the first naturalists, — *the origination of new species by natural causes:* a work which must soon bring about an entire revolution of opinion in favour of the grand principle of the self-evolving powers of nature" (p. 139). We have adopted the italics of the Essayist, who thus clearly indicates his own theory respecting the *modus operandi* in the matter of our "creation." Passing over the manifest unfairness in coupling together the names of *Owen* and *Darwin*, who, as we shall take the opportunity of showing, are *in direct antagonism* on this most important subject, we must first of all consider what is Mr. Darwin's theory, so highly lauded by Professor Powell. We cannot, therefore, do better than state it in his own words, extracted from that volume, which, if it has no rightful claim to the epithet of "masterly," is assuredly a most interesting and bewitching work, and has we fear proved too attractive to many, as indeed it must to all whose faith is not firmly fixed upon the revealed word of God. "I cannot doubt," says Mr. Darwin, "that the theory of descent with modification embraces all the members of the same class. I believe that animals have descended from at most only four or five progenitors, and plants from an equal or lesser number. Analogy would lead me one step further, namely, to the belief that *all animals and plants have descended from some one prototype.* But analogy may be a deceitful guide. Nevertheless all living things have much in common, in their chemical composition, their germinal vesicles, their cellular structure, and their laws of growth and reproduction. Therefore, I should infer from analogy that probably *all the organic beings which have ever lived on this earth have descended from some one primordial form into which life was first breathed by the Creator.*" It is singular to observe the different phases which modern rationalism has undergone. If at one time it assumes that mankind, with all animal and vegetable life, have sprung from "some one primordial form;" at another time it declares that Adam could not have been the parent of the whole human race [1], but that there must have been a multitude of others simultaneously created with him. In short, man's unsanctified intellect prefers the most unreasonable fancy to believing the simple statements of the word of God. The development theory, whether propounded by Darwin, Lamarck, or the author of the "*Vestiges*," which has been quaintly described as a "scheme of creation by which the immediate ancestor of Adam was a chimpanzee, and his remote ancestor a maggot," has been ably exposed by Hugh Miller. He supposes the descendants of the *ourang-outang* employed in some future age writing treatises on geology, and describing the remains of the *quadrumana* as belonging to an extinct order: he pictures Lamarck bearing home in triumph the skeleton of some huge salamander of the Lias, and indulging in the pleasing belief that he possessed the bones of his grandfather, removed of course by many generations; while he justly adds, "Never yet was there a fancy so wild and extravagant but there have been men bold enough to dignify it with the name of philosophy, and ingenious enough to find reasons for the propriety of the name." [2] Mr. Darwin accounts for this marvellous transformation of all animal and vegetable life [3], upon the principle of "*natural selection*." He says, "I will give two or three instances of diversified and of changed habits in the individuals of the same species. When either case occurs, it would be easy for *natural selection* to fit the animal, by some mo-

---

[1] See Essays and Reviews, p. 349. "It is possible, and may one day be known, that mankind spread not from one, but from many centres over the globe."—*Professor Jowett.*
[2] The Old Red Sandstone, ch. iii.
[3] Darwin on the Origin of Species, p. 484.

dification of its structure, for its changed habits, or exclusively for one of its several different habits. . . . In North America the black bear was seen by Hearne swimming for hours with widely open mouth, thus catching, *almost like a whale,* insects in the water" (pp. 183, 184); *ergo,* the black bear and the whale are alike sprung from the same primeval fungus!

Mr. Darwin is not deterred by the natural objection to his extraordinary hypothesis, but admits them with the utmost candour, and dismisses them with charming self-complacency. "It has been asked," he observes, "by the opponents of such views as I hold, how, for instance, a land carnivorous animal could have been converted into one with aquatic habits; for how could the animal in its traditional state have subsisted? It would be easy to show that within the same group carnivorous animals exist, having every intermediate grade between truly aquatic and strictly terrestrial habits, and as each exists by a struggle for life, it is clear that each is well adapted in its habits to its place in nature. . . . If a different case had been taken, and it had been asked how an insectivorous quadruped could possibly have been converted into a flying bat, the question would have been far more difficult, and *I could have given no answer. Yet I think such difficulties have very little weight"* (pp. 179, 180). He adds, "To suppose that the eye, with all its inimitable contrivances for adjusting the focus to different distances, for admitting different amounts of light, and for the correction of spherical and chromatic aberration, could have been formed by *natural selections,* seems, I freely confess, *absurd in the highest possible degree"* (p. 186); and he admits, if it could be demonstrated that any complex organ existed, "which could not possibly have been formed by numerous, successive slight modifications, *my theory would absolutely break down"* (p. 189), though he had previously declared that "he who will go thus far, ought not to hesitate to go farther, and to admit that a structure even as perfect as the eye of an eagle might be formed by *natural selection*, although in this case he does not know any of the transitional grades. His reason ought to conquer his imagination, though I have felt the difficulty far too keenly to be surprised at any degree of hesitation *in extending the principle of natural selection to such startling lengths*" (p. 188).

Startling, indeed, is this theory, so gravely put forth by a man of science, and commended by a professed minister of the Church of Christ, to hear that "natural selection" has the power of producing the highest type of animal life from the lowest type of vegetable life—of converting a mushroom into a man! In order to be consistent in his opposition to the Mosaic record, where the work of creation is said to have been completed in "six days," whatever length of time those "days" may mean, Mr. Darwin advocates another theory, viz. of a countless period of ages, previous to the earliest fossils, and of which there are no remains, or rather none yet discovered, owing, as he expresses it, to "the imperfection of the geological record," to enable *natural selection* slowly to perform her work of changing a fungus into a whale, or an ammonite into an oak. "If my theory be true," he carefully states, "it is indisputable that, before the lowest Silurian stratum was deposited, long periods elapsed, as long as, or probably far longer than, the whole interval from the Silurian age to the present day; and that *during these vast, yet quite unknown periods of time, the world swarmed with living creatures*" (p. 307). He, however, candidly asks, "On this doctrine of the extermination of an infinitude of connecting links between the living and extinct inhabitants of the world, and at each successive period between the living and extinct inhabitants of the world, and at each successive period between the extinct and still older species, why is not every geological formation charged with such links? Why does not every collection of fossil remains afford plain evidence of the gradation and mutation of the forms of life? *We meet with no such evidence, and this is the most obvious and forcible of the many objections which may be urged against my theory.* Why, again, do whole groups of allied species appear, though certainly they often falsely appear, to have come in suddenly on the several geological stages? Why do we not find great piles of strata beneath the Silurian system, stored with the remains of the progenitors of the silurian groups of fossils? For certainly, on my theory, such strata must somewhere have been deposited, at these ancient and *utterly unknown epochs* in the world's history" (pp. 463, 464). If common sense forbids our belief in Mr. Darwin's not original theory of man being formed by the process of "natural selection" from the primeval fungus (though even that must have had a progenitor, which he has omitted to notice), no less strongly does the well-established science of geology condemn his hypothesis of the "utterly unknown epochs" between the igneous or non-fossiliferous rocks and the Silurian system. He asserts it because his " startling theory " requires it ; and if you ask for proof, he is obliged to decline the reasonable challenge, simply because there is none to show. It is well known that the crust of the earth has been sufficiently searched, and the *order* of the different strata, whether with or without fossil remains, has been found to be invariably the same in all parts of the globe, which prevents our reception of the most visionary and improbable idea that has ever entered the mind of man. We have termed Mr. Darwin's theory " not original," because a similar fancy seems to have been broached by Professor Lorenz Oken, A.D. 1810, and likewise by an ancestor of his own,—we believe his grandfather,—about the same time. "Physicophilosophy," said the former, "has to portray the first period of the world's development out of nothing; how the elements and heavenly bodies originated; in what method, by *self-evolution* into higher and manifold forms, they separated into minerals, became finally organic, and, in man, attained to self-consciousness. There are two kinds of generation in the world — the creation proper, and the propagation that is consequent thereupon; consequently, no organism has been created of larger size than an *infusorial point*. No organism is, nor ever has one been, created, which is not microscopic. Whatever is larger, has not been created, but developed. *Man has not been created*, but developed." The latter wrote : " I am acquainted with a philosopher who thinks it not impossible that the first insects were the anthers or stigmas of flowers, which had, *by some means*, loosed themselves from their parent plant; and that *many other insects have gradually, in long process of time, been formed from these;* some acquiring wings, others fins, and others claws, from their ceaseless efforts to procure their food, or to secure themselves from injury."[1]

Before the days of Oken and the elder Darwin, Monsieur Maillet, an ingenious Frenchman of the time of Louis XV., supposed that the whole family of birds had existed at one time as fishes, which, on being thrown ashore by the waves, had got feathers by accident; and that mankind are the descendants of a tribe of seamonsters, who, getting tired of their proper element, crawled up the beach one fine morning, and, taking a fancy to the land, forgot to return. Two centuries ago, a writer named Gerard propounded a theory, somewhat

---

[1] Dr. Darwin's Botanic Garden, Add. Note xxxix.

analogous to the one above, that the bernicle-goose (*Bernicla leucopsis*) was produced from the *ship-barnacle;* and in order to prove his theory, he gives drawings of the different specimens in all their stages, from the mollusc to the bird. His account of this wonderful transition is as follows : — " What our eyes have seen, and hands have touched, we shall declare. There is a small island off Lancashire, called the Pile of Foulders, wherein are found the broken pieces of old and bruised ships, some whereof have been cast thither by shipwracke ; and also the trunks and bodies, with the branches, of old and rotten trees, cast up there likewise ; wherein is found a certain spume or froth, that in time breedeth into certaine shels, in shape like those of the muskle, but sharper pointed, and of a whitish colour ; one end whereof is fastened into the inside of the shell, even as the fish of oisters and muskles,— the other end is made fast into the belly of a rude masse or lumpe, *which in time commeth to the shape and form of a bird:* when it is perfectly formed the shell gapeth open, and the first thing that appeareth is the aforesaid lace or string ; next come the legs of the bird hanging out, and as it groweth greater it openeth the shell by degrees, till at length it is all come forth, and hangeth only by the bill : *in short space after it commeth to full maturitie, and falleth into the sea, where it gathereth feathers, and groweth to a fowle.*"

The most distinguished propounder, however, of the Darwinian theory, we take to be an author towards the close of the last century, more distinguished, perhaps, in the region of politics than of science, and who has thus broadly, yet with refined irony, placed the case fairly before us. " We may conceive," he says, " the whole of our present universe to have been originally concentred in a single point ; we may conceive this primeval point, or *punctum saliens* of the universe, evolving itself by its own energies, to have moved forward in a right line, *ad infinitum*, till it grew tired; after which, the right line which it had generated would begin to put itself in motion in a lateral direction, describing an area of infinite extent. This area, as soon as it became conscious of its own existence, would begin to ascend or descend, according as its specific gravity would determine it, forming an immense solid space, filled with vacuum, and capable of containing the present universe. Space being thus obtained, and presenting a suitable nidus or receptacle for the accumulation of chaotic matter, an immense deposit of it would be gradually accumulated; after which, the filament of *fire* being produced in the chaotic mass by an *idiosyncrasy*, or self-formed habit, analogous to fermentation, *explosion* would take place, *suns* would be shot from the central chaos, *planets* from *suns*, and *satellites* from *planets*. In this state of things, the filament of organisation would begin to exert itself in those independent masses which, in proportion to their bulk, exposed the greatest surface to light and heat. This filament, *after an infinite series* of ages, would begin to *ramify;* and its oviparous offspring would diversify their former habits, so as to accommodate themselves to the various *incunabula* which Nature had prepared for them. Upon this view of things, it seems highly probable that the first efforts of nature terminated in the production of vegetables; and that these, being abandoned to their own energies, by degrees detached themselves from the surface of the earth, and supplied themselves with wings and feet, according as their different propensities determined them in favour of aërial and terrestrial existence; and thus, by an inherent disposition to society and civilisation, and by a stronger effort of volition, became men. These, in time, would restrict themselves to the use of their *hind-*

feet; and their *tails* would gradually rub off, by sitting in their caves and huts, as soon as they arrived at a domesticated state. They would invent *language,* and the use of *fire,* with our present and hitherto imperfect system of *society.* In the meanwhile the *fuci* and *algæ,* with the *corallines* and *madrepores,* would transform themselves into fish, and would gradually populate all the submarine portion of the globe."[1]

We are inclined to imagine that this amusing theory, however opposed it is to *Revelation* and *Science* alike, is a mere *réchauffé* of the ancient doctrine of Metempsychosis, so fully described by Ovid, who quotes a fanatical hierophant detailing the process of his manifold regeneration through various stages of animal and vegetable life. "*A second time was I formed. I have been a blue salmon; a dog; a stag; a roebuck on the mountain; a stock of a tree; a spade; an axe in the hand; a pin in a forceps, for a year and a half; a cock, variegated with white; a horse; a buck, of yellow hue, in the act of feeding. I have been a grain vegetating on a hill, when the reaper placed me in a smoky recess, that I might be compelled freely to yield my corn, when subject to tribulation. I was received by a hen, with red fangs, and remained nine nights an infant in her womb. I have been in Hades, returning to my former state. I have been an offering before the sovereign. I have died. I have revived; and, conspicuous with my ivy-branch, I have been a leader, and by my bounty I became poor.*" Such were the speculations of the heathen of old on the subject of the soul's transmigration, and they appear to have found faithful imitators in the modern Darwinites.

Professor Powell has endeavoured to support this incredible theory of the two Darwins, which *seriously*

---

[1] Poetry of the Anti-Jacobin, p. 128.

attempts to make man and a turnip[1] alike originate from some " one primordial form," by the introduction of the name of Owen, whose authority will be so readily acknowledged by all lovers of scientific truth. Let us, therefore, consider what his opinion really is on the subject at issue. " If," says Professor Owen in the appendix to his Lecture delivered before the University of Cambridge, " the consideration of the cranial and dental characters of the *Troglodytes gorilla* has led legitimately to the conclusion that it is specifically distinct from the *Troglodytes niger*, the hiatus is *still greater that divides it from the human species*, between the extremest varieties of which there is no osteological and dental distinction which can be compared to that manifested by the shorter premaxillaries and larger incisors of the *Troglodytes niger* as compared with the *Troglodytes gorilla*. . . . The unity of the human species is demonstrated by the constancy of those osteological and dental characters to which the attention is more particularly directed in the investigation of the corresponding characters in the higher *Quadrumana*. Man is the sole species of his genus[2], the sole representative of his order and sub-class. *Thus I trust has been furnished the confutation of the notion of a transformation of the ape into man*[3], *which appears from a favourite*

---

[1] This theory reminds us of the witty lines —
  " If a man who '*turnips*' cries,
    Cry not when his father dies,
    'Tis a proof that he would rather
    Have a *turnip* for his father! "

[2] Similar is the testimony of another distinguished anatomist, who cannot be suspected of prejudice with regard to this subject. " The *human species*, like that of the cow, sheep, horse, and pig, and others, is SINGLE; and all the differences which it exhibits, are to be regarded *merely as varieties*." — *Lawrence on Comparative Anatomy*, p. 376.

[3] An allusion to the theory propounded by Lord Monboddo, whom Dr. Johnson described to Mrs. Thrale as " a Scotch judge, who has

old author to have been entertained by some in his day:— 'And of a truth, vile epicurism and sensuality will make the soul of man so degenerate and blind, that he will not only be content to slide into brutish immorality, but *please himself in this very opinion that he is a real brute already*, an ape, satyre, or baboon; and that the best of men are no better, saving that civilising of them and industrious education has made them appear in a more refined shape, and long inculcated precepts have been mistaken for connate principles of honesty and natural knowledge; otherwise there be no indispensable grounds of religion and virtue, but what has happened to be taken up by *over-ruling* custom. Which things, I dare say, are as easily confutable as any conclusion in mathematics is demonstrable. *But as many as are thus sottish, let them enjoy their own wildness and ignorance;* it is sufficient for a good man that he is conscious unto himself that he is more nobly descended, better bred and born, and more skilfully taught by the purged faculties of his own minde.'"[1] Again, the same "acknowledged authority" observes, "As to the successions, or coming in, of new species, one might speculate on the gradual modifiability of the individual; on the tendency of certain varieties to survive local changes, and thus progressively diverge from an older type; on the production and fertility of monstrous offspring; on the possibility, e. g. of a variety of the auk being occasionally hatched with a somewhat longer winglet, and a dwarfed stature;—but to what purpose? *Past experience of the chance aims of human fancy, unchecked and unguided by observed facts, shows*

---

lately written a strange book about the origin of language, in which he traces *monkeys up to men*, and says that *in some countries the human species have tails like other beasts.*"—*Boswell*, vol. iv. p. 73, note.

[1] Owen on the Classification and Geographical Distribution of the Mammalia, pp. 102, 103.

how widely they have ever glanced away from the golden centre of truth. . . . Our most soaring speculations still show a kinship to our nature. We see the element of finality in so much that we have cognisance of, that it must needs mingle with our thoughts, and bias our conclusions on many things. The end of the world has been presented to man's mind under divers aspects; as a general conflagration; as the same, preceded by a millennial exaltation of the world to a paradisiacal state — the abode of a higher and blessed race of intelligences. If the guide-post of palæontology may seem to point to a course ascending to the condition of the latter speculation, it points but a very short way, and in leaving it we find ourselves in a wilderness of conjecture, where to try to advance is to find ourselves 'in wandering mazes lost.'"[1]

We give the mature testimony of another "acknowledged authority" on this subject. "The entire variation from the original type, which any given kind of change can produce, may usually be effected in a brief period of time," says Sir Charles Lyell; "*after which no further deviation can be obtained* by continuing to alter the circumstances, though ever so gradually; indefinite divergence, either in the way of improvement or deterioration, being prevented, and the least possible excess beyond the defined limits being fatal to the individual."[2]

And we add the testimony of one, who, if not so "acknowledged" an "authority" as those we have already quoted, since he dedicates his work to Mr. Darwin himself, can be no unfriendly critic of the subject in question. "It does appear strange," observes Mr. Woolaston, "that naturalists who have combined great synthetic

---

[1] Owen on the Classification and Geographical Distribution of the Mammalia, pp. 58, 61.
[2] Principles of Geology, ch. xxxvi. p. 61, 9th ed.

qualities with a profound knowledge of minutiæ and detail, should ever have upheld *so monstrous a doctrine as that of the transmutation of one species into another*, a doctrine, however, which arises almost spontaneously, if we are to assume that there exists in every race the tendency to unlimited progressive improvement. . . . *The whole theory is full of inconsistencies from beginning to end;* and, from whatever point we view it, is equally unsound from beginning to end." [1]

Thus the "natural selection" theory of Darwin, on which the Essayist fondly relies for overthrowing the plain statements of Scripture respecting " the Origin of Species," is denied and rejected as unworthy of consideration by those "acknowledged masters" of the subject from whose works we have quoted in preference to any mere assertion of our own. At the same time, we cannot forbear remarking upon the boundless credulity which the disciples of the rationalistic school in general, and Professor Powell in particular, display when any theory, however wild and unfounded it be, is propounded by a human creature like Darwin, or Lamarck, or the author of the " Vestiges of a Natural History," compared with the " painful scepticism" they exhibit towards those rational statements which claim to be made on the authority of the Creator Himself.

We would, however, fain hope, as we catch a glimmer of light towards the close of the Essay which we have thus examined, that better feelings actuated the late Professor Baden Powell before being summoned to that bourne whence there is no return; and that " the spirit of faith," which we rejoice to find him saying " discovers continually increasing attestation of the Divine authority of the truths they include" (p. 144), may have had its

---

[1] Op. Cit. pp. 186–8.

due effect upon his own soul previous to that unseen future when faith and hope shall cease, as being no longer required, or rather as being absorbed in that boundless love, which, as being "the greatest," or most lasting, will abide for evermore.

MOSAIC COSMOGONY.

CHAP. IV.

We now arrive at a break, or, as the geologists would term it, "a fault," in the series of Clerical Essayists. Mr. Goodwin, the author of the "Mosaic Cosmogony," being a layman, is necessarily less open to the same amount of censure to which his brother Essayists have been exposed, the public naturally and very properly making a distinction between those who may be described as lawfully exercising the right of free warren in their Biblical investigations, and others who are bound not only by their profession in general, but by their obligations as clergymen of the Church of England in particular, to stand up in defence of the inspiration, the perfection, and the scientific accuracy of God's word as revealed to man.

Nevertheless, Mr. Goodwin, without propounding any peculiar theory of his own, has contented himself with the part of a true Ishmaelite in raising his hand not only against "the Mosaic Cosmogony," as set forth in the two first chapters of Genesis, but against the most eminent geologists, who have endeavoured to show the harmony which exists between the statements in Scripture and the discoveries of modern science. It would have been a happy thing for the author of the Essay before us if he had only attained to the reasonable decision of the

German philosopher Fichte, when he returned this answer to the question which he himself propounded: — "Who educated the first human pair? A spirit took them under his care, as is laid down in an ancient, venerable, original document, *which contains the deepest and the sublimest wisdom, and presents results to which all philosophy must at length return.*"[1] Why this frank admission on the part of one distinguished for his rationalism? Simply because, in reference to the subject before us, scientific truth, rightly understood, is in reality religious truth. Ought we not therefore to echo the sentiment of that great writer, who, without possessing a revelation from God on high, could yet declare? — "Than Truth, no greater blessing can man receive, or the gods bestow."[2]

Hence, as one more eminent than Plutarch has well observed in later times, "Truth is compared in Scripture to a streaming fountain; if her waters flow not in a *perpetual progression*, they sicken into a muddy pool of conformity and tradition."[3] Nothing can be more convincing as regards the force of this remark of our great poet than by contrasting the wonderful advance in every department of science during the last three centuries, with that "muddy pool of conformity and tradition," which existed and flourished when Galileo was condemned by the gross ignorance of the Church of Rome for asserting what is now recognised as one of the elements of astronomical science, though still (if rumour does

---

[1] Quoted by Dr. Dereser of Breslaw in his translation of the Bible, with annotations by himself and others, vol. i. p. 16. John Gottlieb Fichte died A.D. 1814, and there is good reason to believe that several years before his death he renounced the sceptical opinions for which he had been once unhappily famous.
[2] Plutarch, De Iside et Osiride, § 1.
[3] Milton's Areopagitica.

not belie him) consistently denied by the present papal representative in the sister kingdom of Ireland.[1]

Mr. Goodwin, eschewing all notice of the eighty futile attempts by the members of the French Institute, and to which we have already called attention [2], to find a system in accordance with their preconceived notions, all hostile to the Mosaic record, makes the following candid statement:—"It must be observed that in reality two distinct accounts are given us in the book of Genesis, one being comprised in the first chapter and the first three verses of the second, the other commencing at the fourth verse of the second chapter and continuing till the end. *This is so philologically certain that it were useless to ignore it.* But even those who may be inclined to contest the fact that we have here *the productions of two different writers*, will admit that the account beginning at the first verse of the first chapter, and ending at the third verse of the second, is a complete whole in itself. And to this narrative, in order not to complicate the subject unnecessarily, we intend to confine ourselves. It will be sufficient for our purpose to inquire, whether this account can be shown to be in accordance with our astronomical and geological knowledge." [3]

Here are three statements or deductions. We question the first, deny the second, and propose to examine the third. We cannot accept his proposed division in the first two chapters of Genesis, as our future remarks will show, nor can we admit that there are " two *distinct* accounts "

---

[1] "A living ecclesiastic," says Hugh Miller, " of the Romish Church in Ireland, Father (now Archbishop) Cullen, holds that the sun is possibly only a fathom in diameter." — *Testimony of the Rocks*, p. 381.

[2] See p. 198.

[3] Essays and Reviews, p. 217.

of the act of the demiurgic creation as recorded by Moses. We not only "contest the fact" of its being the production of "two different writers," but we may remark that the Essayist has, with the usual caution of sceptics, abstained from advancing the slightest ground for this preposterous dogma, which nobody with the slightest pretensions to Biblical criticism will admit for a moment. He might with equal reason dogmatically affirm that the first and second books of Paradise Lost were not written by Milton, as put forth this unfounded and unsupported theory of "the two distinct accounts" of creation in Genesis being "the productions of two different writers." And we readily accept his challenge by endeavouring to show that the one uniform account of creation, as set forth in the first two chapters of Genesis, is, like every other statement in Holy Scripture, in perfect accordance with all real *Science*, as far as astronomical and geological discoveries have extended.

There have been three different modes of interpreting "the Mosaic cosmogony" as set forth in the Bible, which may be thus summarily defined.

First. "The old views," to which, according to Mr. Goodwin, "the Romish Church adheres to the present day" (p. 208), which interpreted the passage "In the beginning God created the heaven and the earth" to mean about 6000 years ago, when all the geological strata, together with the present animal and vegetable life, were first called into existence by the fiat of the great Creator. Voetius a Dutch divine of the seventeenth century defined "the old views" in the following manner: — "We affirm that the sun flies round the earth every twenty-four hours, and that the earth rests immovable in the centre of the universe, with all divines, natural philosophers and astronomers, Jews and Mahomedans, Greeks and Latins, excepting one or two of the ancients, and *the modern followers of Copernicus.*"[1] There is, however, good reason to believe that some of the ancients had a right conception of the face and shape of the earth nearly 2000 years before the time of Copernicus, if we admit the proposed rendering of a passage in Plato's Timæus with Aristotle's comment thereon. For thus the former expressed himself on the subject: " He made the earth to be the nurse of mankind, *and by her rotation* (ιλλομένην) *round the cosmical pole*, the guardian and creator of day and night." And thus the latter comments upon it: " All those who do not make the earth the centre of the system, *make her rotate round the centre;* and some even of those who place her at the centre say she rotates (ἴλλεσθαι) round the cosmical axis, as we read in the Timæus."[2]

Second. The modern opinion, which may be said to have prevailed as scientific discoveries were made, and which, confining the work of creation, as described in the first chapter of Genesis, to six natural days of twenty-four hours' duration, extends the expression "In the beginning," to a period of indescribable length, and sufficiently long to allow for the very slow formation of the various strata in the earth which the *Science* of geology has brought to light.

Third. Another and still newer opinion is that which would account for the enormous time required for the formation of these strata by understanding each of " the six days," to mean periods of *undefined* length.

Let us consider which of these three opinions mostly accords with what Scripture has revealed, and modern science confirmed.

§ 1. It is certainly much to be lamented that well-intentioned but grievously mistaken persons have imagined

---

[1] Gisb. Voetii, Disput. Theol. vol. i. p. 637.
[2] Aristotle, De Cœlo, ii. § 13.

that the science of geology, which, if compared with its elder sister astronomy, may be still described as in its infancy, militates in any degree against the unerring word of God. We admit that geological speculations have done so, as we have before noticed, and may continue so to do; but the *Science* of geology never can, because the correct definition of that term necessarily forbids it. When, however, we find professed ministers of the gospel defending what they honestly believe to be the cause of truth, at the expense of common sense, as well as the plain inference from Scripture, we are compelled to declare such interpretations and explanations of the sacred text do more harm than good to the cause which the advocates of the same are very properly anxious to defend. Take for instance the following:—In the St. Petersburg Museum there is to be seen the skeleton of a mammoth (of so gigantic a size that the skeleton of a large elephant which stands beside it bears the relative proportion to it which a pony thirteen hands high does to a brewer's dray horse), discovered some years ago in a glacier in Siberia, with *the flesh so well preserved* that the wolves and bears were found holding a festival on its carcase. Yet a writer, who terms his work "A brief and complete Refutation of the Anti-Scriptural Theory of Geologists,"[1] has the confidence to argue in defence of his mistaken theory that this "*mammoth had not necessarily been a living creature* (but that) it was *created under the ice*, and preserved in that peculiar form of preservation instead of being transmuted into stone, like the rest of its class."

Or consider the way in which the late Dean of York endeavoured to reconcile the formation of the strata of

---

[1] See a work with that title, "By a Clergyman of the Church of England," London, Wertheim and Mackintosh, 1853.

the carboniferous era at the time of the Deluge, with his theory that all the fossils discovered are not older than the human race, and that the creation of the heavens and the earth commenced 6000 years ago. We state it in the words of that eminent Christian geologist, whose powers of description elicited such warm praise from Dr. Buckland, at the Glasgow meeting of the British Association for the advancement of science. "The Dean," wrote Hugh Miller in his inimitable style, "conceives that at the commencement of the Flood, when torrents of rain were falling upon the land, numerous submarine volcanoes began to disgorge their molten contents into the sea, destroying the fish, and all other marine productions, by the intensity of the heat, and at the same time locking them up in strata formed of the erupted matter. This process took place ere the land-floods, laden with the spoils of island and continent, and the accompanying mud and sand, could arrive at the remoter depths; which however they ultimately reached, and formed a second formation, overlying the first. There were thus two formations originated—a marine formation below, and a terrestrial or fresh-water formation above; but as these two deposits could not be made to include all the geological phenomena with which even the Dean was acquainted, he had nicely to parcel out the work of his volcanoes on the one hand, and that of his land floods on the other, into separate fits or paroxysms, each of which served to entomb a distinct class of creatures, and originate a definite set of rocks. Thus, the first work of his volcanoes was to form the Transition series of strata. As a commencement of the whole, the internal fire blew up from the bed of the ocean, in tremendous explosions, vast quantities of pulverised rock mixed with clay, which, slowly subsiding, and covering up, as it sank, shells, stone-lilies, and trilobites, formed the Silurian rocks. A second explosion brought up the vents of the volcanoes to the level of the ocean; and while the old red sandstone, thus produced and charged with fish killed by the heat, was settled on their flanks, *they themselves, as if seized by black vomit, began to disgorge in vast quantities, coal in the liquid state.* Very opportunely, just ere it cooled, enormous quantities of vegetables, washed out to the sea by the extraordinary land-floods, were precipitated immediately over it; and sticking in its viscid surface, or sinking into its substance through cracks formed in it during the cooling, they became attached to it in such considerable masses, as to lead long after *to the very mistaken notion that coal itself was of vegetable origin.* Then there ensued another deposit of red sand, with salt boiled into it, and then a deposition of lime and clay. The land-floods still continuing, the great sauroid reptiles which had haunted the rivers and lower plains, began to yield to their force, and their carcases, floating out to sea, sank amid the slowly subsiding lime and clay, now known as the Lias. The volcanoes, too, were still very active, and the lighter shells, ammonites, and the like, which had been previously bobbing up and down on the boiling surface, now sank by myriads; for the viscid argillaceous mud thrown up by the fiery ebullitions from beneath stuck fast to them, and dragged them down. Then came the formation of the Oolite, rolled into little egg-like pellets by the waves; and, last of all, the greensand and chalk; after which the waters ran off, and sank into the deep hollow which now forms the bed of the ocean, but which, previous to the cataclysm, had been the place of the land. The Dean, as he went on, fell into some little confusion regarding the true place of some of his animals, such as the megatherium, which arrived in his arrangement a little too soon. He spoke, too,— if a newspaper report is to be credited,— of a heavy creature soon overtaken and drowned by the rising waters, which he termed the *ptero-dactylus*, and which does not seem to have turned up, either in the body or out of it, since it was lost on that memorable occasion. Nor did he make any provision in his arrangement for the formation of the various Tertiary deposits. But then all these are slight matters, that could be very easily woven into his hypothesis. As the flood rose along the hill-sides, first such of the weightier animals would perish as could not readily climb steep acclivities; and then the oxen, the horses, the deer, and the goats, with the lighter carnivora, who, as they would die last,— some of them not until the final disappearance of the hill tops,— would of course be entombed in the upper deposits. Such is the hypothesis of the Dean of York — an hypothesis of which it may be justly affirmed, that it is well nigh as ingenious as the circumstances of the case permit, and against which little else can be urged than that it must seem rather cumbrous and fanciful to the class who don't know geology, and, on the whole, somewhat inadequate to the class who do." [1]

Had these worthy clergymen, and those who agree with them in supposing that the heavens and the earth, with all its fossil remains, have been called into being within the last 6000 years, paid a very moderate amount of attention to what Scripture teaches on this point, they would have escaped the exposure to which they have fairly laid themselves open, on the part of one who was pre-eminently competent to discover the accordance between *Revelation* and *Science*, as the writings of the late Hugh Miller manifestly prove. When we remembered that the Holy Spirit has used the same term, "In the

---

[1] The Testimony of the Rocks; or Geology in its Bearings on the Two Theologies, Natural and Revealed, pp. 391—397.

beginning," to define the time when God called the heavens and the earth into existence, and also the period of the begetting of the Eternal Son[1], we see at once the impossibility of accepting the theory which limits the stupendous work of creation to the time when man was originally formed. Why should those excellent Christians, who do not doubt for an instant the fact of the great Creator having existed *from all eternity*,—why should they reject, as preposterous, the idea of going back millions of years in the history of his works? It will be sufficient, however, at present, to bear in mind that those who contend in favour of the heavens and the earth having been called into existence about 6000 years ago, are contradicting the express testimony of Scripture.

§ 2. "Geology," said Sir John Herschel, "in the magnitude and sublimity of the objects which it treats, undoubtedly ranks, in the scale of the sciences, next to astronomy." When this *Science* had attained such an interesting position, which it may be considered to have done at the beginning of the present century, it was natural that the interpretation of Genesis i. 1, for dating the creation of the heavens and the earth *within* 6000 years, was given up by every scientific investigator of the works, as well as of the word of God. At the same time, such eminent men as Chalmers and Buckland, who combined the study of geology with the deepest respect for the *Revelation* which God had given to man, were satisfied with understanding that passage of Scripture to express the undefinable period during which all the geological strata were formed; but the six days of the demi-urgic creation were to be understood as natural days of twenty-four hours each,— comprising the entire work

---

[1] Compare the language of the Psalmist, ii. 7, and of Isaiah, xliii. 13, with that of St. John, i. 1: "In the beginning was the Word," &c.

of creation, as regards the present animal and vegetable life, — and that the latest of the geologic ages was separated by a great chaotic gap from our own. This was what Hugh Miller once accepted as a satisfactory solution of a confessedly difficult subject. He subsequently rejected it on mere geological grounds. But as we are chiefly concerned with its theological bearings, it will be sufficient, for the present, to remark that the limitation of the word "day," as used in the first chapter of Genesis, to a period of twenty-four hours, must be rejected, for both positive and negative reasons. Reserving the former for future notice, we may safely assume, respecting the latter, that since a day of twenty-four hours is a mere definition of limited time to express one revolution of the earth on its axis, during which it receives and loses the benefit of that "greater luminary," which God appointed "to rule the day," and which did not take place until what is termed "the fourth day" of creation, we have no Scripture warrant for assuming that the three previous "days" to that arrangement, on the part of the Almighty Creator, are to be understood in the same limited sense as that which the word now bears.

§ 3. Hugh Miller, dissatisfied with the above interpretation of limiting the days of creation to twenty-four hours each, adopted the theory of considering them to represent periods of *undefined* length, during which the whole of the present geological strata, with their fossil remains, were formed. This has been thus stated and answered by Dr. Buckland: "A third opinion has been suggested, both by learned theologians and geologists, and on grounds independent of one another, viz. that the days of the Mosaic creation need not be understood to imply the same length of time which is now occupied by a single revolution of the globe, but successive periods, each of great extent; and it has been asserted that the order of succession of the organic remains of a former world accords with the order of creation recorded in Genesis. This assertion, though to a certain degree apparently correct, *is not entirely supported by geological facts*, since it appears that the most ancient marine animals occur in the same division of the lowest transition strata with the earliest remains of vegetables; so that the evidence of organic remains, as far as it goes, *shows the origin of plants and animals to have been contemporaneous:* if any creation of vegetables preceded that of animals, no evidence of such an event has yet been discovered by the researches of geology. Still there is, I believe, no sound critical or theological objection to the interpretation of the word 'day' as meaning a long period; but there will be no necessity for such extension, in order to reconcile the text of Genesis with physical appearances, if it can be shown that the time indicated by the phenomena of geology may be found in the undefined interval following the announcement of the first verse."[1]

Agreeing with Dr. Buckland that there is "no sound critical or theological objection to the interpretation of the word 'day' as meaning a long period," though differing from Hugh Miller as to its being of *undefined* length, we shall endeavour to show, by a minute examination of what is said in the first chapter of Genesis on the subject, that the literal statements of Scripture are in such exact and perfect agreement with the discoveries of modern science that we may fairly point to their accordance as one of the strongest proofs of the Pentateuch being, as it professes to be, the inspired word of God. This, of course, is in direct antagonism to the opinions of Mr. Goodwin, who considers "the Mosaic account to be simply the speculation of some early Copernicus or

---

[1] Bridgewater Treatise, vol. i. pp. 17, 18.

Newton, who devised a scheme of the earth's formation, *as nearly as he might in accordance with his own observations of nature, and with such views of things as it was possible for an unassisted thinker in those days to take*"[1]

Genesis i. 1.—"In the beginning God created the heavens and the earth," is the first utterance of the Divine mind, according to the rendering of our admirable authorised version. Were there no more in this sentence than what is conveyed by the English translation, we admit the case would not appear as strong as it really is, when we refer to the original. Nevertheless, as we have already remarked, the very expression, "In the beginning," used here and by St. John, to define the period when " the Word was," is sufficient proof that it must have reference to what we vainly attempt to describe as the commencement of eternity, and can have nothing to do with any limit of time, according to the feeble and imperfect standard of man. The Hebrew, however, shows this still plainer. According to the celebrated French philologist D'Olivet, the root of the word translated, "In the beginning," consists of the two letters א and ש,—the former signifying " a principle " or " centre," and the latter, when coupled with it, meaning, " a portion of a circle with a radius." So that the word may be understood to refer to "a power emanating from a centre;" and the more sublime and exact rendering would be, " In his principiating energy." *Blessing* might also be understood or implied in the term, in which case the recondite meaning of this first sentence of the Mosaic cosmogony would run, " In the principle of his blessing and energy," &c. The Hebrew word for " God " being in the plural number, followed by a verb in the singular, is a clear indication of

---

[1] Essays and Reviews, p. 217.

the Trinity in Unity[1] being referred to, as every Jew, when "the veil is removed from his heart in reading Moses,"[2] is only too ready to admit. The verb "created" means original formation, and is distinct from another verb used in the same chapter, which signifies reformed, or "made," as our translators have properly rendered it. The expression, "the heavens and the earth," falls very short of the full force of the Hebrew original. Literally it would be, "the *essence* of the heavens and the *essence* of the earth." Alexander, an Hebrew professor, in commenting on the verse, observes, "את[3], according to the Jewish commentators, is always an implication; here it is a tacit inference of all the hosts of heaven; and in every other place it *implies something more than is expressed.*" The omission of so important a word in our version has prevented the English reader from realising the full force of the original, and has helped, as we believe, to preserve the delusion under which some men in the present day are labouring, in supposing the original creation of the heavens and the earth took place about 6000 years ago. Keeping, therefore, to the letter as well as to the spirit of Scripture, we may paraphrase the first two verses of

---

[1] It is remarkable that the chief heathen cosmogonies, whether Hindoo, Chinese, Pythagorean, Orphic, or Platonic, so far as regards the Being who was considered as the animating Soul and demiurgic Principle of the Universe, seem to be contained in the words of the oracle which Patricius cites from Damascius:—"*Through the whole world shines a triad, over which presides a monad.*" — *Damas. apud Cudworth, Intell. Syst.*

[2] 2 Cor. iii. 15.

[3] Buxtorf, in his Talmudic Lexicon, says, "The particle את, with the Cabalists is often mystically put for *the beginning and the end*, as Alpha and Omega are in the Apocalypse." The Syriac version has *yoth*, which signifies essence, or substance, and is very properly translated in Walton's Polyglott, "Esse cœli et esse terræ."

Genesis as follows:—" In the very commencement of His work, manifesting power and blessing (when the Logos was), Elohim, i. e. the Trinity, or the three Persons united in Godhead, originally created the essence of the heavens and the essence of the earth. Afterwards the earth became waste and desolate, when chaos existed upon the surface of the deep. And the Spirit of Elohim brooded upon the surface of the waters." It will be seen that the rendering of verse 2 is somewhat different from our English version, which reads the passage, "And the earth was without form and void," as if the two verses were in immediate connection, as regards time; whereas we believe the first verse clearly points to the original creation of the universe, and the second refers to the period when God thought fit to prepare the earth for the habitation of man. The translation we have adopted has the sanction of Dr. Dathe of Leipzig, a cautious and judicious critic, does no violence to the Hebrew idiom, and is the only way of reconciling Scripture with the discoveries of geology.

Let us hear what *Science* teaches us respecting the *essence* of the heavens and of the earth, which God called into existence at the commencement of the manifestation of his creative power. We learn that our solar system consists of three differently-constituted parts, viz. the sun; the planets, with their respective satellites; and comets. And we have proof that those beautiful stars, with which the heavens are bespangled on every side, and which appear to us with such different degrees of lustre, are bodies possessing inherent light, and therefore have been appropriately termed suns to other systems,— each one having, as we may infer from analogy, its attendant train of primaries, and their satellites. Of the constitution of comets, it is not necessary to say much. We know but little of them, but, happily, sufficient to correct the vulgar prejudice in former times[1] respecting their evil effects, as well as the mistaken idea concerning the possibility of the earth being annihilated, upon coming into contact with one of them. There is a case on record in which a comet is believed to have passed among the satellites of Jupiter without affecting them in the slightest degree, although the comet itself, by the attraction of the planet, was so strongly affected that its orbit was completely changed. And it has been assumed that our earth might pass safely through the nucleus of a comet without being affected any more than London by a November fog. As all the works of God have their respective uses, we may accept the theory of Sir Isaac Newton, in regard to comets. "As the seas are necessary," he observes, "to the constitution of our earth, in order that the sun, by his heat, may exhale from them a sufficient quantity of vapour, which, being collected in clouds, may descend in rains and water, and nourish all the earth, for the production of vegetables ; or being condensed by the cold summits of mountains, may run down in springs and

---

[1] As late as the present century we find a writer in the "Gentleman's Magazine," for 1818, gravely ascribing the badness of the harvest, the paucity of wasps, the blindness of the flies, and the frequency of the birth of twins (a woman at Whitechapel that year had four children at a birth ! !), to the influence of the great comet of 1811. That of 1668 was discovered to have produced a remarkable epidemic among cats in Westphalia. The comet of 1456 was thought to presage the terrible success of the Turks, who had recently taken Constantinople and struck terror into the Christian world; and drew down upon, we may suppose, its head and tail alike the thunders of the Church, as Pope Calixtus II. exorcised the Turks and the comet in the same Bull. To the comet of 590 was ascribed a fearful plague which prevailed in that year, in the crisis of which the patients were seized with paroxysms of sneezing, often followed by death. The usual benediction "God bless you!" addressed by the bystanders to the sufferer, is said to have originated a custom which has been continued to the present day.

rivers; so comets seem to be required for the conservation of the seas and fluids of planets, in order that, from their condensed exhalations and vapours, the water consumed in vegetables and putrefaction, and converted into dry earth, may be continually replaced and supplied."

With regard to the constitution of the Sun, our conception of its structure would naturally lead us to suppose it a solid globe of burning material emitting light and heat, just as a red-hot ball of metal invariably displays. There was one person, however, some centuries ago, who appears to have had clearer conceptions of the real nature of the Sun.[1] Humboldt quotes from the writings of Cardinal Nicolaus de Cusa, who lived in the fifteenth century, which show the opinion he entertained of its constitution. He considered that the body of the sun itself was only "*an earth-like nucleus*, surrounded by a circle of light as by a delicate envelope; that between them was a mixture of *water charged clouds*, and clear air similar to our atmosphere; and that the power of radiating heat to vivify the vegetation of our earth, does not appertain to the earthly nucleus of the sun's body, but to the *luminous* covering by which it is surrounded." A wonderful idea this, considering that it was entertained previous to the invention of the telescope, by whose aid these crude thoughts concerning the physical condition of the body of the sun have been amply verified under

---

[1] A trial, which took place in this country towards the close of the last century, affords a curious illustration of the opinions of our fathers regarding the sun. A certain Dr. Elliott maintained, in the year 1787, that the light of the sun arose from what he called a dense and universal twilight, and he also believed that the sun might be inhabited. When tried subsequently at the Old Bailey for having occasioned the death of Miss Boydell, Dr. Simmons, and other friends, successfully contended that he *was mad*, upon the grounds that his theory regarding the light of the sun abundantly proved it!

the searching investigations of Sir W. Herschel and M. Arago. According to the present condition of our astronomical knowledge, the sun is composed, as the latter writes,—"1st. Of a central sphere which is *nearly dark;* 2nd. Of a vast stratum of clouds, suspended from the central body which it surrounds on all sides; 3rd. Of a photosphere, or in other words, a luminous sphere inclosing the cloudy stratum, which in its turn surrounds *the dark nucleus.* The total eclipse of the 8th of July, 1842, afforded indications of a third envelope, situated above the photosphere, and formed of dark, or faintly illuminated clouds. These clouds of the *third* solar envelope, apparently situated during the total eclipse on the margin of the sun, or even a little beyond it, gave rise to those singular rose-coloured protuberances, which so powerfully excited the attention of the scientific world in 1842."

Sir W. Herschel calculated that the light reflected outwards by the clouds of the inferior stratum, was equal to 469 rays out of 1000, or less than half the light of the outward stratum, and that the light reflected by the opaque body of the sun below was only seven rays out of every 1000; a proof that the *light* of the outward stratum, and consequently its *heat*, must be extremely small upon the dark body of the luminary, which we see through what are called the solar spots, but now proved to be openings in the luminous stratum. We may then safely assume that the great luminary which hath been appointed by God to rule the day, is, in a material form, of the same nature as the earth, with the addition of being surrounded by a phosphorescent envelope, and by like reasoning, that the fixed stars, or suns to other systems, are composed in a similar way.

But it is the constitution of the planet we inhabit, with which we are more particularly concerned, and of which we have necessarily more certain knowledge than any other part of creation. Notwithstanding the idea, which was once entertained by Halley in the seventeenth century, and which has been resumed in our own day [1], of the essence, or interior of the earth, consisting of a hollow sphere peopled with plants, animals, and even two small revolving planets, prospectively named Pluto and Proserpine, it is now generally admitted that the vast interior of our planet consists of liquid fire. The experiments made by M. Arago in the gardens of the Observatory at Paris, with thermometers sunk in the earth at various depths, by which it appears that the heat increases on an average of 1° for every 54·5 feet, prove that our globe once existed as an intensely heated body in a fluid state, though the period when it was entirely incandescent must have been so remote as to defy all calculation. In some carefully conducted experiments during the sinking of the Dukingfield Deep Mine — one of the deepest pits in England — it was found that a mean increase of about 1° in seventy-one feet occurred, which would require a depth of between fifty and sixty miles before arriving at fluidity. Mr. Fairbairn, however, pointed out in his inaugural address at the meeting of the British Association in the year 1861, that even "this deduction requires

---

[1] Humboldt amusingly relates in his "Cosmos" (vol. i. p. 163), that the entrance of this tunnel to the earth's interior was supposed to be near the North Pole, whence the polar light emanates, and that he and Sir Humphry Davy were publicly invited by Captain Symmes to conduct an exploring expedition to this *terra incognita*. Holberg, a learned Norwegian of the early part of the last century, published a witty satire in Latin on the institutions, morals, and manners of the inhabitants of the Upper Crust, combining in his title " a new theory of the earth, with his subterranean journey, and a history of the fifth monarchy still unknown." Yet notwithstanding, the theory has been revived, as we have seen, in the enlightened nineteenth century.

to be modified by other considerations, viz. the influence of pressure on the fusing points, and the relative condensity of the rocks which form the earth's crust." So that *Science* does not yet enable us to speak with certainty of the depth of the earth's crust, and consequently we must wait the result of the experiments which are being now carried on by Mr. Hopkins [1], before we have anything like certain data to go upon for estimating the time it took in forming.

Now heat, according to the theory of Bacon and Newton, being derived from the same origin as light, viz. vibrations of the ethereal fluid, propagated through space with inconceivable velocity, we may believe that to be the essence of the heavens and the earth, which the great Creator of all (one of whose chief characteristics is light, as we learn by *Revelation* [2]) called into existence " in the beginning " of the manifestation of His power. In course of countless ages this heat-spot or fiery mist gradually cooled at the surface, probably by exposure in space, contracting in dimensions as it cooled and hardened.[3] By experiments on the rate of cooling lavas and melted basalt, it has been calculated by M. Boné that

---

[1] Sir R. Murchison, in his address to the Geological Section of the British Association, A.D. 1861, stated that Mr. Hopkins considers that the thickness of the earth's crust must be two or three times as great as that which has been usually considered to be indicated by the observed increase of temperature at accessible depths beneath the earth's surface.

[2] 1. Ep. John, i. 5.

[3] As the coal of Baffin's Bay and of the torrid zone alike prove by the fossil forms which they contain, that more than a tropical temperature once existed in the regions of perpetual frost, it can only be explained upon the principle of the *internal* heat of the earth, which during the early ages of the carboniferous era must have had so much thinner a crust than now, and must have received heat from another source than that which God has ordained at this present time.

9,000,000 of years are required for the earth to lose 14° Reaumur, and that the time which must have elapsed in passing from liquid fire to a solid crust, may be estimated at 350,000,000 years. This primary crust, composed of the *plutonic*, or older igneous, and the *volcanic*, or more modern rocks, including granite, serpentine, greenstone, porphyry, basalt, lava, and others, forms the solid framework of our globe, and shows internal marks of having once existed in a state of igneous fusion. Above these are found the metamorphic rocks, such as mica gneiss, mica, hornblende, &c., all alike being destitute of any sign of organic life, and are variously described as Azoic, or Hypozoic, or non-fossiliferous. How long a period elapsed between the first cooling of the fiery fluid, and the first appearance of organised life, we have not the most remote idea, as we have no basis for a calculation; but judging from the previous rate of cooling, according to the estimate already given, as well as from the time required for the formation of certain fossiliferous strata which we shall have occasion hereafter to notice, it must have been a period of enormous duration.

The fossiliferous rocks, with upwards of sixty different strata in various groups, extending from the Cambrian with the first symptom of life, to the Pleistocene, the nearest to the present alluvial surface, have been usefully divided by geologists into three series, consisting of the Palæozoic or Primary, Mesozoic or Secondary, and the Cainozoic or Tertiary. It is not our purpose to examine at any length the different geological strata[1] into which

---

[1] M. D'Orbigny has shown, in his *Prodome de Palæontologie*, that there have been at least twenty-nine distinct periods of animal and vegetable existence. If, however, we count all the different geological strata separately which envelope the earth, we find the whole number amounts to upwards of sixty. There is a curious analogy in com-

these series have been divided; it will be sufficient if we notice, very briefly, the conclusions at which geologists have arrived respecting the time required for the formation of some small portions of the present crust of the earth, which, as we have already remarked, has been estimated at about two hundred miles in depth, of the eight thousand which constitute the diameter of the globe. Thus Mr. Babbage considers it as a truth supported by irresistible evidence, that "the formation even of those strata which are *nearest the surface*, must have occupied vast periods, *probably millions of years*."[1] "The great tract of peat, near Stirling, has demanded two thousand years," observes Mr. Macculloch, "for its registry is preserved by the Roman works below it. It is but a single bed of coal: shall we multiply it by 100? We shall not exceed—far from it—did we allow 200,000 years for the production of the coal series of Newcastle, with all its rocky strata. A Scottish lake does not shoal at the rate of half a foot in a century; and that country presents a vertical depth of far more than 3,000 feet, in the single series of the oldest sandstone. No sound geologist will accuse a computer of exceeding if he allow 600,000 years for the production of this series

---

paring these with the number of heavenly bodies in our solar system, which may be worth noticing, Omitting the secondaries, such as the moons which certain of the larger planets possess, the whole number of the heavenly bodies in the solar system yet discovered, amount to sixty-six or sixty-seven. If we add the different non-fossiliferous rocks to the fifty-nine superincumbent strata, which together form the whole crust of the earth, we have about the same number; from which we might infer a fresh exercise of creative power for every additional coating with which the earth is covered. Scripture seems to allude to these various formations in the expression of the Psalmist, "Thou *renewest* the face of the earth" (Ps. civ. 30); every geological strata being a fresh face of the earth renewed by Almighty Power.

[1] Ninth Bridgewater Treatise, p. 79.

alone. Yet what are the coal deposits, and what are the oldest sandstone, compared to the entire mass of the strata?"[1] Speaking of the Cretaceous group, Hugh Miller says: "All our geologists agree in holding that the chalk was deposited in an ocean of very considerable depth, and of such extent, that it must have covered, for many ages, the greater part of what is now southern and central Europe. . . . What chiefly distinguishes the true chalk from any of its modern representatives is the amazing number of microscopic animals which it contains. On a low estimate half its entire bulk is composed of animalculites of such amazing minuteness, that it has been calculated by Ehrenberg that each cubic inch of chalk may contain upwards of a million of the shells of these creatures. Here is then a new association with which to connect the chalk cliffs of England. Every fragment of these cliffs was once associated with animal life; that impalpable white dust which gives a milky hue to the waves as they dash against them, consists of curiously organised skeletons; even the white line which I draw along the board, were our eyes to be suddenly endowed with a high microscopic power, would resemble part of the wall of a grotto covered over with shells."[2] Even this is exceeded, so far as the size of the animalculæ is concerned, as Fullom, in his "Marvels of Science," after contending justly that these remains, so many fathoms deep, "must have been millions of years accumulating," points to the "Tripoli stone, which is formed of exquisite little shells, so minute and so numberless, that a cube of one-tenth of an inch, is said to contain 500 millions of individuals."

Such is the answer we may give to those who still

---

[1] System of Geology, vol. i. p. 506.
[2] Sketch Book of Popular Geology, pp. 114, 115.

cling to the anti-geological hypothesis of the essence of the heavens and earth having been called into existence only 6000 years ago. If we invoke the aid of *Science*, and point to the impossibility of condensing the actual phenomena of the fossil strata into the space of sixty times 6000 years, we are met, as a writer in the *Christian Observer* (April, 1839, p. 212), has pointed out, in the following way. Having called the attention of an advocate of the anti-geological theory to a lofty inland rock composed of one vast mass of shells, and asked him whether he thought these enormous depositions were to be attributed to the deluge, his reply was to this effect : " How do I know but that in those early days the powers of nature were so prolific, *or rather, that there was so constant a miracle,* that this rock, which would require an enormous period to grow by ordinary accretion, *might be generated in a day; each plant and animal going through all its stages of life and death in the fraction of a moment,* if necessary to produce the effect."[1] The narrator very justly asks, " But why should it be necessary ? Or, what ' effect ' did my friend mean, except the support of a popular interpretation ? I almost believe that, if my friend had been pressed with an argument from Euclid, he would have replied, '*But how do we know that antediluvian circles or angles are like ours.*' "

If any farther proof were required to convince any

---

[1] Dr. Pye Smith in his admirable and comprehensive work entitled, " Geology and Scripture," calls attention to the work of a clergyman, who attempts to account for the possibility of nature effecting in 6000 years, what science, and we may add the Bible, teaches must have taken millions, upon the known instances of accelerated speed, in motion and mechanical operations, *by the steam-engine.* Without stopping to notice the want of analogy in this case, it is curious to observe the shifts to which the anti-geologists are put by their mistaken attempts to divorce *Revelation* and *Science.*

reasonable investigator of the harmony which must exist on this, as on every other subject, between *Revelation* and *Science*, and that "in the beginning," when the essence of the heavens and the earth were created, means more than 6000 years ago, we have a sure one in the known velocity at which light travels. This discovery, which has conferred such a high fame upon Roemer, a Danish astronomer of the 17th century, has supplied us with the means of grasping, in some measure, both the infinity and the antiquity of creation, as it has, by common consent, been adopted as the unit in all computations whose object is to gauge the universe. "The distance of the sun and the stars is ascertained by a yard measure," says Professor Airy[1]; and proceeding from such a simple experiment, *Science* has been enabled to point with unerring accuracy, to the respective distances of not only the earth and all the planets from the sun, but also of our solar system from those fixed stars which are hung on every side around. And since the distance of these latter are so enormous, it has been found convenient to express it by the rate at which light passes from them to us, in preference to attempting to record it in numbers of miles. Thus, e.g. if light, which travels at the astounding speed of 192,000 miles each second of time, passes from the sun to the earth in eight minutes, we are enabled to show that it requires a period of more than three years for its transmission, at the same rate, from the nearest fixed star to our solar system.[2]

---

[1] Lectures on Astronomy, p. 4.
[2] The celebrated Bessel of Königsberg, was the first to discover a parallax for any of the fixed stars; having found it for a small star, the second nearest to our system, known by the name of No. 61 in the constellation Cygnus. The parallax was found to be about $\frac{0}{10}$ of a second, corresponding to a distance of 63,000,000,000,000 miles, and

Sir William Herschel calculated that the time required for the transmission of the stellar light from the grand nebulæ in Orion, which is invisible to the naked eye, amounts to 60,000 years. And Professor Struve has published a table of the time required by stars of different magnitudes for the passage of their respective emissions of light to our sun, commencing with one of the first magnitude, whose distance from our system is 986,000 times the radii of the earth's orbit, requiring 119,700 years for the transit of light, and advancing to one of the ninth magnitude, which is 224,500,000 times the radii of the earth's orbit, and requires a period (so enormous that it cannot be thought of without exciting overwhelming feelings of awe) of 28,257,180 years[1], before the light which has left that distant heavenly body can have reached our comparatively tiny globe.

Thus *Science* affords us unanswerable proof that the first sentence in the Book of *Revelation* declares the high antiquity of this globe we inhabit; and the second sentence, which affirms that the earth subsequently became " waste and desolate," or " without form and void," according to our translation, denotes the chaotic gap previous to the Spirit of Elohim brooding upon the face of the waters, when God began to prepare it for the habitation of man. It is interesting to trace the order and amount of creation through the long series of the geological ages, from the period when the little annelide or sand-boring worm was the sole tenant of this wide earth, until the conclusion of what is termed the ter-

---

requiring a period of more than nine years for the transmission of its light to our earth.

[1] See a report upon the state of astral observation, made to Count Ouvaroff, Minister of Public Instruction and President of the Imperial Academy of Sciences, by Professor F. G. W. Struve, May 19th, 1847, Petersburg.

tiary system, as it will be found how regular is the arithmetical progression of animal life, which has been still preserved for the use of man. Thus in the Eocene, the lowest formation of the tertiary, only 3 per cent. of living species of animals have yet been discovered; in the Meiocene, 25 per cent.; in the Pleiocene, 70 per cent.; and in the Pleistocene, that which comes nearest to our own, no less than 95 per cent. of existing species have been found. If we contrast the number of species in the older fossiliferous strata, which, as Sir Roderick Murchison tells us, " often contain *vast quantities* of organic remains," while " *the number of species* is much smaller than in more recent deposits,"[1] with the present abundant fauna, which include 1000 species of mammalia, 6000 of birds, nearly the same number of fishes, and upwards of 500,000 of other species, such as insects, conchylia, and zoophytes, we see how gradually the great Creator has adapted the earth under its present form for the use and habitation of man. We understand then the first two verses in Genesis to be a very brief record (its brevity compared with other cosmogonies is a testimony to its inspiration and its truth) of all creation, from the beginning of eternity through the countless roll of the geological ages, until, after the last *bouleversement* which our earth has witnessed, God deigned to adapt it to the special use of beings whom He created in the image and likeness of Himself.

Adopting the metaphor of Kazivini, an Arabian writer of the thirteenth century, let us imagine what an inhabitant of some distant world would have seen, had he visited this earth at intervals during the existence of some of the different geological series, which are so succinctly and yet so truly described in the first

---

[1] Silurian System, p. 583.

two verses of the Bible, " Countless ages before man was created," he might be supposed to say, " I visited these regions of the earth, and beheld an interminable ocean of granite, seething and glowing like molten ore, in every cleft and volcano ; and the raging flood beneath heaves and falls, and the waters which have fallen from the mists hiss over the awful scene, while the Great Creator is laying the foundations of the earth in the shape of the igneous rocks ; and signs of life there were none. And after many ages had rolled away I again visited the earth, and saw the first signs of organic life—the seas swarming with species of zoophytes, radiata, molluscs, annelides, and crustacea, amongst which was seen the three-lobed trilobite, with its beautifully jointed shells (admirable contrivances for combining simultaneous protection with freedom of movement), a possible emblem of that Triune Creator who had called them all into being. And after the lapse of many ages, I found the earth teeming with the most luxurious vegetation, such as is now unequalled in the jungles of our tropical countries,—ferns, reeds, and club mosses nearly fifty feet in length and upwards of four in diameter. And when I again visited the same place I found it tenanted by monsters of the reptile tribe, the ichthyosaurus, the megalosaurus, and the iguanodon, combining the bulk of an elephant with the shape of an alligator (whose length has been variously estimated from forty to seventy feet), so gigantic that nothing of the present race can compare with them, basking on the banks of its rivers and roaming through its forests ; while through the tree-fern groves flitted a huge, flying lizard (pterodactyl), like a monster bat with wings stretching upwards of twenty-seven feet across, and its capacious jaws furnished with full sixty teeth, like those of a crocodile. And thousands of years rolled by, and when I returned I beheld animals of colossal magnitude, but of a totally different shape from what I had before seen, herds of deer of enormous size, elephants twice as large as those in the present day, the megatherium, and the dinotherium, the tapir, and the mastodon, whose teeth were of 20lbs. weight, and which in size attained a length of upwards of twenty-five feet. And another epoch passed away, and I came to the scene of my former contemplations and all was changed. Herds of deer were still to be seen, but they were of a different size, and were accompanied with horses, and oxen, and swine, and sheep; and in command of all I found one whom I recognised as 'being made in the image and likeness of God.'"

In the *Mosaic Cosmogony* we have a statement respecting the twofold manifestation of "light" to our world. In the first, which has been already noticed[1], we have the simple record of the way in which God commanded light to affect the chaos which then existed. In the second, the appointment of that great luminary on the fourth "day" of creation to rule the day, from whose beams we have light and heat, and by whose influence we have the promise fulfilled, that "while the earth remaineth, seed time and harvest, and cold and heat, and summer and winter, and day and night, shall not cease."[2] In both we have undesigned testimony to facts which it was impossible for human skill to discover, and therefore the narrator must have been directly inspired by God. Thus the twofold sources of light, as described in *Revelation*, are not only in perfect accordance with *Science*, but that which is independent of the sun's rays, and which under the name of stellar light, has been winging its ceaseless flight through millions of years from those distant worlds above, has

---

[1] See p. 199.   [2] Genesis, viii. 22.

been now proved by its operation in one of the bygone geological ages, to have been of incalculable blessing in supplying the daily wants of civilised man. If such an one as we have already supposed, had been permitted to visit this earth during the period when it flourished under the gorgeous flora of the carboniferous era, when what is now called England was favoured with a climate, and covered with a vegetation, far greater and far more luxuriant than the tropical regions in the present day, could he have conceived that it was all purposely designed for the future use of man? Yet what is it that warms our houses, cooks our dinner, lights the streets, puts in motion the vast machinery of our manufacturing districts, and enables us to fly through space with the speed of the swiftest bird? What is it that does all this? Why, *light* bottled up in the earth for millions of years; *light* absorbed by plants and vegetables, which is necessary for the condensation of carbon during the process of their growth, if it be not carbon in another form, and which after being buried in the earth for long ages in fields of coal, is liberated, and made to work, as we see it, in supplying the various wants of mankind. This most striking idea, which originated with that eminent engineer, the late George Stephenson, illuminates at once an entire field of *Science*, and helps to confirm the truth of the *Mosaic Cosmogony*, which would naturally, had it been the work of uninspired man, have attributed the existence of light to its one sole visible source, viz. the luminary which God appointed to rule the day.

Before entering upon the consideration of the second important matter in the *Mosaic Cosmogony*, viz. the exact meaning of the word "day," as used in the first chapter of Genesis, it is right to notice a criticism of Mr. Goodwin's upon the two words which are used by the sacred writer to express the distinction between *creating* and *making*. The Essayist observes, that "it has been a matter of discussion amongst theologians whether the word 'created' (Heb. *bara*) here means simply formed or shaped, or *formed out of nothing*" (p. 218). And he adds, in a foot note, "That it does not necessarily mean to make out of nothing appears from verse 21, where it is said that God created (*bara*) the great whales; and from verses 26 and 27, in the first of which we read, 'God said, Let us make (*hasah*) man in our image,' and in the latter, 'So God created (*bara*) man in his image.' In neither of these cases can it be supposed to be implied that the whales, or man, were made out of nothing." The better way of explaining the distinction between *bara* and *hasah* would be by understanding the former to refer to *original creation*, "whether out of nothing, or out of pre-existing matter" is, as Mr. Goodwin says, "immaterial;"[1] the latter to express *appointing*, or applying to a certain purpose what had existed in a previous creation. Thus, e. g. in verse 1, God is said to have originally created (*bara*) the essence of the heavens and of the earth; in verse 16, "God made (*hasah*) two great lights," i. e. He appointed what He had previously created for a definite purpose to rule the day and night when earth was about to become the habitation of man; in verse 21, "God created (*bara*) great whales," i. e. created for the first time a fish, of which,

---

[1] In the first instance of the word being used in Scripture, it must of course refer to creation "out of nothing," as Maimonides says, "It is a fundamental principle in our law, that God created this world from nothing."—*More Nevochim*, par. ii. c. 30. And speaking of other opinions prevalent in the world he adds, "Those who believe in the law of our master Moses, hold that the whole world, which comprehends every being except the Creator, after being in a state of non-existence, received its existence from God—being called into existence from nothing."—*Ibid.* c. 13.

we believe, no fossil has been discovered in any of the geological strata, and of which there was no need until earth became inhabited, when both the bone and the flesh of this monster of the deep afforded such an abundant supply to meet the wants of civilised man; in v. 25, "God made (*hasah*) the beast of the earth," i. e. re-stocked the earth with animals, which had, of different shape and size, existed there long before; in vv. 26 and 27, we read, "God said, Let us make (*hasah*) man in our image," and "So God created (*bara*) man in his own image." From this double announcement we draw the conclusion, that there may be a reference in the first instance to God's intention to make man, as He had before created a certain order of beings, viz. the angels; and in the second, that He originally created man, not out of nothing, but out of the dust of the earth, when He placed the first "living soul"— an immortal being, upon earth. Finally, we read in the summary of creation given in chapter ii., that "God rested from all His work which He had created (*bara*) and made (*hasah*). These are the generations of *the* heavens and of *the* earth when they were created (or in their creation, *bara*) in the *day* that the Lord God made (*hasah*) earth and heavens." By this we understand a double reference to a double act of creation on the part of the Almighty; first, the original creation of the universe, and then the "six days" preparation of the earth for the habitation of man[1], when God made or arranged what He had long before created, for such a purpose. All this critical accuracy in the account of the *Mosaic*

---

[1] It is worthy of note that the Divine approbation, "God saw that it was good," is expressed at the end of every day's work, save the *second*, which may be explained upon the ground that the earth was not prepared for the habitation of man until the third day, when the expression is twice repeated.

Cosmogony is additional confirmation to its having been revealed to the sacred writer by the Creator of the Universe.

We must now turn our attention to the consideration of the word "day," as used in the scriptural account of creation. We have already noticed some of the various opinions respecting it. Some interpret the word to mean exactly twenty-four hours; others, a defined time of 1000 years; while a third class understand it as a period of indefinite length, for which there is authority in the passage which has just been quoted, when the original generations of the heavens and of the earth " were created *in the day* that the Lord God," &c. Now, considering that our application of the word "day" to a period of twenty-four hours is dependent upon the revolution of the earth on its axis in connexion with its orbit round the sun, which was not apparent before the fourth day of creation, we are not necessarily obliged to limit the word in the *Mosaic Cosmogony* to the time which is assigned to it now. Moreover, as the word "day" is used assuredly in Scripture with other meanings, representing both indefinite periods and periods limited to 1000 years [1], it is not contradicting the sure testimony of Scripture to accept any of those definitions with a view to understanding the true meaning of any words we meet therein. And we therefore reject the imputation which Mr. Goodwin has brought against "conscientious" interpreters of Scripture, when he says, " They evidently do not breathe freely over their work, but *shuffle and stumble over their difficulties in a piteous manner;* nor are they themselves again until they return to the pure and open fields of Science" (p. 250).

Let us, however, undeterred by the remarks of our

---

[1] Compare Isaiah, xlix. 8, with 2 Peter, iii. 8.

Essayist, endeavour to show how, in this instance (as we are firmly persuaded in every other), *Science* and *Revelation* may be completely reconciled. It is stated, that after the work of the six days' creation was accomplished, " God rested on the *seventh day* from all His work which He had made." Is there any means by which we may ascertain the exact duration of this rest, and consequently the scriptural definition of the word " day," as it is used in the first chapter of Genesis ? We conclude there is. It has been universally believed by Jews and Christians for many ages, as gathered from a variety of passages in Scripture, that the period allotted to man, in his present condition on earth, consists of 6000 years ; and the Bible chronology, notwithstanding " Bunsen's Biblical Researches," shows that this limit has nearly expired. This, with the addition of the coming Millennium, would make, in all, a period of 7000 years, at the expiration of which, we are taught in Scripture, that Christ's kingly connexion with earth will cease, as it is said : " Then cometh the end (of this age), when He shall have delivered up the kingdom to God, even the Father, . . . that God may be all in all."[1] The Father will then resume His work, as we conclude, from which He has been resting so long a period. And thus we gather from *Revelation* that " the seventh day," or resting time, as we might term it, of the demiurgic Creator, means a period of 7000 years. Hence it may be logically proved, that *each* of the " six days," mentioned in the first chapter of Genesis, represents a period of equal duration. And a simple multiplication sum shows that nigh 50,000 years will have rolled away, since the Almighty fiat went forth, " Let there be light," and God prepared the earth for man, when " time shall be no more," by " God being all in all."

---

[1] 1 Corinthians, xv. 24, 28.

Now, how does *Science* agree with *Revelation* in this conclusion? We believe that the *sole* test by which the duration of earth's present surface, or what the geologists call "The Post-Tertiary System," can be ascertained, or even surmised, is by estimating the age of the Falls of Niagara, which reason tells us must have been cutting through their rocky bed of Silurian strata without a moment's intermission, as age after age has rolled by, since they assumed their present magnificent appearance. Other tests which have been proposed for a like object, such as attempting to calculate the time required to form the coral reefs of the Pacific, or the Delta of the Mississippi, or the Nile, or the Ganges, or any other river, necessarily fail through the impossibility of making any correct estimate of the annual rate of such sub-aqueous deposits, and also from our not knowing whether the origin of such work may not belong to an earlier formation than our present Post-Tertiary System. Sir Charles Lyell, the greatest living authority on such a subject, states, in his "Principles of Geology," that after the most careful inquiries which he was enabled to make on the spot, in 1841, he came to the conclusion, that the average of *one foot* a year was the rate at which the waterfall has been cutting through its stony bed. He further adds, that " it would have required 35,000 *years* for the retreat of the Falls, from the escarpement at Queenstown (a distance of seven miles), to their present site."

We know, from the Mosaic Cosmogony, that the earth did not exist in its present appearance until the *third* of the six days' creation, as it is written, " God called the dry land Earth; and the evening and the morning were the *third* day."[1] Supposing, then, we are right in our estimation respecting each " day " representing a period

---

[1] Genesis i. 10, 13.

of 7000 years, a simple multiplication sum, 7000 × 5 (the number of "days" in the Mosaic record to be accounted for since the preparation of the earth for man), would give the same result of 35,000, as the number of years required by geology from the formation of the Falls of Niagara unto this present time. And thus *Science* and *Revelation*, without any attempt at a "spurious reconcilement," as Professor Jowett terms it, are shown on this point to be in perfect harmony together, and sufficiently refute the dictum of the same writer, who speaks of "the explanations of the first chapter of Genesis having slowly changed, and, as it were, *retreated* before the advance of geology."[1]

The common objection to this view respecting the meaning of the word "day" in the first chapter of Genesis, rests upon the command to keep holy the Sabbath day:—"For in six days the Lord made heaven and earth, the sea, and all that in them is, and rested the seventh day: wherefore the Lord blessed the Sabbath day, and hallowed it."[2] Whence it is naturally argued that our warrant for observing a weekly Sabbath of twenty-four hours' duration, depends upon God's rest from his work for a similar limited period. "But," as Hugh Miller has justly observed on this subject, "I know not where we shall find grounds for the belief that that Sabbath day during which God rested, was merely commensurate in its duration with one of the Sabbaths of short-lived man,—a brief period, measured by a single revolution of the earth on its axis. We have not a shadow of evidence that he resumed his work of creation on the morrow. The geologist finds no trace of post-Adamic creation; the theologian can tell us of none. God's Sabbath of rest may still exist; *the work of* RE-

---

[1] Essays and Reviews, p. 341.   [2] Exodus, xx. 2.

DEMPTION *may be the work of His Sabbath day.* . . . The collation of the passage (given above) with the geologic record seems, as if by a species of re-translation, to make it enunciate as its injunction, Keep this day, not merely as a day of memorial related to a past fact, but also as a day of co-operation with God in the work of elevation, in relation both to a present fact and a future purpose. God keeps His Sabbath, it says, in order that He may save. Keep yours also, in order that ye may be saved. It serves, besides, to throw light on the prominence of the Sabbatical command, in a digest of law, of which no part or tittle can pass away until the fulfilment of all things. During the present dynasty of probation and trial, that special work of both God and man on which the character of the future dynasty depends, is the Sabbath-day work of saving and being saved. . . . Man, when in his unfallen state, bore the image of God, but it must have been a miniature image at best; the proportion of man's week to that of his Maker may, for aught that appears, be mathematically just in its proportions, and yet be a miniature image too,— the mere scale of a map, on which inches represent geographical degrees. All these week-days and Sabbath-days of man which have come and gone since man first entered upon this scene of being, with all which shall yet come and go, until the resurrection of the dead terminates the work of redemption, may be included, and probably are included, in the one Sabbath-day of God."[1] We should have preferred to define the duration of God's rest-day, compared with man's, as "*perfectly* just in its proportions," in place of the expression " mathematically," which the distinguished geologist, from whose work we have quoted, uses, though it was natural for Miller, who

[1] Footprints of the Creator, pp. 307—310,

adopted the theory of "the six days" creation representing periods of undefined length, to select such a time; but knowing that all God's ways and works are *perfect*, and that any multiple of seven is the emblem of perfection, we think the evidence we have adduced, and the harmony which has been shown to exist between the scriptural and the Mosaic record on the duration of the word "day,"[1] is sufficient to prove that it means none other than the period of 7000 years, during which God is said to rest, while the grand work of man's redemption is commenced, carried on, and perfected, when the Redeemer, having seen of the travail of His soul, and being satisfied, shall deliver up the kingdom, in the exuberance of His joy, to the Father, that "God may be all in all."

Let it not, however, be supposed that the expression "God rested" denotes anything like either weariness or inactivity. "The Creator of the ends of the earth fainteth not, neither is weary,"[2] but rather as it is elsewhere said, "He rested and was refreshed."[3] God's rest is not a cessation from all work, is not a rest of inactivity, but rather a rest in activity, as our Lord declared, "My Father worketh *hitherto*, and I work,"[4] by which we

---

[1] The expression "the evening and the morning were the — day," lit. "and there was evening and there was morning," used to denote the completion of each of the "six days'" creation, is omitted in respect to the *seventh*; from which we may infer, with reason, that it was not completed when Moses lived, and is current *now*. Further, the fact that the cardinal "*one*," and not the ordinal "*first*," as in our translation, is used by Moses, "and there was evening, and there was morning, *one* day," denotes the peculiarity of that day — that it was a day *sui generis*, as commentators have justly described it — dies unicus, prorsus singularis" (Maurer). "Ein einziges Tag" (De Witte), an only day; or, "Einzig in seiner Art" (Hitzig), the only one of its kind.

[2] Isaiah, xl. 28.   [3] Exodus, xxxi. 17.   [4] St. John, v. 17.

understand the perpetuity of preservative governance unceasingly exerted by Jehovah for the benefit of His creatures. The Apostle alludes in 2 Cor. v. 17 to that " new creation," which is an assurance to us that in the spiritual world the creative power of God is ever in exercise, as a recent writer on this subject has justly observed, " There is a restoring process, a building up from the ruins of the fall—a Divine purpose and a Divine *work* in raising man to a higher level than that on which the material creation placed him. In this the Father *worketh;* and this is the work which He hath committed to the Son—the work of the one is a reflex of that of the other—a work in which the profoundest rest is not excluded by the highest activity." [1]

The grand error which pervades Mr. Goodwin's Essay on " the Mosaic Cosmogony" is that which is unhappily common to most of his clerical companions, viz. the inability to believe that Moses, like all the other sacred writers, wrote by the direct inspiration of God, and consequently, in Science and in history, as in doctrine, could have written nothing but the truth.[2] " Why should we

---

[1] Macdonald's Creation and the Fall, p. 106.

[2] No stronger evidence of Moses having written by the direct inspiration of God is to be seen, than in the contrast which the marvellous simplicity of the Biblical cosmogony presents to the silly tales of other cosmogonies, which are in reality the rationalistic ideas of an age later than Moses, conceived by those who did not possess a revelation from God. Will the following compressed statement of Hindoo philosophy, which Sonnerat exhibits, satisfy the rationalists of the present day as being nearer the truth than the Mosaic cosmogony? " On the death of Brahma, all the worlds will suffer a deluge : all the Audons will be broken : and Cailasa and Vaicontha (the Paradise of Vishnu floating on a sea of milk) will only remain. At that time, Vishnu, taking a leaf of the tree called Allemarou, will place himself on the leaf under the figure of a very little child, and thus float on the sea of milk sucking the toe of his right foot. He will remain in this posture, until

hesitate," he asks, " to recognise the *fallibility of the Hebrew writers* on this head (physical science)? . . . It has been popularly assumed that the Bible, bearing the stamp of Divine authority, must be *complete, perfect and unimpeachable in all its parts*, and a thousand difficulties and incoherent doctrines have sprung out of this theory.

. . . The treatment to which the Mosaic narrative is subjected by the theological geologists is anything but respectful. The writers of this school as we have seen, agree in representing it as a series of elaborate equivocations, a story ' which palters with us in a double sense.' But if we regard it as the speculation of some Hebrew Descartes or Newton, promulgated in all good faith as the best and most probable account that could then be given of God's universe, it resumes *the dignity and value of which the writers in question have done their utmost to deprive it*. . . . . No one contends that it (Scripture) can be used as a basis of astronomical or geological teaching, and those who *profess to see it in accordance with facts*, only do this *sub modo*, and by processes which despoil it of its consistency and grandeur, both which may be preserved if we recognise in it, *not an authentic utterance of Divine knowledge, but a human utterance*, which it has pleased Providence to use in a special way for the education of mankind " (pp. 251—253). " The plain meaning of the Hebrew record is unscrupulously tampered with, and in general the pith of the whole process lies in divesting the text of all meaning whatever. We are told that Scripture, not being designed to teach us natural philosophy, it is in vain to attempt to make out a cosmogony from its statements. If the first chapter

---

Brahma anew comes forth from his navel in a tamarind flower. *It is thus, that the ages and worlds succeed each other, and are perpetually renewed."—Sonnerat*, vol. i. p. 226, *apud Moor's Hind. Panth*. p. 103.

of Genesis convey to us no information concerning the origin of the world, its statements cannot indeed be contradicted by modern discovery. But it is absurd to call this harmony. Statements such as that above quoted are, we conceive, little calculated to be serviceable to the interest of theology, still less to religion and morality. Believing as we do, that if the value of the Bible as a book of religious instruction is to be maintained, it must be not by striving to prove it scientifically exact, at the expense of every sound principle of interpretation, and in defiance of common sense, *but by the frank recognition of the erroneous views of nature which it contains"* (p. 211). We agree so far with the Essayist that the object of Scripture is not so much to teach astronomy, or geology, or any physical science, as it is religious and moral truth; but we are at issue with him and his fellow-sceptics on the grand matter, which separates the theological and the rational geologists by an impassable gulf, viz. the possibility of God's word containing any "erroneous views" whatever. When we find him speaking of " the fallibility about the Hebrew writers," and the Bible being " the speculation of some Hebrew Descartes or Newton," in short " a human utterance," in place of being " an authentic utterance of Divine knowledge," and condemning " the popular" opinion which considers it " complete and perfect and unassailable in all its parts," —when we see him accusing the theological geologists of having " done their uttermost to deprive the Bible of its dignity and value," and for " professing to see it in accordance with facts"—when we find him stamping their modest and devout attempts to show the perfect " harmony" between *Revelation* and *Science* with the usual proud dictum of his school as " absurd,"— we can only commiserate the infatuation, and expose the ignorance which in defence of a bad cause he has so unrighteously displayed. "The fool hath said in his heart, There is no God;" and it is only a question of degree, not of principle, on the part of those who, whilst they acknowledge the irresistible evidence in proof that "He is," forget that "He is a rewarder of them (only) who diligently seek after Him."[1] Those only can be said to seek after Him diligently who gladly and in faith recognise the all perfect harmony between His word and His works, instead of exposing their deplorable scepticism in the way our Essayist has done. Happy are the persons who, feeling their high privilege to contemplate the *works* of God, are well assured at the outset that they can never contradict His *word*. The book of nature and the book of revelation equally lie open to our inspection. God has endowed us with faculties by which we can interpret the one, and has given us His Spirit to enable us to comprehend the other. By making *Science* a handmaid to religion, and not the reverse, as unhappily the rationalistic school of the present day seem disposed to do, geology becomes in reality a new evidence to *Revelation*. The true conclusions which are drawn from it have broken the arms of the infidel; and when we meditate upon the great events which they proclaim, the mighty revolutions which they indicate, the wrecks of successive creations which they display, and the immeasurable cycles of their chronology, the period of man's tenancy of earth shrinks into nothing; his most ancient kingdoms are but of yesterday; the gorgeous temples of Egypt, and the palaces of Assyria sink into insignificance beside the mighty sarcophagi of the fossil-dead.

Let us remember, then, to our comfort that *Revelation* and *Science* are, as Dr. Pye Smith expressed it, "both beams of light from the same sun of eternal truth," and

---
[1] Heb. xi. 6.

we may feel satisfied with the thought of Chalmers that " Christianity has everything to hope and nothing to fear " from the advancement of the latter. For sure we are that the Scriptures present no bar to the most comprehensive and searching investigation on the part of those who gladly seek to know the harmony which exists between His word and his works. " Science has a foundation," observes Dr. M'Cosh, in his Method of the Divine Government, " and so has Religion. Let them unite their foundations, and the basis will be broader, and they will be two compartments of one great fabric reared to the glory of God. Let the one be the outer and the other the inner court. In the one let all look and admire and adore; and in the other let those who have faith kneel and pray and praise. Let the one be the sanctuary where human learning may present its richest incense as an offering to God, and the other, the holiest of all, separated from it by a vail now rent in twain, and in which, on a blood-sprinkled mercy-seat, we pour out the love of a reconciled heart, and hear the oracles of the living God."

STATEMENTS OF THE REMAINING ESSAYISTS.

CHAP. V.

HAVING thus endeavoured to show the harmony which exists between *Revelation* and *Science*, in respect to the three prominent subjects mooted in the foregoing Chapters,—viz. the Chronology of Scripture as regards the age of man upon earth in contradistinction to the theory of Bunsen; the origin of species, in opposition to the views of Darwin and his predecessors; and the Mosaic cosmogony, as literally set forth in the first chapter of Genesis,—we proceed to an examination of certain statements put forth by the remaining authors of "Essays and Reviews."

§ 1. One of the most important subjects treated of by the Essayists is unquestionably the regard which we, who profess to be believers in Christianity, are bound to entertain towards Holy Scripture, as containing the revealed will of God to His fallen creatures: and it is a significant proof of the lofty position which England now holds amongst the nations of the earth, to trace it to the almost universal feeling which exists amongst us of the necessity, as well as the propriety, of making the Bible the basis of our national education.

It was a wonderful step in the right direction for man, unaided by a revelation from on high, to attain, when the Grecian sage, in the plenitude of his intellectual powers, gave utterance to that memorable sentence, which was subsequently recorded on the Temple at Delphos, γνῶθι σέαυτον[1]; but it fell infinitely short of that higher knowledge which we are bound to seek respecting, not ourselves only, but Him who hath made us all. Hence, while we must admit, in a sense, the truth of Dr. Temple's dictum, that "the great lever which moves the world is knowledge, the great force is the intellect,"[2] we cannot help thinking that it is a mournful sign of the times for a Christian teacher to exalt the omnipotence of human learning in such a prominent way. Gibbon's celebrated remark, that "man has two sorts of education — one from his teachers, the other, and more important, which he gets from himself," may be applied here. For the soul of man in a healthy condition, which in other words is the intellect sanctified by the Spirit and consecrated to the service of God, is not only delighted with knowledge, but also with the very act of learning. To see and confess the smallness of our range is the necessary and proper result of our acquirement of true knowledge. "What we know is little, what we know not is immense," was the confession of a great mind.[3] "I am but as a child," said one still greater[4], "standing on the seashore of the vast undiscovered ocean, and playing with a little pebble which the waters have washed to my feet."

That such an admission, viewing it in its proper light, can only proceed from an intimate acquaintance with that one great Book, in which God has revealed His will to man, is what Dr. Temple cheerfully admits. "Men are beginning to take a wider view than they did. Physical science, researches into history, a more thorough knowledge of the world they inhabit, have enlarged our philosophy beyond the limits which bounded that of the

---

[1] Xenophon's Memoirs of Socrates, lib. iv. § 10.
[2] Essays and Reviews: The Education of the World, p. 48.
[3] La Place. [4] Sir Isaac Newton.

Church of the Fathers. God's creation is a new book to be read by the side of His revelation, and to be interpreted as coming from Him. In learning this new lesson, Christendom needed a firm spot on which she might stand, and has found it in the Bible" (p. 44). The complete accordance between *Revelation* and *Science* is a subject of such vast importance, that too much cannot be said about it. Hence we can gladly assent to Dr. Temple's inference, that the ποῦ στω of Christendom can be found only "in the Bible." But when he appears to identify the Bible, the Word of God, with conscience, the voice of man, we are constrained, in all fidelity, to reject his views. "We use the Bible," he argues, "not to override, but to evoke the voice of conscience. When conscience and the Bible appear to differ, the pious Christian immediately concludes that he has not really understood the Bible. Hence, too, while the interpretation of the Bible varies slightly from age to age, it varies always in one direction—the current is all one way: it evidently points to the identification of the Bible with the voice of conscience" (pp. 44, 45). Part of this quotation agrees with what was so ably put forth by Bishop Butler about a century ago. "If," said that profound divine, "in Revelation there be found any passages, the seeming meaning of which is contrary to natural religion, we may most certainly conclude such seeming meaning not to be the real one. But it is not any degree of a presumption against an interpretation of Scripture, that such interpretation contains a doctrine which the light of nature cannot discover, or a precept which the law of nature does not oblige to."[1] The remainder, however—viz. the identification of the Bible with the voice of conscience—is Dr. Temple's own definition, to which we may fairly take

---

[1] The Analogy of Religion, pt. ii. c. 1.

exception. Conscience, when it is a waking and speaking one, is an inestimable blessing—(Arminius called it "a paradise")—that is, a conscience not only quick to discern what is evil, but to shun it, as the eyelid closes itself against a grain of dust. Conscience, when it has fair play, is indeed a most valuable monitor; but, like a legitimate monarch, when overborne by passion or unhinged by prejudice, it may be too often dethroned. If we could, to adopt the language of the Psalmist[1], "take to ourselves the wings of the morning, and dwell in the uttermost parts of the sea," conscience, like the Omnipresent One, would be ever with us, for our happiness or our misery. If, to continue the metaphor, we say, "The darkness shall cover us, and the night shall be light about us," in regard to Him to whom "darkness and light are both alike," conscience would never leave us. We cannot escape its power, or fly its presence. It is ever with us in this life, will be with us at its close; and in that solemn scene which yet lies further onward, when the thoughts of all hearts shall be revealed, we shall still find it face to face, to reprove us wherever it has been violated, and to console us so far as grace may have enabled us to profit by it. But this is not the Bible; and he who attempts to identify the one with the other labours under a most fatal mistake. The utility of the Bible consists in the practical application of its holy doctrines and its moral precepts to our own individual conscience, as our Lord taught when on earth—"Search the Scriptures; for in them ye think ye have eternal life; and they are they which testify of me."[2] There is such a variety and such a fulness in them, that our limited reasoning powers are utterly inadequate to fathom their exceeding great depths. As one of old justly contended, "The Word of God, by

---

[1] Psalm, cxxxix. 9—12. [2] St. John, v. 39.

the mysteries which it contains, exercises the understanding of the wise; so usually, by what presents itself on the outside, it nurses the simple-minded. It presents in open day that wherewith the little ones may be fed; it keeps in secret that whereby men of a loftier range may be held in suspense of admiration. It is, as it were, a kind of river, if I may so liken it, which is both shallow and deep, wherein both the lamb may find a footing, and the elephant float at large." [1]

Thus the utility of the Bible, as containing the entire Revelation of the Divine mind, is seen alike in its wonderful simplicity, as well as in its matchless perfection, unapproached and unapproachable by all the science and wisdom of the world. Its high sublimities, its holy morality, its comprehensive depths, its majestic poetry, its glorious principles, its divine precepts, its holy doctrines, and its blessed examples, have never been equalled by man, however tender his conscience, apart from the power and teaching of the Spirit of God. In itself, as having, according to the illustrious Locke, "God for its author, salvation for its end, and truth, without any mixture of error, for its matter," the Bible contains everything necessary by man to be known, and by man to be performed. Every sentence is unquestionably an emanation of Deity, and every human being is interested in the meaning thereof. And therefore, with peculiar propriety, did the translators of our noble authorised version, which has better stood the test of unlimited criticism during the last three centuries than any other book in the world, affirm that, in giving forth this noble translation of the Divine will for the use of the nation at large, in order that " every man in our own tongue, wherein we were

---

[1] Epistle of Gregory the Great " to my fellow-bishop Leander," § iv. Prefixed to his Exposition of the Book of Job.

born,"[1] might read the wonderful works of God, it was "opening the window, to let in the light—breaking the shell, that we may eat the kernel—putting aside the curtain, that we may look into the most Holy Place—removing the cover from the well, that we may come by the water" of life, and taste and drink, and be satisfied for ever. If any further testimony were needed to express the overwhelming importance and value of that blessed gift to the English people, we have it in the candid admission of the most distinguished of the band of seceders who have quitted that eminent branch of Christ's Holy Catholic Church, which has been planted in this country ever since the first century, for the fallen and doomed Church of Rome. "Who will not say," asks Dr. Newman, "that the uncommon beauty and marvellous English of the Protestant Bible is not one of the great strongholds of heresy in this country? It lives in the ear like music that can never be forgotten, like the sound of church bells which the convert hardly knows how he can forego. Its felicities seem to be almost things rather than mere words. It is part of the national mind, and the anchor of national seriousness. The memory of the dead passes into it. The potent traditions of childhood are stereotyped in its verses. The power of all the griefs and trials of a man is hidden beneath its words. It is the representative of his best moments; and all that there has been about him of soft, and gentle, and pure, and penitent, and good, speaks to him for ever out of his English Bible. It is his sacred thing, which doubt has never dimmed, and controversy never soiled. In the length and breadth of the land, there is not a Protestant with one spark of religiousness about him, whose spiritual biography is not in his Saxon Bible."

---

[1] Acts, ii. 8.

Another of the Essayists appears to have a somewhat facile conscience respecting the honour due to Holy Scripture, as containing the revealed will and word of God, when we recollect his status and his obligations as a clergyman of the Church of England. " It has been matter of great boast within the Church of England," observes Mr. Wilson, in his Essay on " The National Church," " in common with other Protestant Churches, that it is founded upon the 'Word of God,' a phrase which begs many a question when applied collectively to the books of the Old and New Testaments, a phrase which is never so applied to them by any of the scriptural authors. . . This declaration (viz. Art. VI. of the Church of England) may be expressed thus: the Word of God is contained in Scripture, whence it does not follow that it is co-extensive with it. The Church to which we belong does not put that stumbling block before the feet of her members; it is their own fault if they place it there for themselves, authors of their own offence. Under the terms of the sixth Article, one may accept *literally, or allegorically, or as parable, or poetry, or legend,* the story of a serpent tempter, of an ass speaking with man's voice, of an arresting of the earth's motion, of a reversal of its motion, of water standing in a solid heap, of witches, and a variety of apparitions. . . *Many evils* have flowed to the people of England, otherwise free enough, from an extreme and too exclusive scripturalism. The rudimentary education of a large number of our countrymen has been mainly carried on by the reading of the Scriptures. . . There is no book, indeed, or collection of books, so rich in words which address themselves intelligibly to the unlearned and learned alike. But those who are able to do so ought to lead the less educated to distinguish between the different kinds of words which it contains, *between the dark patches of human passion and error which form a partial crust upon it*, and the bright centre of spiritual truth within."[1] We reserve the question of inspiration, which is slightly referred to in the above passage, for further consideration; but we cannot omit to notice the skilful way in which the Essayist attempts to evade its force by his allusion to the "Word of God." This phrase, he says, is never applied to the books of the Old and New Testament by any of the scriptural authors, though he admits, in apparent forgetfulness of his previous statement, that " the Word of God is contained in Scripture." We confess we are hardly able to understand this distinction. "The Word of God" is a familiar phrase to denote the revealed will of God conveyed to us in writing, through the instrumentality of fallible men, who wrote as they were moved by the Holy Ghost. We find our Lord using the phrase in this sense, when he speaks of the Pharisees " making *the Word of God* of none effect through your tradition" (St. Mark, vii. 13); or, when He defined His faithful disciples as " My brethren are those which hear *the Word of God* and do it" (St. Luke, viii. 21). St. Luke records in one place, that "the people pressed upon Christ to hear *the Word of God*" (viii. 1); and in another, that " almost the whole city came together to hear *the Word of God*" (Acts, xiii. 44). And St. Paul, in writing to the Corinthians, speaks of certain persons who " corrupt *the Word of God*" (2 Cor. ii. 17); or, " who handle *the Word of God* deceitfully" (2 Cor. iv. 2)— in all which instances the phrase is evidently used in the sense to which the Essayist objects. Further, his assertion, or rather implication, that the Word of God is not " co-extensive with Scripture," seems to be put forth as a loop-hole for getting rid of the honest meaning of that Article on Holy Scripture, to which the

---

[1] Essays and Reviews, pp. 175, 177.

Essayist, as a clergyman of the Church of England, is bound by the most solemn vows. It is impossible to reconcile upon the plain principles of honesty the language of the Sixth Article, that " in the name of the Holy Scripture we do understand those canonical books of the Old and New Testament, of whose authority was never any doubt in the Church," with the subtle suggestion, that " under its terms one may accept *literally*, or *allegorically*, or as *parable*, or *poetry*, or *legend*, the story of a serpent tempter," which, in other words, is God's history of man's fall. If we are at liberty to read this, or any of the other suggested subjects which he mentions, either literally or as a legend, to be received or denied at the reader's pleasure, the same right must be conceded as regards the crucifixion, or any other doctrine or event recorded in Scripture, which may be unpalatable to our preconceived notions of right and wrong. Hence the alternative: either we must accept " all Scripture" to be verily the revealed word of God, containing the truth and nothing but the truth in the plain meaning of the term, and devoid of all " dark patches of human passion and error," save where the effects of sin are exposed and condemned; or we must tacitly acquiesce in such heresies as those of Cerinthus, Montanus, and Arius in ancient times, as well as those of Socinus, Johanna Southcote, and the Mormonites in more modern days.

With regard to the harmony which exists between *Revelation* and *Science*, no one can withhold his assent to a proposition of Professor Jowett, in his Essay on " The Interpretation of Scripture," viz. " That any true doctrine of inspiration (of Scripture) must conform to all well-ascertained facts of history or science. The same fact cannot be true and untrue, any more than the same words can have two opposite meanings. The same fact cannot be true in Religion when seen by the light of faith, and untrue in Science when looked at through the medium of evidence or experiment. . . . There is no need of elaborate reconcilements of *Revelation* and *Science*; they reconcile themselves the moment any scientific truth is distinctly ascertained."[1] Yet, when he comes to apply his canon of interpretation, we are at issue with him on most things which he has put forth on this subject. He writes: "Almost all intelligent persons are agreed that the earth has existed for myriads of ages;" but he omits to notice, as he should have done, that in this there is a perfect harmony, not a "spurious reconciliation," between the language of *Revelation* and the discoveries of *Science*, as we have shown at length when reviewing the Essay on "The Mosaic Cosmogony." And he continues: "The best informed are of opinion that the history of nations extends back some thousand years before the Mosaic chronology.[2] Recent discoveries in geology may perhaps open a further vista of existence for the human species, while it is possible, and may one day be known, that mankind spread not from one but from many centres over the globe; or, as others say, that the supply of links which are at present wanting in the chain of animal life may lead to new conclusions respecting the origin of man" (p. 349). This appears to be a timid avowal of a mixture between Rationalism and Darwinism, which it would be creditable to the writer if it were more boldly declared. It is scarcely necessary for us to add, that, as

---

[1] Essays and Reviews, p. 348.
[2] This is a favourite subject of scepticism with Professor Jowett. Further on he observes that "the time will come when educated men will no more think that the first chapters of Genesis relate *the same tale* which geology and ethnology unfold, than they now think the meaning of Joshua, x. 12, 13, to be in accordance with Galileo's discovery" (p. 419).

it is contrary to the express teaching of *Revelation*, it must be unscientific, and is untrue.

"The question of inspiration" is another subject on which we find ourselves at issue with the learned professor. He opens his battery with unshrinking boldness by asserting that, " *For any of the higher or supernatural views of inspiration, there is no foundation in the Gospels or Epistles.* There is no appearance in their writings that the Evangelists or Apostles had any inward gift, or were subject to any power external to them different from that of preaching or teaching, which they daily exercised ; nor do they anywhere lead us to suppose that they were free from error or infirmity. St. Paul writes like a Christian teacher, . . . more than once correcting himself, *corrected, too, by the course of events in his expectation of the coming of Christ*" (pp. 345, 346). . . . .
" The interpretation of Scripture has nothing to do with any opinion respecting its origin. The meaning of Scripture is one thing; the inspiration of Scripture is another. It is conceivable that those who hold the most different views about the one may be able to agree about the other. Rigid upholders of *the verbal inspiration* of Scripture, and those who deny inspiration altogether, may, nevertheless, meet on the common ground of the meaning of words. If the term inspiration were to fall into disuse, no fact of nature, or history, or language, no event in the life of man, or dealings of God with him, would be in any degree altered. *The word itself is but of yesterday*, not found in the earlier confessions of the reformed faith ; the difficulties that have arisen about it are only two or three centuries old. Therefore, the question of inspiration, though in one sense important, is to the interpreter as though it were not important. He is in no way called upon to determine a matter with which he has nothing to do, and which was not determined by fathers of

the Church. And he had better go on his way and leave the more precise definition of the word to the progress of knowledge and the results of the study of Scripture, instead of entangling himself with a theory about it" (p. 351). . . . . "The word ($\theta \varepsilon \acute{o} \pi \nu \varepsilon \nu \sigma \tau o \varsigma$), 'given by inspiration of God,' is spoken of the Old Testament, and is *assumed to apply to the New*, including that Epistle in which the expression occurs, 2 Tim. iii. 16" (p. 360). We trust this is a fair statement of Professor Jowett's views on the important subject of the inspiration of the Scriptures, including both the Old and the New Testament. We have desired to gather his opinion, and to state it in his own words fully, before proceeding to point out the tremendous gulf which separates him and his brother Essayists from those who believe Scripture to be, not the work of fallible man, but the revealed will of the living God. The Essayist has given two or three instances of differences amongst the Evangelists, which he considers a sufficient proof that such writers could not have been inspired by God. He observes, that "One supposes the original dwelling-place of our Lord's parents to have been Bethlehem (Matthew ii. 1, 22); another Nazareth (Luke ii. 4). They trace his genealogy in different ways. One mentions the thieves blaspheming; another has preserved to after-ages the record of the penitent thief. They appear to differ about the day and hour of the crucifixion" (p. 346). It is needless to answer these objections to the inspiration of the sacred writers, as any one moderately acquainted with the Gospels would naturally anticipate the reply; but we have given them merely to show the reasoning of the semi-sceptical school against one of the most cherished truths of our holy religion.

With regard to the question of *inspiration* itself, we can readily admit, with the Essayist, that the word, as used conventionally[1] in the present day, is of modern origin, or rather we might term it modern in its application. We find it used in another sense by the compilers of our Book of Common Prayer, as the expression in that very beautiful Collect, which precedes the Communion Service, " Cleanse the thoughts of our hearts by the *inspiration* of the Holy Spirit, that we may perfectly love Thee," is evidently a prayer for the ordinary gifts of the Spirit, as distinct from those which are termed extraordinary, with which the sacred writers were necessarily endowed when they spake as they were moved by the Holy Ghost. Neither would we contend for the necessity of " verbal inspiration," if by that expression Professor Jowett means what the judicious Hooker, in one of his admirable works, describes as " syllabic inspiration,"[2]

---

[1] When Mr. Pitt, in the peroration of his great speech on the Abolition of the Slave Trade, depicting the prosperity of Africa in the evening of her day, with that rare felicity of quotation for which he was so eminently distinguished, introduced the famous lines from the Georgics of Virgil:

"Nosq; ubi primus equis oriens afflavit anhelis,
Illic sera rubens accendit lumina Vesper,"—

a thought suggested by the first ray of the rising sun, which darted through the window of the House of Commons,—it is related, that Mr. Windham, then in opposition, was so moved as to clap his hands, exclaiming in rapture—" *Inspiration! Inspiration!* " But this is very different from that " inspiration " which Bishop Stillingfleet happily described as " a Urim and Thummim upon the whole of Scripture, light and *perfection in every part.*"—*Origines Sacræ*, p. 613. Ed. 1675.

[2] Hooker's words are as follows: " This (1 Cor. xi. 12, 13) is that which the Prophets mean by those books written full within and without, which books were so often delivered them to eat, not because God fed them with ink and paper, but to teach us that so often as He employed them in this heavenly work, they neither spake nor wrote any word of their own, but uttered *syllable by syllable, as the Spirit put it*

and from whom we are so unwilling to appear to differ in the slightest degree, but which cannot stand, for this simple reason, that the four Gospels relate, not a fact, but a transcript of the very words in the Greek language which Pilate ordered to be placed on the cross, and they all four record it differently: e.g.

St. Matt. Ουτος εστιν Ιησους ο βασιλευς των Ιουδαιων.
St. Mark. Ὁ βασιλευς των Ιουδαιων.
St. Luke. Ουτος εστιν ο βασιλευς των Ιουδαιων.
St. John. Ιησους Ο Ναζωραιος ο βασιλευς των Ιουδαιων.

Now, were the theory of *syllable* or *verbal* (which are one and the same) inspiration true, surely, on such a memorable occasion as this, the Evangelists would have been moved by the Holy Ghost to recount the exact number of words and syllables which the Roman Governor ordered to be inscribed on that cross whereon the Saviour of mankind offered the perfect sacrifice of Himself for the sins of the world. In saying this, do we in anywise lessen our feelings of inexpressible reverence for the *plenary* inspiration, as it has been appropriately termed, of every portion of the Sacred Oracles of God? God forbid. We cannot find language sufficiently strong to express our firm belief, that all the writers of both the Old and New Testament were equally moved by the Holy Ghost to set forth and to declare, on every subject which is there introduced, whether it be doctrine, prophecy, history, chronology, philosophy, or science, the truth, the whole truth, and nothing but the truth. It is scarcely necessary to add, that inspiration, as defined either by Professor Jowett or the rationalistic school generally, is of a very

---

into their mouths, no otherwise than the harp or the lute doth give a sound, according to the discretion of his hands that holdeth and striketh it with skill." — *Sermon on Part of St. Jude*, § 4.

different nature from the above. When we find one of the leaders of that school asserting that "Milton, and Shakspeare, and Bacon, and Canticles, and the Apocalypse, and the Sermon on the Mount, and the eighth chapter to the Romans, are, in our opinion, all inspired. Inspiration signifies that action of the Divine Spirit by which, *apart from* all idea *of infallibility*, all that is good in man, beast, or matter, is originated and sustained,"[1]—we detect at once the great gulf which separates the teaching of the Rationalists on the subject of the inspiration of Scripture from that of the Catholic Church in all ages. The man who places the words of Shakspeare or Bacon on a par with those of our Divine Master, or the author of the Epistle to the Romans, proves that his idea of inspiration is not a spiritual but an intellectual gift. Perhaps one of the strongest evidences in proof that the sacred writers were inspired in a very different way from the most intellectual of mankind, whether Christian or heathen, is seen, not merely in the different way in which sin, both original and actual, is treated by the one and the other, but by the gigantic and ceaseless efforts which Pagan and Papal persecutors, in ancient and modern times, have made to prevent the circulation, and to destroy the existence, of that which condemns so strongly our inherent self-righteousnes, viz. the word of God. It is not too much to say, that had one tenth part of the care and trouble been taken to destroy the works of either Plato or Cicero, or Shakspeare or Bacon, shortly after the time they were respectively composed, as was taken either during the time of the Diocletian persecution or at the commencement of the Reformation in the sixteenth century, to root out the Scriptures from the possession of living men, there would not have been a trace or vestige

---

[1] Macnaught on the Doctrine of Inspiration, p. 192.

that such philosophers had ever existed, except so far as their works might have been quoted or referred to by contemporary writers. How little do many readers of the Bible reflect what it must have cost the Christians of the early ages merely to rescue the sacred treasure from the rage of the heathen. Isaac Taylor, in his work on "Ancient Christianity," justly remarks, that, "In that fresh morning hour of the Church, there belonged to the sincere followers of Christ a fulness of faith in the realities of the unseen world, such as, in later ages, has been reached only by a very few eminent and meditative individuals; the many felt a persuasion which is now felt only by a few." How touching is the account which Anthony Dalaber, a young Oxford undergraduate, gives of the persecution which the Papal authorities were beginning to make on account of the recent introduction of the translated Scriptures into that famous University. Speaking of the departure of his friend, Master Garrett, he says, "When he was gone down the stairs from my chamber, I straightways did shut my chamber door, and went into my study, and taking the New Testament in my hands, kneeled down on my knees, and with many a deep sigh and salt tear I did, with much deliberation, read over the tenth chapter of St. Matthew's Gospel, praying that God would endue his tender and lately-born little flock in Oxford with heavenly strength, by His Holy Spirit, that quietly, to their own salvation, with all godly patience, they might bear Christ's heavy cross, which I now saw was presently to be laid on their young and weak backs, unable to bear so huge a burden without the great help of His Holy Spirit."[1]

The fatal error of Professor Jowett, on the subject of inspiration, consists in his inability to distinguish be-

---

[1] Froude's History of England, vol. II. ch. vi.

tween the action of the Holy Ghost upon those who were "moved" to convey the revealed Will of God to man, and who were so far infallible, and those lesser gifts of the Spirit, the author of every good thought, or word, or work, which multitudes of what are commonly called "uninspired" men are privileged to possess. For example, there is a very beautiful passage in the essay on which we are now commenting: "It is, perhaps," says the author, "the greatest difficulty of all to enter into the meaning of the words of Christ, so gentle, so human, so divine, neither adding to them, nor marring their simplicity. The interpreter needs nothing short of 'fashioning' in himself the image of the mind of Christ. He has to be born again into a new spiritual or intellectual world, from which the thoughts of this world are shut out. It is one of the highest tasks on which the labour of a life can be spent, to bring the words of Christ a little nearer the heart of man."[1] This is very beautiful and very true, and must be the thoughts of a man, we would fain hope, influenced by the Spirit of God, though differing in quantity, and in quality, from the extraordinary gifts with which the "holy men" were endowed, who, when engaged in writing the oracles of God, "spake as they were moved by the Holy Ghost." The Essayist, however, will not assent to this distinction, for he declares that "the word (θεόπνευστος) 'given by inspiration of God,' is spoken of the Old Testament, and *is assumed to apply to the New*, including that Epistle in which the expression occurs;" and he is venturesome enough to assert that the writings of the most eminent of the authors of the New Testament, the Apostle Paul, prove his non-inspiration according to the common use of the term, by "the course of events *correcting* his expectation of the coming of

---

[2] Essays and Reviews, p. 380.

Christ." We need scarcely add that there is not the slightest ground for this accusation, and the Essayist, with his usual caution, has avoided quoting any text in proof of his "painful scepticism," but contents himself with supposing that his *ipse dixit* will be accepted, to the detriment of the infallible word of God.

Let us, however, consider what St. Paul really taught on the subject of what is generally called the *plenary*[1] inspiration of the Bible. "All Scripture is given by inspiration of God, . . . that the man of God may be perfect, throughly furnished unto all good works." (2 Tim. iii. 16, 17.) It will of course be objected, by Professor Jowett and his school, that the expression, "all Scripture," cannot refer to the New Testament which was not then completed, but must be confined to the Old; and as this opinion has been held by some commentators, it may be right to mention the grounds for believing that the Apostle included both, in so far as the latter was then written. St. Paul had just before stated that Timothy had known, from a child, "the Holy Scriptures" (τὰ ἱερὰ

---

[1] The Rev. B. Cowie, in his Address on the Chief Points of Controversy between Orthodoxy and Rationalism, to the Fellows of Sion College, London, March 25th, 1861, says, "I receive the Bible generally as the word of God, and I believe that it is θεόπνευστος. But if you go beyond what the Church has decreed and talk of '*verbal*' inspiration, and '*plenary*' inspiration, you are importing into the discussion words which are neither in the Bible nor in the forms of the Church; and you have no right whatever to set *them* up as standards of orthodoxy. You make *your* interpretation of inspiration the standard, and not *inspiration* itself;"—which is so far true; yet are we obliged to adopt the use of the well known term "*plenary*," in order to distinguish it on the one hand from "*verbal*" inspiration, which cannot be sustained, and on the other from those intellectual gifts, with which such men as Milton and others were endowed, and which the Rationalists confidently assume to be the same as the gifts of the sacred writers, who were "filled with the Holy Ghost."

γράμματα), which, doubtless, meant the Old Testament, in the knowledge of which Timothy's mother, who was a Jewess, would naturally instruct her child. But the next verse, beginning, "All Scripture," contains a general statement, and, therefore, the Apostle uses another term (πᾶσα γραφὴ), which was purposely meant to include every writing inspired by the Spirit of God to the time when that Epistle was penned, and as it was probably the last Epistle which St. Paul wrote, the whole of the New Testament had been completed, with the exception of the writings of St. John. This will appear more evident if we read the passage literally and without the particle καὶ, which is omitted in almost all the *versions*, and by many of the *Fathers*, and certainly does not agree well with the text. Hence, the Greek may be rendered, "Every writing *God-breathed* is profitable for doctrine," &c. The Syriac version renders θεόπνευστος *written by the Spirit*, and the Ethiopic, *by the Spirit of God*. Knowing, therefore, that the Apostles had been *breathed upon* by the God-man Christ Jesus, and had been "filled with the Holy Ghost," according to the Saviour's promise, as was visibly manifested on the day of Pentecost[1], their writings must necessarily come under the term "God-breathed," and, as such, "*profitable*," yea, and at that time more profitable than those of the Old Testament, "for doctrine and instruction in righteousness." In the writings of the New Testament, as of the Old, there is an instinctive evidence that they are not the work of man, and those who are not wilfully blind to the truth, gladly recognise in them the handwriting of that "friend which sticketh closer than a brother," without needing to be told of the human channel by which they have been conveyed to us. There

---

[1] St. Paul, though not called until after Pentecost, was "not a whit behind the very chiefest Apostles." 2 Cor. xi. 5.

is a Urim and a Thummim, in the true sense of the term, upon the whole of Scripture, light and perfection in every part of it; and it behoves every one who is anxious for the honour of God, as well as for the welfare of his fellow-creatures, to rise, as Chalmers has expressed it, "like a wall of fire around the integrity and inspiration of His word."

An eminent statesman of the last century, when addressing the House of Commons, on the subject of a petition from certain clergymen to be relieved from the subscription, which, since the Reformation, the Church has very properly required of those who enter the ministry, defined the Bible on this wise:—"The Scripture is no one summary of doctrines regularly digested, in which a man could not mistake his way; it is a most venerable but most multifarious collection of the records of the divine economy; a collection of an infinite variety of cosmogony, theology, history, prophecy, psalmody, morality, apologue, allegory, legislation, ethics, carried through different books, by different authors, at different ages, for different purposes and ends."[1] Had Professor Jowett, and the other authors of "Essays and Reviews," gone no further in their attempts to undermine the vitality and power of the Scriptures than the illustrious layman whose words are quoted above, no charge could have been substantiated against them, as the Church of England, while affirming that "Holy Scripture containeth all things necessary to salvation, so that whatsoever is not read therein, nor may be proved thereby, is not to be required of any man that it should be believed as an Article of the Faith," has carefully abstained from determining anything respecting the history, the prophecies,

[1] Edmund Burke on Clerical Petition for Relief from Subscription, Feb. 6th, 1772.

or the scientific statements contained in the Oracles of God; leaving it to the unfettered courage of her faithful children to defend, as best they may, the claim which Scripture, in its entirety, makes to be the inspired word of God, against the hostile assaults of subtle adversaries, or of accomplished and pretended friends.

"None are so blind as those who refuse to see," is an old adage, with much of truth in it; and our Essayist is a striking example of this in his repeated errors on the subject of inspiration. Speaking of "the results of historical inquiries," of what is recorded in the Bible, he observes, they "*cannot be barred by the dates or narrative of Scripture, neither should they be made to wind round into agreement with them. . . .* The recent chronological discoveries from Egyptian monuments do not tend to overthrow revelation, *nor the Ninevite inscriptions to support it.* The use of them on either side may, indeed, arouse a popular interest in them; it is apt to turn a scientific inquiry into a semi-religious controversy. And to religion either use is almost equally injurious, because seeming to rest truths important to human life on the mere accident of an archæological discovery. Is it to be thought that Christianity gains anything from the deciphering of the names of some Assyrian and Babylonian kings, contemporaries chiefly with the later Jewish history? As little as it ought to lose from the appearance of a contradictory narrative of the Exodus in the chamber of an Egyptian temple of the year, B.C. 1500.[1] This latter supposition may not be very probable. But it is worth while to ask ourselves the question, whether we

---

[1] We do not know to what Professor Jowett here alludes, whether it be to the "Exodus Papyri," published by Mr. Heath, or something else; but we have already adduced ample proof that every real Egyptian discovery bearing upon the subject does "not contradict," but does confirm the truth of the Biblical narrative of the Exodus.

can be right in maintaining any view of religion, which can be affected by such a probability" (p. 350). Religion, or in other words, the "plenary" inspiration of Scripture, assuredly does not depend upon "such a *probability*," but it is the *certainty* of the agreement between the statements in the Bible, on every subject therein mentioned, with recent archæological discoveries, that constitutes one of the proofs of inspiration, which, though not wanted by the humble and sincere believer in Revelation, are sufficient to put to shame the infidel, the sceptic, the rationalist, and the miserable quibbler, who, in the superciliousness of his own little mind, and the unconscious magnitude of his profound ignorance, fancies he has detected a flaw in the unerring word of the Almighty and Infinite Jehovah.

We meet Professor Jowett's "painfully sceptical" insinuations by a direct negative. We confidently affirm that the recent chronological discoveries from the Egyptian monuments *tend to support revelation*, and the Ninevite inscriptions amply confirm the same. It is unnecessary to repeat what has been so fully considered in our examination of "Bunsen's Biblical Researches," with respect to the Egyptian monuments being in perfect harmony with Scripture history and Scripture chronology, though we may add another instance of the value and importance of such proofs, by referring to Champollion's discovery of the name of "Judah" on the Temple of Karnak. On one of the walls of that most splendid of Egyptian structures, originally built by Amenophis III., the successor of the Pharaoh who was drowned in the Red Sea, there is a representation of sixty-three prisoners being presented to Pharaoh Shishak by his god Amunra. Amongst them is a turreted oval or cartouche, which the genius of Champollion enabled him to decipher as "Judah Melika," signifying the kingdom (not the king) of Judah; for the final hieroglyph is as determinative of the country, as the *turreted* cartouche is of a captured fortress enclosing foreign prisoners. Now, the statement in Scripture exactly harmonises with the induction from the Egyptian hieroglyph. "It came to pass, that in the fifth year of King Rehoboam, Shishak king of Egypt came up against Jerusalem, because they had transgressed against the Lord, with twelve hundred chariots and threescore thousand horsemen: and the people were without number that came with him out of Egypt: and he took the fenced cities which pertained to Judah, and came to Jerusalem.... So Shishak king of Egypt came up against Jerusalem, and took away the treasures of the house of the Lord, and the treasures of the king's house; he took all: he carried away also the shields of gold which Solomon had made."[1] By this it appears that the fifth year of King Rehoboam synchronised with the reign of Pharaoh Shishak, which agrees with the chronology of Manetho, Bunsen *non obstante;* and thus we have a proof of the value of Egyptian discovery in an important synchronism between the reigns of two kings, in contradiction to Professor Jowett's inference. And more than this, since it is evident from the account in the chronicles of the kingdom of Judah, that only the city was captured by Pharaoh Shishak, but not the person of King Rehoboam, so we find, by a careful criticism of the hieroglyph, that the Egyptian record of the same perfectly agrees thereto, inasmuch as the country, and not the individual king, is described as having been conquered by the power of Egypt.

So likewise with reference to "the Ninevite inscriptions," the discovery by Dr. Hincks of the name of "Jehu, the son of Omri," i. e. of the house of Omri, on the Nimroud obelisk (now standing in the British Museum), who is there represented as acknowledging the

---

[1] 2 Chronicles, xii. 2—9.

supremacy of Temen-Bar[1], the King of Assyria, is one of several proofs in testimony of the connection between Assyria and Israel, which, in the following century (the eighth B.C.), is more particularly mentioned in Scripture, on account of the judgments which the former was permitted to inflict upon the latter. And as it is related in the 2nd Book of Kings that Jehu was guilty of the same idolatry whereby his predecessor, Jeroboam, had made Israel to sin, notwithstanding that he destroyed the worship of Baal, we may fairly conclude that he became for a short time tributary to the King of Assyria, as a punishment, according to the reading of the Nimroud Obelisk. Or, take the confirmation of what is said in Scripture respecting Hezekiah being vanquished by Sennacherib, according to the inscription of the annals of his reign, found by Mr. Layard in his palace at Kouyunjik, and deciphered by Sir Henry Rawlinson. We shall better understand the value of this "Ninevite inscription in support" of the truth of *Revelation*, by placing the two accounts in parallel columns.

HOLY SCRIPTURE.	THE NINEVITE INSCRIPTION.
" Now, in the fourteenth year of King Hezekiah, did Sennacherib King of Assyria come up against all the fenced cities of Judah, and took them. And Hezekiah, King of Judah, sent to the King of Assyria to Lachish, saying, I have offended; return from me: that which thou puttest on me will I bear. And the King of Assyria appointed unto Hezekiah, King of	" Because Hezekiah, King of Judæa, did not submit to my yoke, forty-six of his strong-fenced cities, and innumerable smaller towns which depended upon them, I took and plundered; but I left to him Jerusalem, his capital city, and some of the inferior towns around it. . . . And because Hezekiah still refused to pay me homage, I attacked and carried off

---

[1] There are good chronological grounds for believing that Temen-Bar was on the throne when Jonah visited Nineveh, and if so, must have been the king who submitted to the admonition of the Prophet in a way that few Christian sovereigns have been known to do.

Judah, 300 *talents of silver, and* 30 *talents of gold*. And Hezekiah gave him all the silver that was found in the house of the Lord, and in the treasures of the king's house. At that time did Hezekiah cut off the gold from the doors of the temple of the Lord, and from the pillars which Hezekiah, King of Judah, had overlaid, and gave it to the King of Assyria."[1]

the whole population, fixed and nomade, which dwelt around Jerusalem, with 30 *talents of gold and* 800 *talents of silver*[2], the accumulated wealth of the nobles of Hezekiah's court, and of their daughters, with the officers of his palace, men-slaves and women-slaves. I returned to Nineveh and I accounted their spoil for the tribute which he refused to pay me."

It is impossible to conceive a more undesigned evidence, or a more satisfactory proof of the truth of the historical portion of *Revelation*, than the above Ninevite inscription in support of the same. Again, in the above-mentioned palace of Kouyunjik, a large number of pieces of fine clay have been discovered, bearing the impressions of seals, which once had been affixed, like modern official seals of wax, to documents written on leather, papyrus, or parchment, some specimens of which are now in the British Museum. The greater part bear Assyrian, Egyptian, or Phœnician symbols. Amongst them are two Egyptian impressions of a royal signet, with the name *Shabaka* in a cartouche, with an hieroglyphic inscription above, which reads *Netr-nfr-nb-ar-oht*, i. e. "the perfect God, the Lord who produces things." This Pharaoh *Shabaka* is the same as the second king of the twenty-sixth or Ethiopian dynasty, termed in Manetho's list $\Sigma\epsilon\beta\iota\chi\omega\varsigma$ or $\Sigma\epsilon\upsilon\eta\chi o\varsigma$; in 2 Kings, xviii. 4, "So;" Hebrew, סוֹא; LXX. $\Sigma\eta\gamma\tilde{\omega}\rho$ or $\Sigma\omega\acute{a}$. This seal assumes, therefore, a most important character, in showing the synchronism of the three monarchs of Assyria, Egypt,

---

[1] 2 Kings, xviii. 13—16.

[2] The difference between the 300 talents of silver in the one account, and 800 in the other, may be accounted for by distinguishing between the money and the metal of the Temple.

and Israel; as it must have been affixed to some treaty between the sovereigns of the first two of these kingdoms, after the " conspiracy of Hoshea, King of Israel," mentioned in the Book of Kings, who refused to pay tribute to " Shalmaneser, King of Assyria," when he sent " messengers to So, King of Egypt," for help. This is likewise one of many proofs of the value of the " Ninevite inscriptions." And another seal, discovered at the same place, with a *Phœnician* inscription, singularly confirms the truth of Scripture testimony. According to the alphabet of Gesenius[1], the inscription might be read, phonetically, as *Eldebsh*, or *Elredsh*, or *Eldedsh*, or *Elbrebsh*. Now, Josephus[2] states, that when Shalmaneser invaded Syria and Phœnicia in a hostile manner, as he appears to have done, from 2 Kings, xviii. 5, the King of Phœnicia's name was *Eluleus*, or *Pyas*, or *Pulas*, as various MSS. read it. Further, Menander, who translated the archives of Tyre from the Phœnician into the Greek language, mentions that " the King of Assyria overran all Phœnicia, and *speedily made peace with them all;* and, upon the subsequent revolt of Sidon, and Ace, and Palætyrus, he was assisted by the Phœnicians with sixty ships." This will account for the existence of a Phœnician seal in the palace of Sennacherib, the successor of Shalmaneser on the throne of Assyria, which may possibly represent the name of the king reigning in Tyre at the time when Shalmaneser first overran the country, and who afterwards must have made a treaty of peace with him, the seal to which document exists at this present day. We have thus adduced sufficient evidence in disproof of the Essayist's mistaken idea, that " the Ninevite inscriptions do not tend to support revelation."

---

[1] Script. Ling. Phœn. Monumenta, pars tertia, tab. 1.
[2] Antiq. ix. 14, 2.

Professor Jowett seems to be conscious that his mode of interpreting Scripture cannot be a sound one, and to anticipate the censure which he expected to receive on the promulgation of his unfounded and untenable theory. When he observes, " it is probable that some of the preceding statements may be censured as a wanton exposure of the difficulties of Scripture " (p. 372), he forgets that the exposure is not that of any real difficulty to the humble believer in *Revelation*, but only to those who are oppressed by that " smouldering scepticism " of which he has proved himself so accomplished an adept. " No one," he complacently adds, " is willing to break through the reticence which is observed on these subjects ; hence a sort of *smouldering scepticism*. It is probable that the distrust is greatest at the time when the greatest efforts are made to conceal it. Doubt comes in at the window when inquiry is denied at the door" (p. 373). Prohibition against seeking to know the mind of God, as revealed in His word, has never been the action or the endeavour of Christ's Holy Catholic Church. Such has ever been the exclusive property of the apostate portion of the Church, according to the prophecy, which has received so striking a fulfilment in our fallen sister of Rome. The Church of Christ glories in inquiry, and has ever done so since her Master's virtual command : " Search the Scriptures ; for in them ye think ye have eternal life : and they are they which testify of me."[1] And we know how the Apostles, the inspired founders of the Church, commended " the noble Beroeans" for obedience to the divine command, when they tested the doctrine delivered to them by comparing it with, and interpreting it through, the words of the Old Testament. As an exemplification of " the smouldering scepticism " of the Essayist, and his manifest unfitness as a

---

[1] St. John, v. 39.

sound interpreter of Scripture, we need only adduce one more passage from his Essay, but which painfully manifests the perversion and the confusion of his mental powers. "*The failure of a prophecy is never admitted, in spite of Scripture and of history* (Jer. xxxvi. 30; Isaiah, xxiii.; Amos, vii. 10—17); the mention of a name later than the supposed age of the prophet is not allowed, *as in other writings*, to be taken in evidence of the date (Isaiah, xlv. 1)." (p. 343). Now, considering that the *first* of these instances, quoted in proof of "*the failure of prophecy*," foretold the cessation of the royal line of David as rulers in Jerusalem; the *second* the judgment upon and the destruction of the famous city of Tyre; and the *third* the captivity of Israel by the King of Assyria, one cannot but be amazed at the limited knowledge of history displayed in this opinion, as well as at the temerity with which the Essayist has ventured to put it forth. With regard to his accusation of refusing to allow the mention of a certain king's name in the prophecy of Isaiah to be taken for an evidence of its date, *as in other writings*, this is a mere *réchauffé* argument on his part against the inspiration of the prophet, just as the infidel school in ancient times, and the rationalists in modern, with perverse consistency, have endeavoured to deny the inspiration of the prophecies of Daniel.

Since the very example which Professor Jowett brings forward against the truth of Isaiah's prophecy is in reality one of the strongest evidences in its favour, it will be necessary for us to give it a brief consideration. The prophecies of Isaiah were delivered " in the days of Uzziah, Jotham, Ahaz and Hezekiah, kings of Judah," reigns which occupied, as we know, the whole of the eighth century B.C. At some time or other of that century, probably during the reign of the last-mentioned king, and therefore towards the close of that century, Isaiah was inspired to prophesy: "Thus saith the Lord, Thy Redeemer . . . of Cyrus, or Coresh (Hebr.), *my shepherd*, he shall perform all my pleasure; even saying to Jerusalem, Thou shalt be built; and to the Temple, thy foundation shall be laid. Thus saith the Lord to His anointed, to Cyrus (Coresh), whose right hand I have holden, to subdue nations before Him; and I will loose the loins of kings, to open before Him the two-leaved gates; and the gates shall not be shut."[1] As Cyrus' permission to rebuild the Temple of Jerusalem, as recorded by Ezra (i. 1, 2), occurred within a year or two of the fall of Babylon, which took place B.C. 538, it is a very natural objection, both for the infidel and the unhappy man whose brain is bewildered by a "smouldering scepticism," to make, that such a clear and positive announcement of an historical event could not have been recorded until after the event had taken place; but when we know the intense care which was taken by the Jews to preserve the purity of the text, together with the fact that both the internal and external evidence is overwhelmingly convincing in disproof of this *modern* objection, (for we do not believe that the opponents of Christianity, in ancient times, rejected Isaiah as they did Daniel), we may dismiss it with a sigh at the marvellous infatuation which has beclouded the mind of the Essayist, while we proceed to point out very briefly the evidence which this prophecy affords that Isaiah wrote by the direct inspiration of God.

We hold it to be an incontrovertible fact that, as long as the daily service of the Temple was carried on, including the seventy years' intermission during the Babylonish captivity, since many of the elders amongst the Jews lived through that unhappy period in their history, it was impossible that any interpolations of the Old

---

[1] Isaiah, xliv. 24, 28; xlv. 1.

Testament could have taken place; as all which have crept into the text must have done so subsequent to the destruction of Jerusalem and its Temple by the Roman invasion. The LXX. translators in the third century B.C., with the exception of the word "shepherd," which our present copies render φρονεῖν instead, give the passage as it stands in the Hebrew, translating the Hebrew Coresh, as we have before noticed, by its Greek equivalent, κυρος, or Cyrus. Josephus, in the first century of the Christian era, relates, that the cause of Cyrus having given the Jews permission to return to their country, and rebuild their Temple, was in consequence of "his reading the book which Isaiah left behind him of his prophecies; for this prophet said that God had spoken thus to him in a secret vision: 'My will is, that Cyrus, whom I have appointed to be king over many and great nations, should send back my people to their own land and build my Temple.' This was foretold by Isaiah 140 years before the Temple was demolished. Accordingly, when Cyrus read this, and admired the divine power, an earnest desire and ambition seized upon him to fulfil what was so written." [1]

If we refer to the heathen historians, we have sufficient authority for asserting that the prediction was amply verified by the event, which took place about 200 years after the prophecy was delivered. The name *Coresh*, in the Persian tongue, signifies the *sun*, from which Cyrus had his name, as Ctesias[2] and Plutarch[3] affirm, and has some affinity to the Hebrew word *cheres* (Job, ix. 7) of the same signification; though Scaliger[4] considers the name Cyrus to signify *food* in the Persian language, which answers to the character given him in Scripture, as shep-

---

[1] Antiq. xi. 1, 2.
[2] Excerpta, p. 648, ed. Gronov.
[3] In Vitâ Artaxerxis.
[4] Emendatio Temp. i. 6.

herd. Justin[1] says he had this name given him whilst he was among shepherds, by whom he was brought up. And Xenophon, in his "Institution of Cyrus," represents him as having been accustomed to say, "That the business of a good *shepherd* and of a good king were very near alike; for a shepherd," he said, "ought to provide for the happiness of his flock, and make use of them consistently with the happiness of those creatures; and that a king ought in the same manner to make men and cities happy, and in the same manner to make use of them."[2] The prophecy, in addition to the title given to Cyrus of being a shepherd, for the purpose of restoring the scattered sheep of Israel to the fold in Jerusalem, which God intended for them, specifies that he was to be a prominent subduer of nations, and that the Lord would "loose the loins of kings to open before him the two-leaved gates." Of the fact, that Cyrus was a great conqueror of many nations, there can be no doubt; and we apprehend that the meaning of God loosing the loins of kings, in order that "the two-leaved gates" should be opened to him in an unusual manner, must refer to what took place in Babylon, at the time when the handwriting appeared on the walls, which announced the destruction of that doomed dynasty, as Daniel relates that " then the king's countenance was changed, and his thoughts troubled him so that *the joints of his loins were loosed*, and his knees smote one against the other."[3] We know from profane testimony, that on that night the gates of Babylon within the city, leading from the streets to the river, were providentially left open, when Cyrus penetrated the city with his army through its channel, in consequence of the general disorder occasioned by the great feast which was

---

[1] Hist. ex Trogo, lib. i. c. 5.　　[2] Cyropædia, lib. viii. § 18.
[3] Daniel, v. 6.

then being celebrated. Had it not been so, the Persians, as Herodotus (i. 191) declares, would have been shut up in the bed of the river, and taken as in a net, and all destroyed. Xenophon relates that, as soon as the noise of the final attack began, "the king (Belshazzar) commanded his attendants to examine what the matter was, who ran out, throwing open the gates. While the Persians, under Gobryas and Gadatas, as soon as they saw them loose, broke in and put an end to the king."[1] The prophecy then of Isaiah respecting Cyrus being the appointed instrument for punishing the King of Babylon, as well as for permitting the captive Jews to return to Jerusalem, and to rebuild their desolate city, is one to which every faithful believer in *Revelation* gladly appeals in proof of the Bible being written by men who were moved by the Holy Ghost to foretell things which would happen after their day; and we must deeply lament, though without surprise, the deplorable scepticism which can induce any man, especially a presbyter of the Church of England, to argue that it was the interpolation of an unprincipled forger, introduced into the book some time after the event which it professes to predict had taken place.

One more instance, in conclusion, we must notice, with regard to Professor Jowett's mode of interpreting Scripture. Speaking of the glorious future which awaits the faithful followers of the Redeemer, on the morn of resurrection, he observes: "A recent commentator appears willing to *peril religion* on the *literal* truth of such an expression as 'We shall be caught up to meet the Lord in the air.' Would he be equally ready to stake Christianity on the literal meaning of the words, 'Where their worm dieth not, and the fire is not quenched?'" (p. 403). Elsewhere he says, "When it is gravely urged that from

---

[1] Cyropædia, lib. vii. § 5.

such passages as 'Kings shall be thy nursing fathers,' we are to collect the relations of Church and State, or from the pictorial description of Isaiah, *that it is to be inferred there will be a reign of Christ on earth*, it is a mere assumption of the forms of reasoning by the imagination" (p. 409). If, by the first of these quotations, Professor Jowett means, as his words seem to imply, that St. Paul's declaration of the future rapture of the Church at the coming of the Lord, as declared in his first Epistle to the Thessalonians, is to be equally discredited with the doctrine of the eternity of punishment to the wicked, we can only lament the blindness of his spiritual vision, and pray that he may be speedily brought to a healthier and better state of mind. In the second quotation we have another of the many instances of the palpable unfitness of the Essayist to be a safe guide in the interpretation of Scripture, as witnessed in the Essay before us. It is as great a mistake to deny that Scripture foretells the future reign of Christ upon earth, as it is to infer the present connection between Church and State from the promise that "Kings shall be thy nursing fathers," which can only pertain to the restoration of the Jews, and has nothing to do with Christianity.

If we wanted to see what Scripture teaches respecting Christ's future reign, it would be sufficient to read attentively, and to accept submissively, without attempting to explain this doctrine any more than other unfathomable mysteries with which the word of God abounds, such clear and positive declarations as these: "Thou hast redeemed us to God by Thy blood, out of every kindred, and tongue, and people, and nation; and hast made us unto our God kings and priests: *and we shall reign on the earth*" (Rev. v. 9, 10). And again it is written, "*They lived and reigned with Christ a thousand years*" (Rev. xx. 4). If language is to be understood in the plain and literal meaning thereof, there can be no difficulty about accepting the above texts, without seeking to make ourselves wise above what is written. And that many of the early Christians so received the doctrine we may fairly conclude by the following extracts from their writings.

Papias, Bishop of Hierapolis, who is said by Irenæus to have been a hearer of the Apostle John, and a companion of Polycarp, declared, as Eusebius tells us, " that there shall be a thousand years after the resurrection of the dead, wherein the kingdom of Christ shall subsist upon this earth." Eusebius, after condemning the doctrine, adds, that " Papias gave occasion to a great many ecclesiastical writers after him to be of the same opinion, who respected the antiquity of the man, as Irenæus and the rest who have maintained that opinion."[1]

Justin Martyr, A.D. 130, in his dialogue with Trypho, the Jew, says, in reply to his opponent's question : " Tell me truly, do you know that this place, Jerusalem, will be rebuilt ; and do you expect that your people will be gathered together, and rejoice with Christ, and with the patriarchs and prophets, and with those of our race, and of those who became proselytes before the coming of your Christ ? "—" I and many others hold these sentiments, and believe, assuredly, that thus it will come to pass, though I have intimated to you that many Christians of pure and pious dispositions[2] do not acknowledge it. But I and those Christians who are orthodox (ὀρθογνώμονες) in all things, know that there will be a resurrection of the flesh, and a thousand years in Jerusalem, rebuilt, and adorned, and enlarged, as the prophets Ezekiel and

---

[1] Hist. Ecc. iii. 31.
[2] Mede supposes that this clause should be read in the negative, which the context appears to support.

Isaiah and the others unanimously declare. A certain man amongst us, whose name was John, one of the Apostles of Christ, in a revelation made to him, prophesied that believers in our Christ should live a thousand years in Jerusalem, and after this should be the universal resurrection and general judgment of all."[1]

Irenæus, Bishop of Lyons, A.D. 180, speaks of the doctrine as something undoubted, questioned only by "some accounted orthodox," and denied by those who held "opinions borrowed from heretical discourses, in ignorance of the dispensations of God, and the mystery of the resurrection of the just, and of the kingdom, which is the beginning of incorruption, by which kingdom those who are accounted worthy are gradually habituated to receive God."[2] The doctrine of Irenæus is, that after the resurrection the saints should also, in different degrees of nearness, according to their deserts, in the holy city, in Paradise, or in Heaven, enjoy the sight of the Lord, " for everywhere shall the Saviour be seen, as they who see Him shall be worthy."[3] For this he quotes certain presbyters who had seen and heard St. John, and whom he distinguishes from Papias. He also observes that "all these and other sayings (of Isaiah) are without controversy spoken of the resurrection of the just, which takes place after the coming of Antichrist, and the destruction of all nations under him, in which the Christians shall reign on the earth, growing by the sight of the Lord, and through Him shall be habituated to receive the glory of God the Father, and shall, in the kingdom, receive conversation and communion and unity of spiritual things with the holy angels."[4]

Tertullian, A.D. 200, taught the doctrine of the millen-

---

[1] Dial. cum Tryph. c. 80.　　[2] Advers. Hær. v. 31, 1.
[3] Advers. Hær. v. 36, 1.　　[4] Ibid, v. 31, 1.

nium in several of his works, as *De Spectac.*, *De Carn. Resur.*, and more especially in his work against Marcion, where he refers to a work *On the hope of the Faithful*, now lost, in which he speaks of having treated the subject more at length. He distinctly limits the joys of the millennium to *spiritual* pleasures, observing, " This Jerusalem, we say, is provided by God for receiving the saints upon the resurrection, and refreshing them with the abundance of all spiritual good things, in compensation for those which in the world we have either despised or lost. . . . We confess our belief in a kingdom promised us upon earth, and before heaven, but in a different state of being, viz., after the resurrection, for a thousand years in the city of Jerusalem, divinely built, ' brought down from heaven,' which the Apostle also calls ' our Mother from above.' This both Ezekiel knew and the Apostle St. John saw."[1]

Commodian, A.D. 250, a Latin author and contemporary with Cyprian, "heartily embraced the doctrine of the expected millennium," according to Lardner[2], as he spake of " the believers' return in the golden age, when the heavenly city shall descend at the time of the first resurrection, and those who were devoted to Christ shall receive good things, as formerly they received evil things, and shall continue for a thousand years."

Victorinus, Bishop of Pettaw, in Germany, A.D. 300, observes, concerning the doctrine, " This is that true Sabbath in which Christ is *to reign* with his elect," as Lactantius at a later period taught, " Christ shall hold converse with men a thousand years."[3]

Lastly, St. Augustine, A.D. 400, whose opinion on the doctrine of the millennium subsequently underwent a

---

[1] Adv. Marc. iii. 24.
[2] Credibility of the Gospel History, pt. ii. c. 49.
[3] De Fabr. Mundi, apud D. Doct. Cave, p. 104.

change, originally taught "That eighth day (St. John, xx. 26) signifies the new life at the end of the world; the seventh signifies the peaceful rest of the saints which shall be on the earth. For the Lord will reign on the earth with His saints, as the Scriptures say, and will have a Church here, where no evil shall enter. For the Church shall appear first in great brightness and dignity and righteousness."[1] After his change (for which he had just reason in the immoderate carnality respecting the doctrine entertained and promulgated by some of his contemporaries), he speaks very tenderly of those who rightly held it, observing that "the opinion would be at all events objectionable, if it were believed that the saints should in that Sabbath have spiritual joys through the presence of the Lord. For we likewise thought so formerly."[2]

Such was the state of the doctrine until the early part of the fifth century, held by most but questioned by some. The first who openly impugned it, as far as we know, was Origen, who carried his system of allegorising almost everything to such an extent, that he even denied the doctrine of eternal punishment. The next was his pupil Dionysius, Bishop of Alexandria, who denied the Godhead of the Holy Spirit. The third was Jerome, who appears to have had no idea of that fundamental doctrine of experimental religion, viz., the "being justified, or accounted righteous before God, only for the merit of our Lord and Saviour Jesus Christ by faith, and not for our own works or deservings," which our Church happily terms "a most wholesome doctrine and very full of comfort," but to have been sunk in the slough of superstition and self-righteousness; yet he candidly admits that the mass of the godly (*plurima multitudo*) in his day were mille-

---

[1] Serm. 259, in die Dom. Octav. Pasch. § 1, 2.
[2] De Civitat. Dei, xx. 7.

narians, and that those who denied the millennium went "contrary to the sentiments of the ancients: of the Latins, Tertullian, Victorinus and Lactantius; and of the Greeks, to pass over others, I will mention only Irenæus, Bishop of Lyons." Every believer in the Catholic faith, then, should remember to his satisfaction and joy that the doctrine of the millennium, or, as it is generally termed in the present day "millenarian views," like the evening star which at one time follows the sun when he sets, and at another precedes him in his rise, appears to have been firmly held by the most eminent of the Fathers in the best and purest days of the Church, after the Sun of Righteousness had been taken from her, until it sunk below the horizon during the darkness of the middle ages, only to reappear with renewed lustre, as it has in our own times, like the bright morning star, to usher in "the glorious appearing of the great God and our Saviour Jesus Christ." And it surely behoves those, who by faith "have washed their robes and made them white in the blood of the Lamb,"[1] not only to be assured that they "dwell in Christ and Christ in them, that they are one with Christ, and Christ with them," but also of all the results flowing from this happy union; to feel not only that they are "heirs" of the Father, and "joint heirs" with the Son, but also to enjoy and to realise daily the privileges of such an exalted position. Nor should we forget to add likewise to the value of this doctrine its *practical importance;* for, assuredly, he who is longing for the Saviour to take him home should be living to God, walking with God, and working for God. Blessed, thrice blessed, are they who long for *home;* for they shall soon go *home.* And they who are in earnest on this subject, will be enabled to realise the force of what has been so well expressed by

---

[1] The true reading of Rev. xxii. 14.

that great master in Israel, whose confessions have afforded such comfort and instruction to the Church for so many centuries :—" O God, Thou hast formed us for Thyself, and our hearts are restless until they rest in Thee."[1]

Another question of great importance relating to Holy Scripture remains to be considered. Have we now a genuine transcript of the Old and New Testaments, as they originally came from the hands of the sacred writers, or must we submit to the accusation of " forgeries" having been designedly introduced into that Book of books, for some special object on the part of those who could be guilty of so great a crime? Dr. Temple appears to lean to the latter opinion. "If," says the Essayist, "geology proves to us that we must not interpret the first chapter of Genesis literally ; if historical investigation shall show us that inspiration, however it may protect the doctrine, yet was not empowered to protect the narrative of the inspired writers from occasional inaccuracy ; if careful criticism shall prove that there have been *occasionally interpolations and forgeries in that Book, as in many others;* the result should still be welcome" (p. 47). The connection between *Revelation* and *Science*, as set forth in the first chapter of Genesis, which the Essayist denies, we have endeavoured already to show, when examining the chapter on " The Mosaic Cosmogony," to which it more properly belongs, and we now content ourselves with quoting, as a contrast to Dr. Temple's misconception of Scripture, the truer philosophical deduction which a distinguished divine has drawn from the same passage of Holy Writ. "It has been said," remarks Dr. Chalmers, "that geology undermines our faith in the inspiration of the Bible. This is a false alarm. The writings of Moses do not fix the antiquity of the globe ; if they fix anything at all, it is only

---

[1] St. Augustine, Confess. i. 1.

the antiquity of the species."[1] We have already attempted to show that "inspiration" has "protected the narrative of the writers" of Scripture equally with "the doctrine" in considering the results of "Bunsen's Biblical Researches." "*Forgeries*" in the Bible we most distinctly deny, and we unhesitatingly challenge the most "careful criticism" to produce any well-authenticated attempt at such in God's word. That there have been *interpolations, omissions,* and *mistakes,* affecting both doctrine and history, in our present copies of the sacred text, every scholar will readily admit, as the following examples may serve to show, but such cannot affect the Scriptures themselves, nor justly expose them to the charge of *forgery;* and it is only in the transmission of them from age to age by fallible men that any failure can be detected.

Let us take an example of each for the purpose of showing how susceptible of rectification they become when tested by fair critical research. We read in the Hebrew text of Exodus, xii. 40, that "the sojourning of the children of Israel who dwelt in Egypt was 430 years." If this means, as is sometimes considered, that it makes the duration of the sojourn in Egypt to extend over the whole of that period (though it may be remarked that this reading does not support the deduction of "the sojourning" and "the dwelling in Egypt" being one and the same thing), it is evident that there must be some *omission* here, because we gather from the inspired history of Moses, in the book of Genesis, that only 215 years elapsed from the time of the call of Abraham until the descent of the Patriarchs into Egypt, and the same number of years from that time unto the Exode, which make together the stated number of 430 years. Hence we find St. Paul, who, equally with Moses, wrote by

---

[1] Lectures at St. Andrews, 1804.

the inspiration of God, declaring that "the covenant, that was confirmed (at Mount Sinai) before of God in Christ, the law, was 430 years"[1] after the time of Abraham. And this interpretation, independent of the Apostle's inspiration, agrees with the true reading of Holy Scripture; for not only does the Septuagint version, which was the authoritative copy of the Old Testament used by our Lord and the Apostles, prove the omission in the received Hebrew text by reading the passage as follows—"the sojourning of the children of Israel, and *of their fathers*, which they sojourned *in the land of Canaan*, and in the land of Egypt was 430 years;" but so likewise do all the MSS. and printed copies of the Samaritan Pentateuch, which is owned by the Jerusalem and the Babylonian Talmuds, by the Mishna and the famous Jewish Rabbi Moses Maimonides, to be the original and ancient character of the Sacred Scriptures. We have shown in a previous Chapter[2] that this reading is the only one which agrees with the chronology of that period, as may be deduced from other portions of the Hebrew text. Hence we are constrained to admit that an *omission* has occurred in our present copies of the Old Testament.

We find another instance of *omission* in the Hebrew text of the 145th Psalm. This, as being the last of the *acrostic* Psalms, should contain twenty-two verses, in accordance with the letters of the alphabet. The one wanting in our present copies should be between vv. 13 and 14, beginning with the letter נ. The LXX., Syriac, Vulgate, and other versions, besides one Hebrew MSS. belonging to Trinity College, Dublin, have the omitted verse, which reads thus, "Jehovah is faithful in all His words; and merciful in all His works."

So we have an instance of *interpolation* in 1 Kings, vi. 1, where the Hebrew text reads, "It came to pass

---

[1] Galatians, iii. 16, 17. [2] See pp. 158, 159.

INTERPOLATIONS IN SCRIPTURE. 307

in the 480*th year* after the children of Israel were come out of the land of Egypt, Solomon began to build the house of the Lord." That the number of years here mentioned, from the time of the Exode to that of the Temple, is an *interpolation*, may be very easily proved, because it contradicts the chronology of that period as set forth both in the Old and New Testament. By comparing the statements in the historical books of the one with St. Paul's speech to the elders of Antioch recorded in the other, it is quite certain that a longer interval elapsed from the Exode to the Temple than the present copies of the Hebrew text allow. Josephus, in the first century, and Theophilus, Bishop of Antioch, in the second, both confirm this by quoting the Syrian records, which mention that Solomon's Temple was built 566 years after the Exodus, and which, in all probability, was the exact number, from the fact of Hiram, King of Tyre, having mainly assisted in its building. If anything further were required to show that this passage contains an *interpolation*, it may be seen in the learned Origen's quotation of the text, who cites it in his commentary on St. John's Gospel as follows: " They prepared stones and timber three years: and in the fourth year, in the second month of Solomon's reign over Israel," &c., omitting all mention of the subsequently interpolated words " in the 480th year." And it is to be observed that in the parallel place of the Book of Chronicles, where the building of the Temple is mentioned, this date does not occur, though in all other places, wherever the years are mentioned in the Books of Samuel and Kings, and the same transactions are related in the Chronicles, we find the numbers set down in both records of what may be termed the annals of Israel. Hence we must conclude that the sentence, " in the 480th year after the children of Israel were come out of the land of Egypt," is an *interpolation* of the present Hebrew text, introduced subsequent to the time of Origen, who wrote his commentary about the year A.D. 230.

Further, as we find instances of *omission* and *interpolation* in the sacred text affecting chronology, and therefore *history*, so may we quote a case of clerical error affecting *doctrine*, but which, upon investigation, may be as easily explained as those to which we have already referred. In Revelation, xxii. 14, the present text reads, " Blessed are they that *do His commandments*, that they may have right to the tree of life," &c., a reading somewhat difficult to explain, as it appears to make our "right to the tree of life" dependent upon something we can " do," or some merit of our own, and therefore contradictory of the emphatic teaching of our Lord in reply to the question put to Him, " What shall we do, that we might work the works of God? Jesus answered and said unto them, This is the work of God, that ye believe on Him whom He hath sent."[1] How touchingly this great doctrinal verity has been illustrated by one of the Church of England's chiefest worthies, whom all parties so justly revere, let the affecting testimony of our admirable Hooker on his death-bed decide. After a life full of " good works " in the service of His master, he thus gave utterance to the feelings of his heart respecting the absence of all human merit in reference to salvation. " Though by the grace of God I have loved Him in my youth, and feared Him in my age, and laboured to have a conscience void of offence to Him and to all men ; yet if Thou, O Lord, be extreme to mark what I have done amiss, who can abide it? And, therefore, where I have failed, Lord, show mercy to me : for I plead not my righteousness, but the forgiveness of my unrighteousness for His merits who died to purchase pardon for penitent sinners." The passage, however, to which we

---

[1] St. John, vi. 28, 29.

are referring is susceptible of easy explanation when we learn the true reading, and the way by which the error of a copyist very naturally crept in. The most ancient MSS., *e.g.* our Codex Alexandrinus in the British Museum, —read the passage " Blessed are they who *have washed their robes*, that they might have a right to the tree of life," &c., a reading which commends itself to our reasoning faculties as the true text, because it is in accordance with the grand fundamental doctrine of the Christian religion, that we are " saved by grace through faith; and that not of yourselves : it is the gift of God : not of works, lest any man should boast."[1] If we compare the two readings as they appear in ancient MSS. which have been handed down to us, we can readily understand how the mistake of the copyist arose, and how a very moderate amount of biblical research enables us to rectify the passage in dispute.

1. Older MS. μακαριοιοιπλυνοντεςταςστολαςαυτωνιναεσταιηεξουσια, &c.
2 Later MS. μακαριοιοιποιουντεςταςεντολαςαυτουιναεσταιηεξουσια, &c.

Thus then the charge against the Holy Scriptures, which the language of Dr. Temple seems to imply, may be rejected as incorrect in every point of view, whether of doctrine, history, or science. What we venture to think is required is patient investigation, fair biblical criticism, and a competent knowledge of independent, and, therefore, unexceptionable authorities, to enable us to decide, first, what really is Scripture, and then will it be to us, as everything inspired by God necessarily must be, the infallible standard of divine truth. And surely it behoves us in all things to test the value of a writing of less authority by the greater, not the reverse, as the Essayists appear generally inclined to do. Between the sacred writings and all human authorities a wide interval neces-

[1] Ephesians, ii. 8, 9.

sarily exists. And it is deplorable to witness how readily, but most unreasonably, a school of theological critics, who have arisen in our day, seem desirous, not merely of setting aside the value of the Sacred Scriptures on matters of history and fact, but of exalting human testimony, however confused and contradictory, and therefore worthy of no regard, above the word of God itself.

§ 2. Having thus examined the opinions put forth by some of the Essayists with regard to Holy Scripture, and the various subjects connected with it, we must notice the view entertained by one of their number respecting the religious faith of that favourite race to whom God first confided, and for a long period confined, the Revelation of Himself. "The conviction of the *unity* and *spirituality* of God," says Dr. Temple, "was peculiar to the Jews among the pioneers of civilisation. *Greek* philosophers had, no doubt, *come to the same conclusion* by dint of reason. To every Jew, without exception, *monotheism* was equally natural."[1] If this is meant to teach that the Jews, with a revelation from on high, denied the plurality of the persons in the Godhead, which, from the allusion to the natural religion of the Greek philosophers, we conclude must be the meaning of the Essayist, we must take leave to notice the fatal mistake embodied in the statement above. It is undoubtedly true that there were some amongst the learned heathen who appear to have had sufficient glimpses of the truth

---

[1] Essays and Reviews, p. 11. We have an instance of an eminent *Latin* philosopher, who apparently came to a different conclusion " by dint of reason," though he admitted the spiritual nature of the Jewish religion. "The Jews," says Tacitus, "acknowledge but one God, and that God a Spirit. . . . Some affirm that they worship Bacchus; but their institutions are very different. Bacchus invented luxurious rites, and a voluptuous religion; while that of the Jews may be said to be as sordid as it is absurd." — *Hist*. lib. v. § 5.

to cause their dedication of an altar " To THE UNKNOWN GOD," as St. Paul found at Athens, and which constrained the great Apostle of the Gentiles to preach, " Whom ye ignorantly worship, Him declare I unto you."[1] The Grecian name EI, " Thou art," inscribed on the temple of Apollo at Delphi, and supposed to be taken from the Saite inscription, " I am," on a much older temple in Egypt, dedicated to the goddess Neith, corresponding with Exodus, iii. 14, and meaning " unchangeable ;" the wonderful hymn to the Creator, composed by Eupolis, one of Socrates's pupils, more than four centuries ere Christ appeared—

> " Thee will I sing, O Father Jove,
> And *teach the world* to praise, and love. . . .
> And yet a greater hero far
> (Unless great Socrates could err)
> Shall rise to bless some future day,
> And *teach to live* and teach to pray—"

sufficiently prove the length to which the Grecian philosophers were enabled to attain in the right direction, according to the Divine appointment, " that they should seek the Lord if haply they might feel after Him, and find Him, though He be not far from every one of us ;"[2] but it is not correct to assume that the Jews were monotheists, in the sense of denying the plurality of the persons in the Godhead, according to the fundamental doctrine of the Christian religion.

All admit that the Old and New Testaments teach one and the same truth, whether it be worded as in the former, " Hear, O Israel! the Lord our God is one Lord ;"[3] or, as in the latter, " God is a Spirit, and they that worship Him must worship Him in spirit and in truth."[4] In perfect harmony one with the other they

---

[1] Acts, xvii. 23. [2] Acts, xvii. 27.
[3] Deut. vi. 4.   [4] St. John, iv. 24.

teach alike that the unity of the Godhead subsists in three distinct persons. The very first declaration in Holy Scripture shows this beyond all doubt. "In the beginning God created the heaven and the earth;" for the very fact of the *plural* form אלהים[1] governing the *singular* verb ברא distinctly implies a plurality of persons in the Divine nature. And that it was so understood by the Jews let the following testify: "Come and see," says an eminent Rabbin, "*the mystery of the word Elohim;* there are *three degrees*, and each degree by itself *alone*, and yet notwithstanding they are all *one*, and *joined* together in *one*, and are not divided from each other."[2] So in Isaiah, xlviii. 16, 17, the doctrine of the Trinity appears to be clearly asserted, and so received by the Jews: "Come ye near unto me, hear ye this; I have not spoken in secret from the beginning; from the time that it was, there am I: and now the Lord God, and His Spirit, hath sent me. Thus saith the Lord, thy Redeemer, the Holy One of Israel; I am the Lord thy God which teacheth thee to profit, which leadeth thee by the way that thou shouldest go." Hence the cabalists, speaking of Jehovah, call "the first person *Ain Soph*, or infinite, who is THE FATHER; the second person *Chochma*, or WISDOM; the third person *Beena*, or UNDERSTANDING, and also *Rooch Hakodesh*, or THE HOLY SPIRIT." Hence in the Book *Zohar*, written while the temple was still standing, a work held in the highest veneration by the people, we find the following, which speaks for itself: "There are *three lights in God;* the ancient light or Kadmon; the pure light or Zach; the purified light or

---

[1] That the word אלהים is of plural number may be proved from its being united upwards of *thirty* times in various parts of the Old Testament with adjectives, verbs, and pronouns *plural*.

[2] Simeon Ben Joachi, Comm. in Levit. § vi.

Mezuchzach, and *these three make but one God.*" So in the Targum of Onkelos we find repeated references to the second person of the Trinity, under the name of the *Dvar* or THE WORD. On Exod. xiv. 31, the learned Jew says, " It is THE WORD, in whom Israel believed as well as in Moses." On Exod. xv. 2, " It is THE WORD that redeemed Israel out of Egypt." On Exod. xxx. 6, " It is THE WORD whose presence is promised in the Tabernacle." Finally, in the Jerusalem Targum, supposed to be written during the Babylonish captivity, we read the author's comment on Exod. xxxiii. 9—11, " THE WORD OF THE LORD hath appeared on three remarkable occasions: first, at the creation of the world; secondly, to Abraham; thirdly, at Israel's departure out of Egypt; and a fourth time he shall appear in the person of the Messiah." And on Genesis, iii. 22, the same commentator has these remarkable words: " Jehovah said, Here Adam, whom I have created, is the only begotten son in the world, as *I am the only begotten Son* in the high heavens." These Jewish testimonies make us reasonably conclude that the spiritually taught portion of God's favoured people were not monotheist in the same sense as the enlightened heathen, or as denying the fundamental doctrine of all true religion, viz., that of the Trinity.

Dr. Temple accounts for the miraculous preservation of God's chosen people through 4000 years of marvellous success and unexampled oppression, according to the Divine predictions, repeated over and over again in Scripture, upon the argument that their " *extraordinary toughness of nature* enabled them to outlive Egyptian Pharaohs, and Assyrian kings, and Roman Cæsars, and Mussulman caliphs" (p. 14). Now we appeal to any reasonable being if this be not the deduction of a sceptic rather than that of a Christian minister, who recognises the supremacy of God's word, whether delivered in a way of doctrine, prophecy, or history? Who can read the affecting account of their predicted sufferings foretold by Moses centuries before the nation existed, which God destined to be the instrument of punishing His rebellious people, and compare it with what secular history relates of its terrible accomplishment in every part of Christendom where they have been scattered, together with their present condition and their glorious future, as is so repeatedly asserted by the prophets in the Old Testament, and say it is "*the extraordinary toughness of their nature*" which has preserved them, while other nations " greater and mightier than they" have risen, flourished, passed away and are remembered no more at all? Where are the mighty nations of Egypt and Philistia, of Assyria and Babylon, of Greece and Rome? Gone, never to return. And the Jews are everywhere now, and if we are to understand Scripture in the plain meaning of language, they will in due time be restored to the land which God gave to Abraham and his seed " as an everlasting possession," with more than their former glory.

Does then the fulfilment of what was predicted by Moses respecting their rejection and their sufferings warrant us to believe literally what the later prophets have foretold concerning their restoration? Let us see. In the 28th chapter of the Book of Deuteronomy, written during the sixteenth century, B.C., we read : " It shall come to pass, if thou wilt not hearken unto the voice of the Lord thy God, that all these curses shall come upon thee and overtake thee. Thou shalt be removed into all the kingdoms of the earth. The Lord shall smite thee with madness, and blindness, and astonishment of heart. Thou shalt be only oppressed and spoiled evermore. Thou shalt become an astonishment, a proverb, and a byword, among all nations whither the Lord shall lead thee. The stranger that is within thee shall get above thee very high, and thou shalt come down very low. He shall be the head and thou shalt be the tail. The Lord shall bring a nation against thee from far, from the end of the earth, as swift as the eagle flieth ; and he shall besiege thee in all thy gates, until thy high and fenced walls come down, wherein thou trustedst, throughout all thy land, which the Lord thy God hath given thee. Thou shalt eat the fruit of thine own body, the flesh of thy sons and daughters, which the Lord thy God hath given thee, in the siege, and in the straitness, wherewith thine enemies shall distress thee. The Lord will make thy plagues wonderful, and the plagues of thy seed, even great plagues, and of long continuance. As the Lord rejoiced over you to do you good, and to multiply you ; so the Lord will rejoice over you to destroy you, and to bring you to nought : and ye shall be plucked from off the land whither thou goest to possess it. And the Lord shall scatter thee among all people, from the one end of the earth even unto the other ; and there thou shalt serve other gods, which neither thou nor thy fathers have known, even wood and stone. And among these nations shalt thou find no ease, neither shall the sole of thy foot have rest ; but the Lord shall give thee there a trembling heart, and failing of eyes, and sorrow of mind : and thy life shall hang in doubt before thee ; and thou shall fear day and night, and shall have none assurance of thy life."

Does history verify the fulfilment of these predictions, which foretold the sufferings of the Jews when scattered throughout the earth ? We have only time to notice a few of the many testimonies which bear ample truth to the correctness of the prophecy. It is universally admitted that the nation from the end of the earth, as swift as the flying eagle, whom Moses predicted as the appointed instrument for executing the Divine wrath upon the children of Israel, can refer to none other than the Roman people, whom one of their historians describe as having " eyes which seemed to be on fire, their countenances wild and their looks furious."[1] When the time had arrived for the accomplishment of the prophecy, in the siege of Jerusalem by Titus, where it is computed from the testimony of Josephus that as many as 1,337,490 perished, and where the horrible occurrence took place of Mary, the daughter of Eleazar, " eminent for her family and wealth," being forced by hunger to feast upon the body of her sucking child, the Jewish historian was compelled to make this memorable admission : " All the calamities which have ever happened to any nation, from the beginning of the world, are not to be compared to those which then befel the Jews."[2] In the following century, when they recovered sufficient strength to raise a rebellion against the Roman Emperor Hadrian, it was only to be if possible more tormented and more destroyed, as Dion Cassius[3], who lived not long after, relates. In the fourth century, Chrysostom, in his oration against the Jews[4], says : " They again rebelled in the time of Constantine ; who, causing their ears to be cropped off, dispersed them as vile fugitives and vagabonds in various countries, where they carried this mark of infamy along with them, that all might be instructed to make no more such attempts." In the beginning of the 11th century they were so persecuted and afflicted through Europe, that, as one of their own historians mournfully confesses, " They knew not what they should do, or which way they should turn themselves." And David Ganz, another of their chroniclers, speaking of the crusades, says, " The Jews felt it a most calamitous time, being robbed and

---

[1] Livy, lib. vii. 33. [2] Preface to the Jewish War, § 4.
[3] Hist. lib. lxix. [4] Tom. vi. ed. Savile, p. 383.

pillaged and killed by the Christian soldiers as they marched along." Gibbon, speaking of the same period, observes : " At Verdun, Treves, Mentz, Spires, Worms, many thousands of that unhappy people were pillaged and massacred; nor had they felt a more bloody stroke since the persecution of Hadrian."[1] Their sufferings at that time so much moved the great St. Bernard, that he wrote to the clergy and people not to persecute them. " For they are," says he, " dispersed into all lands, that while they suffer the just punishment of their horrid wickedness, they may be witnesses of our redemption." They were so persecuted in the twelfth century, that Rabbi Zacut complains of no less than ten grievous persecutions in his own age, to abolish the very name of the Jews out of the world. The historian Hallam, when relating the sufferings of the Jews during the middle ages, says : " They were everywhere the objects of popular insult and oppression, frequently of a general massacre. A time of festivity to others was often the season of mockery and persecution to them. It was the custom at Toulouse to smite them on the face every Easter. At Beziers they were attacked with stones from Palm Sunday to Easter, an anniversary of insult and cruelty generally productive of bloodshed, to which the populace were regularly instigated by a sermon from the bishop. It is almost incredible to what a length extortion of money was carried."[2] Sir Walter Scott, in one of his historical romances, describes the Jews " as a race which, during those dark ages, was alike detested by the credulous and prejudiced vulgar, and persecuted by the greedy and rapacious nobility. Except, perhaps, the flying fish, there was no race existing on the earth, in the air, or on the waters, who were the objects of such an unremitting

---

[1] Decline and Fall, ch. lviii.   [2] Middle Ages, vol. i. pp. 233-4.

and relentless persecution as the Jews at this period. It is a well-known story of King John, that he confined a wealthy Jew in one of the royal castles, and daily caused one of his teeth to be torn out, until, when the jaw of the unhappy Israelite was half disfurnished, he consented to pay a large sum, which it was the tyrant's object to extort from him."[1] Truly it may be said of them, as one of their most distinguished historians has observed: " Kings have often employed the severity of their edicts, and the hands of the executioner, to destroy them : the seditious multitude has performed massacres and executions, infinitely more tragical than the princes. Both kings and people, heathens, Christians, and Mahometans, who are opposite in so many things, have united in the design of ruining this nation, and have not been able to effect it. The Bush of Moses, surrounded with flames, has always burnt without consuming. The Jews have been driven from all parts of the world, which has only served to disperse them in all parts of the universe. They have, from age to age, run through misery and persecution, and torrents of their own blood."[2]

Thus then the present condition of the Jews, so far from being traced to their unusual and " *extraordinary toughness*," as Dr. Temple considers, is the most remarkable testimony to the truth of God's word ; and their wonderful preservation amidst the entire disappearance of other nations contemporaneous with their own when David flourished, amidst the ravages of war, the wear of time, and the ceaseless hostility of the Gentiles, affords us ample assurance that, though they have been, as was predicted, " a byword among all nations," they shall, as Isaiah has foretold, at a time probably not far distant, " build the old wastes, raise up the former

---

[1] Ivanhoe, vol. i. p. 83.   [2] Basnage, Hist. des Juifs, vi. 1.

desolations, and repair the waste cities, the desolations of many generations. In their land they shall possess the double. And their seed shall be known among the Gentiles, and their offspring among the people: all that see them shall acknowledge them, that they are the seed which the Lord hath blessed."[1] The Jews then, we may safely assert, banished and dispersed as they still are throughout the world, bear testimony to the truth of the religion of Christ. Preserved, not by *their toughness of skin*, but by a continued miracle, that they may keep the succession of those who shall one day acknowledge Him whom their fathers pierced and slew, they bear witness to Him unceasingly. Had they been only punished, they would have proved no more than His justice; had they been only preserved, they would have proved nothing more than His power; had they not been reserved in order to acknowledge Christ as the true Messiah in the land which God promised to the seed of Abraham as "an everlasting possession," they could not have proved His mercy and veracity, nor have made Him any reparation for their tremendous crime. Their dispersion proves that He is come, but they have rejected Him; while their preservation shows that He hath not cast them off for ever; but that, as God has said by the mouth of one of His servants, "Behold, at that time I will undo all that afflict thee: and *I will get them praise in every land where they have been put to shame. At that time will I bring you again, even in the time that I gather you: for I will make you a name and a praise among all the people of the earth, when I turn back your captivity* before your eyes, saith the Lord."

§ 3. If Dr. Temple's opinion respecting *Judaism* be erroneous, an examination of what he has put forth with

---

[1] Isaiah, lxi. 4, 7, 9.   [2] Zephaniah, iii. 19, 20.

reference to *Romanism* induces a similar conclusion. "That which religion," he observes, "was to the Jew, law was to the Roman. And law was the lesson which Rome was intended to teach the world. *Hence*, the Bishop of Rome soon became the head of the Church. Rome was, in fact, the centre of the traditions which had once governed the world; and their spirit still remained; and the Roman Church developed into the Papacy, simply because a head was wanted, and *no better one could be found*. Hence, again, in all the doctrinal disputes of the fourth and fifth centuries, the decisive voice came from Rome. *Every controversy was finally settled by her opinion*."[1] Again, he states: "The Papacy of the middle ages, and the Papal hierarchy, with all its numberless ceremonies and appliances of external religion; with its attention fixed upon deeds and not upon thoughts, or feelings, or purposes; with its precise apportionment of punishments and purgatory, was, in fact, neither more nor less than the old schoolmaster come back to bring some new scholars to Christ" (p. 42). Surely this is strange language for a Protestant; much more for a minister of the fairest branch of Christ's Holy Catholic Church in Christendom, whose unceasing adherence to all real Catholic truth, during the eighteen centuries of her existence[2], is the best protest against the novelties, heresies, and attempted usurpation of our fallen and apostate sister, the Church of Rome. That she deserves the title of a *new* church, teaching a *new* faith,

---

[1] Essays and Reviews, p. 16.

[2] It is interesting to remember in this present year of grace, A.D. 1861, that the 18th century of our Church's existence is completed, Christianity having been introduced according to the testimony of Gildas, our most ancient authority on the subject, just before the revolt of Boadicea, A.D. 61, as we have endeavoured to prove in another work, written with the object of showing the Pauline origin of the Church of England.

and putting forth new pretensions, in contradistinction to that bright period of her history, when her "faith was spoken of throughout the whole world,"[1] may be seen in the fact, that the definition of her present belief and teaching, in what is commonly known as "the Creed of Pope Pius IV.," *is not quite three centuries old*, having been ratified as late as December, A.D. 1564. It is scarcely necessary to observe, that, by this suicidal act, in defiance of the positive prohibition of the ancient Catholic Church, as expressed in the seventh canon of the Council of Ephesus[2], she has branded herself as being novel, heretical, and apostate. Her heresy was very clear, when Liberius Bishop of Rome, in the fourth century, became an Arian, though her attempted usurpation cannot be said to have commenced before the beginning of the seventh century, when the Emperor Phocas, that imperial Robespierre, granted the title of "Universalis Sacerdos" to Pope Boniface III., A.D. 607, which title has never been recognised for one day by the Eastern Church, which then formed the largest portion of Christendom. In our own country this usurpation cannot be said to have been attempted for a longer period than the interval between the reign of the miserable King John until the glorious Reformation, and even then with only limited success, as there are many instances, during the reign of the great house of Plantagenet, of resistance to the anti-Catholic and anti-Christian claims of the Bishop of Rome. We think, therefore, that Dr. Temple is mistaken in the

---

[1] Rom. i. 8.
[2] The Council of Ephesus, A.D. 431, decreed that, "Whoever shall dare to compose *any other creed* beside that which was settled by the Holy Fathers who were assembled in the city of Nicæa with the Holy Ghost ... *they shall be deposed*, the bishops from their episcopal office, and clergymen from the clergy." See *Hammond's Definitions of Faith, &c.*; *Conc. Eph.* canon vii.

way in which he has spoken of Rome, whether secular or ecclesiastical.

Let us consider his statements separately. He observes : " *Law* was the lesson which Rome was intended to teach the world. *Hence*, the Bishop of Rome soon became the Head of the Church." The more we analyse this reasoning the more we are struck by the fallacy of the author's logic. Admitted that the Roman people, before the Christian era, proved by their conduct their reverence for law and order, history as well as prophecy shows that the Bishop of Rome made no claim to *that* succession. Their only succession, in respect to " law," was what they adopted from the Roman Emperors, whose grand principle was " legibus solutus," which expression, as Gibbon truly observes, " was supposed to exalt the Emperor *above all human restraints*, and to leave his conscience and reason as the sacred measure of his conduct."[1] *Hence* we find the Bishops of Rome decreeing as follows : " We, according to the plenitude of our power, have a right to *dispense above law*[2] or right," said one.[3] " The Pope may *dispense above the law*, and of wrong make right, by correcting and changing the laws," taught another.[4] " The Pope is *exempted from all law of man*," was the declaration of a third.[5] These claims rested, as Archbishop Ferraris, a great authority, affirms, upon the ground, that the Pope can *modify the Divine law*, since his power is

---

[1] Decline and Fall, viii. 17.

[2] Platina, the eminent Roman Catholic historian, relates concerning one of the Bishops of Rome, that " he (Benedict IX.) appeared to a person after his death in the form of a bear and with the tail of an ass; saying, ' Because I lived like a beast, *without either law or reason*, therefore, at the command of God and St. Peter, whose seat I have defiled, I resemble now a beast rather than a man."

[3] Pope Innocent III. Decret. Greg. b. iii. t. viii. ch. iv.

[4] Decret. Greg. XI. De Transl. Ep. Tit. vii. Gloss., in c. 3, col. 217.

[5] Boniface VIII. in Corp. Jur. Can.

not of man, but of God, and he supplies *the place of God upon earth*, with ample power of binding and loosing."[1]

Now all these things which history records respecting the *past*, prophecy, written, as all admit, centuries before the rise of the Roman Papacy to supreme power, relates as to what was then *future*. For do we not find St. Paul expressly affirming, in his Second Epistle to the Thessalonians, that, previous to the next coming of the Lord Jesus Christ, "the apostasy" would be developed, the prominent signs and characteristic marks of which, as a guide to the faithful in its application, were, that he should have the title of "the Man of Sin,"—that he should exercise supreme authority in the Church of God, far above all temporal powers, and that he should be emphatically ὁ ἄνομος, as claiming to be above all human laws,—whose fall would be finally accomplished at the Lord's appearing? But Dr. Temple and his co-Essayists (Professor Jowett has written upon the Thessalonians, we believe, in an opposite sense) will probably reply : " We do not admit there is any reference to the Church or Bishop of Rome in that prophecy." We can understand such reasoning on the part of Romanists, or of those nominal Protestants (in the widest sense of the term) whose apparent object or necessary result of their logic must be to whitewash Rome from those minatory charges which Scripture brings against her, if language has any definite meaning whatever ; but it is impossible to concede such a right to any minister of the United Church of England and Ireland, one portion of which has once authoritatively declared, that " The Bishop of Rome is so farre from being the supreame head of the vniversall Church of Christ, that his workes and doctrine doe plainely discover him to bee *that Man of Sinne*, foretold in the holy Scriptures, *whome the Lord shall consume*

---

[1] Ferraris, Bibl. Prompt. in Verb. Dispen. § 20.

with the spirit of his mouth, and abolish with the brightness of His comming."[1] We abstain from expressing any private opinion upon this article, but we quote it in order to show the teaching of one of the branches of the Catholic Church, on a doctrine concerning which there is so much error afloat in general, and from which the Essayist has drawn such a mistaken inference in particular.

Dr. Temple continues: " The Roman Church developed into the papacy simply because a head was wanted, and no better could be found. *Hence, again,* in *all* the doctrinal disputes of the fourth and fifth centuries the decisive voice came from Rome." Unable to reconcile the inference of the Essayist, that "a head was wanted," with such passages in Scripture as these, " Call no man your father upon the earth; for One is your Father, which is in heaven. Neither be ye called masters; for One is your Master, even Christ" (St. Matt. xxiii. 9, 10); or " Christ is the head of the body, the Church" (Col. i. 18); and believing that the only headship to which the Church of Rome has ever had any claim, is that of " the apostasy " (Justin Martyr[2] emphatically expressed it "the man of the apostasy"), founded upon his assumption of the title of " Universalis Sacerdos,"[3] as we have before noticed, it

---

[1] Art. 80. Articles of Religion agreed upon by the Archbishops and Bishops and the rest of the Cleargie of Ireland in the Convocation holden at Dublin in the yeare of our Lord God, 1615.
[2] Dial. cum Trypho. § cx.
[3] It is curious to reflect that, when the Patriarch of Constantinople took the same objectionable title, which he did a few years before it was claimed by the Pope, Gregory the Great, then Bishop of Rome was so scandalised at the act, that he wrote, " I confidently affirm that whoever calls himself *Universalis Sacerdos,* or desires to be so called in his pride, is the forerunner of Antichrist, because in his pride he prefers himself to the rest. And he is led into error by a similar pride; for as that *wicked one* wishes to appear a god above all men, so

is necessary to call attention to the mistake which Dr. Temple has made in supposing, that in *all* the doctrinal disputes of the fourth and fifth centuries, the " decisive voice came from Rome."

The great event of the fourth century, after the adoption of the Christian religion by the Roman state, was unquestionably the struggle between Athanasius and the Arians ; and the "decisive voice" came virtually from Alexandria and not from Rome, as we may gather from the Catholic Church having expressed herself for so many centuries respecting the all-important doctrine of the Trinity in the magnificent language of that Creed, which bears the name of Athanasius : whereas the then Bishop of Rome went over to the enemy, turned Arian, and branded himself, and the Church of which he was the first minister for the time being, with the fatal charge of heresy, writing with the accustomed hauteur of the occupant of the Roman see, " Athanasius, who was Bishop of the Church at Alexandria, was condemned by me before I sent the letters of the Eastern Bishops to the Court of the Sacred Emperor, and that he was separated from the communion of the Roman Church, as the whole Presbytery of the Roman Church is witness."[1]

The prominent events of the fifth century were the

---

whatsoever he is who alone desires to be called a Bishop, extols himself above all other Bishops."—Ep. xxxiii. ad Maur. Aug. I. vii. Indict. 15. Gregory Nazianzen, three centuries before the time of Gregory the Great, defined the term " Universalis " on this wise : " That in being made *Bishop of Alexandria* he was made *Bishop of the whole world.*"—Ep. lxix. tom. iii. Ben. ed. p. 161.

[1] Epistle of Liberius, Bishop of Rome to Ursacius, in Hilar. Fragm. vi. 6. The conduct of Liberius elicited from Hilary the following very just rebuke : " This is Arian faithlessness . . . . Anathema ! I say to thee, Liberius, and thy associates . . . . a third time, Anathema ! to thee, prevaricator, Liberius."

Councils of Ephesus, A.D. 431, and of Chalcedon, A.D. 451, both held in Asia, where the voice of Rome had never been recognised as of authority over the whole Church; and the most notable acts of those councils is seen in both of them having prohibited, under the severest penalties, any other creed than the one originally set forth, in the preceding century, by the Council of Nicæa. Their decrees affirm, that "It shall not be lawful for any one to bring forward, or to write, or compose, or teach any other creed, and that they who deliver any other creed to those who are desirous of turning to the acknowledgment of the truth, shall be anathematised."[1] Had the decisive voice come from Rome, at that period of the Church's history, she would not have stultified herself by her suicidal act in the sixteenth, when she did dare to compose another creed, and has thereby inherited the anathema of the Catholic Church of the fifth century.

Dr. Temple farther affirms, that "The Papacy of the Middle Ages, and the Papal hierarchy, was, in fact, neither more nor less than the old schoolmaster come back to bring some new scholars to Christ." If this has any reference to the beautiful metaphor of St. Paul in Galatians iii. 24, where he describes the effect and meaning of the Mosaic dispensation, that "The law was our schoolmaster to bring us unto Christ, that we might be justified by faith," it is singularly inapplicable. For though, in the passage above, the word is translated "schoolmaster," we all know, from its derivation, that it rather meant the pedagogue, or servant who had the care of children, to lead them to and fro from school, than the teacher in the school itself. Even so the Mosaic law did not, like the Gospel, *teach* saving knowledge, but only, as it were,

---

[1] The Definition of Faith agreed upon at the Council of Chalcedon. Act. 5.

gave some hints of the Gospel scheme, and the way of salvation, which was not then fully revealed. By types and figures, by rites and ceremonies, by shadows and sacrifices, it led the Jews to see the pollution of their nature, and their need of blood for the remission of sin; by circumcision, the internal rending of the heart; by the passover, the daily sacrifice, and other offerings, the doctrines of redemption, satisfaction, and atonement; by the brazen serpent, the necessity of looking to Christ for salvation; and, above all, by the conduct of their great ancestor, Abraham, to learn that belief such as he displayed, and unswerving faith in the hour of trial, was the only mode by which a perfectly righteous God could, consistent with His justice, accept and pardon unrighteous and unholy man; in other words, the fundamental doctrine of *justification by faith.*

It is in this especially that the great difference between the teaching of our own Church and that of the Church of Rome consists. We, as a faithful branch of the Catholic branch, teach salvation *one way*, the Papal hierarchy of the Middle Ages taught, as the Church of Rome now teaches it, *another.* And how little "the Papal hierarchy of the Middle Ages" was competent to act the schoolmaster, and to bring some new scholars to Christ, let the following description of it, by Roman Catholic historians, testify: "Fifty popes," says Genebard, "in one hundred and fifty years, from John VIII. till Leo IX., entirely degenerated from the sanctity of their ancestors, and were *apostatical* rather than *apostolical.*" "Many shocking monsters," writes Cardinal Baronius respecting the tenth century, "intruded into the pontifical chair who were guilty of robbery, assassination, simony, dissipation, tyranny, sacrilege, perjury, and all kinds of miscreancy. Candidates, destitute of every requisite qualification, were promoted to the Papal chair; while all the canons and traditions of antiquity were condemned and outraged." Nicholaus de Clemangis, a Romish archdeacon, describes the state of the Church of the Middle Ages, at the close of the fourteenth century, by recording that "*the cardinals* had violated the celibiate vow in all manner of unclean living; that *the bishops* spent their days in hunting and fowling, and their nights in debauchery; that the *regulars* were drunkards and incontinent, living in open sin and shame; that the *monks* were wanderers, and instead of justice, were inflated by pride; and that the *mendicants* were ravening wolves, defiling all things by their flagrant vice." Vincent Ferrarius, a doctor of theology, and present at the Council of Constance, declared, concerning the clergy of the following century, that "The priests fish for honours, but they seek not morals; for they are ignorant, scoffers, illiterate, hypocrites, and simoniacs: they grow worse every day. They are voluptuous, envious, corrupting the whole world. They are obstinate and loquacious, but they never declare God's truth. Christianity would rejoice if, *out of a thousand, she found one devout person.*" From all of which, we should rather conclude with John Robitzana, Archbishop of Prague in the fifteenth century, that "the Papal hierarchy" were so intolerably vicious as to have proved their claim to the title under which he describes the Church of Rome, as "Western Babylon, and the Pope Antichrist, who has overwhelmed the worship of God with a heap of superstitions," rather than the strange deduction which an English presbyter of the nineteenth century has drawn, that it was "neither more nor less than the old schoolmaster come back to bring some new scholars to Christ."

Nor has the Church of Rome become more qualified for teaching the world in this present day than she was in the Middle Ages, if we accept the testimony of one whose other writings at the time, and subsequent secession, prove him at least an unexceptionable witness against that Church, which he has now joined. "In truth," once wrote the noted John Henry Newman, "the Church of Rome is a church beside herself, abounding in noble gifts and rightful titles, but unable to use them religiously; crafty, obstinate, wilful, malicious, cruel, unnatural, *as madmen are*. Or, rather, she may be said to *resemble a demoniac*, possessed with principles, thoughts, and tendencies not her own; in outward form and natural powers what God made her, but ruled within by an inexorable spirit, who is sovereign in his management over her, and most subtle and most successful in the use of her gifts. Thus she is her real self only in name; and till God vouchsafe to restore her, we must treat her *as if she were that Evil One who governs her*." [1]

That Dr. Newman should entertain a different opinion now that he has seceded from the Catholic to the Roman Church is only what we might expect. One of his reasons in justification of the step he has taken, or rather in attempting to defend the Church to which he has allied himself from the awful charge of idolatry, of which she has stood convicted for so many ages, is of so curious a nature, that we cannot forbear noticing it. He attempts to demonstrate the injustice of such a charge upon the following ground: "It is foretold, that under the Gospel dispensation, '*the idols God will utterly abolish*' (Isaiah ii. 18). But if under that dispensation the Roman Church be idolatrous, *then* the idols have *not* been *utterly* abolished. *Therefore*, the Roman Church *cannot* have been idolatrous."[2] Q. E. D. !!!

---

[1] Lectures on the Prophetical Office of the Church, p. 103.
[2] See Stanley Faber's Provincial Letters, p. 222.

There are others besides Dr. Newman, and of a very different school, who appear anxious to defend the Church of Rome from the fatal doom which awaits her, if there be any meaning in the positive declarations of the Apocalypse respecting her. We have already noticed the prevailing opinion of the fifteenth century amongst enlightened churchmen, as expressed by the Archbishop of Prague, that "the Church of Rome was Western Babylon, and the Pope Antichrist [1], who had overwhelmed the Church of Christ with a heap of superstitions." The actions as well as the teaching of the Church of Rome for the last four centuries, have fully confirmed the reasonableness of such an opinion. That the Church of Rome is depicted with a sufficient minuteness of detail to forbid doubt, in the 17th and 18th chapters of Revelation, under the title of "Babylon the Great," no unprejudiced person can for a moment deny. Yet men of entirely different schools have, by some unexplained system of logic, persuaded themselves that it bears some other meaning. E. g. one, who like Dr. Newman, was once a Fellow at Oxford, and who subsequently seceded from the Church of England, though to the other extremity of the pole, having allied himself to the latest formed sect in Christendom, commonly known as "the Plymouth Brethren," has contended, as we have before noticed [2], that the city prophetically described as

---

[1] In speaking of the Pope as Antichrist, we should be careful to remember, that he is only one of many Antichrists. He who is described in Scripture emphatically as "*the* Antichrist," has been defined by the Holy Ghost as including and embracing all the false teachers of a certain doctrine which have appeared since the time of the First Advent. "Many deceivers are entered into the world, who confess not that Jesus Christ is come in the flesh. This is *the* deceiver, and *the* Antichrist."—2 *Epistle of St. John*, ver. 7.

[2] See pp. 20, 21, foot-note.

"the seven-hilled city"[1] and "BABYLON THE GREAT," so far from referring to *Rome*, which the Spirit of God clearly points to as "that great city reigning over the kings of the earth" when St. John lived, it must mean *Babylon on the Euphrates*, where Nebuchadnezzar once reigned!

If we turn to another school of prophetic interpreters, we find them equally at issue with the catholic and spiritual interpretation of "Babylon the Great," as belonging to none other than the Church of Rome. In the last number of the "Westminster Review" we have the most recent display of the qualifications of a rationalistic reviewer, for the office of explaining and interpreting some of the most interesting of the most prophetic portions of Holy Scripture. After the usual fling at "the learned Dr. Cumming, and other distinguished scholars of the same calibre," and after sternly condemning "one of these mystagogues" for renewing the lease of a cottage for ten years, "notwithstanding his conclusion that the world is to come to an end in 1867," the reviewer manifests his qualifications for acting as an impartial censor of others on the subject of prophecy, by denying that the Apocalypse was written by the Apostle St. John ; by affirming that it was composed during the reign of Nero, which he considers *proved* by the "literal" Jerusalem

---

[1] In St. John's age, there was but one great city in the world built upon " seven mountains." The name of each of the seven hills is well known; and by the great Roman poets of antiquity, Virgil, Horace, Ovid, Martial, and many others, it was invariably called " the seven-hilled city." In the present day, a Papal poet of less note, viz. Cardinal Wiseman, has adopted similar phraseology when singing the praises of Pio Nono : —

    " The golden roof, the marble halls,
    The Vatican's majestic walls,
    The note redouble till it fills
    With echoes sweet *the seven hills*,
    ' God bless our Pope, *the great, the good.*' "

being mentioned in the Revelation; by declaring that the annals of Tacitus afford authority for applying the interpretation of the first five heads of the apocalyptic beast, described in the 17th chapter, to Augustus and his successors until Nero, the popular belief of whose resurrection sufficiently fulfilled what is said in Revelation respecting the eighth head of "the beast that was and is not, and goeth into perdition;" and by assuring us that his interpretation of the number of the beast, as ἡ λατίνη βασιλεῖα, whose letters, he adds, "translated into numbers, amount exactly to 666, and the spelling is rigorously correct," must be considered as an *important discovery*, and worthy the attention of "Dr. Cumming and his brother pundits."[1]

Further, in the review of a work entitled, "The Apocalypse Fulfilled, &c. by the Rev. P. S. Desprez," in the same periodical, the editor considers that "Mr. Desprez will have rendered an immense service to the cause of *a reasonable Christianity*[2], if his method of interpreting the Apocalypse should be generally accepted. He will have removed a serious stumblingblock from many well-intentioned persons, and have deprived *clerical charlatans of the means of perpetuating gross imposture and deceit.*" And he declares that "Mr. Desprez's work deals a heavy

---

[1] See Westminster Review, No. xl., Oct. 1861, pp. 451, 472, 476, 483.

[2] As Mr. Desprez consistently maintains, that the resurrection of the dead and glorification of the living, foretold by St. Paul in 1 Thess. iv., 1 Cor. xv., Phil. iii. 20, 21, Rev. xx., and in other places, *took place at the destruction of Jerusalem*, we can appreciate the Westminster Reviewer's definition of "*a reasonable Christianity*," though it is somewhat difficult to understand how Mr. Desprez can swallow some expressions in the Creeds respecting the *future* resurrection of the body, to which he, as a clergyman of the Church of England, has given his assent, and which he is so frequently compelled to maintain by word of mouth.

blow upon the Exeter Hall fanaticism, from which it will not easily recover."[1] Whether Exeter Hall can hope to survive this terrible onslaught, we need not stop to determine; but it may be permitted us to point out some trifling inaccuracies and mistakes of the Westminster Reviewer, which must necessarily invalidate the sweeping condemnation which he so unsparingly bestows upon those who do not assent to his prophetic interpretation.

In the first place, then, considering that Papias, Bishop of Hierapolis, the *contemporary* of St. John, received and used the Apocalypse[2]; that Justin Martyr, who held his controversy with Trypho the Jew at Ephesus, where St. John had been living about thirty years before, affirms that the Revelation had been given to "*John, one of the Apostles of Christ;*"[3] and that Irenæus, the disciple of Polycarp, who was himself the disciple of St. John, declares that "it was seen by that Apostle *no very long time ago, but almost in our own age, towards the end of the reign of Domitian,*"[4] we must reject the theory, whether it be of Dionysius of Alexandria in the eighth century, or of a Westminster Reviewer in the nineteenth, which would ascribe the authorship to another[5], and which antedates

---

[1] Westminster Review, No. xl., Oct. 1861, pp. 551, 553.
[2] Andreas, in Apoc.
[3] Dialog. cum Trypho. § lxxxi.
[4] Contr. Hær. v. 30–3. Compare the statement of Irenæus with the conclusion of Professor Maurice, who speaks, in his "Lectures on the Apocalypse," of "the absence of any evidence for the old tradition that the Apocalypse belongs to the time of Domitian."
[5] There is, perhaps, no book of the New Testament for which we have such clear and numerous testimonies (several besides those adduced above) as we have in favour of the Apocalypse, and immediately succeeding the time when it was written. That doubts should prevail in after ages must have originated, either in ignorance of the earlier testimony, or else from some rationalistic idea as to what an Apostle

it about thirty years, in order to deny the doctrine of the Millennium, and to apply what is said in the Apocalypse respecting the heavenly temple, to the material one which was destroyed by the Roman army shortly after Nero died.

Considering also that the Annals of Tacitus, so far from affording any authority to the Westminster Reviewer for his novel application of the prophecy respecting the *five* fallen heads of the apocalyptic beast, to Augustus and his four immediate successors, do warrant, conjointly with the history of Livy, the ancient interpretation, that they refer to the *five* previous forms of government which had existed in Rome before the Imperial, when St. John lived, since they are specified as *kings, consuls, dictators, decemvirs*, and *tribunes* [1], we must reject this modern and unfounded theory, which seeks to apply the fulfilment of the predictions to the destruction of the temple of Jerusalem by the Roman armies.

Considering, moreover, that the wonderful discovery of the Westminster Reviewer respecting the number of the beast, which by the way is not original, must necessarily fail, simply because Scripture declares it to refer to " the number of a *man*," [2] and not to the

---

ought to have written. It is in vain, however, to argue *à priori*, that St. John *could* not have written this book, when we have the evidence of several competent authorities that he *did* write it.

[1] Livy, vi. 1, and Tacitus, Annal. i. 1.

[2] Apoc. xiii. 18. Many other names, besides the selection of the Westminster Reviewer, have been suggested for the fulfilment of this prophecy from the time when Irenæus in the second century proposed a choice between *Lateinos* and *Teitan*, as fulfilling the required number, down to the period of the Reformation, when *Saxoneios* was adopted by Cardinal Bellarmine " for the satisfaction of Luther ; " or to our own day, when Dr. Newman supposed he had discovered the enigma in the phrase " *the Reformed British Parliament ;* " but all these, and a multitude of other similar fancies, necessarily fail for want of agreeing with

number of a kingdom, as he fancifully suggests, we must decline his mode of interpreting the Apocalypse on that head.

Finally, considering that the Westminster Reviewer's definition of "*a reasonable Christianity*" depends upon Mr. Desprez's mode of interpreting the Apocalypse being the true and correct one, the chief feature of which is that "Babylon the Great" means Jerusalem, and not Rome, it may be well to point out as a justification for the ancient opinion, which appears to have been adopted in modern times by "clerical charlatans" and "Exeter Hall fanatics," that "the woman," or "scarlet lady" of the Apocalypse, as she is sometimes delicately termed, cannot be a symbol of *Jerusalem*, as she was never guilty of "committing fornication," i. e. idolatrous worship, "with the kings of the earth," or of making "the inhabitants of the earth drunk with the wine of her whoredom," since her exclusive religious system forbad such unholy connection. Nor was she ever supported by the temporal power in the mode indicated in the Apocalypse, i.e. both guiding it and upheld by it; nor could it be said of Jerusalem that she was ever "*drunken* with the blood of the saints, and with the blood of the martyrs of Jesus;" and that if she had, it would have caused "wonder" and astonishment to St. John, when such a revelation was made to him; nor

---

the marks by which the Church should know that "the number of the beast" meant the number of some man's name, who would towards the close of this age possess dominion in the Roman empire. And it is somewhat curious to find that, by writing the various names of the present Emperor of the French in the three languages which told the world the death of the Saviour of Men, we have in the Latin tongue, *Louis*, i. e. Ludovicus; in the Greek tongue, *Louis Napoleon*; and in the Hebrew tongue, *Charles Bonaparte*, as the equivalents to the required number 666.

was Jerusalem built upon "seven mountains," as the seat "on which the woman sitteth" is distinctly declared to be; nor could her power be ever said to have extended over "peoples, multitudes, nations, and tongues;" nor, finally, was Jerusalem "reigning over the kings of the earth," either at the time when St. John wrote the Apocalypse, or at any previous period of her history. Since, however, these characteristic marks, by which the Catholic Church was to be forewarned and forearmed, are *completely and exclusively*[1] *fulfilled in Papal Rome*, we must adhere to the ancient interpretation, the Westminster Reviewer and Mr. Desprez *non obstante*, content to bear the reproach of being termed "charlatans" and "fanatics," by those whose "*reasonable Christianity*" has sufficiently exposed their pretensions to being considered faithful interpreters of the prophecies of the Book of Revelation.

If we look to the writings of another of the Essayists, as a true exponent of the principles of a "reasonable Christianity," we find a similar confusion of ideas respecting the tremendous and impassable gulf which separates Catholicism and Romanism. "The recognition of the fact," observes Mr. Pattison, in his Essay on "The Tendencies of Religious Thought in England, 1688–1750," "that the view of the eternal verities of religion which prevails in any given age, is in part determined by the view taken in the age which preceded it, is incompatible with the hypothesis generally prevalent among us as to the mode in which we form our notions of religious truth. Upon none of the prevailing theories as to this mode

---

[1] The author has endeavoured to show this in a pamphlet entitled " *Come out* or *Go out ;* an Explication of Revelation xviii. 4, according to the Douay Version. Addressed to our Roman Catholic Brethren of Great Britain and Ireland," to which he ventures to refer those who may feel interested on the subject.

is a deductive history of theology possible. 1. The Catholic theory, which is really that of Roman Catholics, and, professedly, that of Anglo-Catholics, withdraws Christianity altogether from human experience and the operation of the ordinary laws of thought. 2. The Protestant theory of free inquiry, which supposes that each mind asks a survey of the evidence, and strikes the balance of probability, according to the best of its judgment."[1]

The lamentable mistake in the foregoing passage requires notice. To affirm that the religious truth of any age is dependent upon the one which has preceded it, and to assert that the Roman Catholics hold "the Catholic theory," manifests such ignorance of both the positive and negative sides of theology, that it is wonderful how the Essayist could have committed himself in the way he has done. Truth, whether termed religious or Catholic truth, for they are one and the same, is like its Author, unchangeable. The allowable anagram on Pilate's famous question, "Quid est veritas?" "Vir est qui adest," affords the briefest and yet most perfect reply. Christ Himself is emphatically the truth, true God as well as true man. His gospel comes from the God of truth, and lies in the Scriptures of truth—the whole of it and every part of it in particular are equally true. And the promise which the Saviour made before He laid down His life to redeem a fallen world, was, that after his departure He would send the Spirit of Truth to guide His disciples into all truth, to teach them all things, and to abide with them for ever.[2] Hence truth is the same in this nineteenth century, as it was in the first, when the great Apostle to the Gentiles, as is most probable, delivered the glad

---

[1] Essays and Reviews, pp. 255, 256.
[2] St. John, xiv. 16, 26; xvi. 13.

tidings of salvation to our ancestors in this island. Happy would it be if Mr. Pattison and his school could apply that theory as Clement of Alexandria once recommended —" Philosophy shall submit itself to theology as Hagar to Sarah ; but if it be unwilling to obey, 'cast out the bondwoman.'" Until men consent to make their changeable philosophical speculations succumb to unchangeable theological truth, they cannot escape the errors into which the Essayist has fallen.

Having thus committed himself as regards the way in which the Church has received the eternal truth, which Mr. Pattison assumes to be variable from age to age, so has he erred respecting the application of the "Catholic theory" to those who by courtesy are called "Roman Catholics," but whom, if speaking with philosophic precision, we should prefer to call " Romanists " or " Papists." Never, probably, in the history of the world, has any term been so misapplied as that of the term *Catholic*. It is only natural that the Romanist, when he finds it conceded to him by unthinking Protestants, should make the most of it ; but how any one, capable of reason, should deliberately concede a point of such vital importance, in the way the Essayist has done, is surprising beyond measure. When we remember that the Church of Rome has made the acceptance of the Anti-Catholic creed of Pope Pius IV.[1] a *sine quâ non* for admission to com-

---

[1] Every priest of the Church of Rome is bound by the modern creed of Pope Pius IV. to swear to the gigantic absurdity that he will " *never interpret the Holy Scriptures otherwise than according to the unanimous consent of the Fathers ;*" in which oath we have some rather singular instances of the way in which reason and faith are alike set at nought. We see this in the much controverted text of St. Matt. xvi. 18, which may be said to contain the pivot-doctrine of the Roman Church. The celebrated Papal writer, Father Launoy, when exposing the wilful misrepresentations of Cardinal Bellarmine on the subject,

munion, no one with the slightest pretensions to an acquaintance with what Catholic verities really are will ever make so fatal a blunder as to concede to that once flourishing, but now apostate, branch of the Church of Christ the glorious and unchangeable title of Catholic. If it were necessary to make this matter plain to common understandings, we have only to note the mode in which she has defined the truth according to the founder of the Jesuits, and which has been confirmed and approved by the chief of the Roman hierarchy in England:—" That we may *in all things attain the truth*," taught Ignatius Loyola, " that we may not err in anything, we ought to hold it as a fixed principle, *that what I see white I believe to be black if the hierarchial church so define it to be*."[1] This candid specimen of Rome's love of truth is only to be paralleled by what one of her missionaries in China relates respecting the Imperial Will on a similar theological definition. The late Abbé Huc, in his " Travels in China," reports an interesting conversation between himself and one Ki-chan, a mandarin of letters, about public men in Europe and the Celestial Empire. " Your mandarins," said Ki-chan, " are more fortunate than ours. Our Emperor cannot know everything, yet he is judge of everything, and no

---

gives seventeen extracts from various Fathers, in which *St. Peter is spoken of as the Rock*; eight passages from some of the same writers in which *the Church is said to have been built upon all the Apostles*; forty-four extracts which make *the faith of Peter's confession the rock*; and sixteen passages from many of the same authorities, which declare that *the Church was built on Christ the rock*. Vide Lannoii Opera, t. v. p. 99, ep. vii. lib. v. Col. Allob. 1731. St. Augustine appears to have reached the climax of hermeneutical difficulties, when, after having interpreted this famous text in one place of *Peter* and in another of *Christ*, he adds, " *Let the reader select which of the two meanings he deems the more probable*."—*Aug. Retract*. lib. 1. t. i. p. 32, Ben. ed.

[1] Exercises of St. Ignatius, edited by the present Cardinal Wiseman. Dolman, London, 1847.

one dares find fault with any of his actions. Our Emperor says, '*That is white*,' and we prostrate ourselves and say, '*Yes, it is white.*' He shows us the same object afterwards and says, '*That is black*,' and we prostrate ourselves again and say, '*Yes, it is black.*'"

Such is the prostration or rather perversion of intellect amongst the heathen of China, as well as amongst nominal Christians in connexion with the Church of Rome. It is needless to say that such is not "the Catholic theory," as it has existed from the first, and will continue the same unto the last. We apprehend that Cyprian the martyr, Bishop of Carthage, understood the true Catholic theory in his day somewhat better than the present Rector of Lincoln College, Oxford; and his definition of it is as follows:—"Whereas, there is one Church of Christ, divided throughout the world into many members, and one Episcopate, consisting of many concordant bishops; this man (Novatian, a schismatical prelate), when there is already a divine tradition, and a unity of the Catholic Church already knit together, and combined throughout all parts, would fain establish a mere *human Church*, and despatch *his own upstart Apostles* amongst a multitude of cities, in order that they might lay the novel foundations of this institution of his own."[1]

So again, when the Essayist declares that, "In the Catholic theory, the feebleness of reason is met half-way, and made good by the authority of the Church" (p. 328); he misapplies the term "Catholic," and misunderstands the reasonableness of the Christian religion. It is unquestionably true, as Bacon said, that "he laboureth in vain who shall endeavour to draw down heavenly mysteries to human reason; it rather becomes us to bring our reason to the adorable throne of divine truth." Hence

---

[1] Cyprian, Ep. 52.

we cannot forget that when "the Catholic theory" was first announced by the Apostles at Berœa, and the people who heard them exercised their reason by comparing the preaching of Paul and Silas with the Scriptures, they were commended for so doing : " These were more noble than those in Thessalonica, in that they received the word with all readiness of mind, and searched the Scripture daily whether these things were so."[1]

§ 4. We have spoken of the gulf which separates Catholicism from Romanism. It will be right, therefore, to consider how far the ancient creeds of the Church are distinguishable from that modern creed of the Church of Rome, to which our attention has just been called. Mr. Wilson, in his Essay entitled *Séances Historiques de Genève*, has some remarks respecting one of those ancient creeds, which require some notice. His theory appears to be contained in the following sentence :—" As an indication of a great extent of dissatisfaction on the part of the clergy to some portion, at least, of the formularies of the Church of England, may be taken the fact of the existence of various associations to procure their revision, or some liberty in their use, *especially that of omitting one unhappy Creed.*"[2] We are confident that we do not wrong Mr. Wilson when we assume that his " one

---

[1] Acts, xvii. 11. Contrast this with the Roman Catholic theory as embodied in the teaching of the Council of Trent. " If any one shall presume to read the Holy Bible without permission of the Bishop or Inquisitor, unless he shall first deliver up the Bible to the Ordinary, he must not receive absolution for his sins."— *Conc. Trid. Canon* iv. Or in the Bull of Pope Clement XI., which affirms, " The proposition of Quesnel, that ' it is useful and necessary at all times and in all places, and for all sorts of persons to study, and to know the spirit and piety and mysteries of the Scriptures,' is false, captious, shocking, offensive to pious ears, scandalous, pernicious, rash, seditious, impious, and blasphemous."— *Bull entitled* " *Unigenitus,*" A.D. 1713.

[2] Essays and Reviews, p. 150.

unhappy Creed," which he is so anxious to eliminate from among the standard formularies and authorities of the Church of England, can refer to none other than that which is commonly called *the Athanasian Creed*. We presume that the age is not yet sufficiently advanced in scepticism to warrant his advocating the banishment of either of those Creeds, known as *the Apostles'* and *the Nicene*, especially with the warning of the last century before his eyes; and he therefore thinks he can safely manifest his dislike towards the third, as being more recent, and therefore less defensible, than the other two. Now, we have no hesitation in affirming, confirmed as such an opinion must necessarily be by the position of Christendom at this present hour, that the retention or rejection of the Athanasian Creed is one of the chief causes of the gulf which separates the Churches of England and Geneva, as well as the only way by which we can reasonably account for " the rude shocks " which Christianity has experienced in one of "the strongholds of the Reformation." Experience is singularly uniform on this subject : whether in England, Germany, Switzerland, or America, wherever the Creeds of the Catholic Church have been rejected or set aside, a lapse into Unitarianism, which involves a rejection of those two fundamental truths—the worship of the Trinity in Unity, and the doctrine of the Atonement,—has been the necessary result. Mr. Wilson's admission respecting Switzerland ; the exposure which took place about twenty years ago in England, when "Lady Hewley's Charity" was diverted by the Legislature from its intended course ; the rise of the rationalistic school in Germany ; and the remarkable extension of Unitarianism in the United States of America, alike tell the same tale — that mankind needs some judicious restraints in things spiritual, as well as in things temporal. The definition of " unhappy," which the

Essayist has ascribed to the Athanasian Creed, to the use and approval of which he has freely given his assent and consent, is singularly inappropriate, and might, we apprehend, be more properly applied to the condition of his own mind, since he must be conscious of holding preferment in the Church of Christ on a tenure which in his heart he abhors. We justly contend that the epithet is inappropriate for the double reason—1st, that in the Articles there is the general proposition that "Holy Scripture containeth all things necessary to salvation; so that whatsoever is not read therein, nor may be proved thereby, is not to be required of any man that it should be believed as an Article of the Faith" (Art. VI.); and, 2nd, that in the Athanasian Creed, in particular, there is nothing required to be believed but what may assuredly be proved by Holy Writ. Thus the popular idea to which, we suppose, the Essayist inclines,—that every word of the Creed is to be believed on pain of damnation, —is, in reality, a delusion, when the Creed itself is carefully examined. For all that is required of us, as *necessary to salvation, is,* that *before all things we hold the Catholic Faith; and the Catholic Faith is* explained to be *this— that we worship one God in Trinity, and Trinity in Unity, neither confounding the persons nor dividing the substance;* which is repeated farther on. *So that in all things, as is aforesaid, the Unity in Trinity is to be worshipped. He therefore that will be saved must thus think of the Trinity.* This is what the Creed and Holy Scripture alike require us to believe, if we desire an inheritance in the kingdom of God. What else the Creed contains is only brought as a proof and illustration in support, both of the doctrine of the Trinity, and also that of the Atonement; and therefore, as Wheatly truly observes, "requires our assent no more than a sermon to prove or illustrate a text. The text, we know, is the Word of God, and therefore necessary to be believed; but no person is, for that reason, bound to believe every particular of the sermon deduced from it upon pain of damnation, though every tittle of it may be true."[1]

It may be well, however, before proceeding farther, to attempt to define the meaning of the term, "the Catholic Faith," in its integrity and entirety. "I believe in the Holy Catholic Church," is the teaching of the *Apostles' Creed;* and the Catholic Faith is the embodiment of doctrine which that Holy Catholic Church has alike taught in all ages and in all countries, since the time when the Holy Ghost was given according to Christ's promise, to guide her into all truth, and to abide with her for ever. Hence the ancient definition of *Catholicity* in that well-known canon of Vincent of Lerins[2]— "Always, everywhere, and held by all," which accords with the still earlier canon of Tertullian[3]—" Whatsoever was first, that is truth; whatsoever is later, that is adulterated."

Christendom, as it exists in the present day, consists of three great divisions, which may be described under the general terms of Catholics, Papists, and Non-Episcopalians. By *Catholics* we understand those who have combined Evangelical teaching with Apostolical order; the doctrine of the Trinity, and all its blessed concomitants, together with that three-fold order of ministry which God has appointed for rule in the Church, which has ever existed since the day of Pentecost, and which presents so striking a contrast to the many other systems which have been adopted by Christians, notwithstanding they are all of human invention.

By *Papists* we mean those who recognise the Bishop of

---

[1] Wheatly's Rational Illustration of the Book of Common Prayer, ch. iii. § xv.

[2] Contra Hær. c. iii.   [3] Adv. Praxeam, § ii.

Rome as Head of the Church, in place of Christ; who call him "Father of the Faithful," contrary to the express prohibition of our Lord, who has said, "Call no man your Father upon the earth; for one is your Father, which is in heaven;"[1] and who, in defiance of all antiquity and truth, assume to themselves the exclusive title of *Catholics*, which some Protestants, from ignorance or want of thought, are too ready to concede unto them. But inasmuch as the Church of Rome stands convicted of the threefold sin of *Supremacy, Apostasy,* and *Idolatry*,—whether by the worship of "the Queen of Heaven," or of dead men and women, or the deified wafer,—according to the prophetic announcements of St. Paul and St. John, as set forth in the Epistles to the Thessalonians and to Timothy, and in the Book of Revelation, no one, who can distinguish truth from error, ought to be guilty of so fatal a mistake as to concede to them a title to which they have no claim at all.

By *Non-Episcopalians* we mean that large body of Nonconformists, as they are called in this country, who prefer, for the government of the community to which they respectively belong, anything of human devising rather than that which is of Divine appointment. They may be classified in the chronological order in which these several sections of Christendom arose, as Unitarians, Presbyterians, Anabaptists, Independents or Congregationalists, Wesleyans, Plymouth Brethren, and Mormonites, or Latter-day Saints. We do not mean to say that these various bodies of Christians teach alike on the great doctrines of the Gospel. On some fundamental truths they are at issue among themselves, as much as they differ from the full teaching of the "Catholic Faith." But we suppose we do them no wrong when we say that

---

[1] St. Matt. xxiii. 9.

they, one and all, reject the language and the definitions of the *Athanasian Creed*, together with its use, in the same manner as the Unitarians originally, and the whole body of Non-Episcopalians generally, have confounded the doctrines of Regeneration and Conversion[1], which have always been distinguished and separated in the teaching of Christ's "Holy Catholic Church."

Mr. Wilson, however, appears to consider that this "unhappy creed" is so distasteful to the clergy at large, that it is the chief thing to be got rid of, when "the various associations" which have been formed to "procure a revision of the formularies of the Church" are enabled to carry their theories into practice. We cannot but think that our Essayist is over-sanguine in his conclusions, as we cannot forget the failure of a certain noble Lord, who attempted last year to support the cause of the revisionists before the Legislature, for these two reasons— 1st, that "he believed the *great majority* of the clergy of the Church of England were in favour of revision;" and, 2ndly, that "he was unable to see why he should continue to pray in *bad grammar*," as he considered the language of the Prayer Book to be.[2] We hardly know how the noble advocate arrived at these singular conclusions; for the fact of ten thousand of the clergy having petitioned *against* revision, whereas we believe only about four hundred were found on the opposite side, would seem to

---

[1] The Racovian Catechism, drawn up by Socinus in the sixteenth century, contains the earliest intimation of this error, which has subsequently become the great Shibboleth of the creed of modern Dissenters, and presents an instructive contrast to the language of the most profound theologian given to the Church since the days of St. Paul, the saintly Augustine, who taught, "the Sacrament of Baptism, by which children are regenerated to God, is *one thing*, conversion of the heart is *another*." Compare De Verb. Ap. Serm. viii. 8, with Contr. Don. iv. 24, 25.

[2] Speech of Lord Ebury in the House of Lords, May 1861.

imply that "the great majority" were rather adverse than friendly to the cause which he so incautiously espoused. And the accusation of "bad grammar," which he so unhesitatingly brought against our venerated Book of Common Prayer, we meet by quoting the unexceptionable testimony of a Nonconformist minister, who was considered in his own time a competent judge of the beauty of our Saxon tongue, and who thus expressed himself respecting the merits of our English Liturgy:—"I believe," said Robert Hall, "that the Evangelical purity of its sentiments, the chastised fervour of its devotions, and *the majestic simplicity of its language*, have combined to place it in the very first rank of uninspired compositions."[1]

Possibly, however, the noble Lord would have been content with the novel proposition which his Grace the Primate mentioned during the debate as having been gravely suggested by one of the leaders amongst the revisionists, when he observed that "one of the ablest advocates of revision proposed to place the alterations between brackets, and to leave an *alternative to the clergyman to read whichever sentence he approved*."[2] Surely this curious mode of encouraging uniformity must have come from the other side of the water; but we hardly think, even if acceptable to the Essayist, it would be

---

[1] Speech at the Anniversary Meeting of the Bible Society in Leicester, A.D. 1812.

[2] In considering the subject of Liturgical revision we should never forget to distinguish between lawfulness and expediency, according to the advice which St. Paul more than once repeated in writing to the Corinthians. "I shall, for my part," said Archbishop Laud, "never deny that the Liturgy of the Church of England *may be made better;* but I am sure, withal, it may easily be made worse: this will bring forth a *schism* firm enough to rend and tear religion out of this kingdom, which God, for the merits and mercies of Christ, forbid."
—*Opera*, vol. iv. p. 29.

deemed a satisfactory solution of a difficult problem by either of the three theological schools, into which the Church of England is said to be divided.

Again, Mr. Wilson observes respecting the great Catholic doctrine of *Justification by faith*, that the Lutherans represent it as "having died out shortly after the Apostolic age;" and adds that "it never was the doctrine of any considerable portion of the Church till the time of the Reformation. It is not met with in the immediately post Apostolic writings, nor in the Apostolic writings, except those of St. Paul, nor even in the Epistle to the Hebrews, which is of the Pauline or Paulo-Johannean school. The faith at least of that Epistle, 'the substance of things hoped for,' is a very different faith from the faith of the Epistle to the Romans,—if the Lutherans are correct in representing that to be a conscious apprehending of the benefits to the individual soul of the Saviour's merits and passion" (p. 160). Those who believe in the inspiration of the writers of the New Testament will of course reject this unfounded theory of there being any difference in their teaching, such as the Essayist supposes, much less on such an important doctrine as the mode by which a sinner is accounted righteous before God. Those who are acquainted with the ecclesiastical writings of the sixteenth century, well know that this was the chief point on which Luther made his memorable stand against the Church of Rome; and the manner in which it was received he rightly pronounced to be the sign "*stantis vel cadentis Ecclesiæ.*" And it is difficult to understand how a clergyman of the Church of England, who is compelled to express his adherence to the doctrine of "Justification by Faith only," could express himself in the way he has done on so vital a point of Gospel truth. The catholic teaching of the Church of England is expressed as follows—"We are accounted righteous before God, *only* for the merit of our Lord and Saviour Jesus Christ by faith, and not for our works or deservings. Wherefore that we are *justified by faith only* is a most wholesome doctrine."[1] The anti-catholic teaching of the Church of Rome[2] is expressed somewhat differently : " Whosoever shall affirm that the ungodly is justified by faith only, so that it is to be understood that nothing else is required to co-operate therewith in order to obtain justification ; and that it is on no account necessary that he should *prepare and dispose himself by the effort of his own will;* let him be accursed."[3]

Those who know what the early Fathers taught on this all important and fundamental truth, will stand aghast at the hardihood or the limited knowledge of the person who could venture to write that " the doctrine of justification by subjective faith is not met with in the immediately post Apostolic writings, nor in the Apostolic writings, *except those of St. Paul*, and in fact never was the doctrine of any considerable portion of the Church till the time of the Reformation " (pp. 159, 160).

Let us hear the words of some of the great theologians of different ages, and judge how far this bold assertion is borne out by facts.

Thus Clemens Romanus, in the first century, writes :— " We are not justified by ourselves, neither by our own wisdom, or knowledge, or piety, or *the works which we have done in the holiness of our hearts*, but by that faith by which God Almighty has justified all men from the beginning."[4]

---

[1] Art. xi. " Of the Justification of Man."

[2] *Bishop of Coventry :* " Why will you not admit the Church of Rome to be the Catholic Church ? " *Philpot :* " Because it followeth not the Primitive Catholic Church, neither agreeth with the same, no more than an apple is like a nut."—*The Trial of Martyr Philpot.*

[3] Concil. Trid. Sess. vi. Canon xi.   [4] Ep. ad Corinth. § 32.

Thus Justin Martyr, in the second century:—" Abraham, while he was yet in uncircumcision, was justified through that faith by which he believed in God, and received the blessing, as the Scripture testifies. But he received circumcision for a sign, not for righteousness, as the same Scriptures, and the nature of the thing, forces us to acknowledge."[1]

Thus Origen, in the third century:—"*Justification by faith only is sufficient*, so that if any person only believe, he may be justified, though no good work hath been done by him."[2] And again, " The dying thief was *justified by faith without the works of the law;* because concerning these, the Lord did not inquire what he had done before; neither did he stay to ask what work he was purposing to perform after he had believed ; but, *the man being justified by his own confession only*, Jesus, who was going to Paradise, took him as a companion and carried him there."[3]

Thus Basil the Great, in the fourth century:—"Everlasting rest is laid up for them that strive lawfully in this life; not to be rendered according to the debt of works, but exhibited according to the grace of the very bountiful God to them that put their trust in Him."[4]

Thus Jerome, of the same century:—" If we consider our own merits we must despair."[5] And again, " When the day of judgment or of the sleep of death shall come, all hands shall fail; because no work shall be found worthy of the justice of God."[6]

Thus Chrysostom, in the same century:—" Although we suffered a thousand deaths, although we performed all

---

[1] Dial. cum Trypho. § 23.
[2] Comm. in Rom. iii. 28.
[3] Comm. in Luke, xxiii. 43.
[4] Comm. in Psalm cxiv.
[5] Comm. in Esai. c. lxiv.
[6] Ibid. c. xiii.

virtuous actions, we should yet fall far short of rendering anything worthy of those honours which are conferred upon us by God."[1] And again, " It is of God, since it is not of works (which would require spotless perfection), but *by grace we are justified,* where all sin is blotted out."[2]

Thus St. Augustine[3], in the same century, and we prefer in this instance to give his own words:—" Nullane igitur sunt merita justorum? Sunt planè quia justi sunt. Sed ut justi sunt. Sed ut justi fierent merita non fuerunt. Justi enim facti sunt, cùm justificati sunt, sed sicut dicit Apostolus, *justificati gratis per gratiam ipsius.*"[4] And again, " Neque ex lege justitia, neque per naturæ possibilitatem, sed *ex fide et dono Dei* per Jesum Christum Dominum nostrum."[5]

Thus Cyril of Alexandria, in the fifth century :—" Evangelical preaching is *grace by faith,* justification in Christ, and sanctification through the Holy Spirit."[6] And again, " The law proclaimed before that those who were shut up under sin should be *justified by faith in Christ alone.*"[7]

Thus Theodoret in the same century :—" The salvation of men depends upon the sole mercy of God, for we do not obtain it as the wages of our righteousness, but it is the gift of God's goodness."[8]

---

[1] De Compunc. ad Stelechium, tom. vi. ed. Savile, p. 157.
[2] Homily ii. on 2 Ep. to Cor. v.
[3] Elsewhere St. Augustine pronounces the doctrine of Justification by Faith to be " VERA ET PROPHETICA ET APOSTOLICA ET CATHOLICA FIDES," which golden sentence the Benedictine editors have given in capital letters. Liber de Corruptione et Gratiâ, tom. x. p. 75, Ben. ed.
[4] Ad Sextum, Epist. 194, tom. ii. Ben. ed.
[5] Ad Innoc. Epist. 177.
[6] Comm. in Esaiam, l. iii. tom. ii. p. 402, Lut. 1638.
[7] De Ador. in Spir. et Verit. l. xv. tom. ii. p. 527.
[8] In Sophoni, c. iii.

Thus Gregory the Great in the sixth century:—"All the righteousness of man is proved to be unrighteousness, if it be strictly judged."[1]

If we pass on from the Fathers of the first six centuries to the Middle Ages, we find about the year A.D. 1100, there was a form of consolation to the dying, said to have been written by Anselm, Archbishop of Canterbury, and printed A.D. 1476, in Germany, which will afford us some insight into the mode of teaching the doctrine of "Justification by Faith" by the few enlightened men who contended for the Catholic faith amidst the almost universal darkness of Popery. It was in the following words:— "Go to, then, as long as thou art in life, put all thy confidence in the death of Christ alone—confide in nothing else—commit thyself wholly to it—roll thyself wholly on it. And if the Lord will judge thee, say, 'Lord, I put the death of our Lord Jesus Christ between me and Thy judgment, otherwise I contend not with Thee.' And if He say, 'Thou art a sinner,' reply, 'Put the death of our Lord Jesus Christ between me and my sins.' And if He say, 'Thou has deserved damnation,' let thine answer be, 'Lord, I spread the death of our Lord Jesus Christ between me and my demerits ; I offer His merits I should have had and have not.' And if He still insist that He is angry at thee, reply again, 'Lord, I put the death of our Lord Jesus Christ between me and Thine anger.'"

We think this is sufficient to show that the Essayist is not borne out in his assertion that the doctrine of Justification by Faith "never was the doctrine of any considerable portion of the Church till the time of the Reformation."

This is a sufficient reply to the lamentable error and

---

[1] Moral in Job. lib. ix. c. 14.

confusion into which Mr. Wilson has fallen respecting the grand Catholic, and, therefore, unchangeable, doctrine of *Justification by Faith* only for the merits of our Lord and Saviour Jesus Christ, and not for our own works or deservings.

The difference between the unchangeable "Catholic theory" on the subject of man's justification, as stated above, and the teaching of the Roman Church on the same all-important doctrine, will be seen by a reference to the creeds and canons of that fallen communion. "I embrace and receive all and every one of the things which have been defined and declared in the Holy Council of Trent concerning original sin and justification," is the language of the fourth article of the creed of Pope Pius IV. The teaching of the Council of Trent on this subject is as follows:—"Whosoever shall affirm that the ungodly is justified by faith only, so that it is to be understood that nothing else is required to co-operate therewith in order to obtain justification; and that it is on no account necessary that he should prepare and dispose himself by the effort of his own will; *let him be accursed.* Whosoever shall affirm, that men are justified solely by the imputation of the righteousness of Christ, or by the remission of sin, to the exclusion of grace and charity which is shed abroad in their hearts, and inheres in them; or that the grace by which we are justified is only the favour of God; *let him be accursed.* Whosoever shall affirm that justifying faith is nothing else than confidence in the Divine mercy, by which sins are forgiven for Christ's sake; or, that it is that confidence only by which we are justified; *let him be accursed.* Whosoever shall affirm, that a justified man, how perfect soever, is not bound to keep the commandments of God, and the Church, but only to believe; as if the Gospel were a naked and absolute promise of eternal life, without the condition of keeping the commandments: *let him be accursed.*"[1]

The statements put forth by another of the Essayists on this important subject require notice. "'Justified by faith without works,' and 'justified by faith as well as works,' are equally scriptural expressions," observes Professor Jowett in his Essay "On the Interpretation of Scripture," "the one has become the formula of Protestants, the other of Roman Catholics."[2] This is so far true, though an imperfect way of stating a great Scriptural doctrine; but when we find the same writer speaking of "*balancing the adverse statements of St. James and St. Paul*" (p. 366), we discover at once his misunderstanding of the first principles of the Christian religion. No believer in *Revelation* can for a moment admit the possibility of there being any "adverse statements" between two inspired apostles, and it requires no very deep skill in the interpretation of Scripture to discover the way, and the only way, by which the *apparently* (not really) contradictory statements concerning justification can be explained and reconciled. It would have been well for Professor Jowett if he could have received and understood the explanation which two such eminent doctors of early and later days (St. Augustine and Bishop Beveridge) have given of the uniformity of the teaching of the Catholic Church respecting this important matter. "Non sunt," taught the former, "sibi contrariæ duorum Apostolorum sententiæ Pauli et Jacobi, cum dicit unus justificari hominem per fidem sine operibus; Quia ille dicit de operibus quæ fidem præcedunt, is de his quæ fidem sequuntur." The latter observed, "It is by faith

---

[1] Conc. Trid. Session vi. Canons 9, 11, 12, 20.
[2] Essays and Reviews, p. 331.

and not by works that man is accounted righteous in heaven; but it is by works only and not by faith that a man is esteemed righteous upon earth." What, therefore, the Essayist terms "the formula of Protestants," is really Catholic, true, and right; and we venture to remind him that this must be his own opinion likewise, for, as a clergyman of the Church of England, he has sworn that the doctrine of being "justified by faith *only* is a most wholesome doctrine," since "we are accounted righteous before God *only* for the merit of our Lord and Saviour Jesus Christ by faith, and not for our own works or deservings."[1] What he calls "the formula of Catholics," or, in other words, the mode of a sinner's justification as taught by the Church of Rome, is anti-Scriptural, anti-Catholic, and untrue.

§ 5. If we have exposed the lamentable mis-statements of certain of the Essayists in their inability to distinguish between the teaching of the Catholic and the Roman Churches on the doctrine of man's justification, or being accounted righteous by God; still more strange and deplorable is the mental confusion of another Essayist respecting the religion known as *Buddhism*, as we gather from a statement put forth on this subject. "It would not be very tasteful," observes Mr. Wilson in his Essay on "The National Church," "as an exception to this description (of the religion of the Roman empire) to call *Buddhism the Gospel of India*, preached to it five or six centuries before the Gospel of Jesus was proclaimed in the nearer East. But on the whole it would be more like the realities of things, as we can now behold them, to say that the Christian revelation was given to the Western world, *because it deserved it better*, and was more prepared

---

[1] Art xi. Of the Justification of Man.

for it than the East."[1] We do not know upon what ground the Essayist is warranted in affirming that the religious principles or practices of the West "deserved" Christianity "better" than the East. The picture which St. Paul has drawn, in the first chapter of the Epistle to the Romans, of the Paganism which pervaded the civilised world in his day, and which too closely resembles the religion of human nature without a Divine Revelation, militates most strongly against his theory. But we cannot condemn too strongly his profanation and desecration of our honest Saxon term for "good news," though partially veiled by a negative, when he speaks of "Buddhism *the Gospel of* India."

Let us consider what this "Buddhism" really is. Kæmpfer, in his History of Japan[2], supposes that the principal object of worship in India, the Sacred Bull, was derived from Egypt, having been instituted by their great *Budha Siaka*, who died, according to their *Soncarad* or ecclesiastical record, near the beginning of the sixth century B.C. As this agrees with the time of the conquest of Egypt by Cambyses, who heaped such indignities upon the religion of the Egyptians, it is probable that it was some priest of Memphis to whom the Indians gave the name of *Budha Siaka*, or great saint, who fled at that time to India, and taught, with other superstitions, the

---

[1] Essays and Reviews, p. 156.
[2] Vol. i. p. 38. Sir William Jones places the origin of Buddhism about a thousand years before the Christian era; and supposes the system to have been introduced by a younger Buddha, whom he distinguishes from that earlier Buddha who is placed by the Hindoo records in the age of the Deluge. The Buddhists, who once reigned in Gour and throughout North India before their extermination by the Brahmins, may be regarded as the unsuccessful reformers of a degraded superstition, which it were profanation to compare in any way to the "Gospel" of Christ.

worship of the Bull Apis.[1] The four Vedas, or the first class of their Shasters, which are said to contain eighteen distinct kinds of knowledge, of course claim a much higher antiquity for the religion of India. There is a good story told of a learned professor from America having gravely requested Sir William Jones to search among the Hindoos for the Adamic Books, upon the same principle, we may conclude, which induced the Welsh antiquarian to display his pedigree before King James, *in the middle* of which was discovered an instructive annotation : "About this time it is supposed that Adam lived." The amazing credulity of sceptics and unbelievers in every thing except the records of the Sacred Scriptures is notorious. There is no doubt, however, that the age of the Vedas is considerably older than the time of Buddha, who merely grafted an additional superstition upon others equally bad, and considerably older; and if we accept the conclusion of that profound Oriental scholar, whose name we have just mentioned, we may allow them an antiquity of 3000 years, which would place them about two or three hundred years after the time of Moses.

But the question which concerns us is the religion of the Hindoo, which, if it may not be called "the Gospel of India," fell only one degree short, according to the Essayist, of the intellectual heathen worship of Greece and Rome. Like the Mahommedan, the Hindoo in theory acknowledges one Supreme Being as

---

[1] We have a strong confirmation of this in the way in which the Sepoy troops, who were marched from India at the beginning of this present century to take part in the campaign of Egypt, immediately recognised their ancestral idols when they arrived on the banks of the Nile, paying them the same adoration which the ancient Egyptians were accustomed to perform. See *Alison's Hist. of Europe*, vol. v. ch. xxxiv.

the ground and foundation of his religion. *Ek Brumho dittyo nashti*, "One God, and beside him no other," has become a proverb, and is in the mouth of every Brahmin priest. This Supreme Being, called *Brahm*, whom we must be careful to distinguish from *Brahma* an emanation from the former, and the first person in the Hindoo Trinity, is represented in the Shasters as possessed of all the Divine attributes, which are ascribed in the Bible to Jehovah. They declare, however, that being all spirit, without form, and therefore devoid of qualities, a multiplication of him is rendered necessary. Hence the Brahmin rejects the God of the Scriptures, because it appears impossible and irrational for him to believe that spirit can act and create, without being united with matter. After a sleep of many ages, which is considered as the highest beatitude, the Vedas declare that *Brahm* awoke, and feeling desire arising within, exclaimed, "Let me be many." Forthwith he took upon himself a material form, and henceforth he resembles a spider, sitting in the centre, spinning out his endless threads, and fastening what he produces from himself to the right and left, towards all quarters of the infinite vacuum.

The cosmogony of the Shasters, which reminds us somewhat of the Darwinian theory, may be described as follows:—All the germs of the world, which subsequently came into existence, were condensed in the shape of an egg[1], of which *Brahm* took possession in the form of

---

[1] This resembles the Egyptian cosmogony, as it appears on the coffins of the period of the twelfth dynasty, when Joseph was viceroy of Egypt. Part of the twenty-sixth chapter of the funeral ritual, as translated by Dr. Hincks, contains this dogma, alluded to in the Orphic Cosmogony: "I am the Egg of the Great Cackler. I have protected the great Egg laid by Seb in the world: I grow, it grows in turn: I live, it lives in turn: I breathe, it breathes in turn."

THE RELIGION OF BRAHMANISM.

Brahma. One thousand *jugs*, which equal 300,000,000 years, elapsed before the egg was hatched. During that period it floated like a bubble upon the mighty deep. At length it broke, and Brahma sprang to light; having 1000 heads with an equal number of eyes and arms to enable him to undertake the work of creation. Similarly with this incarnation, another monster appeared from the same egg, whose hairs were forest trees, his head the clouds, his beard the lightning, his breath the atmosphere, his voice the thunder, his eyes the sun and moon, his nails the rocks, and his bones the mountains of the earth. The egg being thus hatched, *Brahm*, as creator, retired from the scene and relapsed into his former state of somnolent blessedness. The earth is represented as a flat plain of circular form, measuring 400,000,000 miles in circumference; and resting upon an enormous snake with a hundred heads, which is itself supported by a gigantic tortoise. When the former shakes one of his heads, an earthquake is thereby caused; an original idea certainly, reminding us of the waggish mode of accounting for the juicy substance in the interior of the cocoa-nut.

Besides *Brahma*, there are the emanations from him called *Vishnu* and *Shiva*, which together form the Hindoo Trinity. *Brahma*, the creator, is usually represented in the form of a man with four faces, the symbols of omniscience, and riding upon a goose. In no part of India is a temple to Brahma to be seen, and the reason of this neglect is that he was convicted of every species of profligacy and wickedness, and in some passages the Shasters emphatically denominate him "the father of lies." *Vishnu*, the preserver, is represented in the form of a black man, with four arms, riding upon Gururu, an animal half-man and half-bird. Divine homage, however, is not paid to him in this form, as he is worshipped only in his incarnations, such as *Ram* and

Krishna. He is said to have appeared nine times already upon earth, and the tenth incarnation is expected at some future period. *Shiva,* the destroyer, the third person in the Hindoo Trinity, appears as a terrible deity. In his right hand he holds a trident; his countenance is horrible; his necklace consists of human skulls; his bracelets, earrings, and other ornaments, are made up of poisonous snakes. Though *Shiva* is considered generally as the destroyer; he appears frequently in the Shasters as creator; which the Brahmins explain as follows : " So long as the world lasts, there can be no destruction, it is merely dissolution; and the same elements return, but probably in different forms, into existence."[1] Hence destruction becomes according to such pantheistical notions, nothing but renovation or re-production, which reminds us of Professor Baden Powell's dictum that "creation is only another name for our ignorance of the mode of production;"[2] or of Mr. Darwin's favourite hobby of "*natural selection.*" Thus Shiva displays his power in destruction and creation at the same time; when his thunderbolt strikes human life, he restores the same by metempsychosis, transmigration, or new birth. This triad of gods, *Brahma, Vishnu,* and *Shiva,* with their consorts *Saraswati, Durga,* and *Lackhi,* are said to have produced the 300,000,000 of gods with which the deluded Hindoo has furnished his pantheon. And we think it would be well if those who profess Christianity at home did but act up to their obligations of doing all that lies in their power to dispel the

---

[1] The Pythagorean notion, that nothing is annihilated, but that it only changes its form, and that death is reproduction, was clearly of Egyptian origin. It used to be typified in Egypt by the figure of an infant at the extremity of a tomb beyond the sarcophagus of the dead.

[2] Essays and Reviews, p. 139.

moral darkness which the following anecdote too mournfully testifies as existing throughout Hindostan. " You tell me, Padre," said a native convert to an English missionary, " that there are millions called Christians in England, while so very few come here to teach us the way to heaven. When you write home to your friends, tell them that though there are yet 300,000,000 idol gods which can neither see nor speak, and whom the people ignorantly worship, who knows but at the day of judgment God may give each of these idols a tongue to speak in condemnation of the lukewarmness of English Christians towards India ? "

One of the many evils connected with the Hindoo religion, and one of the chief hindrances to the spread of the true (not the "Buddhist") Gospel in India, is the distinction of *caste*. The Shasters teach that *Brahma*, by means of successive emanations from himself, called various classes of mankind into existence. First the *Brahmin* escaped from his mouth, as the representation of God in human form. The nature of his birth signified him to be, not only the highest and most exalted of all human beings, but likewise the intended teacher, and the mediating priest between the gods and mankind. From the arm of Brahma, as defender of the body, sprang the *Ksethryo*, the warrior-caste, which was appointed to protect the people by his powerful arm, and to defend his brethren against the oppression of the wicked. From Brahma's breast issued the *Vyasa*, or caste of tradesmen, whose duty was to provide for the wants of mankind ; and from the humblest member, his foot, came the despised *Sudra*, or the servile caste, whose task was to perform every kind of menial labour for their nobler-born brethren, both at home and in the field. So unchangeable is this institution of caste in the estimation of the Hindoos, and so firm is their belief in its appointment being of Divine origin, that a transition from one caste to another is absolutely impossible. A sovereign cannot purchase the Brahminical thread, which is the badge of their dignity, for the wealth of the world. And just as a turnip can never become a man (Darwin *non obstante*), so neither can a *Sudra* be turned into a *Brahmin*, i. e. transmigration is not recognised in this present world. In the future the philosophic principles of the Darwinian school may possibly prove true according to the Hindoo theory, only in a somewhat inverse order. For if a poor despised Sudra has happened to injure or offend a haughty Brahmin, the revenge of the hateful priest pursues the poor wretch into the other world. If a Sudra meets a Brahmin in a disrespectful manner, after death he becomes a tree; if he ventures to cast an angry glance at him, *Yama*, the god of the lower regions, will tear out his eyes; or if he beat the Brahmin with only a single straw, he will in the course of twenty transmigrations be turned into an impure beast.

India, like Europe in the Middle Ages, is a paradise for the priests. When Hindooism was at its zenith, the Brahmin could not be punished. Though he had committed every crime under the sun, no prince dared to execute him. All the offerings which the Hindoo presents to his gods fall, as a matter of course, to the Brahmin. The dying Hindoo, who leaves him in his will some of his goods and cattle, will, freed from sin, enter forthwith into Shiva's paradise. He who sells his cow, which is considered a sacred animal, will go to hell; but if he only make it over to a Brahmin, he is sure of heaven. Polygamy prevails to a great extent among the highest classes, viz. the Coolin Brahmins, many of whom possess between twenty and thirty wives, or even more. An English missionary mentions that once on a journey he met such an one, who complained to him, "I have only three wives, but my brother has ten." This profligate custom has produced an abundant crop of wickedness in India, as it invariably has done wherever practised, whether amongst the Turks in the East, or the Mormons in the West. Of all India's degraded and demoralised sons, the Brahmin priest is the most deeply debased. Mr. Holwell, an English judge at Calcutta, said concerning them, " During five years in which I occupied the chair in the criminal court of that city, a case of murder or other crime never came under my notice for investigation where a *Brahmin* was not the guilty party, or had not his share in the case."

One or two extracts from the *Vedas* will enable us to form some idea of the prayers which the Hindoos are taught to use, and which some philosophers at home will doubtless consider so suitable to the wants of mankind, as to forbid any attempt to replace " the Gospel of India" by the introduction of Christianity. " O Ugni," are the words of a prayer, " god of the fire, pray repose upon this chair of kusu grass; I invite thee to taste the clarified butter; *thou hast thy dwelling in the mind, and everywhere;* make my desire known to God, that my offering may be accepted, and that I may obtain honour among men." Another is as follows: " O Indra, give us riches without measure, consisting of gold, oxen, provisions, and long life. We ask more riches of Indra, whether you obtain them from men, or from the inhabitants of heaven, or from the infernal regions,—wherever you may get them; *only make us rich.*"

One characteristic feature of Hindooism is that its votaries appear to have lost all distinction between the Creator and the creature. Many professed Christians have spoken with enthusiastic admiration of the Hindoo writings, asserting that they contain the most sublime doctrines, and inculcate the purest morality; but they would speedily find this to be an egregious error, if they would allow the Brahmins to expound their own Shasters. "During my stay in India," writes a German missionary of the Church of England, "I often looked out for a Cornelius, and one day I thought I had found one. I was arguing with a number of Hindoos. When they could proceed no further, they said, 'Come to our holy father; he is one of the wisest and holiest of men, he will soon silence you.' Coming to the man, I found he was a *Fakeer*, a worshipper of *Shiva*. I asked him, 'Whom do you worship?' He replied, 'God.' 'Who is God?' I said. He arose from his seat, laid his left hand upon his breast, pointed with his right to heaven, and lifting up his eyes, said, 'I worship God, the eternal, the infinite, omnipotent, omniscient, and omnipresent; the holy, just, and righteous; the Creator of heaven and earth, the Supreme Ruler of all things; He it is whom I worship.' I rejoiced at this sublime declaration, and wishing to hear these beautiful words once more, I repeated my question, 'And who is that adorable Being whom you worship?' The Fakeer pointed to himself, and replied, '*I am He, He that speaks in me; I am that Being, I am a part of Him, I am He.*' When we know their systems, it is easy to silence them; and of late I have found it sufficient to ask two questions, which no Brahmin was ever able to answer. I ask, 'Who speaks in us?' Every Hindoo will reply, 'God.' My second question is, 'Who tells lies?' The Hindoo will say, 'God.' Upon this we need but look the man in the face, and ask him, 'Is God a liar?' And ninety-nine out of a hundred will call out, 'No! God is no liar; we are the liars, the sinners.'"[1] Another missionary, of German birth, also a clergyman of the Church of England,

---

[1] Recollections of an Indian Missionary, by the Rev. C. B. Leüpolt, pp. 25—29.

after long experience of the Hindoo religion, thus testified to the unsuitability of Buddhism in any way being "the Gospel for India;" and as his remarks bear upon the question of rationalism, we would commend them to the careful consideration of the Essayist, and those who think with him. "On returning to my native country, after fourteen years' absence, I was astonished to find that *a system of heathenish origin* had gained its admirers and followers in Protestant Germany. The prevailing system of our modern infidel philosophers is pantheism in principle; the personality of God is denied. I told my countrymen, he that desires to learn the true character of this philosophy, separated and denuded of all Christian ideas, together with its moral bearing, should go to Bengal, and, settled on the Ganges, among the *Brahmins*, who have known it for thousands of years, and *developed it to perfection*, I feel assured the sight of their horrid, idolatrous ceremonies would shake his whole being. He certainly would return home, radically cured of all pantheistical ideas; he would be compelled, in putting his hand on the Bible, to exclaim, *here* is life and truth, which satisfies the soul, and rejoices the heart; *there* is falsehood, corruption, and death."[1]

§ 6. We must notice before we close some of the statements respecting the "negative theology" system, as it has been appropriately termed. Mr. Wilson, in his Essay on "The National Church," has declared that the rapid spread of this "negative theology" amongst us, so far from being attributable to the researches of "German Biblical critics," as some imagine, is "rather owing to a spontaneous recoil, on the part of large numbers of the more acute of our population, from some of the doctrines which are to be

---

[1] A Course of Lectures delivered on Indian Missions, by J. J. Weitbrecht.

heard at church and chapel; to a distrust of the old arguments for, or proofs of a miraculous revelation; and to a misgiving as to the authority, or extent of the authority, of the Scriptures. In the presence of real difficulties of this kind, *probably of genuine English growth*, it is vain to seek to check that open discussion out of which alone any satisfactory settlement of them can issue."[1]

In placing "doctrines which are to be heard at church and chapel" in the same category, the Essayist appears to confound things which essentially differ. We do not mean that many Catholic truths may not be heard at chapel as well as church, but we have no guarantee that nothing but what is truth should be heard there; whereas at church, if any minister preaches what is contrary to the truth, he does it of his own *proprio motu*, against the declared teaching of his church, and by that act renders himself liable to trial, and, if guilty, to punishment and deprivation. On the other hand, at chapel, one may hear not only much that is professedly contrary to Catholic truth, but if any Nonconformist minister preaches extreme "negative theology" to his congregation, who, heretofore, may have professed the most rigid orthodoxy according to their use of the term, there is no authority to restrain, condemn, or suspend him. In one chapel we see the doctrine of the Trinity denied; in another that of infant baptism; in a third the threefold order in the ministry, as it has ever existed in the Church of Christ[2]; in a fourth, the need of

---

[1] Essays and Reviews, p. 151.

[2] This is what a saint of old, who received his crown of martyrdom within perhaps a dozen years of the death of St. John, taught on the subject of Episcopacy: "It is fitting that we should not only be called Christians, *but be so*. As some call their ruler Bishop, and *yet do all things without him*, I can never think that such as these have a good conscience, seeing they are not gathered together *completely* according to the command of God."—*Ignatius ad Mag.* iv.

any ministry at all, according to the novel system of the Plymouth Brethren; until, at length, the danger of innovation, and of departing from Catholic truth is seen in all its naked deformity, by the climax of religious infidelity having been attained in the wicked follies of American Mormonism.

Plunged, however, in fatal error, as the Unitarians of the sixteenth and the Mormons of the nineteenth centuries unquestionably are, neither of them can be said to belong to that school known under the name of Rationalists, or the students and promoters of the "negative theology," which the Essayist has pronounced to be "the spontaneous recoil from some of the doctrines which are to be heard at church and chapel," on the part of those who boast themselves to be wise in the things of this world. Believing this rationalism or "negative theology" to be a feeble and unscientific attempt to paint religion in *chiaro oscuro*, from which all revealed truth is eliminated and left out, we are content to let its advocates speak for themselves, in order that we may see the substitute which some amongst us with marvellous subtilty would fain introduce in place of "the glorious gospel of the blessed God."

"The religion of types and notions," says one of its advocates, "can travel only in a circle from whence there is no escape. It is but an elaborate process of self-confutation. After much verbiage it demolishes what is created, and having begun by assuming God to be angry, ends, not by admitting its own gross mistake, but by asserting Him to be changed and reconciled."[1]

"The Christian teacher," said another, "saw that God incarnates himself in man, and evermore goes forth anew to take possession of the world. He said, in this jubilee

---

[1] Mackay, Progress of Intellect, ii. 504.

of sublime emotion, '*I am divine; through me, God acts; through me, speaks. Would you see God, see me; or, see thee, when thou also thinkest as I now think.*'"[1]

Kant advances a step further in the "negative theology" speculation, and manifests his "distrust" of anything like "miraculous revelation," by daringly affirming that "Christ's healing the sick was by medical skill; raising the dead, premature interment; feeding five thousand people, the rich sharing with the poor; stilling the tempest, by steering round a point which cut off the wind; our Lord's death, a mere swoon, restored by the warmth of the sepulchre and the effect of the spices," &c. &c. All such blasphemous follies may be sufficient to satisfy the disciples of that incredulous school to which the Essayists appear to lean, though of course rejected as absurd, and so manifestly absurd as not to need refutation, by every sane and thoughtful Christian.

Another of the Essayists expresses himself respecting what is virtually "negative theology" on this wise:— "Our conduct," observes Mr. Pattison in his Essay "On the Tendencies of Religious Thought in England," "was thought of, not as a product or efflux of our character, but as regulated by our understanding; by a perception of relations, or a calculation of consequences. *This intellectual perception of regulative truth is religious faith. Faith is no longer the devout condition of the entire inner man.* Its dynamic nature and interior working are not denied, but they are unknown; and religion is made to regulate life from without, through the logical being and attributes of God, upon which an obligation to obey him can be raised."[2] In this we have the fatal mistake which

---

[1] Emerson's Christian Teacher. Essays, p. 511. Compare this with Buddhism as defined by one of its votaries at p. 364.
[2] Essays and Reviews, pp. 275, 276.

is so common to men who are content with natural religion in place of spiritual—who exalt the head, and forget that the sum and substance of Divine truth may be said to consist in God's invitation to man, "My son, give me thy heart." The real Pelagian, who denies the corruption of the human heart, as an inheritance handed down from our first parent, naturally places the head, the intellect, the brain, first and foremost in his standard of religious truths. And it would have been a happy thing for himself and others if the Essayist, in place of committing himself, as he has done, with regard to Jeremy Taylor, had learnt a lesson of wisdom which another great divine of the same age has given on this subject. "There is nothing more easy," observes Bishop Hall, "than to say divinity by rote, and to discourse of spiritual matters from the tongue or pen of others; but to hear God speaking to the soul, and to feel the power of religion in ourselves, and to express it out of the truth of experience within, is both rare and hard." Or consider the teaching of another distinguished minister of the present age on the same subject: "To make the wisdom of the New Testament," says Chalmers, "our wisdom, and its spirit our spirit, and its language our best-loved and best-understood language, there must be a higher influence upon the heart than what lies in human art or in human explanation. Till this is brought to pass, the doctrine of the Atonement, and the doctrine of conversion, and the doctrine of fellowship with the Father and the Son, and the doctrine of a believer's progressive holiness under the moral and spiritual power of 'the truth as it is in Jesus,' will, as to his own personal experience of its meaning, remain so many empty sounds, or so many deep and hidden mysteries."

Such, however, is not the theology of the Rector of Lincoln College. After quoting Cudworth, who had rightly taught that the faith mentioned in Scripture as "the substance of things hoped for, and the evidence of things not seen," was "not a mere believing of historical things, and upon artificial arguments or testimonies only, but a certain higher and diviner power in the soul that peculiarly correspondeth with Deity,"[1] the Essayist proceeds to erect his theological structure upon the foundation of *reason*, in place of that *faith* which is, as Scripture tells us, both the gift and the fruit of the Spirit, and without which it is impossible to be accepted of or to please God. "The inner light, or witness of the Spirit," says Mr. Pattison, "in the soul of the individual believer, had fallen into discredit, through the extravagancies to which it had given birth. It was disowned alike by Churchmen and Nonconformists, who agreed in speaking with contemptuous pity of the 'sectaries of the last age.' *The reaction against individual religion led to this first attempt to base revealed truth on reason.* And for the purpose for which reason was now wanted, the higher, or philosophic, reason was far less fitted than that universal understanding in which all men can claim a share. The 'inner light,' which had made each man the dictator of his own creed, had exploded in ecclesiastical anarchy. The appeal from the frantic discord of the enthusiasts to reason must needs be—not to an arbitrary or particular reason in each man, but to a *common sense*, a *natural discernment, a reason of universal obligation*. As it was to be universally binding, it must be generally recognisable. It must be something not confined to the select few, a gift of the self-styled elect, *but a faculty belonging to all men of sound mind and average capacity*. Truth must be accessible to the bulk of mankind" (p. 291).

No one can fail to perceive that such theology is in

---

[1] Intellectual System, Preface.

direct antagonism to what St. Paul taught; and we conclude, if the Essayist were pressed for a reply, he would be constrained to answer that the Apostle was not infallible, or else that we must accept his words in a non-literal and non-natural sense. Let us hear what he, who spake, as we know, by the Holy Ghost, really taught on this momentous and all-important subject. "We speak the wisdom of God," says St. Paul, " in a mystery, even the hidden wisdom, which God ordained before the world unto our glory; which none of the princes of this world knew; for had they known it, they would not have crucified the Lord of Glory. But, as it is written, Eye hath not seen, nor ear heard, neither have entered into the heart of man, the things which God hath prepared for them that love Him. But God hath revealed them unto us by his Spirit: for the Spirit searcheth all things, yea, the deep things of God. For what man knoweth the things of a man, save the spirit of man which is in him? Even so the things of God knoweth no man, but the Spirit of God. Now we have received, not the spirit of the world, but the Spirit which is of God; that we might know the things which are freely given to us of God. Which things also we speak, not in the words which man's wisdom teacheth, but which the Holy Ghost teacheth, comparing spiritual things with spiritual. But the natural man receiveth not the things of the Spirit of God; for they are foolishness unto him; neither can he know them, because they are spiritually discerned."[1] Here it is clear that the Spirit of God teaches that the self-styled *rationalist* of all ages and all countries would learn truth by his own ratiocinations, receive nothing by faith, nor own any need of supernatural assistance. This was very much the character of the pretenders to philo-

---

[1] 1 Corinthians, ii. 7—14.

sophy, and the learned Grecians in those days, as it is of the German neologians in the present. Such do not and cannot understand *the things of the Spirit of God*. *Revelation* is not with them a principle of *Science;* but is looked upon by their distorted vision as delirium and dotage, the extravagant thoughts of deluded dreamers. They cannot receive the precious and really rational truths of *Revelation* in the love of them, so as to approve of and like them, and to be cordially subject to them. Such things are declared to be *foolishness* unto them. They view them as absurd, and contrary to natural reason; they disrelish and reject them as insipid and distasteful, and they often make them the subject of banter and ridicule, through want of spiritual perception. At most, they can only know the literal and grammatical sense of the words of the inspired writers, or only in the theory, notionally and speculatively, not experimentally, spiritually, and savingly; because such things only are *spiritually discerned* in a spiritual manner, by a spiritual light, and under the influence and by the assistance of the Spirit of God. As there must be a natural visive faculty to discern natural things, so there must be a spiritual one to discern and approve of spiritual things, which the natural man, leaning upon his own unsanctified reason, has not. There is an anecdote related concerning Mr. Pitt, of more authenticity, we apprehend, than the one which Mr. Pattison gives of the same person, whom he represents as saying that Butler's *Analogy* " is a dangerous book, raising more doubts than it solves " (p. 306); that having once accompanied Mr. Wilberforce to hear the celebrated Cecil preach, and who was peculiarly happy on the occasion in setting forth, with great power, the truths of the everlasting Gospel, he frankly confessed, in answer to the anxious question of his friend, that, " though he had paid close attention to the sermon, he could not understand at all what it meant."

The late Professor Blunt, of Cambridge, distinguished alike for his learning, sobriety, and devotion, has recorded his impressions concerning the absolute impossibility of the minister of Christ effecting anything without the illuminating power of the Spirit, that it would be well if the Rector of Lincoln College, in the sister university, would ponder over and profit by the advice given by one who has a claim to be heard. "If the parish priest," he observes, "when sitting by the sick man's side, finds his ideas stagnant, and his feelings unmoved,— no power to address him and no knowledge of what to say,— he has reason to suspect that he has work to do nearer home, before he can be of much use there: that he must *first* be converted himself, and *then* strengthen his brother." Or, if we are content to accept the dying testimony of a layman of rare intellectual gifts, let us hear the last words of Dr. Gordon, of Hull, a glorious specimen of *the Christian philosopher triumphing over death:*—"All human learning is of no avail. Reason must be put out of the question. I reasoned, and debated, and investigated, but I found no peace till I came to the Gospel as a little child, till I received it as a babe. Then such a light was shed abroad in my heart, that I saw the whole scheme at once, and I found pleasure the most indescribable. I saw there was no good deed in myself. Though I had spent hours in examining my conduct, I found nothing I had done would give me real satisfaction. It was always mixed up with something selfish. But when I came to the Gospel as a child, the Holy Spirit seemed to fill my heart. I then saw my selfishness in all its vivid deformity, and I found there was no acceptance with God, and no happiness except through the blessed Redeemer. I stripped off all my own deeds — threw them aside — went to Him naked. He received me as He promised He would, and presented me to the father; then I felt joy unspeakable, and all fear of death at once vanished." This is admirable, faithful, and rational in the true sense of the term, and not in the distorted sense of the Neologian school of the present day. It is a candid avowal of one conscious that He was soon to appear before the awful Being, who knows and will judge the secrets of all hearts, and that nothing can avail but the internal testimony of the Spirit, which, as St. Paul affirms, " itself beareth witness with our spirit, that we are the children of God," and which has the same effect, only in a more perfect degree, of what the Apostle, in the same epistle, presents as the result of natural religion. " For when the Gentiles," he says, " which have not the law, do by nature the things contained in the law, these having not the law, are a law unto themselves: which shew the work of the law written in their hearts, their conscience also bearing witness, and their thoughts the meanwhile accusing or else excusing one another." [1] It is, however, beyond all question true, that although there is in mankind a sort of natural conscience which confesses a distinction between good and evil, there is nothing in the heart of any man, who has not the teaching, sanctifying, and internal witnessing power of the Spirit, which corresponds with the principle of what the same Apostle calls " delighting in the law of God after the inner man." Here, the charmer may charm never so wisely, but in vain ; the minstrel may exert his utmost skill, and pour forth strains sweet as the melodies of heaven ; but there is no chord which vibrates to his touch, when he appeals to sinners, dead in trespasses and sins, in praise of the beauty of holiness, and the loveliness of spiritual religion. In the book of the Prophet Isaiah we thus find the Holy Ghost characterising the faithful

---

[1] Compare Romans, ii. 14, 15, with Romans, viii. 16.

people of God: "Hearken unto me, ye that know righteousness, the people in whose heart is my law."[1]

The internal witness of the Spirit is the one grand esoteric doctrine of Christianity. What the Eleusinian mysteries were to the Grecian philosophers, that it is to the earnest disciple of Christ, with the wide difference which must ever exist between truth and error. It is in short what the Psalmist terms "the secret of the Lord," which, he adds, "is with them that fear Him."[2] And it is the antithesis to the lamentable philosophy of our Essayist, which can advance no further than " to suggest that either religious faith has no existence, or that it must be reached by some other road than that of the 'trial of the witnesses.' It is a *reductio ad absurdum* of common-sense philosophy, of home-baked theology, when we find that the result of the whole is that 'it is safer to believe in God, lest, if there should happen to be one, he might send us to hell for denying his existence.' (Maurice, Essays, p. 236.)"[3]

There was truer philosophy in the happy reproof which Bishop Atterbury gave to a sceptical soldier, who once boasted in his presence that the only prayer he could find time to utter before an engagement, was "Oh God, if there be a God, save my soul, if I have a soul," by observing that he once had a friend, who, under similar circumstances, prayed, "Oh! God if I forget Thee, do not Thou forget me," though whether such faith would come under the description of the Essayist's " home-baked theology," we can scarcely take upon ourselves to say. We do not for a moment imagine that Mr. Pattison, or any of the clerical Essayists, are yet prepared to go the same lengths which the more advanced members of his

---

[1] Isaiah, li. 7.   [2] Ps. xxv. 14.
[3] Essays and Reviews, p. 296.

school have already avowed, as we may learn from the terms which foreign rationalists do not hesitate to apply to some of our most cherished principles. Thus, at Gröningen, in Holland, our recognition of the Bible as God's Word is called "Bibliolatry," the inspiration of the New Testament, "Apostle-deification," and the Doctrine of the Atonement, "Blood Theology;" but we cannot avoid observing how clearly the statements they have put forth, and the onslaught they have made on much that is contained in the unerring word of God, tends in that dangerous direction.

That Mr. Pattison's leanings are unhappily so directed, we conclude from the manner in which he permits himself to speak of a " godless orthodoxy, threatening in the present day, as in the fifteenth century, to extinguish religious thought altogether ; when *nothing is allowed in the Church of England, but the formulæ of past thinkings, which have long lost all sense of any kind.*"[1] It is needless to remark that this declaration, so contrary to fact, would be discreditable to any one who is desirous of testing the requirements of our Church upon the common principles of truth and justice ; but proceeding from the quarter it does, it reflects alike upon its authors and the school to which he belongs. But it may be said that we, as clergymen of the Church of England, bound by the same moral obligations as the clerical Essayists, are not the best judges of the failings of our brethren. Let us therefore take the most unexceptionable witnesses that can be found of the tendency of these "Essays and Reviews," as they appear to those without our communion. If the old adage of the Roman poet be true, *Fas est ab hoste docere*, the opinions of those, who certainly are no friends of the Church of Christ, but who

---

[1] Essays and Reviews, p. 297.

appear to entertain a very reverential regard for the Essayists, may be accepted as a significant proof of the morality and effect of their writings in general. " Our satisfaction and our sympathy" (with the Essayists), observes a recent reviewer of their work, " which would else be complete, are weakened when we call to mind the conditions under which these great truths and noble sentiments have been given to the world by Mr. Jowett and the *enlightened men* associated with him in the volume before us. The beliefs which these men avow are *in open contradiction*, if language is to bear its natural meaning, with the creeds which they have deliberately pledged themselves to accept. This is *a painful part* of the subject, which we would gladly avoid; but it is one of which the moral bearings are so important, that we cannot refrain from uttering what seems to us the obvious dictate of common sense and simple veracity. Let us, however, be understood as clearly distinguishing between the *person* and the *thing*. The position occupied by these distinguished men, in their academic and clerical relations, as it presents itself to our minds, is *indefensible, logically and morally*. But we should be sorry to believe, and we do not believe, that it appears in the same light to them." [1]

"No fair mind," says another, " can close this volume, without feeling it to be, at bottom, *in direct antagonism to the whole system of popular belief*.... In object, in spirit, and in method, no less than in general design, *this book is incompatible with the broad principles on which the Protestantism of Englishmen rests*. The most elaborate reasoning, to prove that they are in harmony, can never be anything but futile, and ends in becoming sincere. The

---

[1] National Review, No. xxiii. Old Creeds and New Beliefs, pp. 162, 163.

mass of ordinary believers may well ask to be protected from such friends as *their worst and most dangerous enemies.* Of one thing we may be quite sure, that the public will never be brought to believe that the Bible is full of ' untruths ;' that it does not contain authentic or even contemporary record of facts, and is a medley of late compilers, and yet withal remains the Book of Life. Yet all this our Essayists call on them to admit. The men and women around us are told that the whole scheme of salvation has to be entirely re-arranged and altered. *Divine rewards and punishments, the fall, original sin, the vicarious penalty, and salvation by faith, are all, in the natural sense of the terms, denounced as figments or exploded blunders.* The Mosaic history dissolves into a mass of ill-digested legends, the Mosaic ritual into an Oriental system of priestcraft, and the Mosaic origin of the earth and man sinks amidst the rubbish of rabbinical cosmogonies." [1]

If the opinion of a foreign friend of the Essayists, occupying a more advanced position on the broad road of scepticism than they have yet attained, be worth listening to, let us attend to the following : " The Essays," writes an American, " a book published by six very influential and learned clergymen, and one layman of the Established Church, is a work of the greatest importance and significance. It sets aside the old theology entirely, and *propounds the rational views of Paine and Voltaire,* with just that mixture of cloudiness which you might expect from persons who, while they see the folly of the old superstitions, yet remember that they are clergymen, and feel that they are but partially independent and free. We are on the eve of a great religious revolution. But few of the high and mighty ones speak so freely as we

---

[1] Westminster Review, No. xxxvi. Art. Neo-Christianity.

do, *but they think freely.* Many of our great writers cling to the doctrine of God and of a future state ; *but they have no more faith in the Divine authority of the Bible,* or in the supernatural origin of Christianity, than I or you. The works of Baden Powell, Professor Jowett, &c., are doing a world of good. The Oxford Essays are creating quite a sensation. The good time seems to be really drawing nigh."[1]

Or if the opinion be of weight concerning the writings, not of the Essayists themselves, but of their co-rationalists in Germany, by one whose name ranks high with that school, let us hear what Strauss has said upon this subject:—
"To no one is the Apostle's Creed or the Augsburg Confession any longer an adequate expression of his religious consciousness. *No one believes any longer in any of the New Testament miracles* (to say nothing of those of the Old), from the supernatural conception to the ascension. He either explains them away into natural events, or understands them as legends. And if this be the case with thoughtful laymen, it stands no better with the clergy. Wherefore, then, these subterfuges? Why this hypocrisy before others and themselves? Is it worthy of men, in their relations with religion, to make out their case before her like a crouching and artful slave, *with half words and empty evasions?* Why not boldly speak out at once? *Why not confess to one another, that while they can no longer recognise in the Bible anything more than a mixture of poetry and fact,* and in the Church dogmas only symbols, that still retain a certain significance, they nevertheless continue attached with unaltered reverence to the moral contents of Christianity, and the character of its founder, so far as its human outline can yet be traced, amidst the cloud of marvels in which his

---

[1] National Reformer, Nov. 24th, 1860

earliest biographers have wrapped it? But it may be asked, ought we in that case still to be called Christians? I know not. But is the name everything? This I know, that we shall then become once more true, honest, unsophisticated, and therefore better men than before. Moreover, we shall remain Protestants, yea, then *for the first time real Protestants.*"[1]

In opposition to this daring mixture of rationalism, infidelity, and self-delusion, let us hear the opinion of one to whom Bunsen confessedly bowed as the greatest of modern authorities on this same subject. "In my opinion," wrote the illustrious Niebuhr, "*he is not a Protestant Christian* who does not receive the historical facts of Christ's early life, in their literal acceptation, *with all their miracles*, as equally authentic with any event recorded in history, and whose belief in them is not as firm and tranquil as his belief in the latter; and who has not the most absolute faith in the articles of the Apostles' Creed, *taken in their grammatical sense;* who does not consider every doctrine and every precept of the New Testament as undoubted divine revelation, in the sense of the Christians of the first century, who knew nothing of Theopneustia. Moreover, a Christianity after the fashion of the modern philosophers and pantheists, without a personal God, without immortality, without human individuality, without historical faith, is no Christianity at all to me, though it may be a very intellectual, very ingenious philosophy. I have often said, *I do not know what to do with a metaphysical God, and that I will have nought but the God of the Bible, who is heart to heart with us.*"[2]

---

[1] D. F. Strauss, On the Select Dialogues of Ulrich von Hutten, Vorrede, p. xlix.
[2] Niebuhr's Life and Letters, vol. ii. p. 123.

Commending the opinions of the illustrious Niebuhr, as well as those of the German rationalists and English reviewers, to the attention of Mr. Pattison and his brother Essayists, we must protest against their ungenerous treatment of Butler, Paley, and other divines, respecting the " evidences" adduced by them in behalf of the truths of the Gospel, to say nothing of their suspicious silence respecting the still stronger evidences which this present age has been privileged to receive. The remark of one of the Fathers—" If you are a believer as you ought to be, and love Christ as you ought to love Him, you have no need of *miracles*, for these are given to unbelievers,"[1] —may be equally applied to the *evidences* of the Christian religion. To such disciples, who thus manifest by their humility the highest order of grace, there is no need of treating the great Author of *Revelation* otherwise than as we treat a friend in whom we have perfect confidence. *We take Him at His word.* But to those who prefer to be ranked in one of the three schools of error, either as rationalists, semi-sceptics, or thorough infidels, evidences in confirmation of the truth are valuable to confront, confound, and to overthrow the petty arguments which the Essayists and their sympathisers have brought against the Bible. Hence it is as satisfactory, as it is natural, to find that the evidences, which such masterly writers as Bishop Butler and Paley adduced during the last century in behalf of the truth, have been amply enlarged by the advance of *Science* and of antiquarian research during the present. It is not too much to say, that the very rocks of Behistun, the stones of Nineveh, and the tombs of Egypt can no longer hold their peace; but that, according to the appointed time of Him who " worketh all things after the counsel of his own will," they have risen, as it

---

[1] Chrysos. Hom. xxiii. in Johan.

were, as this sceptical age is drawing to a close, in their majesty and strength, to rebuke the folly and the blasphemy of those who have either played the part of the infidel, or denied the existence of God.

§ 7. In conclusion we may point to the picture which Mr. Pattison has attempted to draw of "the Evangelical School," though he admits its unfinished condition, as a fresh instance of the cloudy state of the author's mind, and of the mystic darkness with which, like the cuttle fish when pursued, he and his brother Essayists have enveloped themselves when treating of the fundamental truths of our religion. " Because legal preaching, as they (the Evangelical and Methodist generation of teachers who succeeded the Hanoverian divines) phrased it, had failed, they would essay Gospel preaching. The preaching of justification by works had not the power to check wickedness, therefore justification by faith, the doctrine of the Reformation, was the only saving truth. This is not meant as a complete account of the origin of the Evangelical School. It is only one point of view—that point which connects the school with the general line of thought this paper has been pursuing. This doctrine of conversion by supernatural influence was, in some way or other, preaching—preaching, too, not as rhetoric, but as the annunciation of a specific doctrine—the Gospel. They certainly insisted 'on the heart' being touched, and that the Spirit only had the power savingly to affect the heart ; *but they acted as though this were done by an appeal to the reason, and scornfully rejected the idea of religious education.*"[1] This concluding sentence betrays at once the animus of the Essayist's mind respecting the Catholic nature of Evangelical truth in general, as well as the conduct of the Beveridges, the Romaines, the Scotts, the Cecils, and the leaders of the

---

[1] Essays and Reviews, p. 326.

Evangelical School in the eighteenth century in particular. The introductory prayer of the Communion Service, which the Church so lovingly instructs her children to offer, "Almighty God, unto whom all hearts be open, and all desires known, and from whom no secrets are hid; cleanse the thoughts of our hearts *by the inspiration of thy Holy Spirit*, that we may perfectly love Thee, and worthily magnify Thy holy name, through Christ our Lord,"—is the real key to the understanding of the motives, the actions, and the marvellous success of the Evangelical School towards the close of the last century. To assert that they acted as though "heart conversion," as the great Augustine terms it, were effected by appealing to the reason, and that they scornfully rejected the idea of religious instruction, is so preposterous that it does not need refutation.

Did the Essayist know anything of "the inspiration of the Spirit" in the sense in which our Church uses the expression; had he any of that internal witness, of which St. Paul speaks, in his own heart, he would not have committed the lamentable blunder he has done in writing on a subject which he has proved himself so incompetent to judge and to teach. The work of the Spirit in the awakening, renewing, sanctifying, teaching, guiding, edifying, and building up of every human being who is "meet for the inheritance of the saints in light," as contrasted with anything like appealing to reason in the sense of the rationalistic school of all times, may be truly characterised as the pivot doctrine of the Evangelical School of the eighteenth century. And until that great but elementary truth is fully realised, there can be no perception of the motive power which actuates the faithful disciple of Christ of all ages and in all places. The manner and way of the Spirit's action upon the soul is truly mysterious, and we cannot attempt to unveil it. As the dew, which falls from heaven in the stillness of the night, is found at morning light hanging upon the leaves, and enriching the arid soil, and we naturally wonder whence it came and who hath begotten it, so is the way of the Spirit's dealing with the soul of man. And although this important work may have been unaccompanied by any marvellous phenomena, or voices from heaven, or any external visions, such as the shepherds saw when keeping their watch by night in Bethlehem's fields; nevertheless to such an one in the inward man it is declared, " I bring thee good tidings of great joy, for unto thee is born this day the Saviour, which is Christ the Lord." To the soul of the awakened sinner has this testimony been borne, and " the record is that God hath given to him eternal life, and this life is in His Son " (1 John, v. 11).

Whereas, on the other hand, he who is content with letting his religious faith rest upon the reasoning powers of his own corrupt and unsanctified mind, and who is destitute of the witness of the Spirit, from whom alone, as our Church teaches, " all good things do come," absolutely knows nothing of the power of the Gospel, or its overwhelmingly great and glorious design. Such an one may discuss its evidences, may speculate upon its doctrines, may fancy that he can reason about its truths, and even may observe its institutions; but as long as he is without its immortalising principle, he can only be compared to a man amusing himself with the leaves, instead of feeding on the fruits, of the tree of life.

Laus Deo!

INDEX.

ABR

ABRAHAM's birth, time of, 95; in Egypt, time of, 97; his contemporaries in Babylon and Persia, 99
Abydos, tablet of, discovered by Mr. Banks, 113
Airy, Professor, mode of ascertaining the distance from the sun, 247; his opinion respecting the supposed occultation of Aldebaran by Venus, 90
American tradition of the flood, 85
Anselm, Archbishop of Canterbury, on justification, 352
Apophis, Pharaoh, patron of Joseph, 121, 122
Apocalypse, date of, 19, 20, 333
Apostasy, meaning of the term in Scripture, 179
Archives, Roman, the testimony of, to the crucifixion, 194
Aristotle's interpretation of Plato's cosmogony, 227
Athanasian Creed, the requirements of, 343
Atterbury, Bishop, anecdote of, 375
Augustine, St., on truth, 5; his opinions on the Millennium, 302

BABBAGE, Mr., on the length of the formation of the earth's crust, 244
Beast of the Apocalypse, the number of his name, various interpretations concerning, 334
Berosus on the Noachian Deluge, 80, 81; in harmony with the Scripture account of the flood, 86, 88; on the early history of Babylon, 93
Bessel, his discovery of a parallax to a fixed star, 247
Birch, Mr., reading of the hieroglyph respecting the great famine in Egypt, 127; decipherment of the Karnak obelisk at Rome, 138

CHE

Blunt, Professor, on conversion, 372
Bohlen, the German rationalist, his scepticism, 96
Brahmin, an Indian, on the English Bible, 6
Buckland's, Dr, refutation of Hugh Miller, 234
Buddhism, religion of, described, 356-365
Bunsen, Dr. Arnold's opinion of, 24; on Daniel's four empires, 31; respecting biblical chronology, 58; on the gradual formation of language, 72; duration of Israel in Egypt, 105; discovery of King Goose in the Book of the Dead, 116; misapplication of the great famine in Egypt, during the reign of Sesortosis I., 127, 128; his denial of Pharaoh being drowned in the Red Sea, 148, 149; his denial respecting the age of Moses, 151; his charge against the Usserian chronology, 158
Burke, Edmund, his definition of Scripture, 285
Butler, Bishop, his analogy of religion quoted, 268
Butler, Professor Archer, respecting the miracles of the Bible, 191

CALLISTHENES on the astronomical records at Babylon, 86
Catholicity defined by Vincent of Lerins, 344
Chalmers, Dr., comparison of Butler and Bacon, 11; his comparison of revelation and science, 265; on geology and Scripture, 304; on spiritual truth, 369
Champollion on the harmony between the records of Scripture and Egypt, 92, 93
Chedorlaomer, King of Persia, time of, 100

C C

China, seven years' famine in, 131
Chinese tradition of the flood, 82
Chinese chronology in harmony with Scripture, 94; teaching in harmony with that of the Jesuits, 339
Chronology of Scripture confirmed by science, 59; of the Bible, compared with that of Bunsen, 64; of the Hebrew text superior to all others, 65; of the Septuagint erroneous, 67; of Archbishop Usher, 68; of Clinton, 69; of the ancient Persians, 71; biblical, from the time of the Exode to the building of the Temple, 159–162
Chrysostom on miracles, 380
Clement of Alexandria on philosophy and theology, 337
Comets, mistaken opinion concerning, 238
Confusion of tongues, 73
Conscience, the power of, 269
Cosmogonies, the principal heathen, in harmony with Scripture, 236
Cosmogony of the Hindoos referred to, 261; the Orphic quoted, 358
Cosmos Indicopleustes, his allusion to the flood, 81
Cowie, Rev. B., on the inspiration of Scripture, 283
Crucifixion, date of, 39, 43
Cuneiform inscription at the India House respecting the building of Babylon, 33
Cyprian, his definition of the Catholic Church, 340
Cyrus, prophecy concerning, by Isaiah, 294–296; capture of Babylon, 297

Day, meaning of the word in Scripture, 255
Daniel, genuineness and authenticity of, 25–32; third ruler in Babylon, how explained, 35
Darwin on the existence of man in Egypt, 76; his "Origin of Species" quoted, 209–213
Desprez, Rev. P., his interpretation of the Apocalypse, 332
Diodorus Siculus on difficulties of Egyptian history, 61; on the early discovery of America, 85
D'Aubigny on the different periods of animal and vegetable existence, 243
Dyaks of Borneo, their tradition of the flood, 83
Dynasty, the 18th of Egyptian kings, 136

Earth, the, its internal heat, 241–243
Ebury, Lord, his attempt to promote Liturgical revision, 346
Egypt, destruction of the first born, 146
Egyptian history in harmony with Scripture, 114, 115; priesthood, great change in their position under the rule of Joseph, 126; great famine in Egypt, 127–130
Egyptians in Assyria, 153
Elliott, Dr., deemed mad on account of his scientific opinions regarding the sun, 239
Emerson on the negative theology, 367
England, time when the Gospel was first preached in, 320
Ephesus, council of, condemnatory of the Church of Rome, 321
Eratosthenes, great difference between him and Manetho, 61; Egyptian chronologers, contradictions of, 63; account of the flood, 83; in harmony with Scripture, 88 ; different modes of writing in the country, 92
Essays and Reviews, the teaching of, described by the National Review, 376 ; by the Westminster Review, 377; by an American Rationalist, 378
Eupolis, his hymn to the Creator quoted, 311
Eusebius on the old Chronicle of Egypt, 73; testimony to Sanchoniatho, 80
Evangelical school, the, teaching of, 383
Evidence, the, to Scripture from prophecy, 172; from miracles, 187; from science, 197

Fichte, John Gottlieb, his testimony to the Bible, 224
Fleming, his work on prophecy referred to, 184
Flood, the, universality of, 79
Fullom's "Marvels of Science" quoted, 245
Futurists, the, their mistaken interpretation of Scripture, 180

Genesis, i. 1, 2, explanation of, 237
Geology defined by Sir John Herschel, 232
Gibbon, his scepticism, 193; treatment of Tertullian, 193; his character described by Porson, 193
Goodwin, Mr., on the Mosaic cosmogony, 223, 225; his scepticism, 263
Gordon, Dr., on Christian philosophy, 373

INDEX.

GRE

Greek tradition of the flood, 84
Gregory the Great, his view of Holy Scripture, 270; his condemnation of the claim to universal supremacy, 324

HALL, Bishop, on vital religion, 369
Hall, Robert, his eulogy on the English Liturgy, 347
Hieroglyphic record of a great famine in Egypt, deciphered by Mr. Birch, 127
Hincks, Dr., his reading of the Nimroud Obelisk in the British Museum, 288
Hindu tradition of the flood, 82
Hooker on the inspiration of Scripture, 278
Hopkins, Mr., on the thickness of the crust of the earth, 242
Horner, Leonard, on the alluvial soil of Egypt, 75
Horsley, Bishop, on Justification, 48
Humboldt invited to visit the earth's interior, 241
Hyksos period, the, explanation of, 62, 100, 110

IGNATIUS on Episcopacy, 366
Inscription on the Cross, 279
Inspiration of Scripture, meaning of the term, 278; how used by St. Paul, 283
Irenæus, his testimony respecting Polycarp, 177; his opinion of the Millennium, 300; on the date of the Apocalypse, 333
Isaiah, 53rd chapter of, prophecy in, 15
Israelites in Egypt, duration of, 105–109, 117, 135; proof of their existence in Egypt, 111; their arrival in Egypt, supposed painting of, 124; painting of making bricks in Egypt, 141, 142

JEWS, restoration of, taught literally, symbolically, and figuratively in Scripture, 178; ancient tradition amongst them, that it would synchronise with the fall of Rome, 178; their doctrine of the Trinity, 312; their sufferings foretold in the Book of Deuteronomy, 315; how fulfilled during the Christian dispensation, 316–319
Johnson, Dr., his argument respecting miracles, 188
Jonah, miracle respecting, 45
Joseph in Egypt, 101, 102, 111, 122–133; his tomb discovered, 132
Jowett, Professor, his scepticism as re-

MAS

gards the origin of man, 210, 256; and of Scripture, 275; on the interpretation of Scripture, 274; his view of the inspiration of Scripture, 276, 277; his scepticism as regards prophecy, 293; his assertion of adverse statements in Scripture, 354
Justification by faith, harmony of St. Paul and St. James respecting, 49; as taught by the Fathers, 349–351; explained by St. Augustine and Bishop Beveridge, 354
Justin Martyr, his apology quoted, 194; his opinion of the Millennium, 299

KANT on the negative theology, 367
Karnak, chamber of, discovered by Mr. Burton, 113; contains an inscription of a King of Egypt's war against Canaan, 175

LAUD, Archbishop, his opinion respecting Liturgical revision, 347
Lepsius on the sojourn of Israel in Egypt, 105
Light, speed at which it travels, 203; its utility defined by George Stephenson, 252
Locke, his definition of the Bible, 270
Longevity, modern instances of, 103
Lyell, Sir Charles, on the origin of species, 220; his conclusion respecting the age of the Falls of Niagara, 257

MACCULLOCH, Mr., on the formation of the coal beds, 244
Mackay on the negative theology, 367
Maitland, Dr., on Daniel's Four Empires, 32
Mammoth, a, the skeleton of, at St. Petersburg, explained by a clergyman, 228
Man, his origin, theory concerning, as propounded by Darwin, 212; by Professor Oken, 213; by Dr. Darwin, sen., 214; by Mon. Maillet, 214; by Gerard, 215; by the author of the Anti-Jacobin, 216; by Ovid, 217; by Lord Monboddo, 218; rejected by Owen, 219, 220; by Sir Charles Lyell, 220; by Wollaston, 221
Man of Sin, the Prophecy concerning, applied by the Church of Ireland to Rome, 323
Manetho, the Egyptian historian, 59
Martyn, Henry, his argument with the Mahometans respecting miracles, 196
Masorah, Jewish, on Prophecy, 18

MAU

Maurice, Professor, on the date of the Apocalypse, 333; his scepticism, 375
M'Cosh, Dr., on the harmony between Revelation and Science, 265
Menes, proto-monarch of Egypt, 62
Müller, Professor Max, on the one primeval language, 72
Millennium, the, ancient opinions concerning, 299–303
Miller, Hugh, his refutation of Darwin, 210; the same of Archbishop Cullen, 225; of the late Dean of York, 231; his own hypothesis respecting the Mosaic cosmogony, 233; on the formation of the chalk cliffs of England, 245; his explanation of God's resting time, 259
Mosaic cosmogony in harmony with science, 235, 251, 253, 254; record, the different opinions respecting, 227, 232
Moses, his mighty deeds in Egypt, 140, 141
Murchison, Sir Roderick, his Silurian system quoted, 249

Newman, Dr., his description of the English Bible, 271; his description of the Church of Rome, 329; his defence of the Church of Rome, 329
Newton, B. W., on Babylon the Great, 21, 331
Niagara, age of, in harmony with the Mosaic record, 258
Niebuhr, his noble defence of Christianity, 380
Ninevite inscriptions in harmony with Scripture, 289

Oppert, Mon., discovery of a cuneiform inscription respecting the deluge, 89
Oracles, heathen, their failure, 183
Origen on 53rd of Isaiah, 16
Osburn's Monumental History of Egypt, 62; respecting unburnt bricks in Egypt, 77; on the duration of the Israelites in.Egypt, 105
Oxford, introduction of English Bible at, 281

Parker, Theodore, his denial of miracles, 196
Pattison, Rev. H., his hypothesis respecting religious truth, 336; his misapplication of the term Catholic, 340; on the negative theology, 368; on the

ROM

witness of the Spirit, 370; his denial of freedom in the Church of England, 376; his opinion of the Evangelical School, 382.
Pearson, Bishop, unfairly treated by Dr. Williams, 14
Pharaoh, the, that knew not Joseph, 133, 137; Pharaoh's daughter, who preserved Moses, 139; of .the Exode, 144, 149
Pharaohs in Egypt, double line of contemporary, 113
Phoenician inscriptions in harmony with Scripture, 291
Pitt, Mr., anecdotes concerning, 278, 372
Platina, his story concerning Pope Benedict IX., 322
Plato, respecting the rotation of the Earth, 227
Pliny, his wonderful tales respecting whales, 46
Pope Pius III., his Bull of universal excommunication, 181
Powell, Professor Baden, on the evidence of Christianity, 172; his opinion respecting miracles, 189, 190, 195; his scepticism in regard to the origin of man, 208
Predictions, uninspired, respecting Russia and Rome, 185, 186
Prophecy of Genesis iii. 5, 173; respecting the downfall of Egypt, 175
Pye Smith, Dr., his work on geology quoted, 246; his definition of Revelation and Science, 264
Pyramids, mention of, in Job, 132
Pythagorean notion, the, of annihilation referred to, 360

Rabbinical version of the history of Jesus, 22, 23
Ramesses, Pharaoh, hieroglyph of, in Syria, 155, 156
Rock, the, different interpretations of the Fathers concerning, 338
Roemer, his discovery of the speed of light, 247
Rome, the Church of, her mysterious nature, 182; her heresy in the fourth century, 321; her present condition described by Dr. Newman, 329; with regard to the unanimous consent of the Fathers, 338; her opposition to the Bible, 341; convicted of apostasy, 345; opposed to the Catholic Church, 349; her teaching on the doctrine of Justification, 353; Bishops of, above law, 322 ; their character during the middle ages, 327, 328

INDEX.   389

RON

Rongé, De, his translation of the Sallier papyri, 118; and of an Egyptian romance, founded on Joseph's history, 123
Rosetta stone, quotation from, 126

SANCHONIATHO respecting the origin of man, 80
Scripture and Science, harmony between, proved by Gen. i. 3, 199; Lev. xvii. 11, 199; Deut. xxxii. 2, 200; Job xiv. 7, 9, 200; Job xxvi. 7, 201; Job xxviii. 23, 25, 202; Job xxxviii. 31, 202; Psalm cxlvii. 16, 204; Prov. viii. 27, 204; Eccl. i. 5, 6, 205; Eccl. i. 7, 206; John xix. 34, 207
Scripture, instances of omissions in, 305, 306; of interpolations, 307; of faulty readings, 308, 309
Seventy weeks, the, interpretation of, 36, 43
Shiloh, the, prophecy concerning, 10, 174
Shepherds an abomination to the Egyptians, how explained, 117
Shishak, Pharaoh, his capture of Jerusalem, 163, 288
Socinus, the introducer of the modern interpretation of Regeneration, 346
Solomon's temple, date of, 157
Strauss, his rejection of the Bible, 379
Struve's, Professor, table of time for the transmission of stellar light, 248
Stuart, Professor Moses, on various readings in Scripture, 15
Summary respecting Bunsen's Biblical researches, 164-168
Sun, opinions respecting the, entertained by Nicolaus de Cusa, 239; by Sir W. Herschel and M. Arago, 240
Syrians, the, effeminacy of, 155

TACITUS, his description of the Jews, 117, 310; his account of the different forms of government in ancient Rome, 334
Taylor, Isaac, on the preservation of Scripture, 281
Temple, Dr., on forgeries in the Bible, 304; on the interpretation of the Bible, 268; his mode of accounting for the preservation of the Jews, 313; on the supremacy of the Church of Rome, 320-324; considers the Papacy as a schoolmaster, 326

ZAP

Tertullian on truth, 4; his opinion on the Millennium, 301; respecting the rapid spread of Christianity, 192; his Apology quoted, 194
Theology, how blasphemed in Holland, 376
Truth defined by Tertullian, 4; by Plutarch, 224; by Milton, 224; famous anagram on, 337; travestied by Ignatius Loyola, 339
Tyrian annals respecting the building of the Temple, 161

VAN Mildert, Bishop, his opinion of the Church of Rome, 179

WESTMINSTER Review, the, its interpretation of the Apocalypse, 332-335
Wilkinson, Sir Gardner, on the alluvial soil of Egypt, 75; his explanation of Heliopolis, 119
Wilson, Rev. H. B., his scepticism as regards Scripture, 94, 272; his opposition to the Athanasian Creed, 341; his views on the doctrine of Justification, 348; his opinion of Buddhism, 355; on the negative theology, 365
Williams, Dr. Rowland, on Providence, 5; respecting English rationalists, 7; his opinion on the Bible, 8; on the prophecy of the Shiloh, 9; his opinion of Butler, 11; contempt for Keith, 12; on Isaiah liii., 13; on the prophecies of Psalms xxii. and xxxiv. 17; on Messianic prophecies, 21; on the Prophet Daniel, 23, 24; denial of Daniel's prophecies, 35; rejects the personality of Jonah, 43; on Justification, 47; on the doctrine of the Trinity, 50; on the Athanasian Creed, 51; estimate of Bunsen, 60; his condemnation of Bunsen, 169
Wiseman, Cardinal, his song upon Pio Nono, 331
Word of God, the, how used in Scripture, 273, 274

YORK, the late Dean of, his theory respecting the deluge, 228, 231

ZAPHNATH-PAANEAH, Joseph's name, how explained, 122

www.ingramcontent.com/pod-product-compliance
Lightning Source LLC
Chambersburg PA
CBHW030428300426
44112CB00009B/907